Detroit Monographs in Musicology/Studies in Music, No. 35

Editor
J. Bunker Clark
University of Kansas

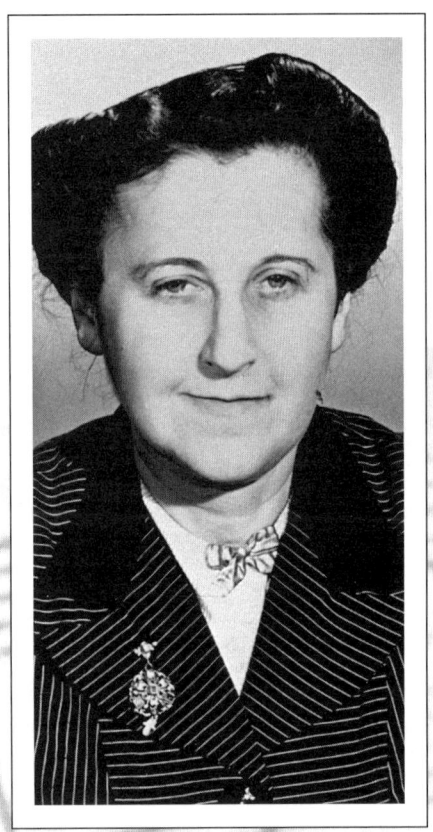
Irene Geiringer

Karl Geiringer

Joseph Haydn and the Eighteenth Century

Collected Essays of Karl Geiringer

edited by Robert N. Freeman

HARMONIE PARK PRESS   WARREN, MICHIGAN   2002

Frontispiece:

Irene Geiringer

Karl Geiringer
Courtesy of the Karl Geiringer Estate

Copyright © 2002 by Harmonie Park Press

Printed and bound in the United States of America
Published by
Harmonie Park Press
23630 Pinewood
Warren, Michigan 48091

Publications Director, Elaine Gorzelski
Editor, J. Bunker Clark
Cover design, Mitchell Groters
Book design and Typographer, Colleen McRorie
Music typesetting, Don Harris

Library of Congress Cataloging-in-Publication Data

Geiringer, Karl, 1899-
　　[Essays. Selections]
　　Joseph Haydn and the eighteenth century : collected essays of Karl Geiringer / Robert N. Freeman [editor].
　　　　p. cm. — (Detroit monographs in musicology/Studies in music ; no. 35)
　　"Bibliography of the works of Karl Geiringer relating to Haydn / compiled by David Malvinni and Martin Silver" (p.).
　　Includes index.
　　ISBN 0-89990-112-3
　　1. Haydn, Joseph, 1732-1809—Criticism and interpretation. 2. Music—18th century—History and criticism. I. Title. II. Series.

ML410.H4 G44 2002
780'.92—dc21

2002027251

*My second great love, next to musical instruments,
belonged to the work of Haydn.
At all times it has been close to my heart and mind.*
—This I Remember, *107*

Contents

Illustrations   ix
Music Examples   xi
Foreword   xv
Preface   xvii
Abbreviations   xxiii

Part 1: Haydn's Artistic and Human Personality

1. Joseph Haydn — 3
2. The Portrait of Haydn Over the Course of Time — 9
3. Haydn and His Viennese Background — 19
4. Haydn's Autograph Remarks in His Music Manuscripts — 41
5. Haydn's Sketches for *The Creation* — 45
6. Joseph Haydn, Protagonist of the Enlightenment — 55

Part 2: Haydn at Work: Specific Fields of His Production

7. The Small Sacred Works by Haydn in the Esterházy Archives at Eisenstadt — 67
8. Haydn as an Opera Composer — 77
9. From Guglielmi to Haydn: The Transformation of an Opera — 97
10. Haydn and the Folksong of the British Isles — 103
11. Haydn: The London Symphonies — 125
12. The Complete String Quartets of Joseph Haydn — 133

Part 3: Haydn and His Contemporaries

13	A Birthday Cantata by Pietro Metastasio and Leonardo Vinci	159
14	Gluck and Haydn	171
15	Concepts of the Enlightenment as Reflected in Gluck's Italian Reform Opera	175
16	Gluck's *Telemaco*	181
17	Emanuel Bach and the Music of the Viennese Classical Triad	195
18	Stephen and Nancy Storace in Vienna	203

Part 4: On Haydn Scholars and Scholarship

19	Robert Sondheimer	213
20	Donald Francis Tovey	215
21	Anthony van Hoboken	217
22	Joseph Haydn Institute, Cologne	221
23	Hungarian Academy of Science	231
24	H. C. Robbins Landon	235

Bibliography of the Works of Karl Geiringer Relating to Haydn   241
    Compiled by David Malvinni and Martin Silver

Indexes
    Names and Places   249
    Compositions by Haydn   257
    Doubtful and Spurious Works Attributed to Haydn   261

Illustrations

Figures

	Irene Geiringer and Karl Geiringer	*frontispiece*
1.1	Haydn, portrait by Thomas Hardy, 1791	2
2.1	Autograph of the First Commandment from the canon cycle *Die zehn Gebote*, Hob. XXVIIa:1	11
2.2	The second through fourth variations from the String Quartet, op. 76, no. 3 ("Emperor")	12
2.3	Haydn's portrait from 1765	12
2.4	Haydn's portrait after Johann Carl Roesler, by Philippe Trière (1800)	13
2.5	Haydn's portrait after Johann Carl Roesler, anonymous (Daniel Caffé?)	13
2.6	Haydn's portrait after Johann Zitterer, color print by M. Jaffé	14
2.7	Haydn's portrait after Johann Zitterer, engraving by Johann Neidl (1800)	14
2.8	Haydn's portrait from a wax medallion by Sebastian Ihrwach (1803)	15
2.9	Haydn, copper engraving by Friedrich Ludwig Neubauer	15
2.10	Haydn, drawing by George Dance (1794)	16
2.11	Haydn's death mask	16
7.1	Title page of a Litany in C, Hob. XXIIIc:C2, by Haydn	74
7.2	Bass part of a *Mottetto di Sta. Thecla*, Hob. XXIIIa:4*, showing Haydn's autograph signature	75
8.1	Haydn, "Dica pure," insertion aria, Hob. XXIVb:8	91
10.1	Title page of Thomson's first collection of Scottish airs arranged by Haydn (1802)	107
10.2	Illustration for Haydn's arrangement of "On Ettrick Banks," Hob. XXXIa:151	123
11.1	Beginning of Symphony no. 94, "Surprise" (1791)	127
13.1	"Concert" [Fête musicale] by Giovanni Paolo Pannini	160
13.2	Same, detail	161
16.1	*Telemaco*, Italian-German synopsis, printed textbook, Vienna 1765	185
16.2	*Telemaco*, act 1, scene 1 (Oracolo, meas. 205ff.) from the autograph fragment (cf. NA, 47)	192
16.3	*Telemaco*, act 1, scene 1 (Oracolo, meas. 205ff.) from the score (cf. NA, 47)	193
18.1	Anna Selina Storace, by Pietro Bettelini	204
18.2	Stephen Storace, *Gli equivoci*, act 1, scene 2, no. 3, "Il ciel che tutto vede," from the Ms. score	208-09

Table

10.1	Nos. 201-365 of the Folksongs of the British Isles in the Haydn-Elssler Catalog of 1805	115-17

Musical Examples

Examples

3.1	Biber, from the *Night Watchman Serenade*	20-23
3.2	Caldara, from *Il giuoco del quadriglio*	24-25
3.3a	Haydn, Concerto in C major, Hob. XVIII:1, Finale	29-31
3.3b	G. M. Monn, Concerto in D major, Finale	32-34
3.4	Haydn, German Dance, Hob. IX:12, no. 4	37-39
5.1	*The Creation*, no. 28, final form	46-47
5.2	*The Creation*, sketch for no. 28 (Österreichische Nationalbibliothek, Ms. 16835, f. 1r)	47-48
5.3	*The Creation*, sketch for no. 28 (Ms. 16835, f. 6v)	49
5.4	*The Creation*, sketch for no. 16 (Ms. 16835, f. 17v)	49
5.5	*The Creation*, no. 16, final form	49
5.6	*The Creation*, sketch for no. 16 (Ms. 16835, f. 17v)	50
5.7	*The Creation*, no. 16, final form	50
5.8	*The Creation*, sketch for no. 19 (Ms. 16835, f. 16v)	50
5.9	*The Creation*, no. 19, final form	51
5.10	*The Creation*, no. 17, final form	51
5.11	*The Creation*, sketch for no. 17 (Ms. 16835, f. 15r)	51
5.12	*The Creation*, sketch for no. 1 (Ms. 16835, f. 19v)	52
5.13	*The Creation*, no. 1, violin 1, meas. 3-4	52
5.14	*The Creation*, no. 1, bassoon, meas. 21-22	53
5.15	*The Creation*, sketch for no. 1, clarinet (Ms. 18987)	53
6.1a	Symphony no. 1, movement 2, meas. 1-28	57-58
6.1b	Symphony no. 49, movement 1, meas. 1-16	58-59
6.1c	Symphony no. 8, movement 1, meas. 1-21	60
6.1d	Symphony no. 49, movement 2, meas. 1-13	61-62
6.2a	String Quartet in C major, op. 33, movement 1, meas. 1-4	62
6.2b	String Quartet in C major, op. 33, no. 3, movement 1, meas. 87-97	62-63
7.1	*O Jesu te invocamus*, introductory violin subject	68
7.2	*Agite properate ad aras convolate*, Elssler incipit	71
7.3	"Offertorio de Sancto vel Sancta," excerpt from the solo bass part	73
8.1	*La canterina*, act 1, scene 1, "Che visino delicato," meas. 1-39	79-82
8.2	*La canterina*, act 2, scene 2, "Non v'è chi mi aiuta," meas. 1-16	82-85

Examples

8.3	*L'infedeltà delusa*, act 1, scene 4, "Come piglia sì bene la mira," meas. 1-28	86-88
8.4	*Armida*, overture, opening theme	90
8.5	*L'anima del filosofo*, act 2, scene 2, "Del mio core il voto estremo"	92-95
10.1	Ending of "Fair Helen of Kirkconnell"	118
10.2	Ritornello for "Fy Gar Rub"	119
10.3	New version of the ritornello for "Fy Gar Rub"	119
10.4	Introduction to "Muirland Willy"	119
10.5	New version of introduction to "Muirland Willy"	120
10.6	"Roslin Castle"	121
10.7	"Cauld Kail in Aberdeen"	121
10.8	"The Birks of Invermay"	121
10.9	"Robin Adair"	121-22
10.10	"The Bonnie Wee Thing"	122
12.1	String Quartet in A major, op. 2, no. 1, movement 1, meas. 37-41	134
12.2	String Quartet in E major, op. 2, no. 2, Finale, meas. 36-43	135
12.3	String Quartet in E♭ major, op. 2, no. 3, Finale, meas. 1-6	135
12.4	String Quartet in F major, op. 2, no. 4, movement 1, meas. 50-57	136
12.5	String Quartet in D major, op. 2, no. 5, movement 1, meas. 1	137
12.6	String Quartet in B♭ major, op. 2, no. 6, movement 3, meas. 12-16	137
12.7	String Quartet in C major, op. 20, no. 2, movement 1, meas. 1-7	139
12.8	String Quartet in G minor, op. 20, no. 3, movement 3, meas. 1-8	139
12.9	String Quartet in D major, op. 20, no. 4, movement 4, meas. 40-45	139-40
12.10	String Quartet in A major, op. 20, no. 6, movement 3, meas. 1-8	140
12.11	String Quartet in B minor, op. 33, no. 1, movement 1, meas. 78-79	142
12.12	String Quartet in E♭ major, op. 33, no. 2, movement 3, meas. 1-8	143
12.13	String Quartet in C major, op. 33, no. 3, movement 2, meas. 35-42	144
12.14	String Quartet in B♭ major, op. 33, no. 4, movement 1, meas. 1-3	144
12.15	String Quartet in G major, op. 33, no. 5, movement 1, meas. 1-10	145
12.16	String Quartet in D major, op. 33, no. 6, movement 2, meas. 1-5	145
12.17	String Quartet in B♭ major, op. 50, no. 1, movement 3, meas. 56-60	146
12.18	String Quartet in C major, op. 50, no. 2, movement 1, meas. 43-51	147
12.19	String Quartet in E♭ major, op. 50, no. 3, movement 1, meas. 1-8	147
12.20	String Quartet in F# minor, op. 50, no. 4, movement 1, meas. 1	148
12.21	String Quartet in F major, op. 50, no. 5, movement 3, meas. 1-5	148
12.22	String Quartet in D major, op. 50, no. 6, movement 4, meas. 1-2	149
12.23	Sonata, op. 51, no. 1, meas. 2	150
12.24	Sonata, op. 51, no. 2, meas. 1-2	150
12.25	Sonata, op. 51, no. 3, meas. 3-6	151
12.26	Sonata, op. 51, no. 4, meas. 43-46	151
12.27	Sonata, op. 51, no. 5, meas. 18-21	151
12.28	Sonata, op. 51, no. 6, meas. 1-3	152
12.29	String Quartet in G major, op. 76, no. 1, movement 1, meas. 144-47	153
12.30	String Quartet in D minor, op. 76, no. 2, movement 1, meas. 1-2	153
12.31	String Quartet in B♭ major, op. 76, no. 4, movement 1, meas. 1-6	154
12.32	String Quartet in D major, op. 76, no. 5, movement 1, meas. 1-4	155
12.33	String Quartet in D major, op. 76, no. 5, movement 4, meas. 7-12	155

Examples

13.1a-d	Vinci, *La Contesa de Numi*, part 2, accompanied recitative, Mars	166
13.2	Vinci, *La Contesa de Numi*, part 2, aria, Mars	167
13.3	Vinci, *La Contesa de Numi*, part 2, accompanied recitative, Jupiter	167
13.4	Vinci, *La Contesa de Numi*, part 1, aria, Fortuna	167
13.5	Vinci, *La Contesa de Numi*, part 2, aria, Astrea	167
14.1	Haydn, Baryton Trio no. 5, movement 1, principal theme, meas. 1-6	172
17.1	C. P. E. Bach, Fantasia in F major, Wq. 59/5 [H. 279], meas. 27-29	199
17.2	Mozart, Phantasie in C major, K. 394, meas. 43-45	199
17.3	C. P. E. Bach, Cembalo Concerto in D minor, Wq. 23 [H. 427], movement 2, meas. 21-27	201
17.4a	C. F. Gellert, "Bitten," C. P. E. Bach, Wq. 194/9 [H. 686/9], meas. 17-22	202
17.4b	C. F. Gellert, "Bitten," Beethoven, op. 48/1, meas. 26-32	202
18.1	Stephen Storace, *Gli sposi malcontenti*, act 1, "Ah, che invan io piango," Eginia	207
18.2	Stephen Storace, *Gli sposi malcontenti*, "Ad un uom versato," Valente	207
18.3	Franz Xaver Süssmayr, insertion aria, "A un onesto mercadante"	207

Foreword

To have the essays and shorter articles of my late husband Professor Karl Geiringer published in one volume is the realization of a long-cherished dream I have had. This volume, containing a great deal of Dr. Geiringer's Haydn research, will afford professors, musicians, students, and the general reader the most convenient and accessible source of his Haydn material all in one place.

It had been a great pleasure to work with Dr. Robert Freeman, associate professor of music at the University of California at Santa Barbara. His devotion and dedication to this project have been outstanding. He worked incessantly with many articles that had to be translated from the German, he obtained the numerous copyrights that were needed before the articles could be published, and he took care of innumerable details to prepare the work for publication.

I hope this book will be of value for all musicians. It is a great resource for Haydn material as well as an interesting and informative book for music-lovers everywhere.

BERNICE GEIRINGER[†]
11 June 2001

Santa Barbara

Preface

In the weeks and months immediately following Karl Geiringer's death in Santa Barbara on 10 January 1989 there was a strong outpouring of heartfelt expressions of commiseration and eulogy, both private and public, transmitted orally, in manuscript and in the printed media.[1] Over the years Geiringer had given unselfishly of himself in many capacities, such as serving a term as president of the American Musicological Society (1955-56), and had received numerous honors and distinctions,[2] such as his election to the American Academy of Arts and Sciences in 1959 and his decorations from the Republic of Austria in 1969 and 1985. Now it was as if the emotions under-pinning these symbols of appreciation and respect had formed their own energy field. Clearly this humble, witty, erudite, and industrious man had touched the lives of many persons, influenced institutions, and garnered the attention of governments. His students, colleagues, and publishers had seen signs of this emotional bedrock before: the large enrollments in his classes, the insatiable demand for him even as an octogenarian as a lecturer, and the enviable success of his writings attested to by the many reprints, editions, and translations of his books, particularly the one on Haydn. It was in this atmosphere that the idea for the present book began to take shape—an attempt to throw light on the phenomenal influence of this unique individual by collecting, carefully selecting, and making accessible a number of representative writings by him encompassing the entire span of his career, but focusing on one of his favorite and most popular subjects—Joseph Haydn.

Geiringer's training in musicology in his native Vienna under Guido Adler (1855-1941) and Wilhelm Fischer (1886-1962) and in Berlin with Curt Sachs (1881-1959), Hermann Kretzschmar (1848-1924) and Johannes Wolf (1869-1947) during the years of his university study, 1919-23, seemed to prepare him more for a career specializing in the study of musical instruments, iconography, and editing rather than the role of a future world-class Haydn scholar. Indeed, his first publications in the 1920s—excerpts from his dissertation on string instruments in Renaissance painting[3] and his entry in the first edition of Adler's *Handbuch der Musikgeschichte* (Frankfurt, 1924), which catapulted him onto the same stage as Einstein, Fischer, Haas, Ludwig, Sachs, Schering, Wagner, and Wellesz—and subsequent articles written to the end of the decade were confined to these subjects. While these disciplines continued to occupy him throughout his life, two events took place practically back-to-back around 1930 that would dramatically

---

[1] See for example George S. Bozarth, "In memoriam Karl Geiringer," *American Brahms Society Newsletter* 7, no. 1 (1989): 4-5; Robert N. Freeman, "Karl Geiringer (1899-1989)," *AMS Newsletter* 19, no. 11 (August 1989): 13, 19; Freeman, "Karl Geiringer," *Mitteilungen der österreichischen Gesellschaft für Musikwissenschaft* 20 (1989): 7-8; Freeman and others, "Karl Geiringer: 1899-1989, Professor of Music, Emeritus," in *University of California: In Memorium 1989* (Berkeley: Academic Senate, University of California, 1989), 50-51; Theodor Göllner, "Karl Geiringer (1899-1989)," *Die Musikforschung* 42 (1989): 109-10; and Roland Jackson, "A Pioneering Organologist: Karl Geiringer, 1899-1989," *Performance Practice Review* 2 (1989): 144-46. Examples of oral expressions were recorded by Bernice Geiringer in the "Epilogue," in Karl Geiringer with Bernice Geiringer, *This I Remember: Memoirs of a Life in Music* (Santa Barbara: Fithian Press, 1993), 197.

[2] See the lists in Freeman, *AMS Newsletter*, 19, and Geiringer, *This I Remember*, 178.

[3] *Die Flankenwirbelinstrumente in der bildenden Kunst des 14.–16. und der 1. Hälfte des 17. Jahrhunderts* (Ph.D. diss., University of Vienna, 1923); later published as *Die Flankenwirbelinstrumente in der bildenden Kunst der Zeit zwischen 1300 und 1550*, Wiener Veröffentlichungen zur Musikwissenschaft, 17 (Tutzing: Schneider, 1979).

open new additional lines of research: the death of his mentor and long-term librarian and archivist for the Gesellschaft der Musikfreunde in Wien, Eusebius Mandyczewski (1857-1929), and the arrival of the bicentennial of Joseph Haydn's birth in 1932.

The first event led to Geiringer's appointment to succeed Mandyczewski as librarian and curator of the collections for the celebrated Musikfreunde in February 1930. Geiringer's connections with Mandyczewski dated from around 1919 when the elder scholar administered his examination in music history for the state teaching credential. The relationship grew into a respectful one, as can be seen by Geiringer's thoughtful dedication to Mandyczewski on an off-print still preserved by the Musikfreunde (see essay 13), and his willingness, as a fellow contributor to Adler's *Denkmäler der Tonkunst in Österreich*, to complete the preparation of Mandyczewski's edition of Antonio Caldara's *Kammermusik für Gesang, Kantaten, Madrigale, Kanons*, which had to be published posthumously in 1932 as volume 75 (Jahrgang 39) in the series. Most importantly, under the successive tenures of Carl Ferdinand Pohl (1866-87) and Mandyzcewski (1888-1929) as librarians and archivists, vast Haydn resources had been assembled for the Musikfreunde. From within the walls of the Musikverein, the attractive new (1870) home for the Musikfreunde, the most significant advancements in Haydn research were being directed: Pohl's three-volume biography (Leipzig, 1875-82, the third volume completed by Hugo Botstiber and published in 1927) placed Haydn biography on a new, documentary footing for the first time, but, as Hoboken was to point out later in the 1950s, it may have been Pohl's extensive unpublished notes left behind that turned out to be his most valuable contribution to Haydn research.[4] Mandyczewski, on the other hand, turned his attention to Haydn compositions, initiating as general editor the first of three twentieth-century attempts to gather, edit, and publish Haydn's complete works. Although left incomplete, eleven volumes containing forty-nine symphonies, fifty-two keyboard sonatas, songs, and two of the oratorios were brought out by Breitkopf & Härtel in Leipzig between 1907 and 1933. With Geiringer's appointment in early 1930 it seems in retrospect to have been almost inevitable that the legacy of this powerful Haydn research tradition at the Musikverein would be passed on to him.

The second event, the Haydn bicentennial, gave Geiringer the opportunity to utilize the rich Haydn resources preserved in the Musikverein's collections for the first time. The result was a barrage of Haydn publications all timed to appear in 1932: the *Führer durch die Josef Haydn Kollektion im Museum der Gesellschaft der Musikfreunde in Wien*, compiled with his colleague Hedwig Kraus; a review on the state of research for the Haydn commemorative issue of *Die Musik* (see essay 2); a study of the sketches for *The Creation* for Carl Engel's *Musical Quarterly* (see essay 8), likewise a commemorative issue; a brief article on Haydn and opera in *Zeitschrift für Musik*; and finally and most importantly a book-length study of Haydn which inaugurated Ernst Bücken's (1884-1949) new series *Die großen Meister der Musik*.[5] The volume was eventually superseded by a larger work in English published by Norton in 1946, *Haydn: A Creative Life in Music*, the nucleus of what was to be Geiringer's definitive work on Haydn in book form. With its many translations and editions until the last revised and enlarged one, published by the University of California Press in 1982, the year of Haydn's quarter millennium (see the Bibliography), the book had much to do with shaping the twentieth-century view of Haydn.

Having "written important sections of this book," Karl's first wife Irene (1899-1983) was inextricably involved with her husband's work on Haydn. Nevertheless, the couple decided not to include her name as co-author on the title page of the first edition, not because of "her determined protests," as the preface to the book would have it,[6] but because they thought its omission would be better for Karl's career.[7] Her name did appear as co-author, however, in all later editions beginning with the first German translation published in 1959 by B. Schott's Söhne in Mainz. Irene Stekel was born in Cernauti (in German Czernowitz, today's Chernovtsy, Ukraine), a fact that could only further have enhanced Karl's relationship with Mandyczewski, who coincidentally was also a native of this capital of the former Austro-Hungarian crownland of Bukovina. Irene came from a family that excelled in arts and letters: her father was a journalist in Cernauti and then in Vienna where he joined his younger brother Wilhelm Stekel

---

[4] Anthony van Hoboken, *Joseph Haydn: Thematisch-bibliographisches Werkverzeichnis,* 1 (Mainz: Schott, [1957]), x. For more details see Geiringer's review (essay 21), below, p. 215.

[5] 12 vols. (Potsdam: Athenaion, 1932-34).

[6] Karl Geiringer, *Haydn: A Creative Life in Music* (New York: Norton, 1946), 12.

[7] According to a letter to me from Geiringer's son George Gardiner, October 2000.

(1868-1940), who had settled there in the 1880s to study medicine. Wilhelm, who is best known as one of the first disciples of Sigmund Freud, was also an accomplished amateur pianist, violinist, and composer.[8] His son, Irene's cousin, was Eric-Paul Stekel (1898-1978), a professional composer and conductor who founded the Hochschule für Musik in Saarbrücken in 1947 and served as director of the music conservatory in Grenoble after 1951.[9]

Irene had studied philosophy and German literature at the University of Vienna and received her Ph.D. before meeting Karl at the newly established Wiener Philharmonischer Verlag (housed in the Musikverein) where they were both employed between 1923-27. They were married in Vienna on 19 April 1928. As the present collection of essays shows (essay 18), Irene's contribution to her husband's work was not limited to the biographical sections of "all the books," but extended also to collaboration in other forms and on other subjects as well. The precise mechanics of the working relationship of the two were rarely disclosed, even to members of the immediate family.[10] The extent of Irene's contribution to Karl's work on Haydn and other subjects, therefore, has never been and may never be fully determined, properly evaluated, or credited.

Arriving at work the morning after the Nazi annexation of Austria in March 1938, Karl discovered the Musikverein cordoned off by the SS. Shortly, the Geiringers and their children were on their way to London, where Karl secured work at the Royal College of Music and at the BBC and as a contributor to the fourth edition of *Grove's Dictionary of Music and Musicians*. By August 1940 they had immigrated to the U.S., and Karl found temporary employment in the music department at Hamilton College, Clinton, New York before he was appointed full professor at Boston University the following year. He was to remain there for the next twenty-one years.

At forty, both Geiringers had to begin a new life in a new country. It is remarkable how little their work seemed to have been affected at this greater distance from the primary sources. The work product of the Boston period would seem to indicate that the level of their productivity was even raised. Besides the Haydn volume for Norton mentioned above, there was the completion, translation, and publication of the first edition of the book on musical instruments (1943), followed by the companion volumes *The Bach Family* and *Music of the Bach Family* (1954-55).

Karl was invited by the University of California in 1962 to establish the graduate program in musicology at the Santa Barbara campus. Here, as he had in Boston, he continued to produce a steady stream of first-rate doctoral students, while initiating the *Series of Early Music*[11] and creating one of the finest music research libraries on the West Coast, built around the acquisition of the libraries of his colleagues Eric Hertzmann and Leo Schrade. Although there is little hard evidence documenting Geiringer's direct input into its design, the Arts Library, which opened its doors at UC Santa Barbara in 1970, seems to memorialize the interdisciplinary aspect of his work, particularly the interaction between art and music that finds expression at various points in his career beginning with the topic of his Viennese dissertation (see also, e.g., essay 13). It is the only library facility on that campus housed within a department (Music) detached from the main library, which combines two arts with one floor devoted to art history and a second floor to music. The Geiringers' major publications of this period were the excellent study of *Johann Sebastian Bach: The Culmination of an Era* (1966),[12] a vastly revised and enlarged second edition of their Haydn book (1968), and the monumental volumes for the Haydn and Gluck collected editions (*Orlando Paladino*, *Telemaco*, 1972-73).

Few who knew the Geiringers were surprised when the "retirement" from the University of California in 1971 proved to be more of a technicality than a reality—the couple turned their indefatigable energies toward preparing third revised editions of his book on instruments (1978) and their studies of Brahms and Haydn (1981-82). Karl continued to be in demand as a teacher and lecturer, and in these late years his presentations were characterized by a deep love of his subject, a knowledge acquired over a lifetime, and a spontaneous, creative humor that could have come only from his native Austria. It is a testament to his strength and stamina that he survived the loss of Irene (23 September 1983) and lived to see their works translated into a dozen languages and disseminated worldwide.

---

[8] See *The Autobiography of Wilhelm Stekel: The Life Story of a Pioneer Psychoanalyst*, ed. Emil A. Gutheil (New York: Liveright, [1950]).

[9] *MGG*, 12 (1965), col. 1248.

[10] According to the Gardiner letter cited above. A brief description appeared later in *This I Remember*, 48, and closed characteristically with a self-deprecatory remark "The success these books had was probably more due to her contribution than to mine."

[11] (Ann Arbor: University Microfilms, 1968-72).

[12] (New York: Oxford University Press).

The last years of Geiringer's life were brightened by his relationship with Bernice Shapiro, whom he married in 1987. In the spring of the following year the couple was invited to Vienna by the Gesellschaft der Musikfreunde, where Karl presented two public lectures observing the passing of the half century since the Nazi takeover of Austria had forced him to leave the country. A few months after their return to California he passed away peacefully in Santa Barbara (10 January 1989).

In the years since then and her own recent death (11 June 2001), Bernice did much to promote Karl's memory. At UCSB she was instrumental in having one of the large rehearsal rooms in the music building refashioned into an attractive lecture-recital hall that carries his name today, and this became the venue for the prestigious and well-attended Annual Geiringer Lectures that she endowed in 1994.[13] Beyond UCSB Bernice saw to it that new publications relating to Geiringer (the memoirs, the Haydn essays) came to press.

* * * *

Geiringer considered his work on Haydn second only to his research involving the history of musical instruments. He saw the former unfolding in two distinct phases, the first of which he characterized as the attempt "to provide a complete picture of Haydn's artistic and human personality."[14] This included studies that drew attention to what he called Haydn's "workshop" (see essays 1-6) and the Bücken volume of 1932 that portrayed Haydn's life in relatively brief, broad strokes and dealt with his music in a classified manner. By far the most significant achievement along these lines was the enormously successful Norton study of 1946. This book brought forward for the first time the cutting edge of European Haydn scholarship that had appeared in the years since the bicentennial to English-speaking audiences and a younger generation of Haydn scholars represented most notably by Robbins Landon, soon to be counted among Geiringer's pupils. To explore Haydn's biography, Irene was given six times more space than there had been in the earlier Bücken volume, while Karl returned to the five-fold periodization of the master's development that he had devised in 1932 by incorporating the turning points posited by Wyzewa (1900) and Sandberger (1921). But now that decade-by-decade chronology was raised in importance, since it was made to serve as the basic framework within which Haydn's entire œuvre was discussed.

The second phase of Haydn research was to be devoted to a more thorough investigation of "specific fields of [Haydn's] production"[15] These fields or genres turned out to be directly related to those lacunae outlined in the important "portrait" essay published in the bicentennial year 1932 (essay 2): Lieder, church music, and opera. Geiringer's Haydn activities were to be focused on these subjects beginning in the late 1940s, when he commenced publishing his work on the folksongs (see the annotation to essay 10 and the Bibliography), and they perhaps reached their climax with the publication of the multi-volume edition of *Orlando Paladino* in 1972-73 in the new collected edition.

These two lines of investigation, then, formed the central core of Geiringer's Haydn research from which sprung a steady stream of books, essays, encyclopedia entries, catalogs, performing editions, program and liner notes, reviews, and lectures. Viewed in its totality (see the Bibliography), this body of work would have been the envy of any well-established musicologist. But Geiringer's achievement is that much more remarkable because he was producing simultaneously equally significant work in almost the same quantity on a number of subjects from different periods and disciplines: organology, Bach, Gluck, Brahms, et al.

The work on Haydn displays a certain duality. On the one hand, one can not help but notice Geiringer's strong tendency toward consistency which can be exemplified best perhaps by his vigorous attacks on the eighteenth- and particularly nineteenth-century images of the childlike (Charles Burney), happy-go-lucky, Good Old Papa Haydn (the *Altvater* of Robert Schumann) launched in Geiringer's earliest writings ("Portrait," essay 2) and pursued relentlessly in his books from the preface of the first edition of the volume for Norton in 1946 (p. 11) through the last pages of the conclusion to the final third edition, revised and enlarged in 1982 (p. 368). Geiringer points out

---

[13] The participants have been Paul and Eva Badura-Skoda (1994), Margaret Bent, Rosalyn Tureck (1995), Christoph Wolff (1996), Charles Rosen (1997), Lewis Lockwood (1998), Walter Frisch, Otto Biba, Ingrid Fuchs, Vassily Primakov (1999), Laurence Dreyfus and the Phantasm Viol Quartet (2000), and Robert Levin (2001).

[14] *This I Remember*, 142f.

[15] Ibid., 143.

(essay 1, pp. 5, 8) how the nickname became attached to Haydn as a term of endearment by the members of his Esterházy band (who knew the most of Haydn's music) because of his humanity, and how the label was made over to express patronization and contempt by nineteenth-century critics (who knew the least of Haydn's music) because of the style of his music.[16] On the other hand, this penchant for consistency coexisted with a certain eagerness to embrace new discoveries and ideas, and a willingness to make the necessary revisions such discoveries and ideas demanded.[17] No doubt this attribute was related to his close involvement in one way or another with all three of the century's Haydn "rivals"[18]—the major enterprises whose purpose may have been to publish the complete works for the first time, but whose activities were the primary generator of new information about Haydn and his music. In aggregate, these experiences put Geiringer in a unique position to view the rapidly changing reception history of Haydn not only in the twentieth but in the nineteenth and eighteenth centuries as well. He expressed himself specifically on this topic from time to time, while much of his work as a reviewer is informed by these same circumstances.[19]

* * * *

Because he was prolific as an editor and author on such a broad range of musical subjects, the attempt to form a selection from the vast œuvre left by Geiringer even within just one of his principal areas of scholarship, Haydn, would be arbitrary if not undertaken with some kind of guiding principles. To avoid this pitfall, therefore, two criteria were brought into the selection process for the purposes of this volume. First, items were assembled that would represent as far as possible the full scope of Karl's activities as they related to Haydn, which extended from scholarly musicological studies intended for the specialist to public lectures, brochures, and reviews directed toward a wider audience. Then, as a second consideration, versions of essays previously unpublished, long out of print or whose publication was widely spread over time and space, such as the landmark reviews of H. C. Robbins Landon's *Haydn: Chronicle and Works* (essay 24), published over a five-year span in the volumes of *Notes*, were collected. Articles or introductions, such as that to the critical edition of C. W. Gluck's *Telemaco* (essay 16), originally published in German, have also been included here in translation for the first time.

The materials selected in this manner have been brought together under one cover and grouped into four sections, the first two of which reflect the phases described earlier by Geiringer to characterize the development of his own Haydn research. Within these sections each of the individual entries is prefaced with a brief editorial annotation followed usually by a pertinent extract drawn from Geiringer's autobiographical *This I Remember*, which also has been inserted editorially and rendered in italics.

Those who had the opportunity to witness Geiringer's inimitable style of lecturing and reading papers would be the first to recall that illustrations were fundamental to both content and effectiveness of his presentations. Yet these examples were often the first to be removed by editors, presumably for reasons of space, when the presentations were published. Therefore, I have restored musical examples to published lectures where these had been clearly indicated by the author (e.g., essays 3 and 8). It is hoped that their inclusion adds to the value and usefulness of the present volume.

Early on in the course of preparing this book the editorial conclusion was reached that, with the few exceptions noted below, there would be little attempt to modernize Geiringer's work by correcting and updating or presenting opposing viewpoints, etc. The essays cut a wide path of over sixty years (1927-88) through the twentieth century, a period in which not only great strides were made in Haydn research in the areas of biography, chronology, authorship, and, therefore, in the perception of style change, but also extensive development and change were experienced in eighteenth-century musical scholarship as a whole. Geiringer's contribution to this recharged atmosphere was

---

[16] Concerning this issue, see also essay 12, p. 148.

[17] Not surprisingly, these same tendencies can be observed in Geiringer's work on other subjects as well. See for instance the examples cited in "Karl Geiringer (1899-1989)," *AMS Newsletter*, 19.

[18] See Leon Botstein, "The Consequences of Presumed Innocence: The Nineteenth-Century Reception of Joseph Haydn," in *Haydn Studies*, ed. W. Dean Sutcliffe (Cambridge: Cambridge University Press, [1998]), 20.

[19] See for examples essay 2 and the article "Haydns Werk im Lauf der Jahrhunderts," *Neue Zürcher Zeitung* 193 (1972): 43-44.

significant and steadfast, despite seemingly insurmountable political and historical obstacles. It seemed more to the point and to the enhancement of the volume's value in the long term to have these writings stand on their own, reflecting viewpoints and conclusions based upon the state of knowledge of the time in which they were created, rather than perceiving them through a prism revised by later discoveries or reflecting the new or different methodologies that were already emerging in the years immediately before Geiringer's death.

Nevertheless, in a few instances where it was felt current information might add significantly to the appreciation of an essay, comments have been made in the introductory annotations preceding the items (see, for example, essay 13). Elsewhere in the introductory extracts from *This I Remember*, in the texts proper, and in the footnotes, square brackets [ ] have been used to insert corrective or supplementary information such as catalog identifications (e.g., Hoboken numbers). Geiringer gave his own supplementary comments, completions, and occasional catalog identifications as a rule in parentheses ( ), and when these appear in the present essays they have been retained in that form. Likewise, in the music examples reprinted from the *Joseph Haydn Werke* the editorial principles of the Haydn Institute have been retained, including the differentiation of ( ) and [ ]. Otherwise, only minor editorial changes have been made in order to bring a degree of stylistic uniformity to essays that were printed over so many decades by various publishers and supervised by different editors in four countries—Austria, Germany, Great Britain, and America.

The volume concludes with a completely revised and up-dated bibliography of the Geiringers' publications as they pertain to Haydn, compiled by David Malvinni and Martin Silver, and indexes of names and references to Haydn's works.

*   *   *   *

Finally I wish to acknowledge my gratitude to the late Bernice Geiringer as well as the Karl Geiringer Estate, especially George Gardiner, for enabling me to access Karl's and Irene's personal library, notes, recordings, microfilms, photographs, and correspondence. My appreciation is extended to Dr. Martin Bente of the Verlagsleitung of G. Henle, not only for granting permission to reprint numerous excerpts from the *Joseph Haydn Werke* in essay 8, but also for generously waiving all copyright fees. Universal Edition A. G. Wien demonstrated similar generosity in providing examples for essay 3. I am also grateful to Otto Biba, H. C. Robbins Landon, and Martin Silver for their valuable suggestions, and the production staff of Harmonie Park Press, in particular the editorial expertise and sharp eye of J. Bunker Clark. The University of California, Santa Barbara provided two generous research grants in support of this book.

The German texts of essays 2, 4, 13-14, and 16 have been rendered into English by Dr. Therese Ahren-August of Yale University and myself. I take full responsibility, however, for any inaccuracies that may have occurred as a result. Other translators are acknowledged in the annotations. A number of graduate students in musicology at UCSB assisted significantly during the preparatory stages of the volume, and I wish to thank especially Dr. Alicia Doyle, David Malvinni, Denise Odello, Guido Olivieri, and Jeanne Scheppach for their untiring efforts. A special note of thanks goes to Valerie Johnson and my sister Betty Spilker for their careful reading of the final typescript.

ROBERT N. FREEMAN[†]
18 June 2002

University of California, Santa Barbara
October 2001

Abbreviations

A	alto
B	bass
B.-Gl.	Irmgard Becker-Glauch, "Neue Forschungen zu Haydns Kirchenmusik," *Haydn Studien* 2 (1970): 167-241.
Bn	bassoon
ca.	circa
Cb	contrabass, double bass
Cl	clarinet(s)
col(s).	column(s)
cond.	conductor, conducted by
diss.	dissertation
ed.	edition, edited by
f., ff.	folio, folios
fasc.	fascicle
Fl	flute(s), flauto
H.	E. Eugene Helm, *Thematic Catalogue of the Works of Carl Philipp Emanuel Bach* (New Haven: Yale University Press, 1989)
Hn	Horn
Hob.	Anthony van Hoboken, *Joseph Haydn: Thematisch-bibliographisches Werkverzeichnis*, 3 vols. (Mainz: Schott, 1957-78)
HV	"Haydn Verzeichnis," in *Three Haydn Catalogues*, 2nd facsimile ed., ed. Jens Peter Larsen (New York: Pendragon Press, 1979)
K.	Ludwig Ritter von Köchel, *Chronologisch-thematisches Verzeichnis sämtlicher Tonwerke Wolfgang Amadeus Mozarts*, 6th ed., ed. Franz Giegling et al. (Wiesbaden: Breitkopf & Härtel, 1964)
meas.	measure(s)
MGG	*Die Musik in Geschichte und Gegenwart*, ed. Friedrich Blume, 17 vols. (Kassel: Bärenreiter, 1949-86)
Ms., Mss.	manuscript, manuscripts
NA	*Christoph Willibald Gluck: Sämtliche Werke*, ed. Rudolf Gerber (Kassel: Bärenreiter, 1951-)
New Grove	*The New Grove Dictionary of Music and Musicians*, ed. Stanley Sadie, 20 vols. (London: Macmillan, 1980)
n(n).	note(s)
n.p.	no publisher

n.s.	new series
Ob	oboe(s)
op.	opus
r	recto
rev.	revised
S	soprano
sec.	section
T	tenor
Tb	tuba
This I Remember	Karl Geiringer, with Bernice Geiringer, *This I Remember* (Santa Barbara: Fithian Press, 1993)
Trb	trombone(s)
Va	viola(s)
Vc	violoncello
Vc & B	violoncello and basso
Vn	violin(s), violino
Wq.	Alfred Wotquenne, *Thematisches Verzeichnis der Werke von Carl Philipp Emanuel Bach (1714-1788)* (Leipzig: Breitkopf & Härtel, 1905)

Haydn's Artistic and Human Personality

Originally I had tried to provide a complete picture of Haydn's artistic and human personality.
—This I Remember, *143*

Fig. 1.1 Haydn, portrait by Thomas Hardy, 1791

Courtesy of the Royal College of Music, London

Joseph Haydn

Entry first published in *The New Encyclopaedia Britannica*, 15th ed. (Chicago: Encyclopaedia Britannica, 1974), vol. 8, 680-84, and frequently reprinted thereafter through 1995. Reprinted with permission of *Encyclopaedia Britannica*, 15th edition, ©1974 by Encyclopaedia Britannica, Inc. The work list and bibliography have been omitted here.

Closely linked to the flowering of classical music in his eighteenth-century Austria, Franz Joseph Haydn, after experimenting with various stylistic trends prevailing in his youth (the pompous and complex idiom taken over from the preceding Baroque period; the light and gay *style galant*, a style distinguished by formal elegance and clarity imported from Italy and France; and the strongly emotional and expressive *Empfindsamkeit*, or "sensitive style," preferred by North German composers), eventually achieved his own distinctive musical identity by using some elements of all three styles simultaneously. From the age of nearly fifty onward, he wrote his greatest works, which display a classical synthesis of seemingly incompatible characteristics. Inspiration and heartfelt expression were as important to him as the work of an alert intellect. He established a well-balanced mixture of cheerful folk song elements and serious, at times even tragic, moods. Haydn was significantly helped by the younger composer Wolfgang Amadeus Mozart, who at first accepted the older man's guidance and later enthusiastically collaborated with him.

Haydn is often called the father of the symphony and of the string quartet. Although the statement is in the nature of an oversimplification, works of this kind having existed before him, he did endow the two forms with an artistry and significant content that secured for them a high place within musical literature. His last two oratorios, his great symphonic Masses, as well as some of his piano works, songs, and concerti stand on an equally high level. Beethoven was strongly indebted to Haydn, and in the nineteenth century such composers as Franz Schubert, Johannes Brahms, and Anton Bruckner all were to build on foundations erected by him.

Early Years

Education in Hainburg and Vienna. Haydn was born on 31 March 1732, in Rohrau, a village in eastern Austria near the Hungarian border. War was anything but a rarity in the district, and Haydn's ancestors had suffered from invasions by the Turks and by Hungarian raiders. Stubborn tenacity and resourcefulness were needed to survive under such conditions, and these were qualities inherited by Haydn. His parents, like their forefathers, were humble people: his father a wheelwright, his mother, before her marriage, a cook for the lords of the village. Joseph, their second child, revealed, to everybody's surprise, unusual musical gifts, and the parents were at a loss how to provide the proper type of education for him. The problem was solved when a cousin, serving as a school principal and choirmaster in the nearby city of Hainburg, offered to take the boy into his home and train him. The parents, seeing no other way, agreed; and thus Joseph, not yet six years old, left home, never to return to the parental cottage except for rare, brief visits.

From a professional point of view, the move to Hainburg was an important one. The boy sang in the church choir, learned to play various instruments, and obtained a good basic knowledge of music. In other respects, life at Hainburg was less satisfactory. The cousin was poor and his modest salary hardly sufficed to support a growing family. Joseph was not given the love and care a child needs; as he later reported, he received "more floggings than food." But he was able to take such disadvantages in his stride; his nature was endowed with wiry resilience and a contented disposition.

A decisive change in his life occurred when Haydn was eight years old. The musical director of Saint Stephen's Cathedral in Vienna had observed the boy on a visit to Hainburg and invited him to serve as chorister at the Austrian capital's most important church. Haydn's parents accepted the offer with delight, for it secured for their son a thorough musical training and relieved them of all financial cares while he boarded at the choir school. Thus, in 1740 the eight-year-old moved to Vienna full of expectation of the glorious experiences in store for him. He stayed at the school for nine years, acquiring an enormous practical knowledge of music by constant performances but, to his disappointment, receiving far too little instruction in music theory. The pattern of life in Hainburg seemed to repeat itself. Again he had to work hard to fulfill all his obligations as a chorister; again he was badly fed and sometimes suffered, as he reported, from "ravenous hunger." Gradually his voice deteriorated; when it broke, the cathedral choir had no use for him. Seizing on the pretext of punishing a practical joke committed by the high-spirited youth, the director had him expelled from the choir school.

With no money in his pocket and three ragged shirts and an old coat as his only possessions, Haydn at seventeen was left to his own devices. He found a refuge for a while in the humble garret of a fellow musician and supported himself "miserably" with odd musical jobs, performing at dances and serenades, playing the organ at Sunday services, and teaching at very modest fees. Hand in hand with these activities went an arduous course of self-instruction through the study of musical works—notably those of Carl Philipp Emanuel Bach (1714-88)—and of leading manuals of musical theory. A fortunate chance brought him to the attention of the successful Italian composer and singing teacher Nicola Porpora (1686-1768), who accepted him as accompanist for voice lessons, and, in return for this as well as for his services as a valet, corrected Haydn's compositions.

Thanks to tremendous persistence and unflagging energy, Haydn made progress. He was eventually engaged to teach some aristocratic pupils and introduced by them to the music-loving Austrian nobleman Karl Joseph von Fürnberg, in whose home he played chamber music. For the instrumentalists there he wrote his first string quartets, a form that he cultivated throughout his professional career, composing some eighty works in this genre.

Bohemian Post with Count von Morzin. In 1758 Haydn received his first steady appointment. Through the recommendation of Fürnberg he was engaged as musical director and chamber composer by the Bohemian count Ferdinand Maximilian von Morzin, who resided most of the time in his country estate of Lukaveč in western Bohemia. Haydn had an orchestra of about sixteen musicians at his disposal, and, for this ensemble, he wrote his first symphony, the other musical form in which he pioneered. These first attempts in the field of instrumental composition were still conventional in character, yet a certain freshness of melodic invention and sparkle marked them as the work of a future master.

The First Period of Esterházy Patronage

"Papa" Haydn. Haydn did not stay long with Count von Morzin, as financial difficulties forced his patron to dismiss the orchestra. Before long he was invited to enter the service of Prince Pál Antal Esterházy, who had heard his works at Count von Morzin's castle. The Esterházys were one of the wealthiest and most influential families of the Austrian empire and boasted a distinguished record of supporting music and art. Prince Pál Antal had a well-appointed orchestra performing regularly in his sumptuous castle at Eisenstadt, a small town some thirty miles from Vienna. As his aged music director was ailing, the prince had vision enough to appoint the relatively unknown Haydn as assistant conductor. The contract, concluded on 1 May 1761, informs us about the new appointee's duties. While church music was still entrusted to the director, three other spheres of activity were assigned to Haydn: to conduct the orchestra and coach the singers (which meant almost daily rehearsals); to compose the greatest part of the music required; to do administrative work by serving as music librarian, supervisor of instruments, and chief of the musical personnel. Haydn carried out these duties extremely well and even managed to find time to supervise the work of the copyists of music and to tune his own keyboard instruments. His service as chief of personnel revealed tact, good nature, and skill in dealing with people. He exerted himself to support his subordinates against other officials on the prince's staff, and, thanks to his friendliness and his sense of humor, he managed to maintain good relations with staff and employers. The musicians loved and respected their "Papa," as they nicknamed him.

In 1766 Haydn became musical director at the Esterházy court. He raised the quality and increased the size of the prince's musical ensembles by appointing many choice instrumentalists and singers. His ambitious plans were supported by Prince Miklós, who, on the death of his brother in 1762, had become head of the family and maintained his leadership for twenty-eight years. A passionate and discriminating music lover himself, he was able to appreciate Haydn's contributions and created an atmosphere beneficial for the development and maturing of his music director's art. Miklós "The Magnificent," as he was usually referred to, loved splendor and display. Having admired Versailles in France, he decided to match it by a creation of his own. At enormous expense he built in 1766 the splendid castle of Esterháza, situated in the western part of Hungary. Every night a performance of a German play or of an Italian opera would be offered in the palace theater. Haydn, in addition to his other staggering duties, was in charge of all operatic activities. He not only selected, rehearsed, and conducted operas by other composers but contributed more than a dozen musical works of his own. No lesser person than Empress Maria Theresa of Austria testified to the high level of operatic performance achieved in the Esterházy theater. She was once overheard saying, "When I want to hear a good opera, I have to go to Esterháza," a verdict that was not gratifying to the musicians of Vienna.

Operas. Some of Haydn's operas, such as the hilarious *La canterina* (The Songstress) [Hob. XXVIII:2] of 1767 and *Lo speziale* (The Apothecary) [Hob. XXVIII:3] of 1768, are musical comedies; other stage works, such as *L'isola disabitata* (The Deserted Island) [Hob. XXVIII:9] of 1779 and *Armida* [Hob. XXVIII:12] of 1784, are of a serious character. Most significant are those operas in which Haydn succeeded in combining comic and serious elements by conjuring up gay characters contrasted with more earnest-minded ones. One of his last and most successful works for the stage, *Orlando Paladino* (Knight Roland) [Hob. XXVIII:11] of 1782, bore the fitting subtitle of "drama eroicomico" (heroic-comic drama). Even when performing operas by other composers, Haydn made adaptations to render them suitable for the personnnel of the prince's theater. Following the common practice of the time, he often added arias of his own to works by other composers, which were display pieces for the singers and added additional sparkle to the work performed.

In addition to his operatic duties, he composed symphonies, string quartets, and other chamber music. The prince was a passionate performer on the baryton, and Haydn provided for his patron more than 150 compositions featuring this now obsolete cello-like instrument.

Haydn seems to have enjoyed his busy life and served Prince Miklós for nearly thirty years. Living in the country was no hardship for him. He loved hunting, fishing, and other outdoor activities. Nor did he feel cut off from the cultural world, for travelling dramatic troupes often brought works by eminent writers to Esterháza, and he frequently visited Vienna in the prince's retinue.

Friendship with Mozart. On these occasional visits a close friendship developed with Mozart. The fact that Mozart was twenty-four years younger than Haydn did not matter. They felt inspired by each other's work. Mozart declared that he had learned from Haydn how to write quartets and dedicated a superb set of six such works to his "beloved friend." Haydn's music, too, shows in various details the impact of his young friend's idiom. The mature composer was by no means set in his ways; he was flexible and receptive to new ideas, an admirable trait in an artist who had already won wide recognition.

Unlike Mozart, Haydn became internationally famous in his own lifetime. His works were performed throughout Europe and were published in Austria, Germany, Holland, France, and England. He received official commissions from many European music lovers. The city of Cádiz in Spain, for example, commissioned *The Seven Last Words* [Hob. XX/2] for a Good Friday service; the king of Naples requested compositions for the lira organizzata, a hurdy-gurdy (wheel fiddle) with a built-in tiny pipe organ; and the "Paris" Symphonies (nos. 82-87) were composed between 1785 and 1786 for the French capital.

Unhappy Marriage. The success of Haydn's professional career was not matched in his personal life. The girl he loved entered a convent, and her parents induced Haydn, who had just obtained his position with Count von Morzin, to espouse the elder sister. The decision proved disastrous for his realization of a pleasant, peaceful home. No children were born to the couple. Haydn's wife, two years his senior, was quarrelsome and bigoted. She did not understand music and showed no interest in her husband's work. It was reported that her expression of disdain went to the extremes of using his manuscripts for pastry linings or curl papers. As a result the composer was not insensitive to the attractions of other women, and for years carried on a love affair with Luigia Polzelli, a young Italian mezzo-soprano in the prince's service.

English Period

In 1790 Prince Miklós died. His son, Prince Antal, did not care for music and dismissed most of the court musicians. Haydn was retained, however, and continued to receive his salary. No duties were required of him, enabling Haydn to do whatever he pleased. But after such a long time at the Esterházy court, the composer was eager to try a different way of life. He, therefore, considered seriously two tempting offers that were made as soon as his availability was generally known. First, the king of Naples urged him to accept an invitation extended several years earlier to visit his court; second, a violinist and concert manager, Johann Peter Salomon, arrived from England and commissioned, at excellent financial terms, six new symphonies and twenty smaller compositions to be conducted by the composer himself in a series of orchestral concerts in London sponsored by Salomon. Haydn, moreover, was to compose a new Italian opera for the King's Theatre in London, for a fee of £300. Haydn felt far more attracted by the English than by the Italian invitation. He felt it would be great experience to work with a large, excellently trained orchestra and to live in one of the great musical centers of the eighteenth century. Furthermore, he would no longer have to submit to the rigid etiquette of the Esterházy court and continually be reminded of his subservient position.

First Visit to London. Undeterred by the dire warnings of his friends, including Mozart, he left for London. What the prospect of the visit to England meant to him may be realized when one considers that though fifty-eight he had yet to travel beyond the borders of Austria. On New Year's Day 1791 he arrived on British soil, and the experience of the following eighteen months proved as rewarding and stimulating as he had anticipated. The many novel impressions, the meeting with eminent musicians, the admiration bestowed on him had a powerful impact on his creative work. The symphonies written for the first and second visit to London represent the climax in his orchestral output. One admires their virtuosity of instrumentation, the masterly treatment of musical forms, the freely flowing melodic inspiration, and the sense of humor that endeared the works so much to the British audiences. Their popularity is reflected in the various nicknames bestowed on them ("Surprise," "Clock," "Military," "Drum Roll"). As Haydn conducted the works himself, he exercised, in the words of the great contemporaneous British musicologist Charles Burney, "an electrical effect on all present and such a degree of enthusiasm as almost amounted to frenzy." The opera he composed fared less well because the King's Theatre, for which it was commissioned, was refused the license to perform such works. Haydn, however, suffered no financial loss, and the events seems not to have greatly disturbed him.

In England Haydn was feted by famous men as well as by royalty. In July 1791 Oxford University awarded him the honorary degree of Doctor of Music. He performed at the residences of the Prince of Wales and the Duke of York. His diary describes visits at which he was "gloriously entertained," and references to beautiful women he met at such occasions are anything but rare. Sixty years old, his face pitted by smallpox, with a large aquiline nose and too-short legs, he remained attractive to women admirers.

In spite of his great success, Haydn was forced to submit to one of the artistic contests fashionable at the time. A rival music organization, which had failed to induce Haydn to join them, engaged a young pupil of his, one Ignaz Pleyel, to conduct its concert series. A vicious campaign was started emphasizing Haydn's advanced age and the pupil's expertise, but it was to no avail; Haydn could report that he had "kept the upper hand." The concerts he conducted, consisting largely of his own works, continued to be a series of triumphs.

In June 1792 Haydn left London for Germany, as Prince Esterházy wanted the famous composer in his retinue at the coronation of Emperor Francis II in Frankfurt am Main. On his journey he stopped at Bonn where the twenty-two-year-old Beethoven was introduced to him, and it was arranged that the young composer should move to Vienna to receive the aged master's instruction. On July 29 Haydn arrived in Vienna where he was able, thanks to his considerable earnings in England, to buy a pleasant house in the suburb of Gumpendorf. This dwelling still stands today and is the site of a Haydn museum.

Second Visit to London. The composer did not stay in Vienna for long, however. His English admirers urged him to visit London once more, and in January 1794 he left the Austrian capital to return to England until 15 August 1795. Again he won great acclaim. Various members of the royal family made efforts to keep him in England, but Haydn declined because a change had occurred in the leadership of the Esterházy family. Miklós II, the new head of the princely house, was eager to restore the former orchestra under Haydn's direction, and the composer felt compelled to accept the assignment. The duties he now undertook would, of course, not be as burdensome as previously. Moreover, the prince's intention to spend the winter months in Vienna provided a strong incentive. Although Haydn had to separate from the many friends he had made in London, he could look back on the period spent in England as a profitable one. His trunks bulged with no less than 768 pages of music he had written in that hospitable country, and the musical stimulus and the financial rewards for his labor had been gratifying.

The Late Esterházy and Viennese Period

Oratorios. In 1791 Haydn had attended the Handel Commemoration at Westminster Abbey in London. He was deeply moved by the superb rendition of Handel's masterly oratorios and by the veneration with which they were received by the English audience. Deciding to compose in this musical genre, he was able to obtain a suitable libretto, allegedly prepared for Handel himself. After settling in Vienna and resuming his duties for Prince Esterházy, Haydn started work on the oratorio *The Creation* [Hob. XXI:2], the text of which had been translated into German by Baron Gottfried van Swieten. The libretto was based on the epic poem *Paradise Lost* by England's foremost seventeenth-century poet, John Milton (1608-74) and on the Genesis chapter of the Bible. Composing the oratorio provided Haydn with a truly congenial task. He was a deeply religious man who throughout his long career had created Latin Masses of great beauty for the Roman Catholic Church. In the oratorio he could express his gratitude to God in a work with German text and at the same time depict in music the beauties of nature that so greatly delighted him. The years devoted to this task were among the happiest in Haydn's life. He felt uplifted and in communion with the divine spirit. In April 1798 the oratorio had its first performance in a princely palace and produced a profound effect. As a critic wrote: "Three days have gone since that enrapturing evening . . . still the mere memory of all the flood of emotions then experienced constricts my heart." Before long a public performance took place with equal results, and henceforth *The Creation* was again and again performed with great success, the proceeds going, at the composer's request, to charitable institutions.

This encouraged Haydn to produce another oratorio, which absorbed him until 1801. A British text, the poem *The Seasons* [Hob. XXI:3] by the Scottish poet James Thomson (1700-48), was again chosen for the libretto and translated by van Swieten. Though of limited poetical value, the adapted work allowed him to compose delightful musical genre pictures of events in nature. This second oratorio was also triumphantly successful both at court, where the Austrian empress sang the soprano solos, and in public performances.

Haydn's late creative activity, however, was not confined to the oratorio. The six Masses written for his patron Esterházy are among the most significant works of this kind from the eighteenth century. He continued to compose magnificent string quartets and, in 1797, he gave to the Austrian nation the stirring song "Gott erhalte Franz den Kaiser" (God Save Emperor Francis) [Hob. XXVIa:43]. It was used for more than a century as the national anthem of the Austrian monarchy and as the patriotic song "Deutschland, Deutschland über alles" (Germany, Germany above all else) in Germany. It is heard today under many titles as a Protestant hymn in the English-speaking countries. The song was so beloved that Haydn decided to use it as a theme for variations in one of his finest string quartets, the *Emperor Quartet*, op. 76, no. 3.

Honors Bestowed. Not surprisingly, honors from various parts of Europe gladdened the composer in his last years. Stockholm, Amsterdam, St. Petersburg, and Paris made him an honorary member of their music associations, and the French capital had, after the premiere of *The Creation*, a gold medal engraved in Haydn's honor. Nor did

Austria lag behind. In the village of Rohrau, Haydn's birthplace, a monument was erected to its famous son, and Haydn had the gratification of seeing it. The city of Vienna conferred on him the great golden Salvator Medal and named him an honorary citizen. Particularly notable was the Vienna concert of 1808 in celebration of Haydn's seventy-sixth birthday. *The Creation* was performed by eminent musicians in the presence of the ailing composer, carried in on an armchair and seated amid jubilant exclamations among members of the high nobility. Poems were read in his honor, applause shook the hall, and on Haydn's departure Beethoven knelt down and kissed the hands of his former teacher. This was Haydn's last public appearance. Henceforth, conditions in Vienna prevented such outings and undermined the little strength still left to the aged artist. Austria faced the Napoleonic armies in 1809—devastating battles were fought and Vienna was bombarded, a cannon ball falling near Haydn's residence. Napoleon, however, eventually placed a guard of honor outside Haydn's house.

In these turbulent days a moment of joyful respite was granted to the invalid. A French officer called and, professing admiration of Haydn's music, gave a rendering of an aria from *The Creation*, which allegedly made the composer shed happy tears. Soon afterward the singer fell in battle. Haydn survived him by only a few days, dying on 31 May 1809. At the official obsequies, members of the French army joined forces with the municipal militia to form a line before the catafalque. Vienna's cultural elite and high-ranking French officers paid solemn tribute to the genius who had given so much to the musical world.

Reasons for Contemporary Success. The success achieved by Haydn in his lifetime is often attributed to his slow development, enabling music lovers to progress step by step in their understanding of his aims; his long life endowed with creative power up to old age; and, most of all, his attunement to the spirit of the times. Haydn was a true representative of the age of Enlightenment. His positive, optimistic approach to life, his striving for balance between the work of the intellect and the flow of emotions, and his sense of moderation leading to the avoidance of strongly discordant moods found superb expression in his music and thus gave his contemporaries the kind of music they were able to appreciate. Music lovers also found irresistible the nobility and deceptive simplicity of his idiom, sparked by delightful outbreaks of humor. In the nineteenth century the ideals of the Enlightenment no longer were prevailing. The age of Romanticism liked to probe dark and complex moods, morbidity seemed attractive, and emphasis was laid on conjuring up ambivalent emotions in music. To this epoch the gaiety and naturalness of Haydn's idiom seemed to be rather philistine and people patronized "good old Papa Haydn," whose works were, as a matter of fact, hardly known. In the twentieth century there was a reevaluation of his work; and the outstanding intellectual nature of his thematic elaborations, the originality of his modulations, and the artistry and superb craftsmanship of his orchestration were again appreciated.

The Portrait of Haydn
Over the Course of Time

Originally published as "Das Haydn-Bild im Wandel der Zeiten," *Die Musik* 24/6 (1932): 430-36. Reprinted with permission of Dr. Hans Schneider Verlag, Tutzing. This brief but significant essay is one of a flurry of publications Geiringer produced in 1932 for the bicentennial of Haydn's birth that included most importantly the first edition of his book on Haydn for Ernst Bücken's newly established series *Die großen Meister der Musik* referred to in the note on page 10 (see also the Preface). Playing upon the double meaning of "portrait," Geiringer seizes the occasion of the bicentennial to review current and past views of Haydn and his music. A decisively anti-Romantic sentiment reflective of this period of Haydn historiography—see Leon Botstein, "The Consequences of Presumed Innocence: The Nineteenth-Century Reception of Joseph Haydn," in *Haydn Studies*, ed. W. Dean Sutcliffe (Cambridge: Cambridge University Press, 1998), 20—is expressed as Geiringer takes to task the nineteenth-century perspective of "good 'Papa Haydn.'" Even Pohl's biography does not escape criticism. The misinterpretation and near total neglect of the vocal categories (sacred music, opera, Lieder) are singled out. Prophetically it was precisely to these lacunae that Geiringer was to turn his own efforts to produce pioneering contributions after leaving Vienna (see essays 7-10). He bewails the lack of a modern thematic catalog and the slow progress of the current (1932) Breitkopf collected edition, although he could not foresee that the following year it would be discontinued, not to be resumed until the formation of the Haydn Society by H. C. Robbins Landon and Jens Peter Larsen in Boston, 1949—see Christopher Raeburn, "H. C. Robbins Landon and the Haydn Society: A Pioneering Musical Adventure," in *Studies in Music History Presented to H. C. Robbins Landon on His Seventieth Birthday*, ed. Otto Biba and David Wyn Jones (London: Thames and Hudson, 1996), 227-33—the dismal picture ends on an optimistic note of hope for the future. The original oil portrait depicted in the figure on p. 12, now thought to have been executed ca. 1768 by J. B. Grundmann, was subsequently lost in World War II.

When Napoleon occupied Vienna in 1809, he placed an honor guard in front of Haydn's home. This act of grandseigneur-like civility reveals a deeper symbolic significance. The French emperor was paying homage to the master, who—much like Napoleon himself—had soared from the most modest of beginnings to the greatest heights of recognition and reputation within his sphere of influence. Napoleon saluted in Haydn an individual who differed from him to his very core and yet was also, in this one sense, a kindred spirit.

To anyone who follows his story from its beginnings to its finale and climax, Haydn's rise must come as a shock. Slow and steady, with the eternal serenity and irresistible power of a force of nature, Haydn climbs step by step and ceases to rise only shortly before his death. His development lacks sudden surprises as well as setbacks. Climbing upwards seems for Haydn to be the most self-evident and natural form of progression.

The master emerges from the lowliest of origins. The fate of his early childhood was determined by one fact: he was one of twelve children in a family of craftsmen in a tiny village in Lower Austria. Hence it already signifies progress that at five years old he reaches the small city of Hainburg and at eight comes to Vienna as a choirboy at St. Stephen's Cathedral. To be sure, things go badly enough for the boy here as well. "It seemed," as a friend reports from Haydn's own comments, "as if the body along with the spirit were deliberately allowed to starve." Yet despite this the boy is neither broken nor bent. He learns through practice whatever there is to learn, fills in the gaps in his education after leaving the boarding school—despite complete lack of financial means—through self-study of theoretical works, makes his way in the world after a fashion—and stands unsuspectingly at the foot of that ladder that would lead him up to the greatest heights. Haydn comes into contact with the Lord von Fürnberg and thus establishes connections to aristocratic and courtly musical patronage, which at the time offered the artist the greatest wealth of possibilities. Baron von Fürnberg recommends him to Count Morzin; through him

Haydn meets Prince Esterházy, and when the prince and his heir had both passed on, King Ferdinand IV of Naples seeks to bring the composer to his court. Yet Haydn wants even more and turns, at almost the same time that the third estate fights for its rights in the French Revolution, from aristocratic to democratic patronage.[1] He declines the king's offer and sets off to give a concert to the bourgeois public in England's capital city.

The triumphs that Haydn achieves here were thoroughly prepared through the efforts of the Kapellmeister for the Esterházys. The musician who was allowed to compose for others only with the "foreknowledge and gracious permission" of his prince had in the three decades of his appointment become a leading figure in eighteenth-century arts. Placing a spotlight on the good reputation that Haydn already enjoyed early on reveals the following: although a reference in an earlier piano sonata (D major [Hob. XVI:19], composed 1767) to the style of Philipp Emanuel Bach is not to his liking, one reviewer does not dare find fault with the work, only claiming that Haydn had "finely picked apart" and parodied Bach's work. The master's works are soon printed in Holland, France, England; Spain commissions Haydn to write music for a Passion, and her poet Dom Tomás de Yriarte praises the composer in ebullient terms. Even in his own land, the prophet begins to be honored. Vienna requests an oratorio and an opera from him, and the esteemed publishing house Artaria attends to his work. However, all of these successes pale in comparison to the triumph of his visits to England. There is no better measure of the far-reaching effects of Haydn's work there than the great number of concerts, enthusiastically received by the critics, to which the artist is invited again and again. Added to this is the simple fact that in London Haydn reaches the high point of his creativity within the symphonic genre.

The pre-conditions for these triumphs had been present in Haydn's work for some time. It would be one-sided to consider only external factors and overlook internal conditions. Already a decade previous, in the early 1780s, a movement toward expansiveness and universality begins to dominate Haydn's work. In terms of compositional technique, that movement can be explained as a breakthrough of the "motivic work" in Haydn's instrumental production. The sharp division between melodically oriented and merely harmonically supportive voices is eliminated. All parts are used obbligato and animated by motives. Every last effect of the courtly-aristocratic principle of dividing the leading "ornamental" instruments from those merely supporting the "Fundament" is eliminated, replaced by the democratic equality of all parts. Hand in hand with this development, Haydn's expressions become simpler, more popular, more easily understood. He leads emotions back to their least common denominator, as it were, and presents them in a form not only comprehensible to "Kenner und Liebhaber," but rather to all. Yet it is precisely in this manner that he also succeeds in generating effects that extend just as far in breadth and depth.

More than ever before, Haydn, now returned home to Austria, turns his attention to the people as a whole. It is no coincidence that he himself makes the suggestion to compose the Austrian national anthem. At the same time, it is fate that brings Haydn to compose the final oratorio at the immense Handel festivals in England. These festivals, performed by thousands but also attended by thousands of revelers, awaken the deepest resonance in Haydn. His sense of responsibility is then no longer limited to his time but extended into eternity. Thus he composes the *The Creation* and *The Seasons* [Hob. XXI:2-3], works that transcend all social, political, and national boundaries with their gaiety and unaffectedness, their simplicity and strength, their clarity and magnitude.

Haydn's contemporaries soon take notice of this. *The Creation* and *The Seasons* are received with an approval that few other major works of music were granted in their first performances. Haydn now stands at the zenith of his fame. Greater proof than the honors he received from scholarly circles throughout the world, greater still than the performances of the *The Creation* in the capital cities of France and Russia, is the simple fact that the smallest of locales, such as St. Johann in Bohemia, or Bergen on the isle of Rügen, passionately rehearse and perform the oratorio. And just how much Haydn's self-confidence had risen is evident in a seemingly humble but in fact charmingly proud statement by the old master. On the occasion of the performance of the *The Creation* in 1808, buoyed by the approval of the audience, Haydn calls out: "All of it comes not from me, but from above!"

In the history of musical arts, few figures of lasting stature were granted a momentary success as great as Haydn's. For the most part, only mediocrity is immediately honored and appreciated by the public. Yet the whole of Haydn's character enabled an exception in this case. Personality and growth are so successfully formed in him that he escapes the typical fate of the genius to live without the understanding of the rest of the world. His nature is firmly cast, clear, consistent. He affirms life, his mind remains free of ambivalence and strife. Slowly and steadily,

---

[1] For further entries see my biography *Joseph Haydn: Die großen Meister der Musik* (Potsdam: Athenaion, 1932).

without sudden leaps, without surprises but also without setbacks, his growth completes itself. To be sure, his fate does not lack deviations. However, they are prepared long beforehand and have only gradual effects. These characteristics of his nature, to which we must add earthy genuineness and healthy cheer, place the key to success in Haydn's hand. In his early works, the composer expresses himself like all other composers of the period. His style is also the style of his time. Yet he calls attention to himself through his music's fullness of character, its higher potency. Thus he already lays the foundation for his fame in a moment in which his style is still constrained and dependent on countless influences. However, thereafter Haydn develops so slowly from decade to decade, so cautiously, so far from subversively, that not only the youth but also the enemies of progress are capable of going along. To be sure, the expressive touch of the *Sturm und Drang*, the Romantic tendencies that become apparent in his last works, and the strong intellectual impact of his instrumental works, may not have pleased every taste. But Haydn makes up for this more and more through the popular character, humor, and immediate strength of his compositional style. Thus, he finds a comforting resonance where a Beethoven, a Mozart, still encountered indifference and incomprehensibility.

Whatever his age did that was good and right in this sense, however, future generations compensate for it in generous terms. Romanticism does not have much regard for gaiety and naturalness. Through to the present, its superior-minded disdain for good "Papa Haydn" has lent the master's image a decided dimness. The unbroken coherence and uniformity of being is not understood in a time that values dusk more highly than clear light. Romanticism, which sees in Mozart only the brilliant sun-youth, is incapable of finding complete access to Haydn. And the playful view of Haydn's work overall goes so far that Schumann believes it especially important to emphasize when, after a performance of the "Farewell" symphony [Hob. I:45], the moving finale does not cause the audience to break out in laughter.

In this way, the nineteenth century overlooks entirely the numerous Romantic characteristics in Haydn's work. The sentimental wave of the *Sturm und Drang* period, into which Haydn was drawn almost more deeply than Mozart, brought to the surface an abundance of subjective expression in the master's production. Finally it is Haydn's last works that have to provide fertile soil again and again for the seeds of that movement whose representatives later took to the battlefield against Haydn. To select only one example, [Amintore] Galli (*Estetica della musica* [Turin: Bocca, 1900]) correctly designated the portrayal of Chaos in the *The Creation* as the point of departure for Romantic instrumental music.

Fig. 2.1. Autograph of the First Commandment from the canon cycle
Die zehn Gebote, Hob. XXVIIa:1

Reprinted by permission of the Gesellschaft der Musikfreunde in Wien

Fig. 2.2. The second through fourth variations from the String Quartet, op. 76, no. 3 ("Emperor")

Courtesy of Staatsbibliothek zu Berlin—Preußischer Kulturbesitz, Musikabteilung mit Mendelssohn-Archiv

Fig. 2.3. Haydn's portrait from 1765

Reprinted by permission of Dr. Hans Schneider Verlag, Tutzing

Fig. 2.4. Haydn's portrait after Johann Carl Roesler, by Philippe Trière (1800)

Reprinted by permission of Dr. Hans Schneider Verlag, Tutzing

Fig. 2.5. Haydn's portrait after Johann Carl Roesler, anonymous (Daniel Caffé?)

Reprinted by permission of the Leipziger Städtische Bibliotheken/Musikbibliothek

Fig. 2.6. Haydn's portrait after Johann Zitterer, color print by M. Jaffé

Reprinted by permission of Dr. Hans Schneider Verlag, Tutzing

Fig. 2.7. Haydn's portrait after Johann Zitterer, engraving by Johann Neidl (1800)

Reprinted by permission of the Burgenländische Landesmuseen, Eisenstadt

Fig. 2.8. Haydn's portrait from a wax medallion by Sebastian Ihrwach (1803)

Reprinted by permission of Dr. Hans Schneider Verlag, Tutzing

Fig. 2.9. Haydn, copper engraving by Friedrich Ludwig Neubauer

Reprinted by permission of Dr. Hans Schneider Verlag, Tutzing

Fig. 2.10. Haydn, drawing by George Dance (1794)

Courtesy of the Royal College of Music, London

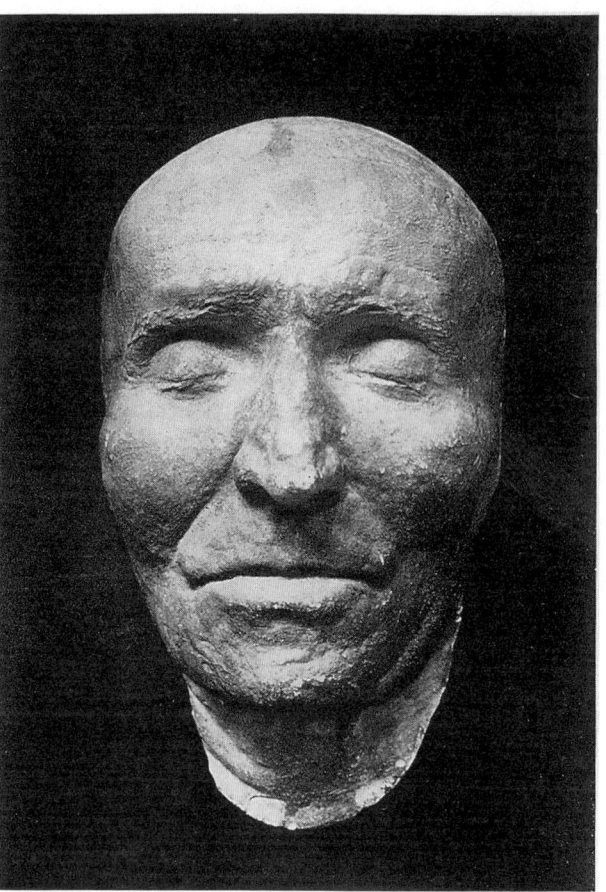

Fig. 2.11. Haydn's death mask

Reprinted by permission of Dr. Hans Schneider Verlag, Tutzing

Attacks on Haydn's sacred music are brought earliest. Haydn's earliest biographers, whose works appeared shortly after the master's death, already seem to defend him against criticisms of a lack of seriousness and a tendency to compose over important textual passages. In the same nineteenth century, in which one [Karl Alexander von] Heideloff rips, with nearly unbelievable vandalism, all of the treasures of the seventeenth and eighteenth centuries out of medieval churches and replaces them with a pseudo-Gothic style of unbelievable dullness, [Anton Friedrich Justus] Thibaut's text *Über Reinheit der Tonkunst* (On purity in musical art) and especially the efforts of the Cecilians lead the charge against Haydn's sacred music. His religious compositions are compared with the *a cappella* music of earlier times and stigmatized as unreligious and decadent.

With the noble frankness of the genius, Haydn himself stated that his dramatic music could only exist with difficulty beside Mozart's. That was to be the end of it, and as a composer of opera Haydn remains—very nearly until the present day—entirely in the shadow of the master from Salzburg. The cheap excuse that his works are inaccessible has been sufficient for performers as well as historians to justify their complete neglect of Haydn's dramatic production. Although the appearance of a new edition of the charming *Lo speziale* (The Pharmacist [Hob. XXVIII:3]), which contains true musical gems, should have attracted interest to the genre, one is still left mainly with excerpts from Haydn's dozen operas. More of the same continues. Haydn's Lieder have been almost entirely overlooked, his piano music criticized for a lack of pianistic spirit. More serious attacks hardly dare to approach the symphonies, but only about a dozen—approximately one-tenth of Haydn's total body of work—are recognized as worthy representatives of this jewel of instrumental music. The string quartet alone is fully understood and appreciated. Yet even here there has been little effort thus far to establish in its entirety this most significant branch of Haydn's production. By publishing the early E♭ major quartet [op. 1, no. 0], I have increased the classic "83" by one, and we cannot doubt that further research will bring more new surprises.

Under these conditions it seems almost fateful that an unlucky star should also shine over the major biography dedicated to Haydn in the nineteenth century. C. F. Pohl completes only the first and second volumes, which appear in 1875 and 1882. The last and most important part of Haydn's life can only be added a half-century later in an information-rich, handsome final volume written by Hugo Botstiber. Moreover, Pohl's method, which offers more of a chronicle of Haydn's time than a portrait of Haydn's life and work, provoked criticism from the very beginning. Spitta already determined that Pohl's work was "not a historical study, nor a biographical one, rather more antiquarian.... The relationship between fore- and background is hardly the right one.... Pohl clears part of the historian's path, but he does not set foot on the path himself." Hence this Haydn biography was unable to promote its subject in the way that Otto Jahn's Mozart biography did two decades previous.

The minimal interest in Haydn's work is also evident in the fact that the collected edition of his works is taken in hand only haltingly. Only the twentieth century assumes this task slowly and hesitantly, and even if Eusebius Mandyczewski presented the discipline with three volumes of highly significant early symphonies and new critical editions of *The Creation* and *The Seasons*, this still cannot obscure the fact that of Haydn's creative work we have completely assessed only—the piano sonata. The lack of a thematic index of Haydn's work stands in immediate relation to this incomprehensible gap. There remains an ignorance of material that the discipline of musicology would not allow for the works of a Praetorius, Lully, or Monteverdi.

As the collected edition makes only insignificant advances (after a pause of many years, two volumes are to appear now—symphonies and Lieder), individual work had to intervene. Works by Haydn were published by various sources and—most surprising for everyone without knowledge of the state of affairs—printed for the first time 200 years after his birth. Hence, to list numerous examples (but with no claim to completeness), A. Schnerich published Haydn's *Kleine Orgelmesse* [Hob. XXII:7], Lenzewski a keyboard concerto in F major [Hob. XVIII:F1], O. E. Deutsch *Minuets* [Hob. IX:20], *Deutsche* [Hob. IX:12], *Contredanse* [Hob. IX:29], and *Zingarese* [Hob. IX:28], Landshoff the "Nelson aria" [Hob. XXVIb:4], Goeyens the concerto for trumpet [Hob. VIIe:1], E. F. Schmid the *Requiem* [Hob. XXIIa:c1] and *Pieces for Musical Clock* [Hob. XIX:1-32], Fitz three string trios [Hob. V:8, V:Es1, XI:1], Balet the trios for flute [Hob. IV:1-4], Gülzow and Weismann the trio sonatas [Hob. V:4, 20, 3, 17, G2, A1]. I edited a concerto for lira [Hob. VIIh:3*], two *notturni* [Hob. II:28*-29*], two *Feldpartien* [Hob. II:41*, 46*] (one of which contains the "St. Anthony Chorale" [Hob. II:46/ii] that Brahms used as the theme of his Haydn variations), an aria, a baryton trio, and the aforementioned string quartet.[2]

Astonishing about these new publications is not the "discovery" of the compositions but rather the current possibility of their appearance in print. This is doubtless proof that interest in Haydn's work has grown. To be sure, the "current occasion"—which plays an ever larger role in contemporary culture—has contributed considerably. Yet it seems as if internal factors were also at work. With the ebb of Romanticism, Haydn's trim freshness and simple unaffectedness have attracted us again. The crystal-clarity of his art is more related to today's art than to Romanticism. It very nearly gives the impression that the purposeful musicality of his compositions could resonate more strongly with the present than works of the nineteenth century.

On Haydn's 200th birthday we have no reason to look back proudly at what has been accomplished. Perhaps, however, we may indulge in the hope that we stand at a turning point. Just as Schnerich succeeded in his fight to undermine gradually the structure of prejudice against Haydn's church music that was built by Cecilianism, so it may gradually be possible today to recover for performance the lost genres in which Haydn composed (including opera, or the compositions for baryton). The future may also bring the possibility of accomplishing the honorable obligations to which musicology is bound. I know that I share with my colleagues the will to devote every effort to deprive the thematic index and the completion of the collected works of their utopian character. Only the interest of wider circles is necessary for this to occur.

---

[2] Among the works I have published, a number of compositions require instruments that are lost to us today. The concerto for lira and the *notturni* each call for the solo use of two "lire organizzate" (hurdy-gurdies into which a small organ works may have been built); in the trio for baryton, the main part is assigned to the baryton, a cello-like stringed instrument with sympathetic strings below the fingerboard, and in one of the *Feldpartien* for eight winds, the bass part is intended for the serpent, a low, holed horn. Of course, these instruments could not be used today and had to be replaced in the arrangement with modern instruments, for which Haydn's own example could be a determining factor. For example, at some time or other he arranged the two parts for hurdy-gurdy with flute and oboe, as he wanted to avoid the possibility that works of his mature period, commissioned by a lira enthusiast, would slip into obscurity along with that fashionable instrument.

In the age of *rinascimento* those monuments of Classical art that best represented the thought of the moment rose from Italy's roots. Likewise, it is not without a deeper significance that Haydn's works are now emerging from archives and libraries and coming to light in somewhat greater volume. The external occasion announced by the return of Haydn's birthday can perhaps be expanded into a birthday of new appreciation. And hence the day of remembrance is closer in spirit to a look forward than to a look back.

Haydn and His Viennese Background

Public lecture, Haydn Conference, Kennedy Center, Washington, D.C., 1975. Originally published in *Haydn Studies: Proceedings of the International Haydn Conference, Washington, D.C., 1975*, ed. Jens Peter Larsen, Howard Serwer, and James Webster (New York: Norton, 1981), 3-13. Reprinted by permission of W. W. Norton & Company, Inc. The musical examples cited in nn. 1-2, 9, and 12 have been supplied by the present editor.

> *In 1975 I attended a large international Haydn Conference at the Library of Congress [recte Kennedy Center, Washington, D.C.]. There I offered the first public lecture, "Haydn and His Viennese Background." Since my time was not limited, the lecture was illustrated with numerous musical examples. I also participated in several working sessions of the Congress and was glad thus to have an opportunity to meet again with old friends working in the same field.—This I Remember, 163-64.*

In order to set the stage for this lecture, I should like to play two brief recorded examples of Austrian music before Haydn. One, written about sixty years before Haydn's birth, illustrates the light and gay spirit of Austrian music and its leaning toward folk art. It is a serenade of Heinrich Biber, sung by a night watchman to the following text:

> Listen, The hour has struck ten [nine].
> Tend the hearth,
> And praise God the Father,
> And our dear Lady [ex. 3.1].[1]

The second, composed in 1734 when Haydn was two years old, exemplifies the highly significant role of Italian music in Austria, and it also illustrates the ruling classes' lively participation in the performance of music. This work was written at the command of the Austrian Empress. The two soprano parts were sung by her two daughters, the Archduchesses Maria Anna and the future Empress Maria Theresa. It is drawn from Antonio Caldara's *Il giuoco del quadriglio*. Four girls are playing cards, but they get bored and decide to dance instead; they sing this "ballo" as they do so [ex. 3.2].[2]

Joseph Haydn was born in the eastern part of Austria, in a region which was inhabited predominantly by German-speaking people. However, the border was not far, and some Hungarians as well as Croatians had settled in the same area. Haydn learned neither the Hungarian nor the Croatian language, but from childhood onward he was familiar with a mixture of peoples.

At the age of eight Haydn moved to Vienna to become a choirboy at St. Stephen's, the capital's magnificent cathedral. In a way, the conditions he encountered there resembled those in his native province. Vienna was

---

[1] The Biber serenade was edited by Paul Nettl and published as no. 112 in Nagels Musik-Archiv (Kassel, [1934]). It was sung by Jakob Staempfli on a Musical Heritage Society recording, *A Concert at Mirabelle Palace in Salzburg* (MHS, [1969?]).

[2] Caldara's *Giuoco* was edited by Eusebius Mandyczewski and Geiringer and published in Denkmäler der Tonkunst in Österreich, vol. 75, Jahrgang 39 (Vienna: Artaria, 1932), 46-61. It was recorded by the Società cameristica di Lugano (Nonesuch 71103, [1966]).

Example 3.1. Biber, from the *Night Watchman Serenade*.

Reproduced from *Heinrich Ignaz Franz Biber (1644-1704): Serenada*, ed. Paul Nettl (Nagels Musik-Archiv, 112), pp. 7-8 (meas. 1-95), by permission of Baerenreiter Music Corporation.

Lost   Ihr   Herrn   Undt

Example 3.1.—Continued

Continued

22 Haydn's Artistic and Human Personality

Example 3.1.—*Continued*

Lost Ihr Herrn Undt last euch sagn, der Ham - mer

der hat Zeh - ne gschlagn, hüets Fey - er, hüets wohl, Undt lo - bet Gott den

Example 3.1.—*Continued*

Example 3.2. Caldara, from *Il giuoco del quadriglio*.

Reproduced from *Kammermusik für Gesang, Kantaten, Madrigale, Kanons* by Antonio Caldara, Denkmäler der Tonkunst in Österreich, vol. 75, Jahrgang 39 (1932), p. 46 (meas. 1-33), with kind permission by Universal Edition A.G. Wien.

Example 3.2.—*Continued*

the capital of an empire in which Czechs, Poles, Croatians, Slovaks, Slovenes, Italians, Hungarians, and others coexisted with the dominant German population. From all corners of the Hapsburg lands people came to settle in Austria's commercial, political, and cultural center. Vienna thus provided a fusion of the most diversified ethnic elements, a harmonious synthesis which exercised a highly beneficial influence on Haydn's artistic development.

In the eighteenth century Vienna was a beautiful place. Following the destruction of large parts of the city during the siege by the Turks, magnificent churches and palaces had been built by such great architects as Fischer von Erlach and Lukas von Hildebrandt. An Italian traveler visiting Vienna in 1718 and comparing it with other European cities emphasized its similarity to the towns of his homeland, exclaiming enthusiastically that one seemed to breathe here something akin to Italian air.[3] Certain Northern features in the architecture, he added, did not reduce, but rather enhanced the city's attractions.

Considerably less enthusiastic was the verdict of the famous "Queen of the Bluestockings," Lady Mary Wortley Montagu, who had visited Vienna two years earlier. In a letter to a friend she wrote:

> This town, which has the honour of being the emperor's residence, did not at all answer my ideas of it, being much less than I expected to find it; the streets are very close, and so narrow, one cannot observe the fine fronts of the palaces, though many of them very well deserve observation, being truly magnificent. . . . For, as the town is too little for the number of the pople that desire to live in it, the builders seem to have projected to repair that misfortune, by clapping one town on top of another, most of the houses being of five, and some of them six stories. You may easily imagine, that the streets being so narrow, the rooms are extremely dark; and, what is an inconvenience much more intolerable, in my opinion, the apartments of the greatest ladies, and even of the ministers of state, are divided but by a partition from that of a tailor or shoemaker. Those that have houses of their own, let out the rest of them to whoever will take them.[4]

Later in the same letter she remarks, however:

> I must own, I never saw a place so perfectly delightful as the Fauxbourg [outskirts] of Vienna. It is very large, and almost wholly composed of delicious palaces. If the emperor found it proper to permit the gates of the town to be laid open, he would have one of the largest and best-built cities in Europe.

Particularly interesting in this letter is the reference to the physical proximity between the residences of the nobility and those of the lower classes. An Austrian attitude seems to be reflected here. The unbridgeable gulf which existed in some countries between the high aristocracy and the common people was not nearly as much in evidence in Austria. The imperial family at times took part in popular festivities; it opened its parks to the citizens of Vienna. Emperor Joseph II is known to have visited peasants and plowed a field. Music, in particular, helped to bridge gaps in social status. Though never oblivious of his humble origins, Haydn learned to move with a certain ease in circles of the highest aristocracy.

The narrowness and darkness of many city streets, which Lady Montagu criticized, induced the Viennese to seek relaxation in the lovely landscape surrounding the imperial city. In the south and west were the green Vienna woods and the undulating foothills of the Alps, in the north the majestic Danube river, in the east the fertile plains leading to Hungary. Abbot Anselm Desing, who offered in 1741 a description of the Austrian capital, had this to report:

> Inside the city the Viennese don't feel well; they love the open air. . . . Walking around and hiking is very common, and there is everywhere ample opportunity for so doing. The nobility at times rides in carriages to the Prater, which is an excessively gay and clean little wood on an island of the Danube. Close by are ordinary walks for pedestrians.[5]

---

[3] Niccolo Madrisio, *Viaggi per l'Italia, Francia e Germania* (Venice, 1718), as quoted in Hans Tietze, *Alt-Wien in Wort und Bild* (Vienna: A. Schroll, 1924), 37.

[4] *The Letters and Works of Lady Mary Wortley Montagu, Edited by her Great Grandson, Lord Wharncliffe*, 3rd ed., ed. W. Moy Thomas, 2 vols. (London: Bickers, 1861), 1:235-36.

[5] *Auxilia historica* (Stadt am Hof nächst Regensburg: J. Gastl, 1741); see Tietze, 43-44.

Haydn and His Viennese Background 27

Thus, love of the outdoors was quite natural to the Viennese. Haydn acquired it, no doubt, in his youth, and the composer of *The Creation* [Hob. XXI:2] and *The Seasons* [Hob. XXI:3] still manifested it near the end of his life. Beethoven, too, was a great hiker who loved to tramp through the Vienna woods.

As we have said, music linked the various social strata. The imperial family took the lead in musical patronage. The achievements of the Hofkapelle won fame throughout Europe. Most of the emperors were accomplished performers, and some were also gifted composers. The aristocracy tried to emulate the imperial family. Several wealthy counts and princes engaged their own bands of musicians, and some of the patrons took active part in the performances. Love of music was equally great among the bourgeoisie. Most young persons learned to sing or to play an instrument, and domestic chamber music was generally cultivated. The French author Marcel Brion rightly stated: "In Vienna, music has always been something far more important than mere entertainment or even aesthetic enjoyment; it was a vital necessity."[6] And in the eighteenth century it was said that in Vienna even the stone angels carved over the doors seemed to be in song.

Haydn strongly felt the magic attraction of this city, to which he returned even after his triumphs won in London. The same is true of Mozart, Beethoven, Brahms, Bruckner, and Mahler, to mention only a few of the great musicians who were not born in Vienna, but who elected to live there.

Operatic performances were particularly enjoyed by the Viennese. Beginning with the works of Cavalli and Cesti in the mid-seventeenth century, a large number of operatic compositions, mostly by Italians in the employ of the Austrian court, were mounted on Viennese stages. The great librettists Zeno and Metastasio were active in Vienna as court poets, while the renowned architects Burnacini and Galli-Bibiena designed the lavish stage sets. Lady Montagu wrote to Alexander Pope of an operatic performance she attended in the garden of the imperial castle La Favorita. "Nothing of that kind," she wrote, "ever was more magnificent; and I can easily believe what I am told, that the decorations and costumes cost the emperor thirty thousand pounds sterling."[7] Significantly enough, nothing is mentioned in this letter about the drama or the music performed. We should not believe, however, that the imperial patron maintained an equally one-sided attitude. After all, the impressive operatic productions in Vienna during the first half of the eighteenth century laid the groundwork for the later climactic achievements of Gluck and Mozart, and indirectly for the work Haydn did for the stage in Esterháza.

In the field of the spoken drama the Viennese showed special liking for comedy. Foreign visitors were shocked at times by the coarseness of the jokes to which elegant ladies and gentlemen listened with obvious enjoyment. Famous buffoons such as Stranitzky, Prehauser, and Kurz-Bernardon were the darlings of Viennese audiences. Simple, popular music was interwoven with the texts of these comedies, greatly adding to their attraction. Young Haydn wrote the music to two of Kurz-Bernardon's comedies. He may also have been the author of other pieces based on comedy texts which have been preserved without the composer's name: compositions in the famous collection *Teutsche Comoedie-Arien* in the Vienna National Library, from which Robert Haas and Eva Badura-Skoda have published interesting excerpts.[8] The peculiar combination of Italian elements with features of Austrian folk music, noticeable in this repertory, conforms to the style of many of Haydn's early compositions.

So far, we have attempted to offer a bird's-eye view of the general social and cultural conditions prevailing in the city where Haydn spent his formative years. Now we have to investigate the specific musical background against which the composer's artistic personality developed. The training which the young choirboy received at St. Stephen's was quite scanty; but in the cathedral, and more still in greater Vienna, he found the atmosphere and the models needed for his general intellectual growth.

The generation of composers active in the mid-eighteenth century attempted to supplant the majestic splendor of Baroque art by the graceful delicacy prevalent in the newly developed *style galant*. Instead of powerful unity of form they wanted unrestrained variety. Strict counterpoint was practically eliminated from their compositions. In instrumental music the Italian *sonata da chiesa* and the French *ouverture* were shunned, because they included

---

[6] *Daily Life in the Vienna of Mozart and Schubert* (New York: Macmillan, 1962), 58.

[7] *Montagu*, 1:237-39.

[8] Robert Haas, ed., *Teutsche Comoedie-Arien*, ed. Robert Haas, Denkmäler der Tonkunst in Österreich, vol. 64, Jahrgang 33/1 (Vienna: Artaria, 1926); Eva Badura-Skoda, "Teutsche Comoedie-Arien und Joseph Haydn," in *Der junge Haydn: Wandel von Musikauffassung und Musikaufführung in der österreichischen Musik zwischen Barock und Klassik, Bericht der internationalen Arbeitstagung des Instituts . . . 29.6.-2.7.1970*, ed. Vera Schwarz, Beiträge zur Aufführungspraxis, 1 (Graz: Akademische Druck- und Verlagsanstalt, 1972), 59-73.

polyphonic sections. Instead, the light and gay *sinfonia* and the colorful suite of dances enjoyed widest popularity. Combinations of these two forms were particularly successful. For orchestral compositions mixtures were mostly chosen in which the *sinfonia* element prevailed. On the other hand the divertimenti, notturni, and cassazioni written for chamber ensemble favored the suite form. An important feature was the gradual growth of the binary structures of individual movements into the highly developed sonata form, a process which went on throughout the whole eighteenth century.

These trends were more or less conspicuous in various parts of Europe. Haydn grew up with them in music of Viennese composers such as Georg Christoph Wagenseil, court composer and the music teacher of Empress Maria Theresa; Georg Matthias Monn, organist of the Karlskirche; Franz Asplmayer, composer of ballets; and others. He shared their efforts and eventually fulfilled their aims.

In the field of keyboard music, which in a wider sense includes the clavier trios, the influence of Viennese music on the fledgling composer is particularly noticeable. The suitelike character of these pieces, which use a minuet as middle or final movement and maintain the same basic tonality in all three movements, as well as the common heading "Partita," are typical features in South German and Austrian keyboard music, particularly of its most representative composer, Wagenseil. But Haydn's musical lanugage was not limited to the light and graceful idiom of the *style galant*. In some early sonatas we already find features of passionate subjectivity which may point to the art of C. P. E. Bach. Without leaving his Austrian base Haydn extended his vistas beyond it.

What a shame that Haydn's early Viennese comedies are lost; we can only conjecture what they may have sounded like! In the works for the stage which he later wrote for Prince Esterházy, he followed traditions of the Italian opera. He embraced in turn its serious and its comic aspects, eventually combining the two features in his greatest dramatic works. Haydn must have first heard Italian operas during his stay in Vienna. He was personally acquainted with Metastasio, who lived for a time under the same roof as Haydn. Moreover, the young musician studied with and worked for the celebrated Neapolitan opera composer and singing teacher Nicola Porpora, who spent several years in the Austrian capital.

In the field of church music Haydn received invaluable practical training while working as a choirboy at St. Stephen's. Thus it was quite natural for him to utilize in his own work in this field the style of religious composition predominant in the capital at that time. Its stylistic features had likewise originated in Italy, but so long before that their origins had almost been forgotten. Solid textures combined with the antiphonal use of different sound groups were first employed in the sacred music of Venice and Rome. They were soon adopted by Austrian composers in an unbroken tradition beginning with the seventeenth-century Masses of Stadlmayr and Christoph Strauss and culminating in the works of the court composer Johann Joseph Fux, who was still alive when Haydn entered St. Stephen's. On the other hand, elements of the Italian opera—the use of arias and duets, brilliant vocal coloratura, and the occasional over-emphasis of purely musical devices—had likewise been adopted by composers of church music active in Vienna. We might only mention Antonio Caldara and Georg von Reutter, the Kapellmeister at St. Stephen's under whom Haydn had to sing. All these features are also to be observed in Haydn's church music, and we may safely state that it originally grew out of his daily occupation in the cathedral.

Let us now attempt to survey the works the young Haydn wrote before he entered the services of Count Morzin. This is no easy undertaking, as the composer's early works strikingly resemble those of his Austrian contemporaries and therefore often present puzzling problems of authenticity. Moreover, very few of the authentic early works can be securely dated. We must therefore be satisfied to state in the most general terms that Haydn wrote solo keyboard sonatas as well as trios for a keyboard instrument accompanied by violin and violoncello ("Basso"). There are string trios for two violins and cello, which some have interpreted as studies for the very important string quartets. The early quartets still clearly show the influence of the suite. They are always in the major mode and contain five movements, two of them minuets. The divertimenti for string and wind instruments may have been written for the fashionable serenades in which the young Haydn took part. It was the custom in Vienna to assemble a group of musicians in front of a fair lady's house to celebrate with music her name-day or birthday. This offered musicians an opportunity to earn a modest fee from the sponsor of such entertainment.

Among Haydn's early compositions is a keyboard concerto, Hob. XVIII:1 in C major, whose autograph has been preserved [ex. 3.3a]. The composer corrected it later and added the date 1756. It may serve as an example of the close affinity of Haydn's early works to those of his Viennese predecessors. I would like to play the finale of this concerto and the finale of a keyboard concerto in D major by Georg Matthias Monn [ex. 3.3b], which was

Example 3.3a. Haydn, Concerto in C major, Hob. XVIII:1, Finale.

Reproduced from *Concerto per l'organo*, ed. Michael Schneider (Partitur-Bibliothek, 3708), by permission of Breitkopf & Härtel, Wiesbaden-Leipzig.

Continued

Example 3.3a.—*Continued*

Example 3.3a.—*Continued*

Example 3.3b. G. M. Monn, Concerto in D major, Finale.

Reproduced from *Wiener Instrumentalmusik vor und um 1750: Vorläufer der Wiener Klassiker*, Denkmäler der Tonkunst in Österreich, vol. 39, Jahrgang 19/2 (1912), pp. 102-03 (meas. 1-64), with kind permission by Universal Edition A.G. Wien.

Example 3.3b.—Continued

Example 3.3b.—*Continued*

probably written a few years earlier. There is no direct connection between the two works—possibly Haydn did not even know the earlier concerto—but in style and content they seem very much alike. (Incidentally, in performances and recordings of these concertos you will sometimes hear harpsichord performing the solo part, at other times an organ. Please disregard this difference. Haydn stated that the work could also be played on the harpsichord, and such exchanges were quite common at the time.[9])

For the church, the young Haydn composed a *Salve Regina* (Hob. XXIIIb:1) for soprano solo, chorus, and organ, and one or two *Missae breves* (short Masses). One of these, the *Missa brevis* in F major [Hob. XXII:1], is certainly a work of Haydn, but the authenticity of the second one, known as *Missa Rorate coeli desuper* (Hob. XXII:3), is doubtful. The thematic beginning of the work is quoted in Haydn's draft catalog (however, entered about fifty years later); on the other hand, manuscript copies name Georg Reutter the Younger or the Vienna court organist Ferdinand Arbesser as the author. Once again it seems almost impossible to distinguish with certainty an early work by Haydn from those of his contemporaries. One argument for the attribution of the little Mass to Haydn is the fact that the work is marred by somewhat primitive and awkward progressions in the vocal parts. It seems quite possible that the fledgling composer was responsible for these shortcomings, but unlikely that a solid craftsman like Reutter or Arbesser could have written them.

As you know, in (or around) 1759 Haydn entered the service of the Czech Count Morzin as music director. When financial difficulties forced the count to dismiss his musicians, the composer quickly found a position as vice-Kapellmeister and soon afterwards as Kapellmeister of Prince Esterházy. Henceforth, up to 1790, Haydn had his residence in the country. But this does not mean that his ties to Vienna were severed. Count Morzin, who lived at his Bohemian castle Lukaveč, liked to spend the winter months in the capital and may have taken some musicians along. When Haydn was subsequently active at the court of the Princes Esterházy in Eisenstadt and at the castle of Esterháza, visits to Vienna occurred from time to time. Although Haydn's duties at the Esterházy court were staggering, he found time to write a large-scale oratorio for Vienna. *Il ritorno di Tobia* [Hob. XXI:1] was premiered in 1775 in the Vienna Kärntnerthortheater for the benefit of a charitable institution. Its great success may have been responsible for the request sent to Haydn in 1776 to write an autobiographical sketch for the publication *Das gelehrte Österreich*, a sort of Austrian *Who's Who*. This article is one of the most important biographical sources available to us. According to tradition (handed down especially by Dies) Haydn was also invited to write an opera for Vienna. He readily undertook this commission, but when he came to rehearse the new work, his competitors let loose such a flood of intrigues that he withdrew his score in disgust. *La vera costanza* [Hob. XXVIII:8] was then premiered, like other Haydn operas, at the castle of Esterháza.[10] The composer also had disagreements with the charitable institution for which he had written *Il ritorno di Tobia*, but all this did not change his strong attachment to the city where he had grown up.

That attachment was further increased by the warm friendship between him and Mozart. The Salzburg composer had moved to Vienna in 1781. Haydn and Mozart established personal relations presumably in 1784 or 1785, and they even had the joy of playing chamber music together. We don't have to quote here the well-known praise of Mozart's work uttered by Haydn to Mozart's father, or Mozart's moving dedication of six quartets to his "beloved friend Haydn." More important still is the fact that in the 1780s the two composers independently—and yet quite often influencing each other—reached a classical maturity of style. In combining the light gaiety of the *style galant* with the tender subjectivity of *Empfindsamkeit*, adding some of the strictness of Baroque polyphony and imbuing the whole with elements of folk music, Haydn—and on a different plane also Mozart—established a classical balance of expression. Vienna, the city in which for centuries various ethnic groups had lived together and harmoniously blended, offered the inspiration for such a fusion of artistic elements. It is unlikely that a similar influence could have been exerted by any other city.

---

[9] The score of the Haydn concerto was first published by Michael Schneider (Wiesbaden: Breitkopf & Härtel, 1953). It was recorded by E. Power Biggs (Columbia ML 6082/MS 6882, [1964]). The Monn concerto for harpsichord was edited by Wilhelm Fischer in Denkmäler der Tonkunst in Österreich, vol. 39, Jahrgang 19/2 (Vienna: Artaria, 1912), 92-106. It was recorded by Janos Sebestyen on *A Gala Dinner Concert at the Court of Vienna* (Turnabout TV-S 34324, [197-?]).

[10] On this subject see Horst Walter's paper in *Haydn Studies: Proceedings of the International Haydn Conference, Washington, D.C., 1975*, ed. Jens Peter Larsen, Howard Serwer, and James Webster (New York: Norton, 1981), 154-57.

About 1780 a very significant practical tie was established between Haydn and Vienna in the form of a business connection with the important publishing house of Artaria & Co. This firm published more than three hundred editions of his works: string quartets, symphonies, *The Seven Last Words* [Hob. XX/2], the late piano sonatas, and many other compositions. The lively correspondence testifies to the friendly relationship between Haydn and Carlo and Francesco Artaria, who were, of course, of Italian extraction. In 1785 Haydn joined the freemasonic lodge *Zur wahren Eintracht* in Vienna. This step was probably taken largely on the recommendation of Mozart. But Haydn, as opposed to Mozart, never had much contact with the world of freemasonry, and it seems doubtful whether the ideas of the order had any influence on his attitude as a loyal son of the Catholic church.

Towards 1790 probably the strongest attraction in Vienna was offered by visits to the home of Dr. von Genzinger, physician to Prince Esterházy. The doctor and his charming wife Marianne were ardent music lovers, and Frau von Genzinger, the mother of five children, was an excellent singer and pianist. In the Genzinger home Haydn found the congenial atmosphere never provided by his own wife, who took no interest whatever in her husband's work. The letters that Haydn wrote to Marianne von Genzinger, first from Esterháza and later from London, are warm, human documents free of the conventional stilted flourishes so often found in correspondence of the time.

Considering this strong attachment to the capital, it cannot surprise us that when Prince Nikolaus Esterházy died in September 1790, and his successor dissolved the Esterházy musical establishment, Haydn's instinctive reaction was to rush to Vienna. After three decades of service to the same family, the composer was suddenly relieved of his duties. But this state of affairs did not last long. Haydn received various offers, and he decided to go to London, where during two memorable visits his symphonic output reached its magnificent climax. We cannot accompany Haydn on his travels to England, but I should like to point out one characteristic feature of the works he performed there. The folkloristic element, which had always been strong in his compositions, is particularly emphasized in the last twelve symphonies. How natural and appealing, for instance, is the Andante theme from Symphony no. 94 in G major ("Surprise"), derived, as E. F. Schmid pointed out,[11] from a German nursery song. An Austrian rustic scene is conjured up in the following minuet, Allegro molto. We seem to witness Austrian peasants vigorously swinging their girls in a spirited folk dance. Austrian folklore, nurtured by the different nationalities of its inhabitants, is also encountered in other symphonies. No doubt the homeland, and with it the center and heart of Austria, were in the composer's mind when he wrote these symphonies intended for English music lovers. The situation was not entirely different a century later, when Dvořák composed his *New World Symphony*.

Between his two visits to England Haydn returned to Vienna. He used the newly won riches for the purchase and remodeling of a comfortable house in the Vienna suburb Gumpendorf. Obviously he intended eventually to retire to his favorite city.

I would like to mention a small, but not insignificant, incident from these years. In autumn 1792 Haydn was asked to provide music for a masked ball to be held at the imperial Redoutensaal (ballroom) for the benefit of artists' widows and orphans. Such a mixture of good fun with charity appealed to the composer, and he accepted the commission without pay (although he made up for it later by selling the music for twenty-four ducats to Artaria). Thus, on 25 November 1792, twelve minuets [Hob. IX:11] and twelve German dances [Hob. IX:12] newly composed by Haydn had their first performance. These enchanting pieces are far too little known, though they are remarkable for their thoroughness of workmanship and delicacy of orchestration. Haydn applied himself to all twenty-four pieces with a zeal which seems out of proportion to the modest task. While in his younger years he had dashed off dance music rather quickly, he now worked more carefully and deliberately. As a matter of fact, more than two dozen sketches for this work have been preserved. The feeling of responsibility, not least after the great success he had won in London, and his desire to present himself in Vienna to best advantage, left their imprint even on so humble a composition as this tiny German dance [ex. 3.4].[12]

With Haydn's return to Vienna after his second visit to London the circle closes. Haydn now chose to reside in the city in which he had grown up. Artistically, he turned over a new leaf. After having achieved his greatest successes in the field of instrumental music, he now wrote chiefly vocal compositions. Elements of folk song

---

[11] Ernst Fritz Schmid, *Joseph Haydn: Ein Buch von Vorfahren und Heimat des Meisters* (Kassel: Bärenreiter, 1934), 302.

[12] Haydn's *Deutscher Tanz* (Hob. IX:12, no. 4) was first published by Otto Erich Deutsch (Leipzig: F. Kistner & C. F. Siegel, 1931). It was recorded by the Philharmonic Orchestra of Vienna, cond. Hans Gillesberger (Haydn Society HSLP 1022, [195-?]).

Haydn and His Viennese Background   37

Example 3.4. Haydn, German Dance, Hob. IX:12, no. 4.

Reproduced from *Tänze und Märsche*, Joseph Haydn Werke, R. 5, pp. 80-81 (Tanz Nr. 4), by permission of G. Henle Verlag, Munich.

Continued

38 Haydn's Artistic and Human Personality

Example 3.4.—Continued

Example 3.4.—*Continued*

Da Capo

and art music reached a magnificent, classical fusion in the song "Gott erhalte Franz den Kaiser," composed in 1797 [Hob. XXVIa:43]. Haydn labored for quite some time on the perfection of this tune, and he made many sketches before it was completed. The result was a song that sounds familiar at first hearing and is never forgotten afterwards, despite—or perhaps because of—its unique melodic invention.

Haydn had always loved Vienna; now, at last, this love was fully reciprocated. The Viennese had learned to appreciate the beauty of his work. In particular, they were delighted by the decidedly Austrian character revealed in the last two oratorios, with their fine sense of humor and deep love of nature. When *The Creation* was heard in the Vienna Burgtheater in 1799 it drew the greatest crowd ever assembled in this theater. The Viennese were so excited about the treat offered to them that they hardly seemed to notice the Russian army under General Suvarov that was passing through the capital on the same day. Performances of *The Creation* and *The Seasons* which Haydn conducted in Vienna for the benefit of widows and orphans netted 40,000 florins for charity.

This brings us to the end of Haydn's career. But the impact of his work was felt in Vienna long after his death. Beethoven revealed in his string quartets and symphonies strong ties with Haydn's music. Schubert, Brahms, Bruckner, and Mahler received vital inspiration from the great old man's work. Even Vienna-born Arnold Schoenberg expressed admiration for the boldness of Haydn's modulations.[13] No doubt the atmosphere and culture of the Austrian capital exercised a decisive influence on Haydn's artistic personality, while his work, in turn, left its imprint on music created in Vienna by later generations.

---

[13] *Structural Functions of Harmony*, rev. ed., ed. Leonard Stein (New York: Norton, 1969), 147-49, 167.

Haydn's Autograph Remarks in His Music Manuscripts

Originally published as "Eigenhändige Bemerkungen Haydns in seinen Musikhandschriften," in *Anthony von Hoboken: Festschrift zu seinem 75. Geburtstag*, ed. Joseph Schmidt-Görg (Mainz: Schott, 1962), 87-92. Reprinted by permission of the Geiringer estate.

For the music lover, examining a Haydn autograph provides a source of stimulation and joy. Although the notes were clearly written in the greatest haste, they are of exemplary clarity, and nowhere can arise any doubt of the composer's intentions. Evidently Haydn had determined his compositions in large part in his mind before taking pen in hand. Subsequent changes are seldom, and once a work is begun, the master also completes it. In impressive fashion, therefore, the music manuscripts reflect the powerfully resolute personality of the composer.

The brief remarks that Haydn liked to insert into the manuscripts offer a noteworthy supplement to the musical notation and complete the image of Haydn's character communicated through his own writings. In this article, as a modest contribution to this well-deserved jubilee dedicated to the consideration of Haydn source materials, these insertions will receive a brief assessment.[1]

Latin entries of religious character, which appear with great regularity, are not unusual in the eighteenth century, and yet we have reason to believe that for Haydn they arose from a profound faith. As a rule the composer places the words "In Nomine Domini" (also in abbreviated form: "In N: D:") at the beginning, while at the end various forms of thanksgiving and praise can be found. Most common is "Laus Deo," but more extended closings also appear on special occasions. In the extensive Latin sacred *Applausus* cantata [Hob. XXIVa:6], for example, the formula reads as follows: "Finis. O:(mnia) A:(d) M:(ajorem) D:(ei) G:(loriam) et B:(eatissimae) V:(irginis) M:(ariae). At the close of the six String Quartets, op. 17, the following notice appears: "Laus Deo et B(eati)S(simae) V:(irgini) Mar:(iae) et om(nibu)s S(anct)is." Notably, in the Quartets, op. 20, which are so very significant for Haydn's development, the final remarks are presented differently in each piece. No. 1 reads "Soli Deo et Cuique Suum," no. 2 "Laus omnip(otenti) Deo"; in no. 3 the joyful exclamation "Gloria in Excelsis Deo" follows the scintillating finale.[2]

An unusual form of the Latin closing prayer can be found in the *Salve Regina* in G minor [Hob. XXIIIb:2]. Pasted into the autograph is the following:

oro te o pIa o DVLCIs VIrgo Vt assIstas CoMposItorI

pIa DVLCIsqVe VIrgo assIste CoMposItorI[3]

---

[1] For their kind assistance with details of the Haydn manuscripts I am indebted to Dr. Irmgard Becker-Glauch of the Haydn Institute in Cologne, as well as Dr. Dénes Bartha, Budapest.

[2] The autograph remarks for the works discussed thus far can be found throughout the Gesellschaft der Musikfreunde, Vienna. Cf. Anthony van Hoboken, *Joseph Haydn: Thematisch-bibliographisches Werkverzeichnis*, vol. 1 (Mainz: Schott, 1957), 385, 389-90.

[3] Tübingen, Universitätsbibliothek.

The sense of these brief fervent prayers emerges from the differential usage of upper- and lower-case characters. If one regards the upper-case letters as Roman numerals and takes them together, each of the two lines comes to 1771, the date of the work's composition.[4] Such amusements were popular at that time, and Haydn seems to have shared this tendency; in addition to the closing already mentioned, on the final page of the *Applausus* a chronogram can be found in which even the composer's name is reproduced in misspelled form in order to establish the desired numeral 1768 as the date of composition. Here it reads:

hVnC appLaVsVM feCIt Ioseph haIDn

Another set of remarks demonstrates the work of the practical musician. In a score of his opera *Armida* [Hob. XXVIII:12],[5] written by a copyist, Haydn inserts in his own handwriting the following, quite urgent performance indication: "NB. In order to attain his aim and true expression in the following passages and several similar ones" (here two musical examples using *fp* are inserted) "the author requests that the first onset of the *forte* be of the briefest duration for all voices, that is as if the *forte* would seem suddenly to disappear." Similarly, the composer gives the following exact performance indication in one of his pieces written for musical clock (Hob. XIX:31): "NB in the fifteenth measure the three middle notes" (an example follows with notes linked by ties) "must be drawn out."[6] As an explanation for one rare, belated correction, Haydn writes in the first movement, meas. 41-42 of his String Quartet, op. 64, no. 3, of the cello part: "in order to play it more easily."[7]

A note in the trio of the minuet of Symphony Hob. I:50 reflects the character of the observant conductor, who does not even leave insignificant details to chance. Here, as a direction to the copyist in the brass and percussion sections: "Tacent. The rests in the trio must be written out, because there is no repetition in the trio."[8]

The instructions in the Symphony Hob. I:62 assume a more personal character; originally, in its first movement there was to be no participation of the flute. When Haydn decided to change this, he wrote a flute part on his own, attaching it to the finale, crossed out the remark "Primo All(egr)o Tacet" in the earlier flute part and wrote over it, "Friend, return to the first Allegro," charming evidence of the kind tone that "Papa" maintained with respect to his musicians.[9]

In the Symphony Hob. I:97, the composer establishes the relation to his impresario and first violinist from London. In meas. 40 of the minuet's trio he requests that the concertmaster play one octave above the other violins and expresses that wish with the following words: "in 8va Salomon Solo ma piano."[10]

These directions take on a monumental form in the well-known instruction booklet that Haydn included in his score of the *Applausus*, when he was unable to attend the performance of the work at the abbey of Zwettl.[11] These extremely thorough explanations offer indispensable help for the investigation into the performance practices of the time.[12]

Various manuscript entries bear witness in a curious sense to a somewhat naïve pride that the artist sensed about his own achievements in counterpoint. This shows itself, for example, in the aforementioned Quartets, op. 20, in which Haydn marks the finales of nos. 5, 6, and 2 with "fuga a 2 soggetti," "con tre soggetti," and even "a

---

[4] In addition there is also a second Latin chronogram, apparently written in another hand, of which the meaning has not yet been clarified.

[5] Previously owned by Sándor Wolf, Eisenstadt. Facsimile of the page in question in Geiringer, *Joseph Haydn*, Die großen Meister der Musik (Potsdam: Athenaion, 1932), 115.

[6] Autograph under private Swiss ownership. Cf. Hoboken, 835f.

[7] Autograph of Rychenberg Foundation, Winterthur. Cf. Hoboken, 417.

[8] Autograph previously under ownership of the Staatsbibliothek zu Berlin. Cf. *Josef Haydn Gesamtausgabe*, ser. 1, vol. 5, ed. Helmut Schultz (Boston: Haydn Society, 1951), 288.

[9] The autograph for the flute part and the Esterházy performance materials in Budapest, Orszógos Széchényi Könyvtár. With regard to the rather complicated state of affairs, cf. Carl Ferdinand Pohl, *Joseph Haydn*, vol. 2 (Leipzig: Breitkopf & Härtel, 1882), 21, 271, and H. C. Robbins Landon, *The Symphonies of Joseph Haydn* (London: Universal Edition, Rockliff, 1955), 367f.

[10] Autograph previously under ownership of Stefan Zweig. Facsimile of the relevant passage is in Landon, 557.

[11] Cf. Leopold Nowak, *Haydn*, 2nd rev. ed. (Zürich: Amalthea, [1959]), 185.

[12] The document is presented in its entirety in Geiringer, *Joseph Haydn: Der schöpferische Werdegang eines Meisters der Klassik* (Mainz: Schott, 1959), 317-19.

4^{tro} soggetti." In order to bring his erudition even more clearly to light, he remarks in the fifth quartet at one stretto, "in canone," and at a point of retrograde motion, "al roverscio" (*sic*). Similar directions can be found in the trios for baryton. Hob. XI:94 contains a minuet with the title "Canone in Diapente," and the finale of Hob. XI:101, a bit primitive from a technical standpoint, boasts as "Fuga a 3 soggetti in contrapunto doppio." In the Symphony Hob. I:70 of 1779 the remark "specie d'un canone in contrapunto doppio" heads the second movement in the original parts.[13]

One other heading, that of the minuet (fourth movement) of the Divertimento in F major (Hob. II:23*), belongs to the set of such "learned" remarks. At the beginning, this dance movement presents the words "Incipit Lamentatio," as its subject is related to the Gregorian chorales sung during the Holy Week lamentations.[14] Yet in terms of content this graceful piece has hardly anything to do with the seriousness of the church.

Particularly illuminating are those remarks which were not meant for other eyes and in which the composer seems to be thinking aloud. Here the humor that is so deeply rooted in the master's character is repeatedly given voice. To view something of a pre-formulation of such expressions, one need only look to the richly ornamented barlines at the end of each movement of Symphony Hob. I:13, which are undertaken with great enthusiasm and gusto.[15]

It is certainly not always easy to trace Haydn's ideas in the marginal comments. In the Farewell Symphony, Hob. I:45, the words "Sapienti pauca" are found in meas. 150-51 of the first movement.[16] Haydn made the same cryptic remark in his London journal, while mentioning a dinner at Stephen Storace's. In both cases he apparently wants to imply that an item not generally known ought to be understandable to the initiated without further explanation. As László Somfai suspects, in the symphony it likely refers to the fact that in the second violin part Haydn writes in the measures in question the more legible note G rather than the F𝄪 (resolving to G♯), which would be indicated in proper musical notation.[17]

Even more difficult to explain are two entries at the opening of the score for the Trios for Baryton, Hob. XI:109.[18] Here, the composer made both an Italian and a Latin remark: "fatto a posta" and "nihil sine causa." It is well known that Haydn occasionally sent his prince these baryton trios in order to put him in a favorable humor for particular reasons.[19] The Trio 109, which the master marked with the words "made deliberately" ("mit Absicht gemacht") and "nothing without a reason" ("nichts ohne Grund") likely served just such a purpose.

His humorous touch is evident in an impish remark at the end of the fugue movement in the String Quartet, op. 20, no. 2. In this autograph, the following words are written under the religious closing phrase "Laus omnip:(otenti) Deo:" "Sic fugit amicus amicum," an original and quite appropriate characteristic of fugue technique.[20]

In his Horn Concerto (Hob. VII d:3*), Haydn confused the systems of the two violins and oboe and noted as an excuse on the upper edge, "written while asleep" ("In schlaff geschrieben").[21]

His striving for a tonal language "from heart—to heart" becomes apparent in a small note in the second movement of the Symphony Hob. I:42 of 1771.[22]

---

[13] Parts to Hob. XI:94 and 101 as well as Hob. I:70, in Budapest, Országos Széchényi Könyvtár.

[14] Fragment of autograph in Tübingen, Universitätsbibliothek. New edition of the Divertimento by H. C. Robbins Landon (Vienna: Doblinger, 1959).

[15] Autograph in Budapest, Országos Széchényi Könyvtár. Cf. Pohl, I, 303.

[16] Autograph in Budapest, Országos Széchényi Könyvtár; facsimile, ed. László Somfai (Budapest: Hungarian Academy of Sciences, 1959).

[17] From a friendly correspondence from Dr. Somfai to this author. Helmut Schultz develops a different theory. In the critical commentary of the collected works, *Joseph Haydns Werke*, ser. 1, vol. 4 (Leipzig: Breitkopf & Härtel, 1933), viii, it is stated: "m. 150-51: With regard to Vl. 2, which is only sparsely marked with C and C, request for the attention of the copyist in the autograph 'Sapienti Pauca.'"

[18] Autograph in Budapest, Országos Széchényi Könyvtár. Facsimile in *Koldály Zoltán: 75. szülestésnapjára*, ed. Bence Szabolcsi and Dénes Bartha, Zenetudományi tanulmányok, 6 (Budapest: Akadémiai Kiadó, 1957), following p. 688.

[19] Here cf. H. C. Robbins Landon, *The Collected Correspondence and London Notebooks of Joseph Haydn* (London: Barrie and Rockliff; Fair Lawn, N.J.: Essential Books, 1959), 12.

[20] Facsimile in Geiringer, *Haydn Meister*, 49.

[21] Autograph, Vienna, Gesellschaft der Musikfreunde. Facsimile in ibid., 92.

[22] Autograph, Budapest, Országos Széchényi Könyvtár. Cf. Hoboken, 47.

Here, Haydn strikes three measures with a bold harmonic modulation and explains "This was for entirely too learned ears." The contrast between a statement such as this and those allusions to the tools of erudition found in the Quartets, op. 20, written in the following year, illuminate the glaring internal contradictions that characterize this period of experimentation in Haydn's production.

Typical not only of Haydn but for the entire Classical era is that a quarter-century later, a remark appears which is related to that of Symphony 42. In the sketches for *The Creation* [Hob. XXI:2], Haydn first drafted a quite complicated version of the chorus "Gesegnet sei des Herren Macht" and then a more simple version, noting that "it is not good to be interesting."[23]

Remarks of this sort demonstrate that for the composer the musical manuscript—even more than for its obvious artistic purpose—also becomes the communicator of illuminating little messages, intended sometimes for others, sometimes for the writer himself.

---

[23] Autograph, Vienna, Österreichische Nationalbibliothek. Facsimile in Geiringer, *Haydn Meister*, plate 10, verso.

Haydn's Sketches for *The Creation*

Reprinted from *Musical Quarterly* 18 (1932): 299-308, by permission of Oxford University Press. Translated by Manton Monroe Marble. Movement and measure numbers of music examples for the "final form" refer to those of Mandyczewski's edition of *Die Schöpfung* for the *Joseph Haydn Werke* XVI/5 (Leipzig: Breitkopf & Härtel, 1922).

"I never did write hastily," Haydn acknowledged to his friend and biographer, Griesinger, "but always composed diligently and deliberately, and set nothing down until I was quite sure of what I had to say." Everything he wrote, from his youth up to the threshold of his complete maturity, bears witness to this manner of creating, so characteristic of his method, ever painstaking, ever mindful of his objective. His original manuscripts, to be sure, were written out in the hastiest possible fashion, yet at all times with splendid clearness and legibility. Moreover it was never his wont either suddenly to discontinue work on a still uncompleted task, as Mozart did, or to be forever changing, eliminating, and erasing, as Beethoven did. Haydn's manuscripts are remarkably conclusive and show that he first put the composition together in his head, complete to the last detail, before he committed it to paper.

This method of composing went through a partial modification during his last creative period. After his return from England, covered with glory, he developed a new and heightened sense of responsibility. He knew that his name was beginning to belong to history, that he was no longer writing for his own time alone but for posterity. Now, all at once, Haydn took to correcting and polishing his work before carrying out the final revisions. These characteristics of his new method are very clearly revealed in a little trio for two flutes and violoncello [Hob. IV:4*], which he wrote in 1794, during his second stay in London.[1] Composed for a special occasion, it was rather tersely put together, and the composer evidently set but scant store by it. Notwithstanding, he reworked the already finished middle movement a second time. The style of this second revision is unquestionably still more concise and pithy. The somewhat perfunctory sonata form of the first draft is converted into the romanza form, and the theme running along in equal 8th notes is made more piquant by bringing in a dotted rhythm. Even to a work of such slight moment, Haydn now applied the new method which made it possible for him to scale the heights of achievement.

At this time also, he began to make use of preliminary sketches. More or less definite and far-carried drafts have come down to us of *The Creation* [Hob. XXI:2], *The Seasons* [Hob. XXI:3], the last Mass [Hob. XXII:14], and of various marches, songs, and canons.[2] Haydn intended these to serve primarily as aids to memory. On the first page of the sketch for *The Creation*, he notes naïvely: "So that I shall remember!" The real value of these memoranda lies in the fact that they differ in characteristic points from the final versions.

---

[1] Manuscript in the Staatsbibliothek zu Berlin.

[2] These are to be found in the collections, among others, of the Österreichische Nationalbibliothek, Vienna; the Staatsbibliothek zu Berlin; Breitkopf & Härtel, Leipzig; the Gesellschaft der Musikfreunde, Vienna; and at Sándor Wolf's, Eisenstadt.

This is true, as we shall see, of the most important of these sketches, those for *The Creation*. Heretofore they have not been examined; for that matter, the whole subject of Haydn's sketches as a field for research has so far been neglected, with the exception of Schünemann's comments on one sheet of a sketch for *The Seasons*.[3]

The sketches for *The Creation* are today preserved as valuable records in the National Library (Österreichische Nationalbibliothek) in Vienna. They fill the first twenty pages of Ms. 16835, a square-shaped volume, which also contains twelve pages of sketches for the last Mass. Manuscript 18987 includes but three pages of a fairly detailed sketch for the orchestral score of the "Chaos."

The distinctness which characterizes the finished manuscripts of Haydn's works is most noticeably missing in these sketches. They were thrown together so hurriedly that in many cases it is hardly possible to decide whether one note or its neighbor was meant. There are also many subsequent corrections. And since ideas and scraps of motives are all mixed up together, and Haydn freely omitted key indications and accidentals, as well as the text in voice passages, the deciphering of these sketches meets with not inconsiderable difficulties. Besides, Haydn's ink has not withstood the effects of light, air, and time. Much that was still legible a century ago is today faded beyond recognition. The copy of *The Creation* sketches, prepared more than half a century ago by C. F. Pohl,[4] is consequently a very valuable document, and it has been drawn upon in this article. Even this, however, clears only a few individual difficulties. Hence, as is always the case in examining sketches, conjectures were not altogether avoidable.

The sketches for *The Creation* show that the spontaneous freedom of expression which stamps the final draft of the work was the product of extraordinarily intense labor. Of that easy reliance on sure instinct which Haydn's youthful works so often reveal, there is here not a trace. With tireless, constantly renewed efforts, he strives for the ultimate in expression. This is perhaps most characteristically shown in the chorus "By thee with bliss," which in its final form presents only a shadowy, psalmodizing substructure for the swelling hymn of the two soloists [ex. 5.1]. Haydn did not arrive at this justly admired color-effect in his first inspiration. As first conceived, this chorus was a not very original, lively movement, opening with motives introduced in imitation, and set, as the harmony shows in the absence of clef and signature, not in C major but in C minor [ex. 5.2]. But Haydn did not let the matter rest there, and the passage appears again on another page in the sketches. Hereafter the piece is treated in C major, the soprano solo already occurs in its present form, and a staff is left open for the bass solo, which is still lacking. The chorus is handled far more simply, if by no means so characteristically as in the final form [ex. 5.3]. Here Haydn appended the words, so indicative of his unsuppressible sense of humor: "that it is not good to be interesting." The obvious premise to this marginal comment he did not set down; the sense of the remark being undoubtedly: the musical example which here follows proves "that it is not good to be interesting."

Example 5.1. *The Creation*, no. 28, final form.

---

[3] Georg Schünemann, "Ein Skizzenblatt Joseph Haydns," *Die Musik* 8/16 (1908-09): 211-22.

[4] Now in the possession of the Gesellschaft der Musikfreunde, Vienna.

Example 5.1.—*Continued*

Example 5.2. *The Creation*, sketch for no. 28 (Österreichische Nationalbibliothek, Ms. 16835, f. 1r).

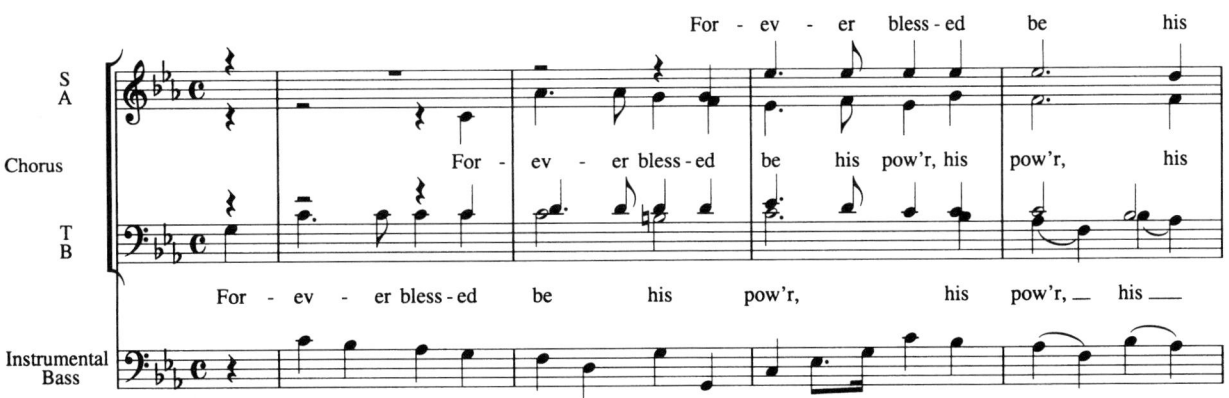

Continued

Example 5.2.—Continued

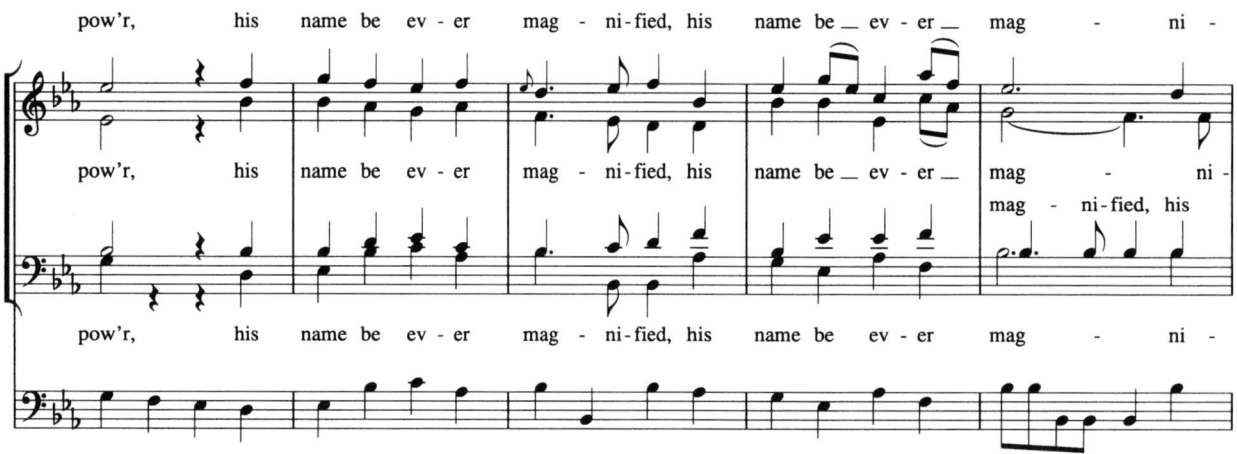

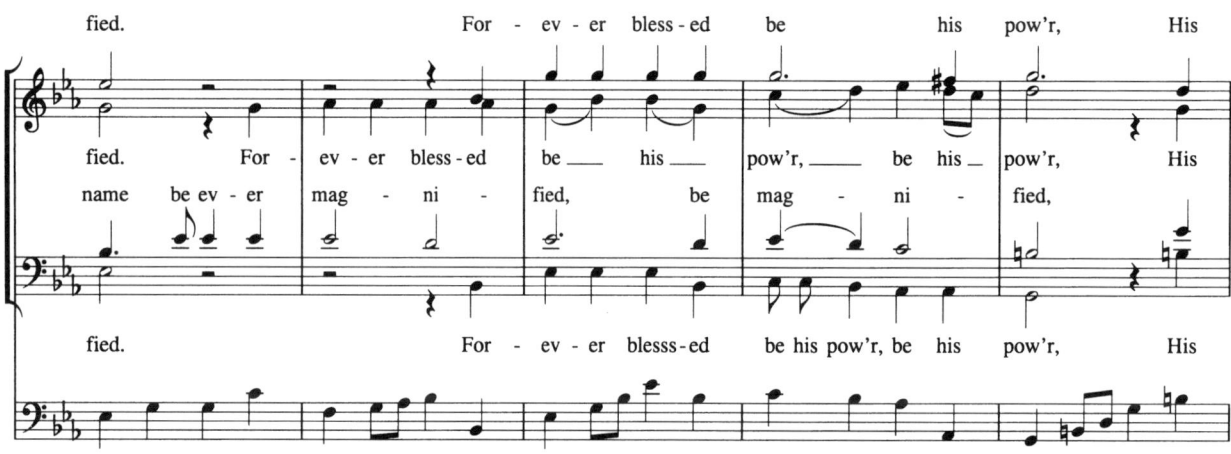

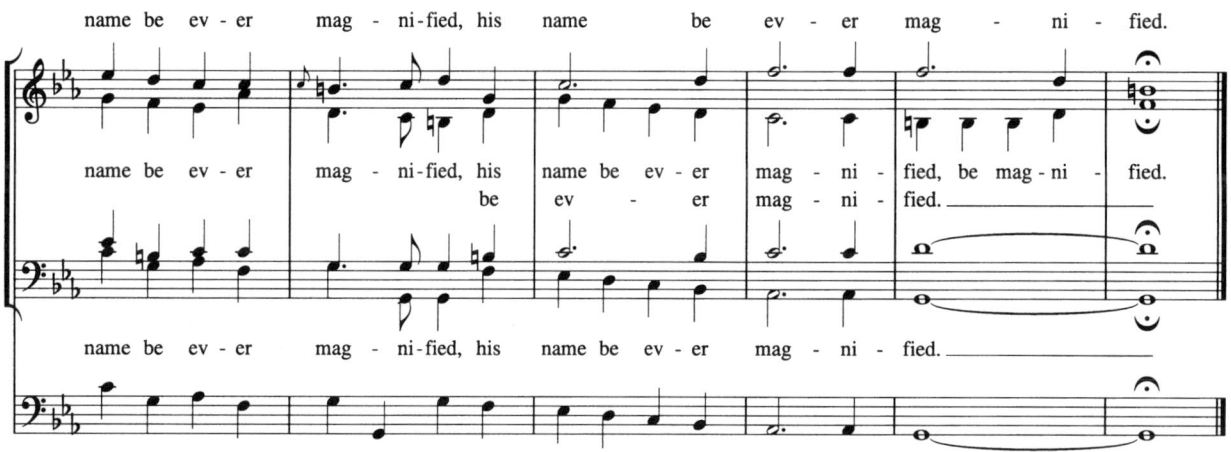

Example 5.3. *The Creation*, sketch for no. 28 (Ms. 16835, f. 6v).

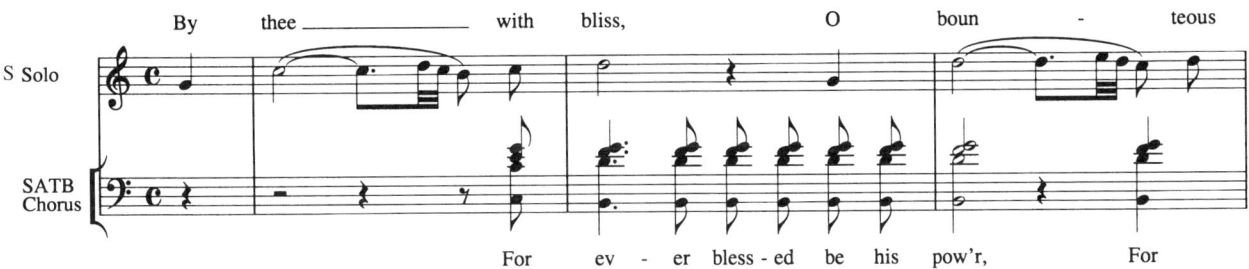
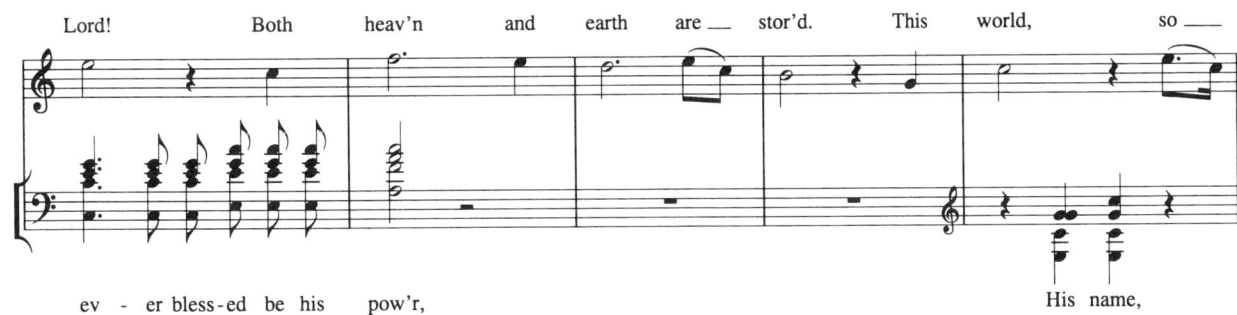

Gabriel's "Bird Aria," no. 16, at the beginning of part 2, especially occupied Haydn's attention. He devoted two pages of these sketches to it. The delineation of the eagle in $\frac{3}{4}$ time in the first draft is particularly interesting. Although at the start there are glimpses of the final form:

Example 5.4. *The Creation*, sketch for no. 16 (Ms. 16835, f. 17v).

Example 5.5. *The Creation*, no. 16, final form.

the passages which follow, all woven about with the coloratura embellishments then in vogue:

Example 5.6. *The Creation*, sketch for no. 16 (Ms. 16835, f. 17v).

are still far removed from the simple naturalness of the last revision:

Example 5.7. *The Creation*, no. 16, final form.

The melodic form of the sketch still belongs to the feeble type of expression of Haydn's Neapolitan opera [*recte* oratorio], *The Return of Tobias* [Hob. XXI:1], written two decades previously, out of which only the strictest self-discipline could ever have led the composer to the vigorous, native simplicity of *The Creation*.

The sketches for the A-major Trio in part 2 are also indicative of Haydn's fond solicitude for the final form of each melody:

Example 5.8. *The Creation*, sketch for no. 19 (Ms. 16835, f. 16v).

Example 5.9. *The Creation*, no. 19, final form.

Here the final form is already clearly presaged, and yet the sketch lacks that last personal token, that genuine Haydn touch in charm and grace of feeling, which distinguishes the ultimate revision.

In view of the care Haydn bestowed on the recitatives and arias in *The Creation*, it is hardly to be wondered at that a number of rough drafts for such parts are also among these sketches. For example, the wonderful "Be fruitful all," which in its final form is accompanied by the lower strings:

Example 5.10. *The Creation*, no. 17, final form.

was originally conceived as a mere *recitativo secco* [ex. 5.11].

Example 5.11. *The Creation*, sketch for no. 17 (Ms. 16835, f. 15r).

For one of the most important parts of *The Creation*, the "Representation of Chaos," there exist quite far-carried sketches. Ms. 16835 presents the first draft. The differences between this sketch and the final form will be apparent after a comparison of a few measures:

Example 5.12. *The Creation*, sketch for no. 1 (Ms. 16835, f. 19v).

* Haydn so vigorously corrected this passage for horn 2, which he later omitted entirely, that his original intention is no longer quite clear.

The unadorned passage for the first violin in the third and fourth measures, which shadows forth the boundless loneliness of uninhabited Chaos:

Example 5.13. *The Creation*, no. 1, violin 1, meas. 3-4.

is missing in the sketch; also the impetuous thud of the orchestra in the fifth measure. The ascending triplet figure is employed rather more often in the sketch than in the final version. Yet it still lacks that compelling organic effect of a completed whole. Haydn brings in these triplets not only on the first and third but also on the second quarter of the measure, whence a sort of syncopated figure results, through an involuntary secondary accent in the middle of the figure:

which is prejudicial to the wraithlike immateriality of the expression. Haydn later avoids this by introducing the triplets mostly on the third, sometimes on the first quarter. In the instrumentation of this significant figure of the accompaniment, too, it was only gradually that he evolved that systematic softening of the orchestral colors which a romantic treatment of Chaos requires. The figure is entrusted to the first violins in the fifth measure of the sketch, to horns 1 and 2 in the sixth, to the clarinets in the eleventh. Later the composer deleted these highlights altogether. The triplets are entrusted to the bassoon, the viola, the violoncello, or at most to the second violins (which unquestionably sound more restrained and subdued than the first). Thus by eliminating the too-substantial colors, Haydn succeeded in dematerializing the tone-quality of the passage. In this draft, only the first part of the "Representation of Chaos" is outlined. The D♭ major part is but indicated (meas. 21ff.). The second sketch (Ms. 18987) presents the first part practically in the final form in which we know it today; but in the contrasting D♭ major portion, which brings the idea of life into Chaos, there is still lacking the significant 16th-note accompaniment in the bassoon, which contributes so substantially to the resolution of the acrid austerity of the beginning:

Example 5.14. *The Creation*, no. 1, bassoon, meas. 21-22.

And it is characteristic that in meas. 49 of the final draft, before the beginning of the coda, Haydn has written a single ascending figure for the bassoon, where originally he had put a frilly flourish for the clarinet:

Example 5.15. *The Creation*, sketch for no. 1, clarinet (Ms. 18987).

Thus, Haydn, even in this instrumental music, worked steadily towards simplification and intensification of expression.

It is not possible to mention here all the plans projected in the pages of *The Creation* sketches.[5] But the characteristic examples adduced will have sufficed to show how rigorously the later Haydn kept himself in hand, how with iron self-discipline he banned from his work all Rococo affectation, even all emotional exuberance, in order to attain the Classic ideal of "noble simplicity and tranquil grandeur." Yet exactly herein lies the achievement of genius, that in the finished work there shall nowhere be perceptible the torment and sweat of the creative process. The final result still possesses for the hearer the dewy freshness of first inspiration. Haydn, who clung to nature and all earthly things more fervently than almost any other composer, succeeded in reflecting here the youthful purity of the universe on the first day of its own creation and so produced a work the influence of which endures unbroken throughout the centuries.

---

[5] Bound in their midst, ff. 9-10, and written in Haydn's own hand, is the complete part for contrabassoon, an instrument not often employed. All the cues have been written out as a precaution against copyists' mistakes. That this part was actually intended for the copyist and not for performance is to be assumed from the master's marginal notation: "Recitative to be written as above." The manuscript of the trumpet part for parts 2 and 3—now in possession of the Conservatoire National de Musique, Paris—contains similar provisions.

Joseph Haydn, Protagonist of the Enlightenment

Geiringer's paper was read at the First International Congress on the Enlightenment organized by the Institut et musée Voltaire and held in Geneva, 1963. It was subsequently published in *Studies on Voltaire and the Eighteenth Century* (Institut et musée Voltaire, Geneva) 25 (1963): 683-90, and is reprinted here with permission of the Voltaire Foundation, Ltd. The English translation of the aria "In native worth" from *The Creation* quoted on page 64 is after A. Peter Brown, ed., *Die Schöpfung* (*The Creation*) (Oxford: Oxford University Press, 1995), 192-95.

An intellectual movement as highly important as the Enlightenment was bound to have a vital impact on the music of the time. Significantly enough, in this era of powerful philosophic activity the distinction between the creative artist and the scholar was often obliterated, and the eighteenth century produced in all countries men who did eminent work both as composers and as theorists. In France, the home of the encyclopedists, Jean-Philippe Rameau, the great harpsichord and opera composer, worked out a monumental theoretical system which up to the present time has served as foundation for our conception of harmony and tonality. Jean-Jacques Rousseau won outstanding success not only as poet and philosopher, but as author of the much performed comic opera *Le Devin du village*; moreover he invented a numerical system for the notation of music which was used in Geneva up to the year 1911. In England Charles Burney was active as composer of clavier, violin, and dramatic music; but it was in the field of musicology that he offered his most important contribution by presenting a *General History of Music*, one of the most significant works of the kind. Johann Mattheson of Hamburg wrote no less than eight operas, twenty-five oratorios, passions, or cantatas, as well as numerous minor works. Yet he found time to demolish Baroque music esthetics in several vigorously aggressive books. In Berlin, where Voltaire's friend King Frederick was ruling, Johann Joachim Quantz, a distinguished flute composer and the teacher of His Majesty, contributed an excellent manual on flute playing, and it is interesting to note that Quantz also improved the construction of his instrument. It seems hardly necessary to point out that Carl Philipp Emanuel Bach, the Prussian ruler's harpsichordist, who counts among the most eminent composers of the time, offered in his *Versuch über die wahre Art das Clavier zu spielen* a standard work of musical theory. In Vienna the imperial court conductor Johann Josef Fux presented in his *Gradus ad Parnassum* an eminent work on counterpoint. Even in Italy the church composer *padre* Giambattista Martini of Bologna grew into an authority on all questions of music history and theory, enjoying in this field greatest respect all over Europe.

Although it would be tempting to follow up such dualistic manifestations of creativity frequently occurring in the era of Enlightenment, it seems more important still to demonstrate that even artists not connected with the contemporary philosophy and not particularly interested in theoretical or pedagogic problems received vital influence from the tenets of the time. Joseph Haydn, the most successful composer of the era, appears to be particularly well suited as the subject of such an inquiry. Although he was not prone to rationalizing or to philosophic speculation, he made the ideas of the Enlightenment his very own. His attitude illuminates the enormous power emanating from the new ideas, a power strong enough to reach a composer working in the seclusion of a Hungarian court, far from any intercourse with the great spirits of the time.

It is interesting to watch from this angle Haydn's creative growth. As a young and immature composer he adopted the *style galant* of the Rococo, and the music he produced was, as a contemporary critic put it, "charming, ingratiating, engaging, naturally humorous and enticing." This description exactly fits the ideas of the Enlightenment which, in the field of music, had started as violent opposition against a style determined by contrapuntal complexities and Baroque pompousness. Avoiding such features, the enlightened musician set himself the aim of producing light, cheerful, and agreeable sounds bound to be pleasing to any sensitive listener, even one lacking technical knowledge. Young Haydn, like many of his contemporaries, accepted this creed and achieved results fulfilling the ideals of enlightened aestheticism. However, it did not take him long to grow away from this state of mind and hereby he revealed again a great composer's sensitivity to the pulse of the time. A reaction was setting in against the gay and superficial idiom of the *style galant*; it was gaining more and more power in the 1760s and thus produced a new phase in the tenets of Enlightenment. If the ideal goal of this movement was to achieve truth in every domain of cultural life, the real nature of man's emotions had to be reflected in the creative arts. In the case of music it was not sufficient for it to be pleasing to the ear; it was, as the English philosopher Daniel Webb put it, "the business of music to express the passions in the way they rise out of the soul." The new movement, which saw in Jean-Jacques Rousseau its guiding spirit, was eagerly accepted by the young progressives.

In German literature, where it was known under the designation of *Sturm und Drang* (storm and stress), it brought forth as epoch-making a work as Goethe's *Die Leiden des jungen Werthers*, exhibiting an unrestrained emotionalism that moved people all over the world to bitter tears, and even to suicide. Haydn may never have heard of Webb, and we don't know how well he was acquainted with Rousseau's ideas or even with Goethe's novel. But he responded to the new trend, and by the end of the 1760s his style had undergone a radical change, so radical that the great French musicologist Théodore de Wyzewa felt justified in speaking of a "romantic crisis" in Haydn's creative life. This term must not be misunderstood, however. No romantic involvement in Haydn's life seems to have been responsible for his changed musical idiom. So far as we know, nothing of the kind happened while Haydn felt compelled to deviate from the ideas of the *style galant*. He did not go through a personal crisis, but thanks to the new movement in the arts, he acquired the courage to break away from the fashionable grace and shallow gaiety and strove truthfully to express what he felt. In this way his idiom gained immeasurably in profundity and power, and Haydn started on the path that would ultimately lead him to a synthesis of the two artistic trends he had followed so far and thus to the mastery of the Classical style.

I would like to illustrate Haydn's artistic development to you by a few examples. I will play to you excerpts from four symphonic movements. In the beginning you will hear the slow movement of his very first symphony [ex. 6.1a] of 1759 to be followed by the slow movement of no. 49 of 1768, the latter known as "La Passione" [ex. 6.1b]. Then we will play the initial Allegro molto from Symphony no. 8, "Le Soir" [ex. 6.1c] of 1761 and finally the corresponding movement from "La Passione" [ex. 6.1d]. Only a few years lie between these compositions, but what a world of difference between them! The Symphonies nos. 1 and 8 show you the enlightened composer of the *style galant*, no. 49 the musician swayed by Rousseau's slogan "back to nature."

There are also other connecting links between Haydn's music and the Enlightenment. The composer is often described as the "father of the string quartet." While a statement of this kind is in the nature of an oversimplification, one has to admit that it was Haydn who endowed the string quartet, conceived for four instruments of equal significance, with an artistry which made it one of the most cherished and important forms of eighteenth-century music. The principle used by Haydn when reaching artistic maturity bears a striking resemblance to the ideas presented by the philosophers of the Enlightenment, ideas that ultimately found their outlet in the French Revolution. Haydn did away with the old Baroque conception of leading and accompanying instruments. To give all four partners in a string quartet the same rights he introduced the device of thematic elaboration. He dissected the main subject, and in most ingenious ways developed the resulting fragments whereby each instrument was similarly entrusted with important utterances. In this way he achieved music of a truly democratic character. Allow me to illustrate this by playing to you a section from a quartet movement. In the Allegro moderato of op. 33, no. 3, known as "The Bird," a twittering motive taken from the main theme is distributed between all four instruments. This is the motive [ex. 6.2a] and its democratic development [ex. 6.2b].

Another facet of Haydn's work embodying ideas of the Enlightenment is its cosmopolitan character. His music received inspiration from Austrian and Croatian folksongs, from Hungarian Gypsy melodies, from Italian opera, French chansons, and British vocal music, these disparate elements being fused through the fire of Haydn's

Example 6.1a. Symphony no. 1, movement 2, meas. 1-28.

Continued

Example 6.1a.—*Continued*

Example 6.1b. Symphony no. 49, movement 1, meas. 1-16.

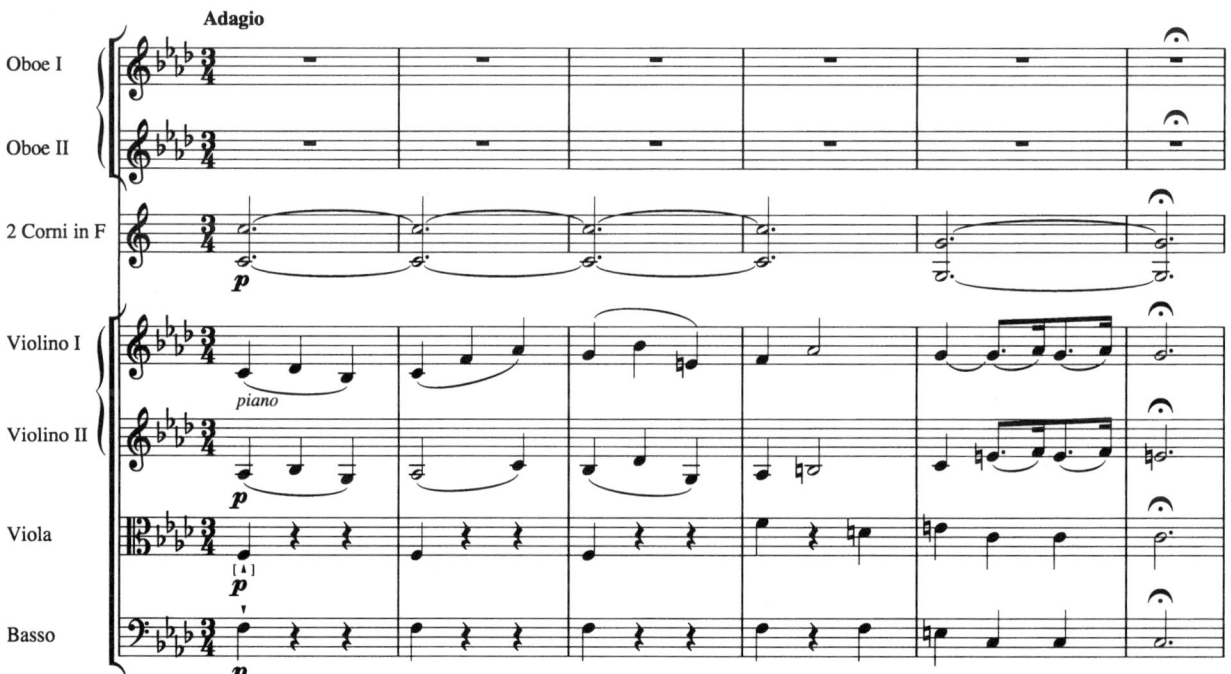

Example 6.1b.—*Continued*

Example 6.1c. Symphony no. 8, movement 1, meas. 1-21.

Example 6.1d. Symphony no. 49, movement 2, meas. 1-13.

Continued

Example 6.1d.—*Continued*

Example 6.2a. String Quartet in C major, op. 33, no. 3, movement 1, meas. 1-4.

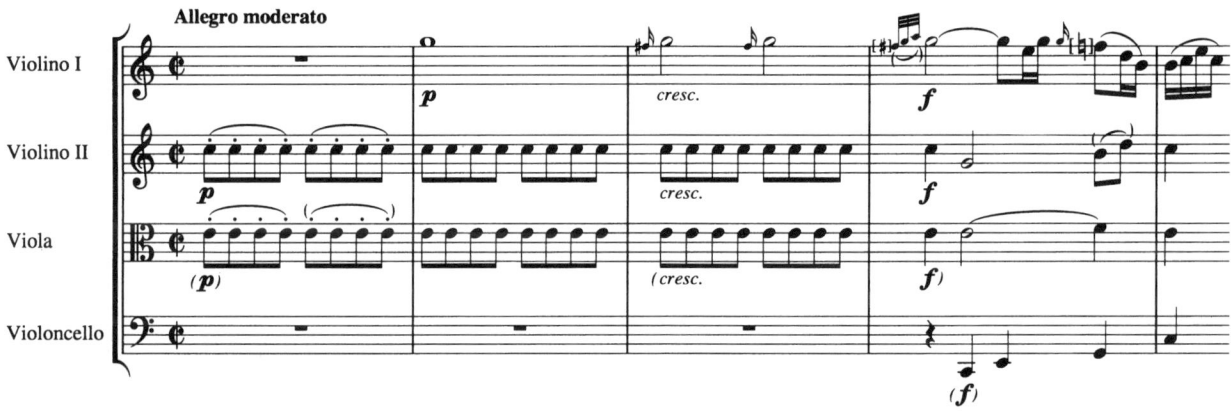

Example 6.2b. String Quartet in C major, op. 33, no. 3, movement 1, meas. 87-97.

Example 6.2b.—*Continued*

genius into a homogeneous entity of supranational character. The understanding of, and love for, his music was not confined to any group of peoples or races. Wherever musical friends of the eighteenth century gathered, the right audience for Haydn's compositions was present. The composer, who had spent thirty years in the service of the Hungarian princes Esterházy and embarked on his first extensive journey when approaching his sixtieth birthday, enjoyed fame in all countries of Europe and even in the New World. Commissions reached him from France, Italy, Spain, Germany, and the British Isles, and he was in active and remunerative business relations with Austrian, German, French, English, and Scottish publishers, occupying in this respect quite an unusual position among the composers of the time. It is significant that when he considered embarking on his first visit to England, and Mozart warned him that he "had no education for the wide world and spoke so few languages," Haydn felt justified in serenely answering "But my language is understood all over the world."

Strangely enough, even Haydn's church music is to some extent connected with the tenets of the Enlightenment. This sounds at first like a paradox, for Haydn was, as we know, deeply religious. He inscribed his manuscripts with an invocation of and praise to God, and we have every reason to assume that Haydn, who as a boy served for several years in the choir of Vienna's largest cathedral, was through his whole life a loyal son of the Roman Catholic Church. On the other hand his sacred music exhibits quite clearly some features of a secular nature. It has been pointed out with full justification that his last Masses display a symphonic character, and the extensive coloratura which he at times assigns to the solo voices point to influences of contemporary opera. Haydn does not hesitate to entrust the chorus with certain sections of the text reserved, according to liturgical precepts, to the priest. At times the Latin text is crowded together as much as possible to abbreviate the composition, and he even uses the expedient of having each of the four voices utter different words simultaneously. In this manner he manages to deal in one of his earliest Masses with well over seventy words in only nine measures of music. On the other hand, the very broadly conceived *Missa Sanctae Caeciliae* [Hob. XXII:5] is so extensive that it cannot possibly fit into the liturgical service. Most of all, the light-hearted mood of some of Haydn's church music is bound to invite criticism from a strictly liturgical viewpoint. Quite rightly Griesinger, a friend of the composer and one of his earliest biographers, stated: "Haydn's attitude towards religion was gay, reconciled and trustful, and this character is also to be found in his composition for the church." There is no doubt that these works contain numbers of exquisite beauty, yet they reveal a freedom of the mind and spiritual detachment characteristic of the enlightened composer whose strong belief in the divine power did not necessarily manifest itself in faithful adherence to liturgical precepts.

The optimism exhibited in Haydn's church music is a basic feature of his personality. And here we see one of the strongest links to the tenets of the time. In spite of life's dark sides, which were only too familiar to one who had led quite an unsheltered existence from his earliest childhood, Haydn fervently believed in goodness, in beauty, and in God's mercy, proofs of which he recognized in all the wonders of the creation which never ceased filling him with joy. Like other protagonists of the Enlightenment he believed in humanity, and a number like the aria "In native worth" in his oratorio *The Creation* [Hob. XXI:2], describing man in his dignity and proud bearing, breathes the very spirit of this great era. Haydn powerfully conveys in music the meaning of the following words:

Mit Würd' und Hoheit angetan,	In native worth and honour clad,
Mit Schönheit, Stärk' und Mut begabt,	With beauty, courage, strength adorn'd,
Gen Himmel aufgerichtet, steht der Mensch,	To heav'n erect and tall, he stands a man,
Ein Mann und König der Natur.	The Lord and King of nature all.
Die breit gewölbt', erhab'ne Stirn	The large and arched front sublime,
Verkünd't der Weisheit tiefen Sinn	Of wisdom deep declares the seat,
Und aus dem hellen Blicke strahlt	And in his eyes with brightness shines the soul,
Der Geist, des Schöpfers Hauch und Ebenbild.	The breath and image of his God.

Haydn regarded his creative work as a service to mankind. He was aware that his music, pervaded by the joy of life and by a strong affirmative spirit, could help in many ways. When in 1802 the man of seventy received a warm letter of thanks from unknown music amateurs in a little town on the North Sea, he answered with words truly significant for his own attitude and for the spirit of Enlightenment as well. Parts of the letter I should like to read now to you in conclusion of my paper:

> You give me the pleasant convicton (which cannot fail to be a most welcome consolation of my declining years) that I am often the enviable source from which you, and so many families susceptible of true feeling, derive pleasure and enjoyment in domestic life. What happiness does this thought cause me! Often, when contending with obstacles of every sort that interfered with my work, often when my powers both of body and mind were failing and I felt it hard to persevere in the course I had entered on, a secret feeling in me whispered: "There are but few contented and happy men here below; everywhere grief and care prevail; perhaps your labors may one day be the source from which the weary and worn, or the man burdened with affairs, can derive a few moments' rest and refreshment." This was indeed a powerful motive to press onward.

Part 2
Haydn at Work: Specific Fields of His Production

My vital interest in Orlando Paladino [Hob. XXIII:11] *was prompted by a kind of second phase in my Haydn research . . . I wanted to investigate more thoroughly the specific fields of his production.*
—This I Remember, *142-43*

The Small Sacred Works by Haydn in the Esterházy Archives at Eisenstadt

Reprinted from *Musical Quarterly* 45 (1959): 460-72, by permission of Oxford University Press. Geiringer initially shared the results of his research in Eisenstadt at the Haydn Congress held in Budapest in September 1959 (see essay 23, p. 232). Having exposed early on "the structure of prejudice against Haydn's church music that was built by Cecilianism" (essay 2, p. 17), Geiringer set out to investigate the smaller church compositions in this pioneering study. His research served as the basis for continuation of the work for the Haydn Institute, Cologne, by Irmgard Becker-Glauch and Marianne Helms. See in particular Becker-Glauch's "Neue Forschungen zu Haydns Kirchenmusik," *Haydn-Studien* 2 (1969-70): 167-241, and Helms, "Kleinere Geistliche Werke," ibid., forthcoming.

> Paul [Henry Lang] *also helped me with a strong letter of recommendation for a coveted Guggenheim grant. This enabled me to travel to Austria during a period of sabbatical leave to study the church music preserved in the Esterházy castle at Eisenstadt. Prince Esterházy, who was an ardent Hungarian patriot, had been annoyed when, at the end of World War I, the Burgenland, which had originally belonged to Hungary, became a part of the new Austrian Republic. He removed all objects of value—among them the precious Haydn original manuscripts—from his castle in Eisenstadt, the Burgenland's capital, and stored them in his Budapest palace. The church music, consisting mostly of eighteenth-century copies, was left behind, as it was considered to be of lesser significance. Ironically, the castle of Eisenstadt with everything it contained was almost the only thing the prince was able to keep after the Second World War, as the Communist regime in Hungary confiscated his Hungarian property. So, in Eisenstadt I was now able to study an important collection of Haydn's music, used in his own time, probably under his supervision. The essay I wrote about this subject was later published in* Musical Quarterly *and the German version in* Kirchenmusikalisches Jahrbuch.—This I Remember, *129-30.*

The Esterházy castle in Eisenstadt, for a long time a center of Haydn research, still contains a collection of valuable manuscripts which have been more or less bypassed by scholars. At the end of the First World War, when a portion of western Hungary, the Burgenland with its capital Eisenstadt, was allotted to Austria, Prince Esterházy removed the bulk of his Haydn treasures to Budapest.[1] However, he left behind the very substantial collection of church music preserved in the Eisenstadt castle. Perhaps he felt it unnecessary to move this music because it was meant for performance and did not contain autographs. In any case, the sacred music of the castle, preserved in beautifully written parts, is still to be found in large cabinets outside the chapel. As was to be expected, this repertory, which is arranged in alphabetical order, includes a considerable number of compositions by Joseph Haydn, among them some surprising items. Neither the political changes nor the years of the Second World War with the subsequent occupation of Eisenstadt by the Russian army seem to have damaged this collection.

The prince's library offers much insight into a field of activity that forms a by-no-means negligible part of Haydn's output. Especially the miscellaneous church compositions assembled there—the "Kleinere Kirchenmusikstücke," as Pohl[2] rather vaguely terms them—deserve our attention. These offertories, graduals, *Salve*

---

[1] There they remained as the prince's possessions until the Communist government took them over and incorporated them into the Országos Széchényi Könyvtár, Budapest.

[2] Carl Ferdinand Pohl, *Joseph Haydn*, 2 vols. (Leipzig: Breitkopf & Härtel, 1878-82).

Regina, etc., have been neglected, while Haydn's contributions to the literature of the Mass have received a fair appraisal.³ Yet these small works, although often written to comply with the exigencies of the day, are much more than mere routine compositions. In particular they help to fill the gap in our knowledge of the formative years in Haydn's artistic growth.⁴

This music preserved in Eisenstadt in fine eighteenth-century copies may be divided into two groups: *contrafacta*-based, according to the custom of the time, on works with non-liturgical texts, and orginal compositions.

Three works based on Haydn's Latin cantata *Applausus* [Hob. XXIVa:6] of 1768, which was written for a prelate's inauguration at the Austrian monastery of Göttweig [*recte* Zwettl], are to be found here.⁵ A sheet of detailed instructions drawn up for his performers by the composer, who was unable to attend the concert, reflects the care he had bestowed on his work,⁶ and it is understandable that after a single performance on the festive occasion some of the main numbers were put to new use. Of these arrangements the offertory *O Jesu te invocamus* [B.-Gl. B/6/d] seems to have been a favorite, since it is preserved in Eisenstadt in two sets,⁷ the violin part of one of them listing no less than twenty-four performances between 28 January 1787 and 20 January 1793. Even after Haydn's death the work continued to be played, as we learn from a terse remark pencilled on the timpani part of the second set: "on 26 March 1827, Ludwig van Beethoven died." Haydn's offertory was also printed by Breitkopf & Härtel, with added German text, as *Allmächtiger Preis dir und Ehre! O Jesu, te invocamus! Hymne für vier Singstimmen mit Begleitung des Orchesters*.⁸ The Haydn-Elssler catalog of 1805 mentions the work,⁹ listing the first three measures of the bass part as no. 2 of the offertories.

This is a gay four-part chorus set in simple harmonies and accompanied by sparkling runs in the two violins. The orchestra comprises in addition two oboes, two trumpets, timpani, bass, and organ.¹⁰ Since wind instruments are mostly used for filling, the orchestral body is very slender. In its construction *O Jesu te invocamus* reveals the compactness favored by Haydn. The work is in da capo form, the main section being in C major, the middle section in A minor; cohesion is achieved through the frequent appearance of the introductory violin subject (ex. 7.1) and its derivatives.

Example 7.1. *O Jesu te invocamus*, introductory violin subject.

This offertory is based on the Latin cantata's final chorus, "O coelites vos invocamus." Musically there is hardly any difference between the two works except for the employment of an independent viola part in *Applausus*. Textually, too, there is great similarity. Frequently the same words or at least the same rhymes occur in both

---

³ Alfred Schnerich, *Der Messen-Typus von Haydn bis Schubert* (Vienna: Selbstverlag des Verfassers, 1892); Carl Maria Brand, *Die Messen von Joseph Haydn*, Musik und Geistesgeschichte Berliner Studien zur Musikwissenschaft, 2 (Würzburg: Triltsch, 1941). Moreover, H. C. Robbins Landon edited two volumes of Masses in the collected edition published by the former Haydn Society, Boston, and the new Haydn Institute, Cologne, respectively.

⁴ My research was undertaken in 1957-58 with the help of a Guggenheim Fellowship. I made the initial trip to Eisenstadt with H. C. Robbins Landon, to whom I am most grateful for his valuable advice. Best thanks are also due to Dr. Werner, attorney of Prince Esterházy, who allowed me to peruse the Eisenstadt church music collection and to make photographs there, and finally to Dr. János Harich, keeper of the prince's archives, who subsequently checked a few items for me.

⁵ The original manuscript of this cantata is preserved in the library of the Gesellschaft der Musikfreunde, Vienna.

⁶ An excerpt from this revealing document was presented in English translation in my *Haydn: A Creative Life in Music* (New York: Norton, 1946). The complete German original is reprinted in my *Haydn: Der schöpferische Werdegang eines Meisters der Klassik* (Mainz: Schott, 1959).

⁷ Nos. 154/69 and 195/73.

⁸ A copy of this fine edition is preserved in Marburg, Westdeutsche Bibliothek (no. 9886).

⁹ On p. 24. Cf. Jens Peter Larsen, ed., *Drei Haydn Kataloge in Faksimile* (Copenhagen: Munksgaard, 1941).

¹⁰ A handwritten score in Vienna, Österreichische Nationalbibliothek (no. 15786) employs two trombones also. These are not to be found in most of the other sets in existence.

works, and it is significant that an attempt was even made to use the chorus from *Applausus* with unchanged text as an offertory.[11]

A somewhat different situation prevails in the offertory *Quae res admiranda* [B.-Gl. B/6/a],[12] for four singers (SATB), two violins, viola, two horns, two trumpets, timpani, bass, and organ, a work by no means as widely known as *O Jesu te invocamus*. It is not often to be found in collections of church music; the Haydn-Elssler catalog does not list it, and it was never printed. This is obviously due to its peculiar character. The offertory starts with an extensive instrumental introduction of almost eighty measures followed by recitatives of the four soloists in alternation and a vocal quartet (Andante), "Christus coeli atria," in which the singers are given virtuoso passages. Thus the work demands well-trained soloists and is not suited for wide circulation. The Andante is again in the customary da capo form with a modulating middle section inclining towards the minor mode and with chromatic progressions. It is noteworthy that the trumpets and timpani prescribed in the recitatives give way to horns in the more *cantabile* quartet. This offertory is based on the beginning of *Applausus*, the recitative "Quae metamorphosis," and the ensuing quartet "Virtus inter ardua." The long instrumental ritornello used as introduction to the whole cantata was—as Haydn pointed out—meant to replace a symphonic movement. Apart from the removal of the two oboes, the instrumentation was left unchanged, and even the viola part appears in both versions. One wonders whether this arrangement was actually made by Haydn.

A third piece derived from *Applausus* to be found in Eisenstadt is an *aria de tempore*, "Dictamina mea" [B.-Gl. B/6/b] for soprano and contralto accompanied by two violins, two violas, two horns, organ, and bass.[13] This offertory too enjoyed great success in the eighteenth century and is preserved in most of Austria's larger church and monastery libraries. The textual resemblance between the two versions is particularly marked here, the *aria de tempore* starting like its model, no. 6 of *Applausus*, with the words "Dictamina mea doceri qui gestit." Merely by including the name of Christ and slightly changing a few sentences the piece was made suitable for divine service. Musically the situation is different, however. The offertory does not use the oboes of the original, and replaces its trumpets with horns. More important still is the change in structure. No. 6 of *Applausus* is in da capo form with a C-major Andante moderato in $\frac{4}{4}$ as the main section, and as middle part an Andantino in $\frac{3}{8}$ starting in C minor and concluding on G. The offertory dispenses with the da capo, and, to round off the work, adds a short Alleluia for soprano and alto solo, mixed chorus, strings, and organ. This Alleluia following the concluding G of the second part is in G major, and thus a composition starting in C major ends surprisingly in the dominant key. The approximate date of the arrangement may be deduced from the fact that a set of parts preserved at Göttweig (no. 289) exhibits the name of a Pater Odo and the year 1771. Evidently the offertory originated between 1768 and 1771, and perhaps it was Pater Odo, who after the performance of *Applausus* at Göttweig induced Haydn to adapt no. 6 as a sacred work. That it was Haydn himself who was responsible for the arrangement is attested by the fact that an autograph of the Alleluia coda has been preserved. The six pages of this interesting document, previously owned by Sándor Wolf, are now to be found in the Eisenstadt Haydn Museum.

The offertory's *cantabile* first part, which through the divided violas and the addition of horns achieves a warm and mellow color, the middle section in minor ("Haec opera Christi") with its thinly veiled dance character, and finally the joyous, youthful Alleluia coda,[14] makes this aria one of the most valuable sacred works of Haydn's middle period.

Another arrangement preserved in Eisenstadt is the chorus *Insanae et vanae curae* [B.-Gl. B/8], available in two sets of parts.[15] This motet, which was also circulated with the German texts *Des Staubes eitle Sorgen* and *Im Augenblick* is an adaptation of the powerful and passionate storm chorus *Svanisce in un momento*,[16] which

---

[11] *O coelites vos invocamus: Offertorium in C de Sanctis a Soprano, Alto, Tenore, Basso, Violino I^{no}, Violino II^{do}, et Organo* (Ignatii Schneller, 1839). Parts in Vienna, Österreichische Nationalbibliothek, no. 27091.

[12] Eisenstadt collection, no. 152/69.

[13] A fourth arrangement, the bass aria "Resonent tympana" (also used with the text "Lauda Sion salvatorem"), which is based on the aria "Non chismaras somniatis" of *Applausus*, is missing in the Eisenstadt collection. A copy dated 1778 is to be found in the monastery of Göttweig (no. 291). Cf. also Vienna, Österreichische Nationalbibliothek no. 21592.

[14] An edition of the Alleluia by this author is in preparation. [The edition appears not to have been published; see Hob. XXIIIc:3.]

[15] Nos. 30/38 and 154/67.

[16] Autograph in Budapest, Országos Széchényi Könyvtár, Esterházy archives.

Haydn added in 1784 to his Italian oratorio *Il ritorno di Tobia* [Hob. XXI:1]. The first part of the "motetto" in D minor depicts humanity's restless search for salvation on earth; the F-major middle section presents as contrast to this a vision of the joys in heaven, whereupon the first section returns to be concluded by a coda in D major blissfully anticipating divine mercy. The impressive composition reveals the masterly touch one admires in the great storm choruses of Haydn's last creative period.

Apart from such *contrafacta* the Eisenstadt collection comprises a sizable number of Haydn's works originally destined for the church. Possibly the earliest among them is a *Salve Regina* in E major [Hob. XXIIIb:1], for solo soprano, mixed chorus, two violins, bass, and organ,[17] which according to the autograph originated in 1756[18] and evidently was still used by Haydn while serving at the Esterházy court. The short composition achieves an effective contrast between the utterances of the soloist, which abound in coloratura, in Neapolitan fashion, and the simply set vigorous choruses. The original manuscript of this early work is somewhat hastily penned and it is therefore remarkable how much care Haydn bestowed on the inclusion of dynamic signs in it. In the very first two measures *forte* alternates with *piano* four times, a youthful exuberance not often to be observed in the composer's works.

A little duet on the German text "Mutter Gottes, mir erlaube" [Hob. XXIIId:2] may have originated in the same period. This naïve *Aria de Adventu*[19] employs soprano and contralto with two violins, bass, and organ. Childlike piety suffuses the tune, which is strophically arranged and reflects the devotion to the Mother of God expressed in a more artistic manner in the *Salve Regina*.

At a somewhat later date Haydn may have composed the exquisite contralto solo *Lauda Sion salvatorem* [Hob. XXIIIc:6*], using for the accompanying body flutes and strings. He achieves delightful effects here by having the singer compete with a violin and the woodwind instruments. A pencilled note on the cover of the first violin part points to the contributions to musical life at the Esterházy court made by the family of one of Haydn's foremost associates. It reads "Tomasini Pepi solo" and evidently refers to Josephine Tomasini, a daughter of Luigi Tomasini (1741-1808), who for nearly fifty years served the court as first violinist and whose performances in Haydn's quartet were superb, indeed unsurpassed, according to the composer's own verdict. After Tomasini's death his family continued to enjoy the prince's support. From 1807 to 1810 his two daughters Elisabeth and Josephine were engaged as singers at court,[20] and it was Pepi (an abbreviation customary in Austria for Josephine) who took over the vocal solo in *Lauda Sion salvatorem*.[21]

Much more extensive is a second *Salve Regina*, in G minor [Hob. XXIIIb:2], which the Eisenstadt collection owns in two sets.[22] The work is scored for four solo voices, mixed chorus, strings (including viola), and organ. At the beginning the keyboard instrument is entrusted with an extensive solo, and subsequently its cantilenas, somewhat reminiscent of the idiom of woodwind instruments, alternate very attractively with the utterances of the vocalists. Solo quartet and chorus are effectively juxtaposed, thus forecasting Haydn's mature style. Following the structure of the text, Haydn built the composition in three movements, the fastest, an Allegro, being in the center, while an Adagio forms the beginning and an Allegretto introduced by a Largo concludes the work.

An autograph of this *Salve Regina* is preserved.[23] It employs a rather curious, though at that time fashionable, method of establishing the year of composition. At the end of the autograph there are two prayers to the Holy

---

[17] No. 4/173.

[18] The autograph is now owned by Darmstadt, Hessische Landesbibliothek, which acquired it from Breitkopf & Härtel, Leipzig. Since the date 1756 was added by Haydn much later (around 1800), it is not fully reliable. Cf. H. C. Robbins Landon, *The Symphonies of Joseph Haydn* (London: Universal Edition, Rockliff, 1955), 58-59.

[19] Eisenstadt parts no. H 22/125. This is probably the "Cantilena pro adventu a due," the musical incipit of which Haydn failed to add to the entry on p. 2 of the so-called *Entwurfkatalog* (cf. Larsen, 4). For unknown reasons the staff reserved for it remained empty.

[20] Cf. Pohl, 1:265.

[21] There is a regrettable discrepancy in the tempo indications between the different parts in the Eisenstadt collection. The first section of this da capo aria is marked Adagio. For the faster middle section the first violin part prescribes Allegretto, the second Allegro, the viola Un poco Allegro, and the organ Un poco vivace (the flutes are silent in this section). Such inaccuracies are rare in the music of the Eisenstadt library; the parts are usually quite reliable.

[22] Nos. 38/175 and 39/175.

[23] In Tübingen, Universitätsbibliothek.

Virgin to accord help to the composer. Each is in the form of an acrostic, its capital letters to be interpreted as Roman numbers which added give the year of composition—1771:[24]

> oro te o pla o DVLCls Vlrgo Vt asslstas CoMposltorl
> pla DVLClsqVe Vlrgo asslste CoMposltorl

The composer's name as well as the date on the title page are evidently not in Haydn's hand. As a matter of fact the "771" seems to have been tampered with; maybe it was subsequently corrected in order to conform with the meaning of the two acrostics at the end. Nor is this the only riddle presented by the autograph. Above the two aforementioned acrostics there is another one in a different hand indicating the year 1791, but rather unclear in its meaning. It reads:

> Ita qVoqVe tIbI preCanDo, eXorat IesV genltrICeM tVVs raffaeL.

One stumbles over the name of Raffael in this acrostic. There was a composer by the name of Ignaz Wenzel Raffael (1762-99) who towards the end of his life resided in Vienna.[25] Was he perhaps the owner of the *Salve Regina* autograph in 1791?

A piece of monumental simplicity is the "Offertorio in Stillo a Capella" *Non nobis Domine* [Hob. XXIIIa:1], mentioned in both the *Entwurfkatalog* and the Haydn-Elssler list of 1805.[26] This curious work employing only four singers and bass revives the idiom of the Baroque motet and is the only composition of its type to be found in Haydn's output. It was probably written in the early 1770s, when Haydn was eagerly experimenting with old forms.[27] The exquisite piece[28] uses a Latin version of the beautiful words of Psalm 115:1 "Not unto us, O Lord, not unto us, but unto Thy name give glory," starting with a fugato and subsequently turning to a homophonic idiom, in which expressiveness is matched by dignity and power. The initial austerity of the tonal language—interestingly deviating from Haydn's later fugues—gradually gives way to an abundance of sound and a powerful climax is achieved.

The offertory *Agite properate ad aras convolate*[29] [Hob. XXIIIa:2] is also known with the text "Animae Deo gratae ovantes jubilate." It is listed in the Haydn-Elssler catalog among the offertories,[30] with an insignificant incipit (ex. 7.2). This is a spirited, festive C-major piece concluding with a jubilant Alleluia. It employs a solo trio of two

Example 7.2. *Agite properate ad aras convolate*, Elssler incipit.

sopranos and tenor whose brilliant coloraturas alternate with the tutti of the four choral parts, which also require virtuosity.[31] Violins, oboes, trumpets, timpani, basses, and organ create an effective instrumental background. Parts

---

[24] Similarly the autograph of Haydn's *Applausus* exhibits at the end a Latin acrostic giving 1768 as the year of composition.

[25] Cf. Robert Eitner, *Biographisch-bibliographisches Quellen-Lexikon der christlichen Zeitrechnung bis zur Mitte des XIX. Jahrhunderts*, vol. 8 (Leipzig: Breitkopf & Härtel, 1903), 113. Maybe he was identical with the Raphael whose ballet *Pygmalion* was performed in 1797 at Eisenstadt. Cf. Hugo Botstiber, *Joseph Haydn: Unter Benutzung der von C. F. Pohl hinterlassenen Materialien weitergeführt* (Leipzig: Breitkopf & Härtel, 1927), 120.

[26] P. 18 of *Entwurfkatalog*, p. 24 of Haydn-Elssler list. Parts are Eisenstadt no. 202/75.

[27] Botstiber's theory (*Joseph Haydn*, 149) that the work originated in 1799 was contradicted by Larsen, who deduced from the nature of the handwriting that the offertory may have been entered into the *Entwurfkatalog* in the 'seventies. Cf. *Die Haydn-Überlieferung* (Copenhagen: Munksgaard, 1939), 235.

[28] An edition of the work by this author is in preparation. [The edition was subsequently published in 1960 by Concordia Publishing House, St. Louis, Missouri.]

[29] Eisenstadt collection no. 155/69.

[30] P. 24, no. 3.

[31] The Eisenstadt parts comprise one first and one second soprano, alto, tenor, bass, as well as a sixth part designated "Alto con Soprano 2do." This last is an alto part in which the slightly modified solos of the second soprano are inserted. Apparently it was used when in the absence of a second soprano the part had to be sung by an alto.

preserved in the monastery of Göttweig and dated 1776 prove the work to have originated in that year at the latest. This is one of Haydn's sacred works that expresses fully his positive and unquestioning faith.

The monumental chorus in da capo form *Ens aeternum* [Hob. XXIIIa:3], using for accompaniment strings, oboes, bassoon, trumpets, timpani, and organ,[32] may have been written as late as 1780. It is a solemn, powerful piece whose bass incipit is listed in the Haydn-Elssler catalog.[33] This offertory, which combines elegance of structure with textural solidity, seems to have enjoyed great favor, since it was published by both Simrock and Breitkopf & Härtel with the German text "Walte gnädig, o ew'ge Liebe" added to the Latin original.

The latest composition in the collection is the mighty *Te Deum* in C major [Hob. XXIIIc:2], composed in 1799. This very concise work confines itself to four-part chorus and orchestra in which the trumpets play an important role, the over-all effect being enhanced through the inclusion of the Gregorian *Te Deum* tune in the middle parts. The concluding double fugue, in which the theme of "in te Domine speravi" is combined with that of "non confundar in aeternum," presents a poetical feature of symbolic significance also to be observed in Bruckner's *Te Deum*.

These last-mentioned compositions may help to restore Haydn's church music to the position it enjoyed in the composer's lifetime. They are powerful and sparkling, built with fine craftsmanship, not hard to perform thanks to their compactness and the economy of means employed. Those critics who take exception to occasional peculiarities in Haydn's setting of the Mass text might derive full satisfaction from these shorter sacred works.

Going through the comprehensive Eisenstadt collection, we are surprised to find a curious gap. We miss one of Haydn's most successful sacred works, the *Stabat Mater* of 1767 [Hob. XXbis], of which the composer was particularly proud. This sweetly sad composition is mentioned in Haydn's autobiographical sketch; he informs Artaria in a letter of 1781 that it was performed four times in Paris and lists it in the catlog of 1805[34] among his great oratorios.

A letter that recently came to light[35] may help to explain the absence of the work in the Eisenstadt chapel. This is, incidentally, an interesting human document because it reveals the shrewd psychological method employed by Haydn in order to wrest permission for a leave from his patron. The letter, dated 20 March 1768,[36] is addressed to the prince's secretary Anton Scheffstoss and reads:

> I believe it is known to you that last year the venerable hymn *Stabat Mater* was set to music by me to the best of my ability and that I sent the work to the outstanding and world-famous Hasse, my sole purpose being that in case I had not adequately expressed words of such deep significance, this defect might be corrected by a master so successful in all his works. The great master against my deserts honored me with ineffable praise and only wished to be allowed to hear the work performed by a competent group of musicians. However, since there is at present a great lack in Vienna of singers *utriusque generis*, my submissively obedient petition is herewith made to His Grace through your good offices to allow me, Weigl and his wife, as well as Friberth[37] to go to Vienna in order to enhance His Grace's honor through his servants' performance on Friday afternoon at the Fratres Misericordiae,[38] Saturday night we would be back at Eisenstadt. If His Grace so command, I could replace Friberth by another singer. Asking you, dearest Mr. Scheffstoss, to expedite my petition, I remain with all veneration,
>
> Your most obedient servant
> Josephus Haydn
>
> P.S. . . . The promised divertimentos will certainly be delivered to His Highness within this week.

---

[32] Eisenstadt parts no. 440/99. Österreichische Nationalbibliothek owns a score of the work (no. 15786) calling for trombones also.

[33] On p. 25 as no. 4 of the offertories.

[34] On p. 63.

[35] Cf. Arisztid Valkó, "Haydn magyarországi múködése a levéltári akták tükrében" (Haydn's activities in Hungary as reflected in archival documents), in *Koldály Zoltán 75. születésnapjára*, ed. Bence Szabolcsi and Dénes Bartha, Zenetudományi tanulmányok, 6 (Budapest: Akadémiai Kiadó, 1957), 627-67. [This is] a study offering several unknown Haydn letters from the Esterházy archives in German as well as in Hungarian translation.

[36] Esterházy archives, fasc. I, 56.

[37] Joseph Weigl was a cellist of the Esterházy orchestra; his wife, Anna Maria (born Scheffstoss) a soprano; Karl Friberth a tenor.

[38] The order of the Fratres Misericordiae (Barmherzige Brüder—Brothers of Mercy) in Vienna was especially dear to Haydn. As a young and struggling artist he had held a position there as violinist. He also maintained close contact with the Eisenstadt monastery of the order. See below.

We do not doubt that Haydn achieved his object. His ambitious patron could not help being pleased with the praise bestowed by the great Hasse on his conductor, and his mood was certainly further mellowed by the promise of some new divertimentos (in all likelihood trios with a part for the baryton, Prince Esterházy's favorite instrument). At the Viennese performance of the *Stabat Mater* Haydn would have used the material from Eisenstadt, and anxious to hurry back so as not to overstay his leave, he may have left the parts behind.

Though it lacks this famous piece, the Eisenstadt collection includes two works of extreme rarity. The "Offertorio de Sancto vel Sancta Concertantes jugiter per calamitatem" [B.-Gl., B/6/C], for bass solo, strings, two oboes, and organ,[39] has not been mentioned by either Pohl or Larsen and does not appear in the very comprehensive list that Larsen and Landon compiled for *Die Musik in Geschichte und Gegenwart*.[40] According to information kindly supplied by Dr. Anthony van Hoboken, the work is also to be found in the monastery of Seckau, again under Joseph Haydn's name, however with the text "Bonitatis totius" and an introductory recitative missing in the Eisenstadt set. Although we have no conclusive evidence for the authenticity of the work, the fact that it is preserved in eighteenth-century parts in a collection of which Haydn was in charge makes it highly probable that it is genuine Haydn. The character of passionate fervor as well as the abundance of Neapolitan coloraturas with enormous skips—up to an octave plus a sixth—in the solo voice (ex. 7.3) point to the earlier years of Haydn's creative career. There is even a decided affinity between this composition in D minor and an Italian aria in the same key displaying an identical heroic mood and using again large melodic skips. Haydn wrote the latter ("Quanti il mar tesori aduna") in 1763 for the secular cantata *Destatevi o miei fidi* [Hob. XXIVa:2], intended to celebrate his patron, and the offertory may have been composed at about the same time.

Example 7.3. "Offertorio de Sancto vel Sancta," excerpt from the solo bass part.

Of greater interest is a more extensive composition which so far has not been discussed in any work on Haydn.[41] It is entitled *Lytania de B:V:M: / in C / 4 voc: / Soprano, Alto Tenore / Basso / 2 Violini, 2 Clariny / Tympano / Organo con Violone / NB In Mater Amabilis, Traverso Solo / Salus infirmorum Org: Solo / Del Sig. Giuseppe Haydn*[42] (see fig. 7.1). The words "Salus infirmorum Org: Solo" were added in another handwriting and evidently by the organist, to refer to his own performance. About the author of these four words there can fortunately not be any doubt; they were written by Haydn himself. He was also responsible for an entry on the right upper corner of the title page: "780.Ch:Fr:M:D:C:" This could be taken to stand for "1780—Choro Fratrum—Maestro di Cappella," and would mean that in the year 1780 the prince's conductor Joseph Haydn supplied this Litany to the chorus of the Brothers of Mercy in Eisenstadt. If this assumption is correct it would indicate that the Litany was performed by the monastic order for which Haydn created, among other compositions, his *Kleine Orgelmesse* [Hob. XXII:7]. The parts were neatly written by a copyist, but Haydn himself made small additions. In the organ part we find for example in the *Salus infirmorum* the entry "Piano Sempre" in the composer's hand. The Litany is simply constructed. Four numbers in C major using full chorus, trumpets, and timpani alternate with movements in related keys, employing a smaller orchestra without trumpets. In one of them a bass solo is accompanied by strings only, in the second contralto and flute compete, while the last and most important one is for chorus and

---

[39] Eisenstadt parts no. 77/61.

[40] 5 (Kassel: Bärenreiter, 1956).

[41] Larsen mentions the incipit in *Drei Haydn Kataloge* (VIII/1:126, 137), on the basis of information supplied by Dr. János Harich, keeper of the Esterházy archives.

[42] Eisenstadt parts no. 196/161.

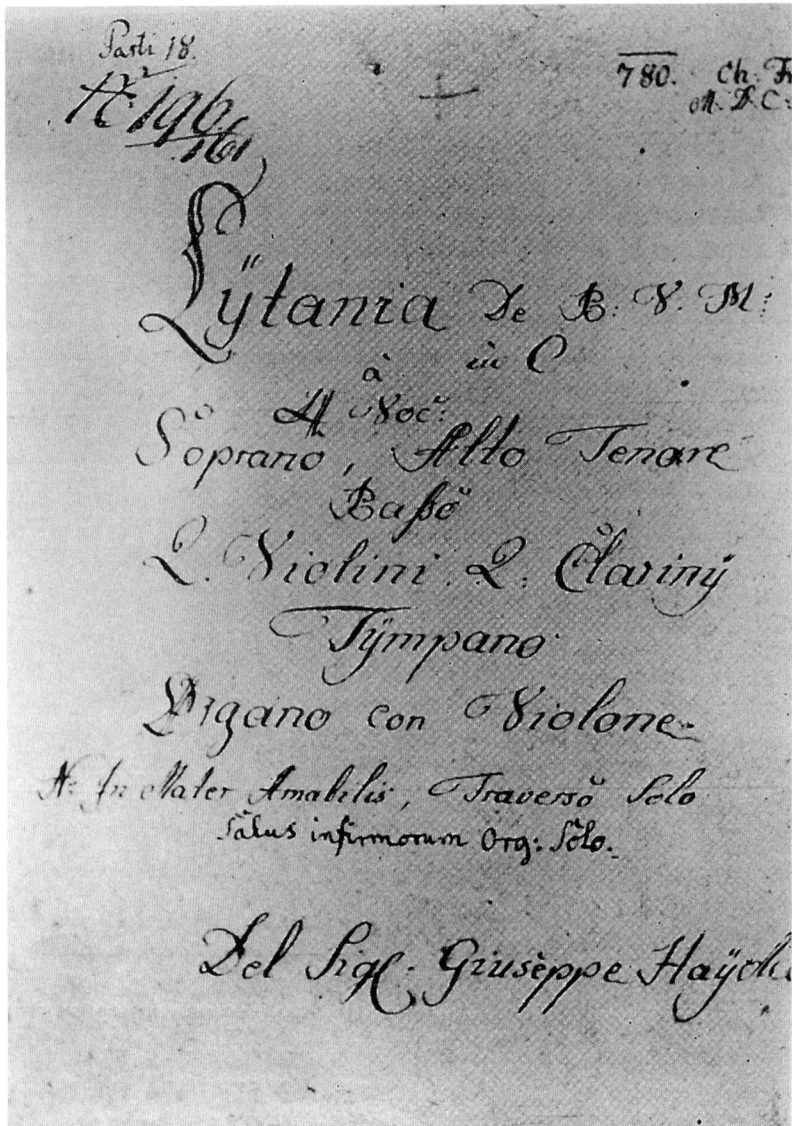

Fig. 7.1. Title page of a Litany in C, Hob. XXIIIc:C2, by Haydn

Courtesy of the Parish church, Eisenstadt

solo organ. Haydn's vocal works using a solo keyboard instrument were all written within a comparatively short period, from 1763 to the middle of the seventies. In all likelihood the Litany belongs there too. Stylistic similarities with the so-called *Grosse Orgelmesse* [Hob. XXII:4] of 1766, which is likewise dedicated to the Blessed Virgin, suggest that the Litany also originated in the middle sixties.

Another work in the collection, listed by Larsen[43] on the basis of the Esterházy inventory, seems to be of doubtful authenticity. It is an *Ave Regina* in F major [Hob. XXIIIb:6*] preserved in the chapel in two separate sets of parts.[44] In both sets we find the indication "del Signore Haydn" without any first name. From long, bitter experience we know that old manuscripts with merely the indication "Haydn" very often are works by Joseph's younger brother, Michael. In the case of the *Ave Regina* in F this seems most likely. The gentle, somewhat languorous sweetness of this brief chorus, accompanied by two violins and organ only, shows greater resemblance to other church works by

---

[43] *Drei Haydn Kataloge*, VIII/2. Cf. also the list of Haydn's works compiled by Larsen and H. C. Robbins Landon in "Haydn, Franz Joseph," *MGG*, 5 (1956), col. 1891.

[44] No. 35/191. It appears once as an independent piece and once as the fifth in a collection of six *Ave Regina*, whose first and sixth are by Albrechtsberger, while nos. 2, 3, and 4 are by Krottendorffer.

the Salzburg composer than to those of Joseph Haydn. It might be advisable to place the *Ave Regina* in F among the doubtful compositions of Joseph Haydn until further evidence is found to prove its authenticity.

Problems of this kind confront the Haydn student in countless Austrian collections, but fortunately sometimes evidence is offered where it is least expected. The Stadtpfarrkirche at Eisenstadt owns a large pile of church music attributed to Joseph Haydn. Leafing through it one finds a *Motetto di Sta. Thecla* for soprano solo, mixed chorus, strings, and organ. The parts are written in a completely uncharacteristic, rather careless hand, and nobody perusing them would expect anything remarkable. However, at the end of the bass part the shock comes, because here we find, without the slightest warning, Haydn's own, very characteristic signature (see fig. 7.2). How it got there is anybody's guess. It may be that the organist of the Eisenstadt city-church approached his famous colleague and asked him which of the manuscripts owned by the church and bearing the composer's name were actually his. Perhaps Haydn then looked them over and when he recognized the *Motetto di Sta. Thecla* as one of his works, wrote his name on the first part that came to his hand.

Fig. 7.2. Bass part of a *Mottetto di Sta. Thecla*, Hob. XXIIIa:4*, showing Haydn's autograph signature

Courtesy of the Parish church, Eisenstadt

This is an attractive little cantata. It starts with a secco recitative for soprano solo which is followed by a da capo aria for the soprano, a simple and gay hymn for mixed chorus forming the conclusion. The melodic language reflects Austrian folksong, and the instrumental introduction of the aria is based on two contrasting subjects, features that make it seem likely that this motet originated at the beginning of the seventies, when Haydn achieved greater independence from Neapolitan models.

The Eisenstadt collections offer a remarkable cross-section of a form of music that for a long time held Haydn's interest. Going through these sacred works, we are allowed most revealing glimpses into the composer's workshop.

Haydn as an Opera Composer

Reprinted from *Proceedings of the Musical Association* 66 (1939-40): 23-32, by permission of Oxford University Press. Haydn's dramatic works were among the lacunae singled out by Geiringer in the seminal "Portrait" article published in the issue devoted entirely to Haydn in Bernhard Schuster's *Die Musik* (1932) (see essay 2, p. 16). From that time forward Geiringer seemed not to have failed to pursue every opportunity to speak and write about the operas and to promote their performance. In this respect he was a pioneer, and early on—perhaps intuitively—he grasped the necessity of investigating the dramatic works in order to gain a fuller understanding of the composer's development. This paper-article and the following essay of 1974 (essay 9) represent just two of his several published efforts in this direction which culminated in the two massive volumes for the *Joseph Haydn Werke*: the edition of *Orlando Paladino* (Munich: Henle, 1972-73) and *Acide und andere Fragmente italienischer Opern um 1761 bis 1763*, co-edited with Günter Thomas (ibid., 1985; see appended Bibliography).

At the time Geiringer wrote this survey, however, hardly any of the over two dozen dramatic works had been published, and the music was known only to a small handful of scholars, of which Geiringer was one. Furthermore, this admirable attempt to survey the core operatic production was made without the advantages of having at hand fundamental monographs on the subject, such as Helmut Wirth's *Haydn als Dramatiker* (Ph.D. diss., University of Kiel, 1940), while two more decades would pass before the landmark archival study *Haydn als Opernkapellmeister* by Dénes Bartha and László Somfai would appear (Budapest: Verlag der Ungarischen Akademie der Wissenschaften, 1960; see Geiringer's review reprinted as part of essay 23, p. 233). Musical examples referred to by the author have been supplied by drawing from the now-complete edition of the operas in the *Joseph Haydn Werke* (with permission, G. Henle Verlag).

The insertion aria "Dica pure" (see fig. 8.1) is now believed to have been composed by Haydn for Pasquale Anfossi's dramma giocoso *Il geloso in cimento* (1785). Haydn's authorship cannot be authenticated.

It is a regrettable fact that the opportunities for hearing, or even for studying, the works of Joseph Haydn still leave much to be desired, and that, in spite of the composer's popularity, today not more than a tenth of his music is ever played, and hardly one-third is accessible in print. The remainder is scattered through the world's libraries in manuscript or in old exhausted editions.

For years past a revival of interest in Haydn's works has been foreshadowed and with that object a collected edition was projected. The first volume appeared in 1908, and since that date only ten volumes have been published. If this edition, which is expected to comprise about eighty volumes, continues to progress at the same speed as hitherto, its completion may be expected in about two hundred years' time!

Among the many unknown works by Haydn are thirteen operas, most of which he wrote whilst in the service of the Princes Esterházy, those passionate devotees of the stage. Daily performances were arranged in the exquisite little theater of the castle Esterháza, which was capable of seating four hundred and possessed a roomy stage equipped with every artistic and technical device of the Baroque period. The dramas were performed by touring companies, but for the operas a special cast was engaged under Haydn's direction. He studied the parts with the singers, rehearsed the orchestra, discussed scenic effects with the stage-manager, and conducted the performances. The results attained the highest standard, and Vienna was not overpleased when the Empress Maria Theresa, after a visit to Haydn's prince, was overheard saying: "When I want to hear a good opera I have to go to Esterháza." In 1784 a pamphlet entitled *Beschreibung des hochfürstlichen Schlosses Esterház* (Description of the princely castle of Esterháza) saw the light. Its anonymous author—probably Prince Esterházy himself—writes about an opera performance at the court of Esterháza:

> Words cannot describe how both eyes and ears are delighted here. When the music begins, its touching delicacy and the strength and force of the instruments penetrate the soul, since the great composer, Haydn, is himself conducting. But the audience is also overwhelmed by the admirable lighting and the deceptively perfect stage-setting. At first we see clouds on which the gods are seated sinking slowly to earth. Then the gods rise upwards and instantly vanish, and then again everything is transformed into a delightful garden, an enchanted wood or, it may be, a glorious hall.

For special festivities, such as the prince's patron-saint's day or the arrival of prominent visitors, Haydn himself composed a new opera, and to such occasions almost all his dramatic works owe their existence. Twice only (if we disregard a lost work of his youth) did Haydn write for other theaters; but in neither case did the projected performance take place. An opera commanded in 1776 by the imperial court was withdrawn by Haydn himself, infuriated at the intrigues of his rival composers, intrigues such as Mozart experienced again and again. And when Haydn, on his first visit to England in 1791, wrote his opera *L'anima del filosofo* [Hob. XXVIII:13] (later entitled *Orfeo ed Euridice*) for the newly-opened King's Theatre, the impresario was refused the necessary permission of the king for its performance. As far as I know, it still awaits its first hearing.

I propose now to give a survey of Haydn's operatic output, but without discussing those works of which the music has not been preserved, namely the marionette operas, Haydn's first dramatic venture *Der krumme Teufel* [Hob. XXIXb:1a], and his Italian comedies of 1762. Of the marionette operas and the comedies only insignificant fragments have survived, while the music to *Der krumme Teufel* is altogether lost. But there are still thirteen operas left, quite a considerable number for a composer whose dramatic works are hardly ever noticed at all in our time. The earliest of these, the Festa teatrale *Acide* [Hob. XXVIII:1], of which only part has been preserved, follows the style of the then fashionable Italian *opera seria*. There are the usual interminable da capo arias, overladen with roulades and coloratura. Such a work was expected to have a happy ending and therefore the hero, Acide, after being murdered by the giant Polyphemus, returns to life in the shape of a fountain, and as a fountain joins vigorously in the final quartet.

No long time elapsed before the unnatural character of this form of opera provoked a reaction in Italy which led to the composition of gay and popular works. Haydn also felt the attraction of this type and his opera *La canterina* [Hob. XXVIII:2] (The singer), composed in 1766, is no mythological drama but a lively farce taken from everyday life. It is an intermezzo, similar in character to Pergolesi's *La serva padrona*. There is no overture, and its two parts are meant to be performed in the intervals of a three-act serious opera. No one could uphold the morality of the plot, for the young vocalist Gasparina thinks it appropriate to encourage two lovers at the same time. Her double dealing is discovered and she is placed in a very awkward position, but she is clever enough to know the old trick. She threatens to commit suicide and pretends to faint, whereupon the fury of her lovers gives way to compassion. They repent of their anger and once more shower gifts upon her. The music is simple and graceful and most economical in form, so as not to interfere with the natural flow of the action.

Madam Elisabeth Forini will sing the first aria from *La canterina* in which Gasparina's chaperone, old Apollonia, teaches her the art of make-up [ex. 8.1]. This simple song-like piece has nothing in common with the pompous da capo arias of the Neapolitan operas. In its light Rococo style it forms an appropriate introduction to the intermezzo.

May I present yet another example from the same work? I must confess to a certain partiality for this intermezzo, since I have been responsible for the first performance of it in both German and French. Here is one of the numbers in which Haydn burlesques the *opera seria*, the plaintive air by which Gasparina designs to move the heart of her offended lover [ex. 8.2, pp. 82-85]. The employment of the melancholy English horn, the gloomy tonality of C minor, the dramatic string tremolo, diminished and augmented intervals, and the deep sighs in the solo voice—all these have an exaggerated plaintiveness by which Haydn succeeds well in his object of ridiculing his model.

It is not surprising that in the long run the superficial gaiety of *La canterina*, which offered no escape for any deeper musical expression, was not more able to satisfy the artistic leanings of a Haydn than was the shallow pathos of the *opera seria*. Although he did not entirely abandon comic opera, he endeavored increasingly to imbue it with warmth and tenderness. His gay characters were more and more contrasted by serious and dignified figures, and thereby a type of serio-comic, or mixed, opera was created, a type which Mozart was to develop to perfection. It was no mere accident that Goldoni, the Venetian poet who was mainly responsible for the division into *parte serie* and *parte buffe*, should have supplied the libretti for the first two works of this group. They are *Lo*

Example 8.1. *La canterina*, act 1, scene 1, "Che visino delicato," meas. 1-39.

Example 8.1.—*Continued*

Example 8.1.—*Continued*

Example 8.1.—*Continued*

Example 8.2. *La canterina*, act 2, scene 2, "Non v'è chi mi aiuta," meas. 1-16.

Haydn as an Opera Composer   83

Example 8.2.—*Continued*

Continued

Example 8.2.—*Continued*

Example 8.2.—*Continued*

speziale [Hob. XXVIII:3] (The apothecary) *dramma giocoso* of 1768, and *Le pescatrici* [Hob. XXVIII:4] (The fishermaids) *dramma giocoso* of 1770 [1769]. They were followed by:

L'infedeltà delusa [Hob. XXVIII:5] (Unfaithfulness deluded), *burletta*, librettist unknown, 1773 [1775].
L'incontro improvviso [Hob. XXVIII:6] (The chance meeting), *dramma giocoso*, libretto by Dancourt-Frieberth, 1773.
Il mondo della luna [Hob. XXVIII:7] (The world of the moon), *dramma giocoso*, libretto by Goldoni, 1777.
La vera costanza [Hob. XXVIII:8] (True faithfulness), *dramma giocoso*, libretto by Puttini and Travaglia, 1779.[1]
La fedeltà premiata [Hob. XXVIII:10] (Faithfulness rewarded), *dramma giocoso*, libretto probably by Lorenzi, 1779 [1780].
Orlando Paladino, *dramma eroi-comico* [Hob. XXVIII:11], libretto by Nunziato Porta, 1782.

In these mixed operas the prominence given to the music and the proportion given to it increase steadily. As Haydn had no chorus at his disposal, he combined his soloists into quartets, quintets, and occasionally even septets and octets. Of special importance are his finales, which show the composer at the height of his dramatic mastery. The tempo, the rhythm, and the number of singers are constantly varied, while the musical unity is always maintained. In each finale a great climax is reached after several retarding episodes. In some of these operas Haydn includes purely instrumental numbers of an illustrative or "program" character, as well as ballets.

The first of these mixed operas, *Lo speziale*, is the only dramatic composition of Haydn that is occasionally played today. In it the composer has written a masterly comedy with music, and every part of the score reveals his peculiar humor and descriptive gift. Mengone's aria in A major, for example, paints the sufferings of indigestion and the soothing effect of rhubarb with a daring realism that makes the piece seem hardly suitable for a refined audience.

The opera *L'infedeltà delusa* was composed to celebrate the visit of the Empress Maria Theresa to Esterháza. From this work the aria "Come piglia sì bene la mira" will now be sung [ex. 8.3]. It deals with a favorite subject of the Rococo. It describes how Cupid, in spite of the bandage over his eyes, does not fail to pierce the heart of his victims.

---
[1] The composition was already started in 1776.

(I was unable to procure the score for today's performance, so we have to manage with a piano reduction which I made at an earlier time.) In spite of the graceful coloratura, the expression here is warmer and deeper than in the arias from *La canterina*.

Example 8.3. *L'infedeltà delusa*, act 1, scene 4, "Come piglia sì bene la mira," meas. 1-28.

Example 8.3.—Continued

Continued

Example 8.3.—*Continued*

In the Turkish opera *L'incontro improvviso*, Haydn treats a subject that has been previously used by Gluck. It is interesting to note how, in rationalist fashion, the clergy are ridiculed here in the person of the roguish monk Calandro. The Goldoni opera *Il mondo della luna* includes an unusually large number of instrumental pieces. Each act is preceded by an orchestral prelude in preparation for the action that follows. There is also a ballet. This is somewhat reminiscent of Rameau's tendencies, which at that time had been adopted in Germany by composers like Jommelli. The opera *La vera costanza* shows some relationship to a work by Mozart. By an odd coincidence the heroine, who from humble beginnings rises to the rank of countess, bears the name of Rosina, and like Rosina in Mozart's *Le nozze di Figaro*, she is attached in deep love and faithfulness to her husband, although the Count, heedless of his own gallant adventures, torments her with his unfounded jealousy. The last of this group is the *dramma eroi-comico Orlando Paladino*, in which stress is laid on the heroic element, so that, whereas in *Lo speziale* one sentimental hero is balanced against three comic personages, in this opera six serious characters are contrasted with two comic parts. One of the latter, however, the cowardly vain braggart Pasquale, is a masterpiece, rivaling his seventeenth-century brother, the Sancho Panza of Cervantes. The cavatina by which Pasquale on horseback, after being heralded by trumpets and horns, boasts of his feats of valor, ranks among the best numbers that the comic opera of the eighteenth century produced.

Haydn's artistic development, as revealed in these mixed operas, led naturally, it would appear, to his reverting to the purely serious type. In 1779—that is, before *Orlando Paladino*—he composed an opera of distinctly serious character, *L'isola disabitata* [Hob. XXVIII:9], which he called an "Azione teatrale," a term Gluck had employed for his *Orfeo ed Euridice* in 1762. Another point in common with the work of that operatic reformer is found in the fact that in *L'isola disabitata* Haydn substitutes for the customary *recitativo secco* with its harpsichord accompaniment, a recitative furnished with a carefully worked-out orchestral accompaniment.

Haydn's last two operas, *Armida* [Hob. XXVIII:12] (1783), and *L'anima del filosofo* (The philosopher's soul, 1791), are also of a serious character. Both are based on subjects familiar to students of Gluck's works, and in them Haydn again adopts the principles and methods of the older composer. What Gluck wrote about his overture to *Alceste*: "Ho imaginato che la Sinfonia debbe prevenir gli spettatori dell'azione, che ha da rappresentarsi, e formarne, per dir cosí l'argomento" (I have considered that the overture should prepare the audience for the action of the drama and give them a kind of outline of the plot) might also have been said of the prelude to Haydn's *Armida*. While in the older Italian operas the overture was entirely independent of the work to follow, in this case Haydn produced a sort of symphonic poem covering the whole plot of the crusader Rinaldo's sinful passion for the lovely sorceress Armida and his eventual return to duty. The opening theme of the overture depicts in its first four measures Rinaldo's carefree life of knighthood and in its second half his youthful longing for love. The energetic second subject portrays the hero's attachment to his military duties, but the development of the movement imports a serious conflict. Abruptly a yearning Allegretto is heard, and this corresponds to that part of the opera in which the hero arrives at Armida's paradise. At last Rinaldo wrenches himself from the arms of the sorceress. The return of the first part then reveals the victory of duty over love, and the overture closes with the Rinaldo theme, but without the love-motive of its second half. This interesting prelude, which in form resembles Mozart's overture to *Il seraglio*, will now be played [ex. 8.4]. It has recently been edited by Hans Gál. The complete original manuscript of the opera *Armida* was sent to this country by the composer himself and was at first the property of the Sacred Harmonic Society of London, from which it passed to the Royal College of Music.[2]

In the latter years of his life Haydn was repeatedly asked to write arias for operas by other composers. One of these, "Dica pure," probably meant for the singer Antonia Flamm, to be included in Martín's successful opera *Una cosa rara*, of 1786, will now be given [see fig. 8.1]. Like many of the compositions that Haydn wrote after he became a friend of Mozart, the aria shows in its melody a certain Mozartian touch. This piece has been edited by Dr. Paul Pisk.

It has often been said that Haydn's last opera, *L'anima del filosofo*, is unfinished. This is not the case, as I am able to state after making a careful examination of the extensive autograph which today is the property of the Prussian State Library in Berlin. The error was due to the fact that in 1805 Haydn published through Breitkopf & Härtel a selection of seven numbers from the unperformed work, together with four arias not included in the original score. This selection was never supposed to be complete and was destined merely for the concert-hall. This

---

[2] Ms. no. 276.

Example 8.4. *Armida*, overture, opening theme.

Fig. 8.1. Haydn, "Dica pure," insertion aria, Hob. XXIVb:8
Courtesy of the Sibley Music Library, Eastman School of Music,
University of Rochester, Rochester, New York

opera, having been composed in London, was the only work of the kind where Haydn had not to take into account the little group of singers of Prince Esterházy's company. So he could make ample use of the chorus which, as in Gluck's operas, plays an important part in the dramatic events. I feel sure that it will be interesting to hear something from an opera so closely connected with this country, even if we have to content ourselves with a piano accompaniment to an aria, the aria of the dying Euridice, a piece of classic simplicity and depth of feeling [ex. 8.5].

We have noticed that each of the three last serious operas by Haydn shows the influence of Gluck. It is a striking proof of Haydn's breadth of mind and keenness of intellect that, at the height of his creative power, and after winning world-wide fame, he had no hesitation in accepting ideas from another composer. On the other hand, the serious subjects treated in these latest operas involved a departure from the simplicity, humor, and naturalness that are the main features of Haydn's art. This may be the reason why *La canterina* and the mixed operas that the composer wrote before attaining his full artistic maturity make a stronger appeal to us today than his last dramatic works. The timid attempts made towards a revival of *La canterina*, *Lo speziale*, *L'incontro improvviso*, and *Il mondo della luna* have met with greater success than a performance of *L'isola disabitata* given by the Vienna Court Opera and concert performances of *Orfeo ed Euridice*. After all, the same can be said of Mozart, whose mixed operas are for good reasons preferred to such serious works as *Idomeneo* or *La clemenza di Tito*.

As Mozart's name has again been mentioned, it seems appropriate to compare the dramatic activities of these two great masters, who incidentally were close friends. Haydn's own opinion in this respect is disclosed in a most interesting letter that he wrote in 1787, from which I should like to read a few passages.

Example 8.5. *L'anima del filosofo*, act 2, scene 2, "Del mio core il voto estremo."

Example 8.5.—*Continued*

Haydn as an Opera Composer 93

Continued

Example 8.5.—*Continued*

Example 8.5.—*Continued*

It is the answer to a request he had received from an official in Prague. He writes:

> You want an *opera buffa* from me. I will send it with pleasure if you care to have it for your own use. But it would not be suitable for a performance at a Prague theater. All my operas have been written especially for our ensemble at Esterháza and could not be produced elsewhere with the same effect. It would of course be quite another matter if I had the pleasure of composing a special work for your theater. In any case that would be a daring enterprise, as the great Mozart can hardly be equalled by anybody. Oh, could I only explain to every musical friend the inimitable art of Mozart, its depth, and the greatness of its emotion, and its unique musical conception, as I myself feel and understand it: every nation should strive to have such a treasure in its midst. It grieves me that this unique Mozart has not yet been engaged by an Imperial or Royal Court. Do forgive this outburst; but I love that man too much.

In fact, Mozart's nature was so versatile that he was able to identify himself with the most different beings, and he could at one and the same time project himself into the mind of Leporello, Octavio, and Don Giovanni, or Figaro and Cherubino. Haydn's character was far less complex, and there were not so many types which he could endow with real life. The rest sing music that is often lacking in true dramatic vigor. Nevertheless, this music is artistically so valuable that whoever takes the trouble to unearth and study these voluminous scores will find his full reward.

From Guglielmi to Haydn: The Transformation of an Opera

Reprinted from International Musicological Society, *Report of the Eleventh Congress, Copenhagen, 20-25 August 1972*, ed. Henrik Glahn, Søren Sørensen, and Peter Ryom (Copenhagen: Wilhelm Hansen, 1974), 391-95. Reprinted by permission of Edition Wilhelm Hansen/Chester Music New York, Inc. (ASCAP).

> ... most important of all, the treasures of the National Library [Budapest] *(largely former Esterházy possessions) were made fully available to us. I luxuriated in studying countless Haydn original manuscripts, the hand-written materials Haydn had used in the performances at the Esterházy Opera House, as well as other treasured documents. In particular, my attention was attacted to the original parts which had been used by the singers in Haydn's opera* Orlando Paladino *[Hob. XXVIII:11]. These valuable documents showed that the soloists were not given piano scores, but simply their own parts, into which the necessary cues were inserted. A figured bass replaced the original orchestral accompaniment. The parts were, moreover, full of little annotations and corrections in Haydn's own hand, and they induced me to deal quite thoroughly with Haydn's* Orlando Paladino *at a later date. . . . Then came* Orlando Paladino, *which I edited again for the collected edition. This took a great deal of time, but I found it most rewarding. The best part of Haydn's extensive original manuscript has been preserved, and it clearly demonstrates how quickly he worked, rarely changing his mind, although he himself occasionally suggested cuts, apparently on the basis of his experience during early performances. A welcome secondary source was also provided by the parts of the singers, which I have already mentioned; and, finally, there was a manuscript score with a German translation of the text that had been sent to Haydn for his approval from a theater in Mannheim. The composer began to correct the German text in accordance with his own ideas, but he did not finish the job. He never returned the score, apparently because he intended to continue his revision at a later time. The score remained in his library, and was taken over first by Prince Esterházy and eventually by the Budapest National Library. Irene and I carried on the revision of the German text as well as we could, and our score with German text was published by Bärenreiter Verlag in Kassel. For the publication of the work in the collected edition I had, of course, used Haydn's original Italian text only.*—This I Remember, *130, 143-44.*

Pietro Alessandro Guglielmi (b. 1728 in Tuscany, d. 1804 in Rome) belongs to the most successful Italian opera composers of the eighteenth century. His dramatic works were performed not only in his homeland, but also in Austria, Bohemia, Germany, and England. Today his claim to immortality is based primarily on the influence his works for the stage exercised on similar compositions of Mozart. In Hermann Abert's biography of Mozart no less than five pages are devoted to an analysis of Guglielmi's operas and their relationship to the works of the Salzburg composer.[1]

Abert does not mention, however, the work of Guglielmi, which primarily concerns us in the present paper. This particular opera may not have been known to Mozart at all, but a direct line leads from it to one of the most important stage works of Haydn.

We know that Guglielmi was active at the King's Theatre in London from 1768 to 1772.[2] During this period more than half a dozen of his operas were performed, and it seems that the greatest success was achieved by a

---

[1] Hermann Abert, *W. A. Mozart*, vol. 1 (Leipzig: Breitkopf & Härtel, 1919), 441-45.

[2] Cf. the article by Emilia Zanetti in *MGG*, 5 (1956), cols. 1054-60.

comedy entitled *Le pazzie d'Orlando* (The madness of Orlando). A libretto with the original Italian text and an English translation was printed in 1771 by W. Griffin, in Catharine Street, Strand, and at the same time Bremner, London, published no less than seventeen "Favourite Songs" and the overture of the opera.[3] The fact that thus a complete bilingual book, and three-quarters of the solo numbers in full score, were made available testifies to the great interest the public took in this work.

The success of *Pazzie* is not altogether surprising. Carlo Francesco Badini, who was later to write the libretto for Haydn's dramatic swansong *L'anima del filosofo* [Hob. XXVIII:13], produced here a rather silly, but at the same time quite effective and extremely funny, text. Its story was based on Ariosto's *Orlando furioso*, an epic poem which was a favorite with operatic composers. The great warrior Orlando, a nephew of Charlemagne, is driven to insanity when his ardent love for the beautiful Angelica is not reciprocated. He can only be cured through the intervention of higher powers. Lully in 1685 and Handel in 1733 wrote serious operas on this topic, with the inevitable happy ending. In Badini's book, on the other hand, the emphasis is on the comical element. Most of the characters are in love with the wrong partners, which creates no end of complications. Orlando's unrequited passion for Angelica forms, again, the core of the work. But this is only a part of the amorous comedy of errors. Angelica has just married the elegant spark Medoro. She loves him dearly, but he has quickly tired of her and started a flirtation with the kitchenmaid Polpetta. This little girl's ambition is to find a husband, but as no proper suitor is available, she puts up with Medoro's advances. There is also the great sorceress Alcina who is in love with Rodomonte, the king of Algeria, but he too has eyes only for Angelica and tells the sorceress in no uncertain terms that he has no intention of getting involved with an ugly witch. The only character who keeps free from amorous entanglement is Polpetta's father, the cook and innkeeper Maccarone. He claims to have earned a doctorate of culinary sciences, and compares the works of art produced in his kitchen with music-dramatic creations. Quite amusing is also a detail which the librettist inserted into the finale of the second act. The sorceress Alcina, unable to cope with the raving of the demented Orlando, holds up to him the head of Medusa, which transforms him into, stone. The other characters feel pity for him, and Alcina relents. She declares that music which has power over wild beasts, woods, and rocks, might also release him. Thereupon Medoro, who pretends to be a true Parisian, tries his luck by singing an aria by Rameau. He is unsuccessful, and Angelica takes over. Her prize song is "Che farò senza Euridice," complete with the music from Gluck's *Orfeo*. The incantation has the desired effect, and Orlando comes back to life. This episode must have particularly amused the audiences which were bound to remember that in the previous year a rather questionable arrangement of Gluck's master opera, made by Guglielmi and Christian Bach, had been performed in the same King's Theatre in which *Le pazzie d'Orlando* was now presented.[4]

Badini's solution of the various problems he set himself in this opera is quite simple, though not entirely satisfactory. Orlando drinks water from the river Lethe and forgets his infatuation with Angelica, but also—to Maccarone's chagrin—to pay his bill at the inn. Angelica herself remembers that after all she is a princess and she tells her flirtatious husband in no uncertain terms that she will send him packing unless he starts to behave. This threat is effective, and Medoro promises to mend his ways. Alcina, Rodomonte, and Polpetta are left to their own devices to sort out their amorous problems.

The music to this book is—as can be imagined—rather lightweight, but far from unattractive. In the few tragic episodes it sounds rather hollow and unconvincing. Particularly appealing are, on the other hand, the sentimental protestations of love which the composer imbued with warmth and real feeling. The best results are achieved in the humorous sections of the score, which Guglielmi enlivens with folksonglike melodies and catchy rhythms. The finales to the first and second acts are effectively built up with striking contrasts in tempo, melody, and meter, while gradually most or all of the opera's characters are employed. The remarkable finale of the third act has the form of a rondeau with solos of each of the singers interrupting the restatements of the tutti ritornello. Joseph Haydn took over text and form of this finale in an opera which we shall presently discuss.

The performances of Guglielmi's opera were not confined to London's King's Theatre. The work moved over to the continent and, as it did so, some of its features underwent characteristic changes. The Bibliothèque Nationale in Paris owns a full score of the opera in manuscript, which was formerly the property of the Bibliothèque du

---

[3] Copies in the Royal College of Music, London.

[4] Cf. Charles Sanford Terry, *John Christian Bach* (London: Oxford University Press, 1929), 177f.

Conservatoire.[5] Obviously this score was based on the one used at the King's Theatre. The names of the singers from the London production precede also the respective arias in the Paris score, but invariably they were crossed out by a later hand, as a different set of artists seems to have been active in the performance for which the Paris score was prepared. A great deal of shortening, especially in the recitatives, is noticeable, and in the third act several scenes are even missing from the copy. Of the final duet between Angelica and Medoro only the voice parts are written down, possibly because the writer was doubtful whether this number would be included in the performance, and he compromised by bringing a skeleton score to paper. Apart from the fact that the Paris score definitely condenses the composition, there is only a single major deviation from the London original. No. 5, a simple and unpretentious aria of Angelica, is replaced in the Paris version by a more ornate and showy cavatina on a different text. Obviously the prima donna's wish caused this change.

A new phase in the history of our opera can be observed in 1775. The University Library in Prague, the present capital of Czechoslovakia, owns a bilingual, Italian-German libretto with the title:

ORLANDO / PALADINO / DRAMMA / EROICO COMICO / DI / NUNZIATO PORTA / DA / RAPPRESENTARSI NEL REGGIO TEATRO DI / PRAGA / SOTTO / L'IMPRESA E DIREZIONE DI / GIUSEPPE BUSTELLI / L'ANNO 1775

Underneath the list of singers it states: "La musica è del celebre Signor Pietr Guglielmi."

A look at the Prague *Orlando* shows that it descended straight from the London *Pazzie*. The outlines of the work, and even the text of many numbers, remained unchanged. Nevertheless, Nunziato Porta—who did not even bother to mention Badini's name any more—had substantially altered the libretto. The former "comic opera" was indeed transformed into a "drama eroico-comico." The serious and sentimental elements in the Badini book were strengthened, the comical features narrowed down. The strong feeling for tenderness and sensibility prevalent at that time induced the new librettist to perform some basic changes in the text.

Angelica and Medoro are husband and wife no longer. This must have seemed too prosaic to the new librettist. Instead they are transformed into a couple of ardent romantic lovers. Medoro is a rather passive and feeble character, but there is no question of infidelity, and throughout the opera he is unwavering in his devotion to Angelica. Similarly the effect of the ridiculous infatuation of Alcina is removed from Porta's libretto. She appears as a superior power, majestically directing the fate of the mortals. These three serious characters, two female and one male, are balanced by three comical characters, two male and one female. The ferocious Rodomonte— a kind of Hercules without brains—has hardly changed from the earlier plot. The "little meat-ball" Polpetta is transformed into the gay and flirtatious shepherdess Eurilla. And there is also a wonderful new personality in the book who inherits some of the features of the old Medoro, and especially of the old Maccarone no longer appearing in Porta's book. This freshly created character is Pasquale, squire of Orlando, an eternally hungry, cowardly braggart who is spiritually related to Sancho Panza and closer still to Leporello. In the middle between these two groups stands Orlando, who, as a true eighteenth-century madman, appears partly pathetic and partly comical.

As to the music, Guglielmi could save several recitatives from *Pazzie*, moreover eight arias, part of the finale to act 1, and the rondo concluding act 3. The rest had to be newly composed. A score of the Porta-Guglielmi opera is preserved in Český Krumlov.[6] It contains also music by Piccini, Paesiello, and Jommelli, thus assuming the character of a pasticcio.

Two years after the Prague performance there appeared in Vienna an Italian libretto with the title:

ORLANDO / PALADINO / DRAMMA / EROICOMICO / PER / MUSICA.[7]

---

[5] Its title is *Le pazzie d'Orlando* and not *Orlando furioso* as stated in Francesco Piovano, "Elenco cronologico delle opere (1757-1802) di Pietro Guglielmi (1727-1804)," *Rivista musicale italiana* 12 (1905): 407-46, and "Notizie storico-bibliografiche sulle opere di Pietro Carlo Guglielmi (Guglielmini) con appendice su Pietro Guglielmi," ibid. 17 (1910): 554-89.

[6] Cf. Anthony van Hoboken, *Joseph Haydn: Thematisch-bibliographisches Werkverzeichnis*, vol. 2 (Mainz: Schott, 1971), 416.

[7] Copy in Österreichische Nationalbibliothek, Vienna.

The names of the librettist and of the composer are not mentioned, nor is the theater indicated in which the performance took place, possibly because this was an unauthorized print. However, the Vienna libretto of 1777 conforms in all essential points to the Prague libretto of 1775. On the other hand, it is known that an opera entitled *Orlando Paladino* was played in Vienna twelve times, beginning on 19 June 1777.[8] Thus we may assume that Guglielmi's work conquered the imperial city. This is also corroborated by a document from the castle of Esterháza. Nunziato Porta, since 1781, was employed by the court of Prince Esterházy as opera director,[9] and it was one of his duties to obtain new operas for the vast repertory of the princely theater. In June 1782 the director sent the following memorandum to the prince:

> On Your Highness' order I wrote seven months ago to Brunswick for the opera . . . "Orlando Paladino" in score and parts. Meanwhile, Mr. Pustelli has died in Vienna and . . . Your Highness agreed . . . to buy the opera . . . in Vienna. May I ask to have the money thus expended refunded to me.[10]

Porta's reference to a purchase of the *Orlando* material in Brunswick is significant, as it is known that Guglielmi spent some time there.[11] We learn also from Porta's letter that the *Orlando* material in Brunswick was identical with that in Vienna. Finally the music was bought from the estate of Mr. Bustelli, who had served as impresario and director of the Prague production. All this points to Guglielmi's authorship of the *Orlando* performed in the Austrian capital.

When Porta's letter was written, the Vienna material was apparently in his hands and a performance of Guglielmi's *Orlando Paladino* was being prepared at Esterháza castle where, incidentally, another Guglielmi opera had gone over the stage in 1778.[12] However, these plans had to be changed, and at this point Joseph Haydn comes into the picture.

News that the Russian Grand Duke Paul and the grand duchess were expected for a visit in Vienna reached the castle. Hopes were entertained that the august couple would also come to Esterháza, especially since they were known to be fond of Haydn's music. For a festive event of this magnitude an opera already known in Vienna was not suitable; the Kapellmeister had to present a dramatic composition of his own. The matter was pressing, and it seemed simplest to use the text of Guglielmi's opera and to write new music to the ready-made libretto.

This was done, and despite the short time available, textual changes were made,[13] occasionally even while the composer was working on his new opera. The autograph score shows in certain places that Haydn first set the old text to music, then often crossed it out and used new words.[14] Ultimately a substantial number of alterations had taken place. Each of Pasquale's arias was given new words, which helped make Orlando's squire one of the most successful figures in Haydn's operatic output. Also, the parts of Angelica and Medoro were substantially enlarged. Basically, however, the former text remained unchanged.

The visit of the grand duke and his wife, planned for October, did not materialize, as the visitors had to leave Austria sooner than anticipated. Haydn's opera was premiered on 6 December 1782, at the occasion of Prince Esterházy's nameday. While it was customary to print 200 copies of a new libretto, in this case 500 copies were produced.[15] The anticipated success presently materialized. *Orlando Paladino* was repeated in Esterháza thirteen

---

[8] Cf. Franz Hadamowsky, *Die Wiener Hoftheater 1776-1961*, Museion: Veröffentlichungen der Österreichischen Nationalbibliothek in Wien, n.s. 1; Veröffentlichungen der Theatersammlung, 4/1 (Vienna: Prachner, 1966), 94.

[9] Cf. Mátyás Horányi, *Das Esterházysche Feenreich: Beitrag zur ungarländischen Theatergeschichte des 18. Jahrhunderts* (Budapest: Hungarian Academy of Sciences, 1959), 144.

[10] Cf. Dénes Bartha and László Somfai, *Die Haydn-Dokumente der Esterházy-Opernsammlung* (Budapest: Hungarian Academy of Sciences, 1960), 96.

[11] Cf. *Riemann Musik Lexikon*, 12th ed., ed. Wilibald Gurlitt, vol. 1 (Mainz: Schott, 1959), 694.

[12] The opera was *La sposa fedele*. Cf. Bartha-Somfai, 91, 200.

[13] Cf. Anthony van Hoboken, "Nunziato Porta und der Text von Joseph Haydns Oper 'Orlando Paladino,'" in *Symbolae historiae musicae: Helmut Federhofer zum 60. Geburtstag*, ed. Friedrich Wilhelm Riedel and Hubert Unverricht (Mainz: Schott, 1971), 170-79.

[14] Cf. the critical commentary to my edition of Haydn's *Orlando Paladino* in *Joseph Haydn Werke*, ser. 25, vol. 11 (Munich: Henle, 1973).

[15] Cf. Horányi, 146.

times during the year 1783 and seven times in 1784.[16] This was the beginning of the work's triumphal progress through Central Europe. In the composer's lifetime it was performed in Pressburg, Prague, Brünn, Vienna, Budapest, Mannheim, Frankfurt, Cologne, Graz, Nuremberg, Berlin, Hannover, Bremen, Leipzig, Munich, Augsburg, Königsberg, Hamburg, Breslau, and Dresden.[17]

No doubt the opera's colorful libretto was—at least to some extent—responsible for this great success. Thus, one of the most important and most enthusiastically received dramatic compositions of Joseph Haydn is based on the collaboration of a rather incongruous trio of Italian craftsmen: the London librettist Carlo Badini, the Neapolitan composer Pietro Guglielmi, and the Esterházy theater-director Nunziato Porta.

If I might be granted one additional minute I should like to present a short aria from Guglielmi's opera. Orlando sees the names of Angelica and her lover Medoro jointly engraved into the bark of a tree, and his jealousy drives him to madness. The identical words were later set to music by Haydn.

---

[16] Cf. Bartha-Somfai, 112-22.

[17] Cf. Alfred Lowenberg, *Annals of Opera, 1597-1944*, 2nd ed., 2 vols. (Geneva: Societas Bibliographica, 1955), 1:396-97.

Haydn and the Folksong of the British Isles

Reprinted from *Musical Quarterly* 35 (1949): 179-208, by permission of Oxford University Press.

Geiringer outlines his involvement with this subject in the extract from his autobiography quoted below. For a discussion of the unique problems with which he was confronted when preparing the edition of the Napier folksongs for the *Joseph Haydn Werke* XXXII,1 (München-Duisburg: Henle, 1961), see the review in essay 22, pp. 223-24. Geiringer's work on the folksong arrangements was followed in part by Hoboken's introduction to the folksong listings in the second volume of his Haydn thematic catalog (see essay 21, p. 219) but especially at the Haydn Institute by Irmgard Becker-Glauch, who reported on her work at the Haydn congresses in Washington, D.C., in 1975 and Vienna in 1982—"Some Remarks about the Dating of Haydn's Settings of Scottish Songs," *Haydn Studies: Proceedings of the International Haydn Conference, Washington, D.C., 1975* (New York: Norton, 1981), 88-90; "Haydns Schottische Liedbearbeitungen für Thomson," *Joseph Haydn: Bericht über den Internationalen Joseph Haydn Kongress, Wien, Hofburg, 5.-12. September 1982* (Munich: Henle, ca. 1986), 110-16. This work was suspended with her death in 1990.

The current name British Library has been substituted for the older British Museum, when appropriate.

> *I had started out with his arrangements of folk songs of the British Isles. I felt particularly attracted to this topic because folk songs always interested me very much and also because Haydn research had consistently neglected it. I knew, of course, that these arrangements were not really representative. Haydn received the melodies without text, and he wrote his accompaniments without any knowledge of the specific character of this kind of music, just providing simple and technically undemanding accompaniments. Nevertheless, I found the problem challenging, and to begin I made a catalog of all the arrangements known to me. This catalog was photographed on a microfilm, and I presented copies of it to the British Museum in London and the Library of Congress in Washington, D.C. Then I wrote a study about the topic for* Musical Quarterly, *and, finally, I edited the first hundred arrangements in a volume of the collected Haydn edition. I continued my work, extending it to some of Haydn's later arrangements. However, questions arose about the authenticity of some of these arrangements. It appears that Haydn occasionally enlisted the help of his pupil Neukomm for this routine work, without indicating this in the manuscripts he delivered. I began to lose interest in the work and first enlisted only the collaboration of the Haydn scholar Dr. Irmgard Becker-Glauch, but eventually I ceded the whole work to her.—*This I Remember, *143.*

Much of Haydn's music is inspired by the folksong of various nations. Austrian, German, Hungarian, Croatian, and even French folklore provide the germ cells for works dating from all periods of his career as a composer. As he grew older his interest in folk music increased and he started to work methodically on songs of the British Isles, arranging a substantial number of them from 1791 to 1805. These arrangements belong to the rather numerous categories of Haydn's works that so far have been insufficiently explored. As is so often the case, one of the main obstacles to systematic exploration lies in the inaccessibility of the material. Only a few libraries own the original printed copies, complete with violin and cello parts, and the small number of European reprints[1]—in some cases with German texts only—offer but a very limited insight into this branch of Haydn's activities.

This study was made with the assistance of grants from the American Philosophical Society in Philadelphia, Pa.

[1] Cf. the Breitkopf & Härtel editon of 1805, the publications of the Universal Edition of 1921 edited by Eusebius Mandyczewski, and the selections presented by Steingräber Verlag in 1927 and edited by Bernhard Engelke.

The older biographies mention these arrangements in a rather vague manner, and it was not until J. Cuthbert Hadden's biography of George Thomson was published in 1898[2] that any details about Haydn's relations with his principal Scottish publisher were made public. Another contribution was made in 1908 by Augustus Hughes-Hughes, who cataloged the manuscripts of Haydn's arrangements made for Thomson and owned by the British Museum.[3] In 1926 Alfred Schnerich[4] reproduced the list of Scottish and Welsh songs from the Haydn-Elssler catalog of 1805, omitting, however, the actual thematic beginnings and replacing them by an indication of the tempo, key, and time signature. A final contribution of great importance was made in 1940 by Cecil Hopkinson and Cecil B. Oldman, who provided a thematic catalog of the printed Thomson arrangements, listing for each song the most important early editions.[5]

The object of the present study is to attempt the coordination of the various results so far obtained and to add new material, so as to gain a comprehensive view of Haydn's work in the field of British folksong.[6] In particular the author has aimed at conducting research along the following lines, which so far have been neglected: 1) a review of the biographical facts and publication of a number of hitherto unpublished Haydn letters; 2) a comparison of the numerous music manuscripts still preserved with the earliest printed editions; 3) an analysis of the Scottish and Welsh songs enumerated in the Haydn-Elssler catalog of 1805,[7] and an indication of the source of each piece; 4) a discussion of the characteristic features of these arrangements.

As a basis for his investigation the author collected photographs of all the Haydn arrangements, both printed and manuscript,[8] with their string parts. He made a complete thematic catalog of the composer's 445 British folk-songs and prepared a selection of some fifty of the most interesting arrangements—among them the valuable *Six Airs with Variations*, as yet unpublished—hoping to be able to publish this additional material in the not too distant future. Meanwhile a microphotograph of the author's catalog has been deposited in the Music Division of the Library of Congress in Washington as well as in the British Library, so as to be available for further research.

In this study only the earliest editions of the printed songs will be cited, the first number indicating the year of publication, the second the volume, the third the page. Of unpublished songs, the number of the manuscript as well as the folio is given. The following abbreviations are used:

Na. for Napier
Th. for Thomson[9]
W. for Whyte
H. for the manuscript Haydn-Elssler catalog of 1805
O. for the catalog of Thomson's printed songs compiled by Hopkinson and Oldman
G. for the manuscript catalog compiled by the author listing all of Haydn's published and unpublished arrangements

---

[2] *George Thomson, the Friend of Burns: His Life and Correspondence* (London: J. C. Nimmo, 1898).

[3] *Catalogue of Manuscript Music in the British Museum*, vol. 2: *Secular Vocal Music* (London: British Museum, 1908).

[4] *Joseph Haydn*, 2nd ed. (Zurich: Amalthea-Verlag, 1926).

[5] "Thomson's Collections of National Song with Special Reference to the Contributions of Haydn and Beethoven," *Edinburgh Bibliographical Society, Transactions* 2, no. 1 (1938-39): 1-64.

[6] The author wishes to express his sincere thanks to all those who helped him in his work, in particular to A. Hyatt King, Cecil B. Oldman, and Bertram Schofield of the British Library; Walter F. H. Blandford, London; Hans Gál and Jean M. Allan, Edinburgh; Harold Spivacke, Richard S. Hill, and William Lichtenwanger of the Music Division, Library of Congress; Carleton Sprague Smith, Music Department, New York Public Library; Richard Appel and Leonard Burkat, Music Department, Boston Public Library; Carlotta Vitali and Estelle Reemie Freeman of Boston University.

[7] A satisfactory reproduction of this part of the catalog is not available. Schnerich's enumeration of the contents is quite insufficient, and Jens Peter Larsen in his facsimile edition of the catalog *Drei Haydn Kataloge* (Copenhagen: Munksgaard, 1941) omits the whole section dealing with the folksongs.

[8] The author found forty-three arrangements made by Haydn that have not yet been published.

[9] Th. 1802, Th. 1804, Th. 1805, Th. 1817, and all later dates refer to editions of Scottish songs published by Thomson. Th. 1809 and Th. 1811 apply to his collections of Welsh songs; Th. 1814 to his Irish songs. Th. W.A. 1817 refers to Welsh Airs, in order to distinguish them from the Scottish songs published in the same year.

The almost half-thousand folksong settings of Haydn represent a considerable slice of the output of his old age and demand more study and attention than was hitherto accorded to them. The author endeavored to explore the field as thoroughly as possible and offers some of the results of his researches in this article. Needless to say, an article, even a long one, can not possibly encompass the multitudinous material collected during this folkloristic excursion; accordingly some of it—especially the collation of the various editions and manuscripts—will have to be presented in another, bibliographical, article. This the author proposes to do as soon as circumstances will permit.

*   *   *   *

The first publisher to commission arrangements of folksongs from Haydn was William Napier. This Scottish musician was born ca. 1740;[10] from about 1773 to his death in 1812 we find him in London, where he was active both as a music publisher and as a member of the King's Band.[11] Napier's most important publication bears the following title: *A Selection of the Most Favourite Scots Songs Chiefly Pastoral, Adapted for the Harpsichord with an Accompaniment for a Violin by Eminent Masters. . . .*[12] The frontispiece, engraved by Haydn's friend Gaetano Bartolozzi, gives the date of publication as 1 February 1790. Four "eminent masters" arranged the songs of this volume. Samuel Arnold, Mus.D. (1740-1802), well known as an operatic composer, better still as an editor of the works of Handel,[13] was responsible for ten of the songs in the volume. Twelve were contributed by William Shield (1748-1829), a successful composer of songs and operas. In 1791 he spent a few days with Haydn at Taplow and afterwards, declared that on this occasion he had learned more about music than in years of study. Charles Thomas Carter (1734-1804), an Irishman well known for his musical comedies, songs, and hymn tunes, supplied twenty-six songs to the collection. The main contributor, represented by thirty-three arrangements, was François Hippolyte Barthélemon (1741-1808), a French violinist and composer, who had moved to England at the age of twenty-three and was one of Haydn's closest friends in London.[14] In spite of the distinguished array of collaborators, Napier's collection apparently did not meet with the success it deserved. Haydn, who arrived in England on New Year's day of 1791, was bound to become acquainted with the publication. Being an intimate friend of Barthélemon and Bartolozzi, and on good terms with Shield and Dr. Arnold, he certainly heard much about the financial misfortune of the *Favourite Scots Songs*. When Napier had the happy idea of trying his luck with the celebrated guest and asked Haydn to arrange a number of Scottish songs for him, probably not much persuasion was needed. Haydn was interested in the prospect of dealing extensively with folksongs, and he was also willing to help a man who had suffered grave financial reverses through sponsoring an important new publication. Before long a new volume of Napier's edition was ready. It bore the title *A Selection of Original Scots Songs in Three Parts, the Harmony by Haydn, Dedicated by Permission to Her Royal Highness the Duchess of York. . . .* As before, the frontispiece was engraved by Bartolozzi, and the date, 1792, appears underneath the picture.[15] This second collection was so successful that Napier was enabled to reprint the first, and to issue a third one, also completely arranged by Haydn. The publisher paid Haydn £50 for the 100 arrangements in the second volume, and, to make up for the modest fee, £100 for the 50 airs of the third, so that the average honorarium was £1, or 2 ducats, each. The third volume, however, seems not to have been as successful as the second. The advance orders may have been disappointing, since the volume contained only half as many songs as its predecessor. It is also worth

---

[10] See Frank Kidson, *British Music Publishers, Printers and Engravers: London, Provincial, Scottish, and Irish from Queen Elizabeth's Reign to George the Fourth's, with Select Bibliographical Lists of Musical Works Printed and Published within That Period* (London: W. E. Hill & Sons, 1900), 80.

[11] See the necrologue in *Scots Magazine*, August 1812.

[12] Kidson, 81, gives the title wrongly, as he confuses the first edition of this work with the second.

[13] Arnold lived at 480 Strand, and therefore was a neighbor of Napier, who had his store at 474 Strand.

[14] Barthélemon is reported to have been partly responsible for the choice of *The Creation* as the subject matter of the first oratorio Haydn wrote after his return from England.

[15] The list of subscribers includes the names of the Queen, the Prince of Wales, the Duchess of York, Mrs. Billington, William Fraser, Walter Scott, Mr. Saloman (probably a misprint for Salomon), and George Thomson.

noting that while the second volume enjoyed a wide circulation and is to be found today in a great number of libraries, copies of the third volume are extremely rare. This third volume, which was dedicated to the Queen, was published in 1794, and closely resembled its predecessor both typographically and musically.

Far more important than Haydn's connection with Napier was his association with George Thomson,[16] who was born in Limekilns, Dunfermline, Scotland, on 4 March 1757, the son of a schoolmaster. At the age of seventeen Thomson came to Edinburgh, where in 1780 he became Clerk to the Board of Trustees for the Encouragement of Arts and Manufactures in Scotland. He remained for fifty-nine years in the service of this institution, which was intended for the promotion of "such undertakings in Scotland as should most conduce to the general welfare of the United Kingdom." How successful Thomson was in his position may be gathered from the fact that his initial salary was £40 a year, whereas he retired in 1839 on a yearly pension of £420. The duties of his office seem to have left him plenty of time for his hobbies: music and collecting. He was a violinist and singer, a collector of valuable stringed instruments, and, most of all, a collector of his native country's folksongs, to which he afterwards added those of Wales and Ireland. Thomson's aim was to make these tunes available to music lovers all over the world, but he soon found out that in order to present them in a form acceptable to his contemporaries he needed the assistance of both poets and musicians. The result was Thomson's association with some of the finest creative minds of his time: Robert Burns, Walter Scott, Haydn, Beethoven, and Weber.

In 1793 Thomson published the first volume of his *Select Collection of Original Scottish Airs for the Voice*[17] (see fig., *opposite*) containing twenty-five songs arranged by Haydn's pupil Ignaz Pleyel. Owing to difficulties with this musician, five years elapsed before a second volume, presenting twenty-five arrangements by the Viennese composer Leopold Kozeluh (1752-1818) could be published. Another collection of twenty-five settings by Kozeluh was printed in 1799, and in the same year a fourth series, comprising eighteen arrangements by Kozeluh and seven by Pleyel, was issued. The hundred songs of these four sets were usually sold in two volumes of fifty numbers each. In 1799 Thomson communicated with Haydn, and in a letter to a friend[18] he describes the beginning of their association as follows: "My first application to Haydn was upon the 30th October, 1799, when I sent him part of the Scottish melodies which in the following summer he returned, united to his admirable symphonies and accompaniments. And from that time we continued in correspondence till the year 1804, when I received the last of his many precious compositions."[19] The letters were at first exchanged with the help of Alexander Straton, secretary of the British legation in Vienna, whose place was later taken by one Charles Stuart. At the beginning of their relations, Thomson asked Straton to get in touch with Haydn in order to settle with him the question of remuneration. The secretary's answer, dated 16 February 1800, is well known.[20] He pointed out that Haydn "seemed desirous of having rather more than two ducats for each air, but did not precisely insist upon this point," and concluded the matter with this statement: "Upon the whole he [Haydn] appears to be a rational animal, whereas all that can be said of the other, I mean Koz[eluh] is, that he is a Bipede without feathers." On 19 June 1800, Straton was in a position to forward thirty-two of Haydn's arrangements to Thomson, but when the latter sent more tunes difficulties arose, since Haydn was not satisfied with the payments. Only after being informed that Thomson intended to make him a present of twelve India handkerchiefs, did he consent to accept the new commission. In December the work was completed, and Haydn sent the last batch of songs to Thomson with the following letter, written in Italian, like most of his communications to his Scottish friend:

> Most esteemed friend:
>
> I am hereby sending you the rest of the Trios[21] and feel quite convinced that they could not be better done, since I have taken great pains to satisfy you, and show the world how far a man can progress in his art, particularly in this type of composition, if he is willing to exert himself. I wish that

---

[16] Cf. Hadden, n. 2 above.

[17] Cf. Hopkinson & Oldman.

[18] Cf. Hadden, 304.

[19] Actually their relation lasted until 1805.

[20] Cf. Geiringer, *Haydn: A Creative Life in Music* (New York: Norton, 1946), 154.

[21] Haydn obviously did not count the original vocal parts.

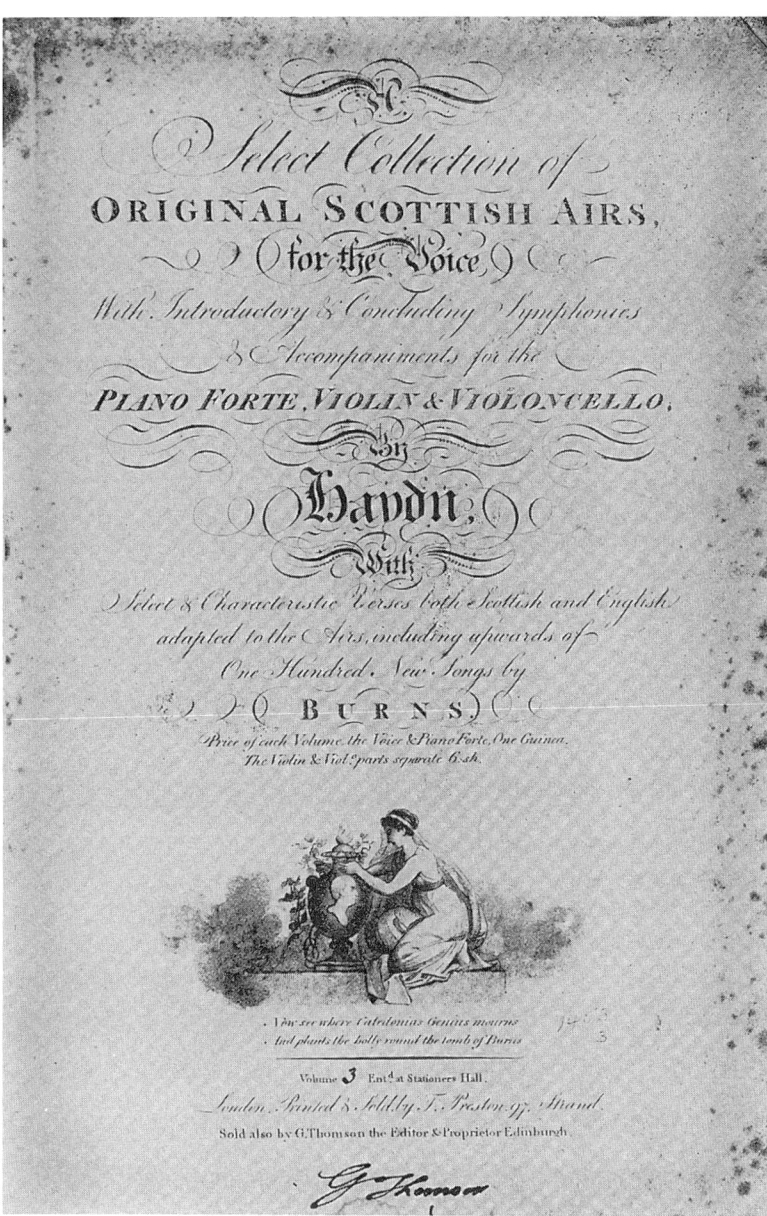

Fig. 10.1. Title page of Thomson's first collection of
Scottish airs arranged by Haydn (1802)

all students of composition would try their hands at this type of music. The fruits of their efforts would surely, in time, be well remunerated. With this work I flatter myself that I shall live in Scotland for many years after my death. I only ask you to send me a copy of the publication when it is printed.

Hoping to receive your kind reply very soon, I am, dearest friend, your sincere and most humble servant,

Vienna, 5 December 1801.   Joseph Haydn[22]

Thomson was greatly impressed by Haydn's remark concerning his reputation in Scotland, and quoted it subsequently in the preface to his publication. Observations of this kind are not rare in Haydn's letters of the period, when he became increasingly concerned with thoughts of death and of the recognition his work would enjoy after he

---

[22] London, British Library, Add. Ms. 35263, f. 136.

was gone. At the same time, however, this letter supplies an amusing proof of the composer's naïve salesmanship, which a man of his worldwide fame hardly seemed to need.

A few weeks later, on 2 January 1802, Haydn sent Thomson an arrangement of "The Blue Bells of Scotland" [Hob. XXX1a:176], adding:

> I would like to have this little air printed by itself and dedicated in my name as a very small gift to the renowned Mrs. Jordan, whom, without having the honor of knowing, I respect deeply for her outstanding abilities and reputation. I did not wish to make a more brilliant accompaniment, which might overpower the expressive and beautiful voice of so pleasing an artist.[23]

Haydn always liked to pay compliments to fair ladies, and it is also significant that the experienced conductor should have anxiously avoided interfering with the singer through too elaborate an accompaniment. Thomson's endorsement of this letter includes the following remark: "with symph. Accomp. & Variations to the Blue Bell." This might be a reference to the holograph version of this song with variations preserved in the British Library.[24] However, Thomson did not see fit to act according to Haydn's suggestion. He included the song as no. 35 in the volume of 1802 and omitted the three variations.

Haydn continued working diligently on the Scottish airs. The following rather curious method was used by composer and publisher. Thomson sent to the composer only the tunes of the folksongs without any text or title. Haydn arranged them for voices and instruments, and returned them to Thomson, who added the headings and supplied the words, using either the original folksong or, mostly, a new poem by one of his collaborators.

From 1802 we have also an undated letter, which, according to Thomson's note on the envelope, was received on 11 February 1802:

> Most esteemed Friend,
>
> I am sending you again ten ariettas and will soon let you have the rest. I also look forward to the fulfilment of your promise and am,
>
> Your most devoted servant,
>
> *I am proud of this work.*
>
> Joseph Haydn[25]

The promise to which Haydn refers apparently concerns the fee, for which he again presses in a letter dated 29 January 1802,[26] stating that he had up to this date delivered forty arrangements. Four days later eighty ducats were handed to him by Mr. Stuart, according to a holograph receipt in German.[27] We learn from this document that Thomson's original offer of two ducats for each arrangement had been accepted by Haydn, who was probably mellowed by the beautiful handkerchiefs he had received.[28]

Through 1802 and 1803 Haydn steadily continued with his folksong arrangements. A memorandum of payments kept by Thomson in his files reveals that by 8 June 1803 Haydn had received £171.16.11 for 158 airs.[29] In addition, Thomson did not forget to keep the old master in good humor by little presents. The following letter written by Haydn shows that Thomson sometimes overshot the mark:

---

[23] London, British Library, Add. Ms. 35263, f. 138, original in Italian.

[24] London, British Library, Add. Ms. 35275, f. 28. The date, 6 February 1805, on this manuscript may be due to the fact that Haydn revised his arrangement when he wrote variations on other Scottish tunes (cf. the subsequent correspondence).

[25] This letter, written in Italian, was made available to me through the kindness of its owner, Miss Elizabeth C. Firestone, of Akron, Ohio.

[26] London, British Library, Add. Ms. 35263, f. 140.

[27] Ibid., f. 142.

[28] Kozeluh was paid slightly less. He got 100 ducats for 64 airs (cf. Hadden, 299). Since three different currencies are mentioned in the Haydn-Thomson correspondence, it may be stated that one guinea was approximately the equivalent of two ducats or ten Viennese florins.

[29] Cf. London, British Library, Add. Ms. 35263, f. 165, and Annex to f. 142.

Most esteemed Sir:

I am sending you for the time being 40 new Scottish arias; before long the rest will be finished too. I thank you infinitely for the payment of the 120 ducats which I have just received from Messrs. Fries & Co. and I kiss you, my dear friend, for the handkerchiefs, which are very beautiful, especially those destined for my poor wife. She has been under the ground these past three years, and I have therefore used them to delight a married lady, who is most accomplished in the field of music. Hoping that you will be satisfied with my work, I am, with all my respect, your most sincere friend,

Vienna, 1 July 1803   Giuseppe Haydn[30]

A few days later Haydn received the third volume of Thomson's publication, containing the first fifty of his arrangements, and wrote: "The copy that you sent me is unequalled as regards printing and beauty of paper. Will you please let me have the first and second volumes together with the fourth . . . I shall be glad to pay the price of the whole set."[31]

These repeated friendly communications written by Haydn early in July may possibly have been due to a certain sense of guilt. Unknown to Thomson, the composer had done similar work for another Scottish publisher, William Whyte of Edinburgh. When Thomson heard about it, he was naturally anything but pleased and apparently asked for an explanation. Thereupon Haydn wrote to him only one day before the letter quoted above, in a rather outspoken manner, as follows:

Vienna, 30 June 1803

Dearest Friend:

I am hereby sending you the rest of the Airs, hoping that you, and all the other lovers of music, will be satisfied with this work. I only regret that in this world I am obliged to serve anyone who will pay me; and, besides, Mr. Whyte gives me two guineas for each Air, which means twice as much [as your fee]. Dearest friend, I wish I were in a position to serve you on another occasion. Meanwhile I am with greatest esteem,

Your most sincere friend and servant,

Joseph Haydn[32]

Perhaps Haydn regretted having expressed himself so bluntly. Anyway, he changed his tactics. According to Charles Stuart,[33] he stressed in a conversation that "being now seventy-four years of age [he was actually seventy-one!] and extremely infirm, he found himself wholly incapable of further application to study, and must therefore beg leave to decline all offers whether on Thomson's part or from any person whatsoever." This procedure proved successful. Thomson agreed to the higher fee and, aware that a charming note from a young lady would please the old master, made his daughter write directly as well. How the publisher exerted himself is shown from remarks he made in a letter to Haydn drafted on 20 December 1803:

Your Ritornelles and Accompaniments delight me so much that I really cannot bear the idea of seeking an inferior composer to finish the work already so nearly done by you. I do flatter myself therefore that you will not give me the pain and mortification of a refusal. I ask it as a most particular favour, and I am willing to pay you 4 ducats for each Air, and as the Airs are in general very short, they will not occupy much of your time. Let me beg then that you will be so good as to do them in your usual charming manner as soon as you can.[34]

---

[30] London, British Library, Add. Ms. 35263, f. 171, original in Italian.

[31] Ibid., f. 172. The letter is this time in French and only signed by Haydn.

[32] Ibid., f. 170, original in Italian.

[33] English letter to Thomson of 6 August 1803, ibid., f. 179.

[34] On the top of the English draft to this letter (London, British Library, Add. Ms. 35266, f. 17) is the note "translated into Italian and sent to M. Coutts to be transmitted through Fries & Co." This seems to have been the usual procedure.

Thomson's appeal was really no longer needed. As soon as the new arrangement came into force, Haydn recovered rather quickly from his infirmity, and he wrote on 18 December 1803:

> My most esteemed Friend,
>
> At last I am sending you the 13 arias you asked for and hope they will give equal pleasure to you and to your dear, dearest daughter, whose hands good old Haydn kisses. A few of these arias have, contrary to my intention, turned out a bit difficult, but when they have been more frequently performed, they will prove to have the same value as the others.[35] I thank you also for the 50 ducats I received from Messrs. Fries & Co. . . .
>
> As I have set so many Scottish airs for you, I am willing, if you so wish, to do yet another twenty-five or more, and if your beautiful daughter desires a few little English songs of my own composition with piano accompaniment, I will quickly send them. . . . I am as always with the greatest esteem,
>
> Your most sincere friend and servant,
>
> Giuseppe Haydn[36]

Needless to say, Thomson did wish him to do more work. So Haydn continued with his Scottish arrangements and sent on April 6 of the following year another batch of fourteen airs. On 10 May 1804 he again wrote a very cordial letter, the draft of which was reproduced by the present author in an earlier article,[37] so that it can be omitted here. The correspondence with Miss Thomson seems to have continued, for Haydn wrote on 30 October 1804 to her father:

> My most esteemed Sir,
>
> At last I send you the desired piece[38] which I received three days ago. On this occasion I thank you infinitely for the payment, i.e. 50 ducats, which I received through Messrs. Fries. I want to see whether I can satisfy your dear daughter, and should like her to choose two or three of the last lot of Scottish songs, according to her taste, and send me just a few measures of the voice parts, so that I can make variations or rondos from them.
>
> I am and will always be, my dear Sir, your most devoted servant,
>
> Giuseppe Haydn
>
> Today I feel rather weak, but I hope, God will give me more strength. I kiss the hands of your dear daughter. When the fourth volume is ready, I beg you to send me a copy. I will very gladly bear the expenses. Farewell.[39]

Thomson was always anxious to have his arrangers write compositions based on Scottish melodies,[40] and apparently his daughter had expressed this desire to Haydn. It seems quite likely that some of Haydn's six airs with variations (cf. p. 122) were the outcome of this correspondence.

Early in 1805 Thomson was deeply shocked to read in a newspaper that Haydn had died. He sent a letter of condolence to Messrs. Fries & Co. and got the following answer dated 9 February 1805: "We have received your Favor of the 7th January and as the celebrated Haydn is not dead as it was generally reported, but only in a weak state of health, we communicated your letter to him and send you enclosed the answer he has dictated to your inquiries."[41] The answer referred to is in French and contains the following remarks:

---

[35] For reasons that will be given later in this study, Haydn considered it necessary to make excuses for the difficulty of some of his accompaniments.

[36] London, British Library, Add. Ms. 35263, f. 196, original in Italian.

[37] "Joseph Haydn's Arrangements of Scottish and Welsh Songs," in *Proceedings of the Music Teachers National Association* 41 (1947): 235-44.

[38] According to Thomson's endorsement on this letter, Haydn sent one air with a simplified accompaniment, for which Thomson had apparently asked.

[39] London, British Library, Add. Ms. 35263, f. 244.

[40] Cf. his correspondence with Beethoven in Alexander Wheelock Thayer, *The Life of Ludwig van Beethoven*, ed. Henry Edward Krehbiel (New York: Beethoven Association, 1921); and Fritz Erckmann, "Beethoven und George Thomson," *Neue Musik-Zeitung* 28, no. 8 (1907):161-65.

[41] London, British Library, Add. Ms. 35263, f. 255.

> Haydn is very touched by the distress which the news of his alleged death has given to Mr. Thomson and this proof of attachment has, if such be possible, further increased the esteem and friendship Haydn will always feel for Mr. Thomson. . . . You will see that he has written his name and the date on the [enclosed] sheet of music, in order better to prove that he is still in this base world. At the same time he asks to have the letter of condolence written by Mr. Thomson copied and sent to him.[42]

Thomson, overjoyed at the turn of events, sent a new consignment of airs to Haydn in April and another one in August, but now the ailing master took his time. On 5 September 1805, Thomson enlisted the help of C. R. Broughton, in the Secretary of State's Office, asking him to induce Mr. Jenkinson, the successor of Charles Stuart in the Vienna Legation, to "call upon the great Haydn, and represent to him as emphatically as possible my [Thomson's] earnest desire, that he would compose Ritornelles and Accompaniments without delay to the 20 Airs which I sent him. . . . Mr. J. may be so good as to ask the Doctor whether the Indian Handkerchiefs I sent him be worn out, and if he would wish to have a few more. . . ."[43] Haydn went on slowly, and in 1806 he had Messrs. Fries inform his Scottish friend that he was unable to continue with the work. Thereupon Thomson got him to sign a formal cession of rights for all his arrangements, totaling 170 Scottish and Irish and 62 Welsh songs.[44] According to a memorandum that Thomson kept in his files, he made in all ten payments to Haydn amounting together to £291.18.1.

While Thomson took good care to preserve all the material suitable for a biographer, William Whyte, Haydn's third publisher of Scottish songs, did not possess his rival's interest in historical documents. We know only that his office was located during Haydn's lifetime at 1 South St. Andrew's Street in Edinburgh[45] and that he apparently communicated with the composer through the master's Viennese publishers, Artaria & Co. The British Library owns the following holograph document written in German by Haydn:

RECEIPT

for the amount of 300 florins which I, the undersigned, received in cash from Messrs. Artaria & Co. as the balance of the 500 florins due me for the Scottish songs of Mr. Whyte of Edinburgh.

Vienna, 3 February 1804　　　　　　　　　　　　　　　　　　　　　　　　　　　Joseph Haydn[46]

Whyte's edition, consisting of two volumes of forty and twenty-five songs respectively, is handsomely engraved, and is more decorative than either the Napier or the Thomson volumes. Its title,[47] however, does not greatly differ from that of Thomson and still more closely do the contents of the two works resemble each other. In the preface Whyte boasts that in rival editions the harmonies were supplied by "composers of various descriptions and degrees of genius and talent. The harmonies of the present are composed exclusively by Haydn, confessedly the first of modern masters." He adds: "It may not, perhaps, be superfluous to say, that he [Haydn] has himself pronounced them to be his best." How unfortunate that the letter of that good businessman, Haydn, to which Whyte apparently refers, has not been preserved!

---

[42] Ibid., f. 251.

[43] London, British Library, Add. Ms. 35266, ff. 70-71.

[44] See letter of July 1806 from Thos. Coutts & Co. to Fries & Co., ibid., f. 91. Thomson's enumeration includes also a song that Haydn sold by mistake to both Thomson and Whyte.

[45] According to the title-page of Whyte's edition of Haydn's songs.

[46] London, British Library, Add. Ms. 35264, f. 8. This receipt has given rise to the generally accepted statement that Haydn was paid 500 florins for the 65 arrangements of Scottish songs he made for Whyte—cf. Frank Kidson in *Grove's Dictionary of Music and Musicians*, 3rd ed., 5 vols., ed. H. C. Colles (New York: Macmillan, 1927-28), 5:713. But 500 florins is approximately the equivalent of 50 guineas or 100 ducats, which would be very meager payment for 65 arrangements. Since Haydn mentioned in his letter of 30 June 1803 to Thomson that Whyte gave him 4 ducats for each song, it is obvious that the abovementioned 500 florins were the honorarium for the 25 songs that appeared in the second volume of the Whyte edition. In all Haydn must have received for his work for Whyte 1300 florins or 130 guineas, and not 500 florins.

[47] *A Collection of Scottish Airs Harmonized for the Voice and Piano Forte, with Introductory and Concluding Symphonies and Accompaniments for a Violin and Violoncello by Joseph Haydn Mus. Doc. . . .*

The preface to the rare first edition of the first volume carries the date 2 July 1804.[48] Most libraries possess only the second edition of this volume, dated 1 March 1806. Confused by this reprint, Kidson[49] and Botstiber[50] have stated that Whyte's publication began to appear in 1806. The second volume, dated 1807, is known only in a single edition. Very likely it was not printed before that year, since in the preface to this volume the publisher

> respectfully apologizes to his Subscribers for the long interval which has elapsed betwixt the publication of the first volume of this work and the present; and for the number of the songs being restricted to twenty-five in place of forty, as was originally proposed. Both cirumstances are to be ascribed to the same cause . . . the precarious health of the illustrious composer, and the delay and difficulty which has attended all communications with the continent of late years.

Among the sixty-five Whyte songs we find a number of tunes that Haydn previously arranged. In most cases, however, the "symphonies" and accompaniments differ from those composed for Thomson, although the voice parts and even the keys are identical. The present author has found a single instance where Haydn made a slip and sent to Whyte and Thomson exactly the same arrangement. The air "Wandering Willie" [Hob. XXXIa:257bis], printed in the second volume of the Whyte collection as no. 45 (G. 382), is to be found with the same introduction, harmonization, and postlude in the main set of manuscript songs Haydn sent to Thomson.[51] It was, however, never published by Thomson, who naturally examined his rival's edition with the greatest care. He also excluded as far as possible other Haydn arrangements of tunes reproduced by Whyte, even though the arrangements were completely different.

*   *   *   *

Not a single manuscript of Haydn's arrangements made for Napier or Whyte has so far come to light. On the other hand, most of the manuscripts of the Thomson songs and a considerable number of arrangements made for Thomson but not published by him, are accessible. A small but completely autograph manuscript belonging to the Bibliothèque du Conservatoire is preserved by the Bibliothèque Nationale in Paris. This autograph[52] was formerly the property of Jean Baptiste Weckerlin, who bought it from a nephew of Haydn's pupil, Sigismund Neukomm.[53] The manuscript is in oblong folio and contains thirteen songs. A note in Haydn's hand on the first page indicates that there were originally twenty-two arrangements in the collection, but nothing is known of the remaining nine songs. All the pieces in the autograph were printed by Thomson in the years 1802 to 1805. The songs are written in full score; the top line is for the violin, the next line for the voice. There follow two lines for the piano, and the lowest staff is for the cello. Each song has the tempo indicated and there are expression marks, but there are no titles or texts in any of the thirteen arrangements, since, as has been mentioned, these were not known to Haydn.

The British Library owns another manuscript of Haydn's folksong arrangements which is entirely autograph.[54] The manuscript also is apparently incomplete, since its eight songs are numbered from 7 to 14 in Haydn's own hand. Its whole aspect resembles that of the Paris Conservatoire manuscript. With the exception of Haydn's no. 8, which is published in Thomson's collection of Scottish songs of 1804,[55] none of these arrangements has so far been printed. Hughes-Hughes states that "they are said to be Welsh," without giving reasons for this assumption. Since no. 8 is a Scottish song, it may be that others in the set are also.

---

[48] A copy is in the possession of Jens Peter Larsen. See his *Die Haydn-Überlieferung* (Copenhagen: Munksgaard, 1939), 137, n. 140.

[49] P. 201.

[50] *Joseph Haydn: Unter Benützung der von C. F. Pohl hinterlassenen Materialien weitergeführt von Hugo Botsiber*, vol. 3 (Leipzig: Breitkopf & Härtel, 1927), 333.

[51] See London, British Library, Add. Ms. 35273, f. 30b.

[52] Ms. 23521, Conservatoire no. 139; old number 24745.

[53] According to a note on the cover of the manuscript.

[54] Add. Ms. 28613.

[55] II/84 (O.68, G.218). Hughes-Hughes's supposition that none of the songs in this manuscript was published by Thomson is therefore incorrect.

As a rule Haydn sent to Thomson not his autograph manuscripts but copies, as he considered it safer not to entrust the originals to the mails.[56] Occasionally he gave away some of the autographs, such as the two sets mentioned before. The copies that Thomson got from Haydn are preserved in the British Library, which keeps them in four volumes under the numbers Add. Mss. 35272-75. The principal writer of the manuscripts is a copyist whom the British Library catalog calls Radnitzky. But when the writing in these volumes is compared with that in the Elssler-Haydn catalog, which is easily accessible in Larsen's facsimile edition,[57] it becomes evident that the main copying was done by the person who wrote the catalog—that is, Johann Elssler. The hands of two other writers are also easily recognizable in these volumes: those of Haydn and George Thomson. The arrangements arrived from Vienna without titles; these were added by Thomson, who inserted the headings to each song in the four volumes.

Add. Ms. 35272 contains forty-one songs in full score; again, as in the autographs, the violin is written on the top staff, then follow the parts for voice, pianoforte, and violoncello. All the pieces in this volume were printed by Thomson in his collections of Scottish songs. Particularly interesting are the last two sheets of the book, written partly by Thomson and partly by Haydn, containing alterations to five songs, which will be discussed later in this study.

Add. Ms. 35273 is the largest collection of Haydn arrangements. It contains eighty-eight songs in full score that Thomson published, one printed by Whyte, and six that have remained unpublished. Mss. 35274 and 35275, almost completely written by Elssler, have the appearance of the printed editions. No. 35274 contains one staff for the voice above two lines for the piano, while separate violin and cello parts for the songs in 35274 are to be found in 35275. Although the manuscripts bear the title "Welsh Airs," a considerable number are Scottish. Fifty songs in these volumes were printed by Thomson, while no less than twenty-three remained unpublished. The end of 35274 presents four versions, partly new and partly corrections, of songs that appear on preceding pages of this manuscript. In addition to the violin and cello parts for the songs of 35274, Ms. 35275 contains all the parts of six hitherto unpublished Airs with variations.[58] Of these the piano and voice parts of "The Blue Bells of Scotland" are autograph, the rest are written by Elssler.

* * * *

The enumeration of Haydn's Scottish, Welsh, and Irish songs in the famous Elssler-Haydn list of 1805 has so far never been properly examined and analyzed. The author of this article did this with the help of a photograph of the catalog in the Library of Congress, which again is a copy of Elssler's original manuscript in the possession of Breitkopf & Härtel in Leipzig.[59] The Haydn-Elssler catalog lists the thematic beginnings of 365 songs, the first 200 with titles, the last 165 without them. The whole group of works is headed "A Selection of Original Scots Songs. The Harmony by Dr. Haydn." This is quite obviously copied from Napier's edition, and indeed the first 150 songs of Haydn's list correspond to the 150 songs published by Napier in the second and third volumes of his edition.[60] After these 150 songs the catalog of Prince Eszterházy has four blank pages,[61] then follows the heading "with Symphonies and Accompaniments," which is apparently taken from the printed edition of Thomson's volume 3 (1802). Haydn's nos. 151-200 are copied from this edition. These fifty songs are listed in the same order and with the same titles as in the printed volume. From 201 on, however, the titles are missing. Obviously the sources for the last 165 entries in the catalog were not printed editions, but Haydn's own autographs. Apart from the three volumes (two by Napier, one by Thomson), which Haydn and Elssler had already consulted, no printed edition had been

---

[56] The statement occasionally made that Haydn kept the autographs of his Scottish songs under glass and framed on the walls of his home is probably due to a confusion with Haydn's canons.

[57] *Drei Haydn Kataloge*.

[58] See below, p. 122. Although the catalog of the British Library indicates that the variations are published, the author of this article could find only the Airs themselves, but none of the variations, in print.

[59] Of the two copies of the catalog that Elssler made, one became the property of Breitkopf & Härtel, the other that of Prince Eszterházy. Cf. Larsen, *Die Haydn-Überlieferung*, 253.

[60] There is just one slight deviation. In copying the beginnings of the songs Elssler omitted by mistake no. 58. He realized this later on and included this song in his list as no. 100.

[61] Cf. Larsen, 252.

seen by them at the time. And since Haydn received from Thomson the tunes for his arrangements without any text or title, he was unable to supply these in his own catalog. A comparison of the catalog with the Thomson manuscripts in the British Library shows a certain resemblance in the order of the songs, but this is not marked enough to lead to the assumption that the catalog is based on these copies. The conclusion is therefore inevitable that Haydn's own autographs, which he had kept while sending copies to the publishers, were the sources of the last 165 numbers of the Haydn catalog. As a negative proof, it should be mentioned that the twenty-one songs of the Paris Conservatoire and British Library, the autographs of which the composer had given away, are missing in the Elssler-Haydn catalog.[62] Apparently the composer had disposed of these autographs before the catalog was made.

In order to save space, the present author will not reproduce the first 200 numbers of the Haydn catalog, which were taken from the printed Napier and Thomson editions. The names of the songs listed therein may be found in the appendix to Schnerich's Haydn biography.[63] On the other hand, table 10.1, reproduced on pages 115-17, sets out for the first time the names and sources of the last 165 entries in Haydn's catalog. It will be found that of these 165 songs, 118 were made for Thomson and forty-seven for Whyte. Of the 118 Thomson arrangements listed by Elssler, twenty-six remained in manuscript, while the other ninety-two were printed. The table shows also that Elssler mixed Thomson and Whyte arrangements freely. As in other types of Haydn's works, the Elssler-Haydn catalog is completely reliable as far as the authenticity of the listed works goes, but at the same time it is incomplete. It omits altogether more than eighty of the arrangements, eighteen of them made for Whyte and the rest for Thomson.

* * * *

The arrangements that Haydn made for Napier were all printed on three staves. The top line is for the violin part; the second and third lines, connected by braces, do not call for a specific instrument. Under the second staff the words of one verse of the text are printed, while the complete poem is reproduced on a separate page facing the music. The third staff always contains a figured bass. Clearly the songs are meant for violin and a keyboard instrument. If, however, a violin is not available, it is often a simple matter for the player of the harpsichord or pianoforte to play the violin part as well as his own. In this case very few "fillng notes" are required, as the violin and voice parts together with the bass produce fairly full harmonies. In a few songs the lowest staff contains occasional dyads, indicating that Haydn considered fuller harmonies necessary. It is important to notice that the composer did not give any specific instruction for performing the bass line. It was of course meant for the left hand of the keyboard instrument player, while the use of a cello seems to have been optional.

The introduction to the first volume of the Napier edition offers some important hints for the execution of this music.

> The accompaniment of a Scottish song ought to be performed with delicacy. . . . The full chords of a thorough bass should be used sparingly and with judgement, not to overpower, but to support and raise the voice at proper pauses. Where, with a fine voice, is joined some skill in instrumental music, the air, by way of symphony, or introduction to the song, should always be first played over; and at the close of every stanza, the last part of the air may be repeated, as a relief to the voice. In this symphonic part, the performer may shew his taste and fancy on the instrument, by varying it *ad libitum*.

A slight note of apprehension may be detected in the preface of the second volume, containing the first hundred Haydn arrangements. The editor seems to be on the defensive, refuting possible complaints by amateurs that the composer's accompaniments were too complicated for the simple folk tunes. The relevant passages read:

> The Editor . . . has . . . to request that those, who are not skilled in the THEORY, as well as in the PRACTISE of Music, will not hastily decide on the merit of the following performance. As the songs are set by the hand of a MASTER, they should be performed with delicacy and precision; and in the Accompaniments the VIOLIN and BASS must be particularly careful not to overpower the voice.

---

[62] Except for no. 10 of the Paris autograph. It is listed in Haydn's catalog as no. 198, since it was printed at the time of the compilation of the catalog and Elssler got its thematic beginning from the Thomson edition.

[63] P. 199.

Table 10.1

Nos. 201-365 of the Folksongs of the British Isles in the
Haydn-Elssler Catalog of 1805 [Hob. XXX1a-b]

H. 201	The Widow's Lament	Th. 1809, v. 1/12; O. 153; G. 281
H. 202	The Lamentation of Britain (unpubl.)	Add. Ms. 35274/23 b; G. 435
H. 203	The March of the Men of Harlech	Th. 1809, v. 1/2; O. 146; G. 274
H. 204	The Blossom of the Thorn	Th. 1811, v. 2/57; O. 179; G. 307
H. 205	Sir Watkyn's Dream	Th. 1809, v. 1/10; O. 151; G. 279
H. 206	Jenny's Mantle	Th. 1809, v. 1/8; O. 149; G. 277
H. 207	The Rising of the Lark	Th. 1809, v. 1/1; O. 145; G. 273
H. 208	Away, My Herd, under the Green Oak	Th. 1809, v. 1/16; O. 155; G. 283
H. 209	Venture Gwen (duet)	Th. 1809, v. 1/9; O. 150; G. 278
H. 210	The Red Piper's Melody	Th. 1811, v. 2/56; O. 178; G. 306
H. 211	New Year's Night	Th. 1811, v. 2/41; O. 173; G. 301
H. 212	The Soldier's Return	Th. 1809, v. 1/11; O. 152; G. 280
H. 213	The Minstrelsy of Chirk Castle	Th. 1811, v. 2/39; O. 171; G. 299
H. 214	Of a Noble Race (duet)	Th. 1811, v. 2/35; O. 168; G. 296
H. 215	The Dimpled Cheek	Th. 1809, v. 1/14; O. 154; G. 282
H. 216	The Flowers of the Heath	Th. 1811, v. 2/43; O. 174; G. 302
H. 217	Come to Battle (duet)	Th. 1809, v. 1/19; O. 158; G.286
H. 218	Towyn Castle	Th. 1811, v. 2/38; O. 170; G. 298
H. 219	Och! Pretty Kate	Th. 1805, v. 4/175; O. 96; G. 246
H. 220	The Dawn of Day	Th. 1809, v. 1/47; O. 147; G. 275
H. 221	The Sweet Melody of North Wales (unpubl.)	Add. Ms. 35274/15 b; G. 428
H. 222	The Crystal Ground	Th. 1809, v. 1/21; O. 159; G. 287
H. 223	Lady Owen's Favourite (unpubl.)	Add. Ms. 35274/20 b; G. 434
H. 224	The Ancient Harmony	Th. 1811, v. 2/59; O. 181; G. 309
H. 225	Winefreda (unpubl.)	Add. Ms. 35274/18; G. 432
H. 226	The Cornish May Song	Th. 1811, v. 2/31; O. 165; G. 293
H. 227	The Rising Sun (duet)	Th. 1809, v. 1/17; O. 156; G. 284
H. 228	The Willow Hymn (unpubl.)	Add. Ms. 35274/17; G. 430
H. 229	O Marion Is a Bonny Lass	Th. 1818, v. 5/218; O/ 125; G. 318
H. 230	Tis Nae Very Lang Sinsyne	Th. 1805, v. 4/187; O. 108; G. 258
H. 231	Sleepest Thou, or Wakest Thou	Th. 1805, v. 4/157; O. 78, G. 228
H. 232	One Morning Very Early	Th. 1804, v. 1/18; O. 57; G. 207
H. 233	The Waefu' Heart	Wh. 1804, v. 1/10; G. 347
H. 234	Sweet Annie	Wh. 1807, v. 2/62; G. 399
H. 235	Hellvellyn	Wh. 1804, v. 1/16; G. 353
H. 236	Up in the Morning Early	Wh. 1807, v. 2/52; G. 389
H. 237	The Flowers of the Forest	Wh. 1804, v. 1/13; G. 350
H. 238	My Apron, Dearie	Wh. 1804, v. 1/23; G. 360
H. 239	My Ain Kind Deary, O!	Wh. 1804, v. 1/8; G. 345
H. 240	The Maid in Bedlam	Wh. 1804, v. 1/22; G. 359
H. 241	Lewie Gordon	Wh. 1804, v. 1/19; G. 356
H. 242	The Lass of Lochroyan	Wh. 1804, v. 1/7; G. 344
H. 243	The Maid That Tends the Goats	Wh. 1804, v. 1/33; G. 370
H. 244	O Phely, Happy Be That Day	Th. 1805, v. 4/160; O. 81; G. 231
H. 245	The Honest Man	Th. 1805, v. 4/163; O. 84; G. 234
H. 246	The Lowland Maids Gang	Th. 1805, v. 4/189; O. 110; G. 260
H. 247	Could I Find a Bonny Glen	Th. 1805, v. 4/181; O. 102; G. 252
H. 248	Bonnie Wee Thing	Th. 1822, v. 1/22; O. 131; G. 324
H. 249	Their Groves o' Sweet Myrtle	Wh. 1807, v. 2/44; G. 381
H. 250	The Shepherd's Son	Wh. 1804, v. 1/40; G. 377
H. 251	Thou Art Gane Awa'	Wh. 1804, v. 1/36; G. 373
H. 252	The Collier's Bonny Lassie	Wh. 1804, v. 1/14; G. 351
H. 253	This Is No Mine Ain House	Wh. 1804, v. 1/38; G. 375
H. 254	The Bonnie Wee Thing	Wh. 1804, v. 1/28; G. 365

Continued

Table 10.1—*Continued*

H. 255	O'er the Muir	Wh. 1804, v. 1/32; G. 369
H. 256	Auld Lang Syne	Wh. 1804, v. 1/24; G. 361
H. 257	Fate Gave the Word	Th. 1804, v. 1/45; O. 62; G. 212
H. 258	There Lived Ance a Carle	Th. 1805, v. 4/182; O. 103; G. 253
H. 259	O What Had I Ado	Th. 1805, v. 4/170; O. 91; G. 241
H. 260	Now Bank and Brae	Th. 1818, v. 5/227; O. 129; G. 322
H. 261	Keen Blaws the Wind	Th. 1805, v. 4/186; O. 107; G. 257
H. 262	John Anderson	Wh. 1804, v. 1/26; G. 363
H. 263	The Soldier's Return	Wh. 1807, v. 2/42; G. 379
H. 264	Galla Water	Wh. 1804, v. 1/30; G. 367
H. 265	Mourn, Hapless Caledonia	Th. 1804, v. 2/87; O. 69; G. 219
H. 266	Up in the Morning (unpubl.)	Add. Ms. 35273/52 b; G. 411
H. 267	The Flowers of Edinburgh (unpubl.)	Add. Ms. 35273/53; G. 412
H. 268	Morag (unpubl.)	Add. Ms. 35273/53 b; G. 413
H. 269	'Twas in That Season	Th. 1804, v. 1/14; O. 55; G. 205
H. 270	Come Rest Ye Here	Th. 1805, v. 4/172; O. 93; G. 243
H. 271	The Banks of the Dee	Th. 1805, v. 4/167; O. 88; G. 238
H. 272	Auld Gudeman	Th. 1805, v. 4/165; O. 86; G. 236
H. 273	What Numbers	Th. 1817, v. 2/79; O. 123; G. 316
H. 274	O Willie Brew'd	Th. 1805, v. 4/179; O. 100; G. 250
H. 275	Come All Ye Jolly Shepherds (unpubl.)	Add. Ms. 35273/58 b; G. 415
H. 276	Charming Anne	Th. 1839, v. 5/150; O. 142; G. 335
H. 277	The Smiling Morn	Th. 1804, v. 1/1; O. 51; G. 201
H. 278	There's Auld Rob Morris	Th. 1804, v. 1/17; O. 56; G. 206
H. 279	I'll Never Leave Thee	Wh. 1804, v. 1/3; G. 340
H. 280	The Rose (unpubl.)	Add. Ms. 35273/66; G. 416
H. 281	Will Ye Go to the Ewe-Bughts	Th. 1804, v. 1/8; O. 52; G. 202
H. 282	Beneath a Green Shade	Th. 1804, v. 2/84; O. 68; G. 218
H. 283	When First I Came to Be a Man	Th. 1805, v. 4/184; O. 105; G. 255
H. 284	Now Wat Ye Wha I Met Yestreen	Th. 1805, v. 4/194a; O. 115; G. 265
H. 285	For the Lack of Gold	Wh. 1804, v. 1/34; G. 371
H. 286	She Rose and Loot Me in	Wh. 1804, v. 1/29; G. 366
H. 287	Gilderoy	Wh. 1804, v. 1/39; G. 376
H. 288	Sae Flaxen Were Her Ringlets	Th. 1805, v. 4/190; O. 111; G. 261
H. 289	Thickest Night	Th. 1805, v. 4/178; P. 99; G. 249
H. 290	O Wot Ye Wha's in Yonger Town	Th. 1804, v. 2/53; O. 64; G. 214
H. 291	Harken, and I Will Tell	Th. 1805, v. 4/177; O. 98; G. 248
H. 292	Of a'the Airts the Wind Can Blaw	Th. 1805, v. 4/159; O. 80; G. 230
H. 293	There's Nought but Care	Th. 1805, v. 4/155; O. 76; G. 226
H. 294	My Nannie O (duet)	Th. 1826, v. 1/4; O. 136; G. 329
H. 295	There Was a Lass	Th. 1805, v. 4/152; O. 73; G. 223
H. 296	Behold the Hour (duet)	Th. 1805, v. 4/154; O. 75; G. 296
H. 297	The Blythe Young Lad	Th. 1839, v. 5/50; O. 141; G. 334
H. 298	O Lassie Art Thou Sleeping Yet?	Th. 1805, v. 4/156; O. 77; G. 298
H. 299	How Can My Poor Heart	Th. 1805, v. 4/161; O. 82; G. 232
H. 300	Hark! The Mavis' Ev'ning sang	Th. 1805, v. 4/166; O. 87; G. 237
H. 301	What Ails This Heart	Th. 1805, v. 4/180; O. 101; G. 251
H. 302	Farewell, Frances	Th. 1809, v. 1/18; O. 157; G. 285
H. 303	Maltraeth	Th. 1811, v. 2/58; O. 180; G. 308
H. 304	David of the White Rock	Th. 1809, v. 1/6; O. 148; G. 276
H. 305	The White Mountains	Th. 1809, v. 1/28; O. 164; G. 292
H. 306	The Flowers of London	Th. 1811, v. 2/34; O. 167; G. 295
H. 307	The Whirling of the Spinning Wheel	Th. 1817, v. 3/96; O. 185; G. 314
H. 308	The Allurement of Love (unpubl.)	Add. Ms. 35274/4 b; G. 417
H. 309	The Marsh of Rhuddlan (unpubl.)	Add. Ms. 35274/6; G. 420
H. 310	The Note of the Black Cock	Th. 1809, v. 1/24; O. 162; G. 290

Table 10.1—Continued

H. 311 I Wish I Were Where Helen Lies	Th. 1805, v. 4/168; O. 89; G. 239
H. 312 The Inspired Bards	Th. 1811, v. 2/36; O. 169; G. 297
H. 313 The Despairing Band	Th. 1809, v. 1/26; O. 163; G. 291
H. 314 The Answer	Th. 1805, v. 4/194 B; O. 116; G. 266
H. 315 Todlin Hame	Wh. 1807, v. 2/61; G. 398
H. 316 From Thee, Eliza, I Must Go	Wh. 1804, v. 1/21; G. 358
H. 317 The Maid of Toro	Wh. 1804, v. 1/37; G. 374
H. 318 Farewell Thou Fair Day	Wh. 1807, v. 2/63; G. 400
H. 319 Shepherds I Have Lost	Wh. 1807, v. 2/54; G. 391
H. 320 The Gaberlunzie Man	Th. 1805, v. 4/191; O. 112; G. 262
H. 321 The Door Clapper (unpubl.)	Add. Ms. 35274/5; G. 418
H. 322 The Britons (unpubl.)	Add. Ms. 35274/5 b; G. 419
H. 323 The Pursuit of Love (unpubl.)	Add. Ms. 35274/10; G. 422
H. 324 The Poor Pedlar (unpubl.)	Add. Ms. 35274/10 b; G. 423
H. 325 The Blossom of the Honeysuckle (unpubl.)	Add. Ms. 35274/11; G. 424
H. 326 War Song of the Men (unpubl.)	Add. Ms. 35274/11 b; G. 425
H. 327 The Melody of Cynwyd	Th. 1811, v. 2/44; O. 175; G. 303
H. 328 The Fairy Banquet	Th. 1811, v. 2/60; O. 182; G. 310
H. 329 The Bend of the Horseshoe (unpubl.)	Add. Ms. 35274/13; G. 426
H. 330 Loth to Be Apart (unpubl.)	Add. Ms. 35274/13 b; G. 427
H. 331 Let My Lass Be Young	Th. 1817, v. 4/193; O. 124; G. 317
H. 332 Our Good King	Th. 1805, v. 4/193; O. 114; G. 264
H. 333 Lassie wi' the Gowden Hair (unpubl.)	Add. Ms. 35274/19; G. 433
H. 334 Gala Water (unpubl.)	Add. Ms. 35274/17 b; G. 431
H. 335 [My Nannie O!] (unpubl.)	Add. Ms. 35274/16 b; G. 429
H. 336 Away to the Oaken Grove	Th. 1809, v. 1/22; O. 160; G. 288
H. 337 Adieu to My Juvenile Days	Th. 1817, v. 3/94; O. 184; G. 313
H. 338 The Flower of North Wales (unpubl.)	Add. Ms. 35274/37 b; G. 436
H. 339 The Song of the Old Man	Th. 1817, v. 3/78; O. 183; G. 312
H. 340 The Lambs Fold Vale	Th. 1811, v. 2/33; O. 166; G. 294
H. 341 The Departure of the King (unpubl.)	Add. Ms. 35274/40 b; G. 438
H. 342 The Happy Cambrians	Th. 1811, v. 2/48; O. 176; G. 304
H. 343 Hunting the Hare	Th. 1811, v. 2/50; O. 177; G. 305
H. 344 The Shepherd's Son	Th. 1822, v. 2/5; O. 132; G. 325
H. 345 No, Henry, I Must Not	Th. 1817, v. 3/120; O. 186; G. 315
H. 346 Over the Stove	Th. 1809, v. 1/23; O. 161; G. 289
H. 347 New Year's Gift (unpubl.)	Add. Ms. 35274/39; G. 437
H. 348 The Delight of Prince Hoel	Th. 1811, v. 2/40; O. 172; G. 300
H. 349 Lochaber	Wh. 1807, v. 2/60; G. 397
H. 350 Of A' the Airts	Wh. 1807, v. 2/66; G. 402
H. 351 O Poortith Cauld	Wh. 1807, v. 22/50; G. 387
H. 352 The Siller Crown	Wh. 1807, v. 2/53; G. 390
H. 353 Saw Ye My Father?	Wh. 1807, v. 2/51; G. 388
H. 354 Bessy Bell and Mary Gray	Wh. 1807, v. 2/58; G. 395
H. 355 Widow Are Ye Wakin?	Wh. 1807, v. 2/59; G. 396
H. 356 Maggy Lawder	Wh. 1807, v. 2/64; G. 401
H. 357 An Thou Wert	Wh. 1807, v. 2/49; G. 386
H. 358 The Palmer	Wh. 1807, v. 2/41; G. 378
H. 359 Nancy's to the Greenwood Gane	Wh. 1807, v. 2/55; G. 392
H. 360 Robin Is My Only Jo	Wh. 1807, v. 2/48; G. 385
H. 361 Tak' Your Auld Cloak	Wh. 1807, v. 2/57; G. 394
H. 362 My Jo Janet	Wh. 1807, v. 2/46; G. 383
H. 363 The Lass of Patie's Mill	Wh. 1807, v. 2/43; G. 380
H. 364 The Day Returns	Wh. 1807, v. 2/47; G. 384
H. 365 Merry May the Maid Be	Wh. 1807, v. 2/56; G. 393

Whatever objections may be imagined, on the first trial, he is confident they will vanish, in proportion as the performer becomes more ready and correct in the execution.

As was customary at that time, the texts of the songs were in some cases "improved," especially if they were likely to offend the modesty of members of the fair sex. The introduction refers to this in a special paragraph, but without mentioning the names of the poets who made the changes.

While in the Napier arrangements a great deal is left to the performers' improvisation, the Thomson and Whyte versions present the complete musical text. Figured basses disappear and the addition of filling notes to the piano part becomes unnecessary. The Whyte songs as well as most editions of the Thomson arrangements contain a separate staff for the voice and below it two staves for the keyboard instrument.[64] This was almost a luxury, since in most cases the upper staff of the pianoforte also comprises the voice part. Violin and cello parts were not included in the score, being printed separately in every case. The great innovation of the Thomson and Whyte editions consisted in the addition of "symphonies," or ritornellos, purely instrumental sections placed at the beginning and end of each song, which make it unnecessary for the player to improvise introductions and postludes. In most cases the symphony starts much as the voice part does, but after a measure or two the composer continues independently of the melody of the song. In these short sections, which are often not more than four to six measures long, Haydn displays a wealth of inspiration. In most cases the postludes show an even greater independence; see for instance the deeply felt ending of "Fair Helen of Kirkconnell"[65] [Hob. XXXIa:236] (ex. 10.1). Haydn, however, was not permitted by Thomson to let his imagination roam too freely. To the song "Fy Gar Rub"[66] [Hob. XXXIa:7] he wrote a ritornello with a rather interesting bass[67] (ex. 10.2). Thomson found this too complicated and copied on a piece of music paper[68] the first notes of the vocal section, adding in Italian in the margin: "I should greatly appreciate a new introduction in a very melodic style. This aria is my favorite." Haydn complied with this wish and wrote on the same piece of paper the following very charming version of the ritornello (ex. 10.3).

Example 10.1. Ending of "Fair Helen of Kirkconnell."

---

[64] The octavo Thomson edition of 1822-24, which aimed at popularizing the songs by presenting them in an inexpensive publication, has only two staves, the right hand of the keyboard part embracing the voice part.

[65] Th. 1804, v. 4/168; O. 89, G. 239. The small notes in our examples indicate those portions of the violin part that do not comform to the piano part. The cello has approximately the same notes as the left hand of the piano.

[66] Th. 1804, v. 2/53, O. 64, G. 214.

[67] London, British Library, Add. Ms. 35273, f. 46.

[68] London, British Library, Add. Ms. 35272, f. 21.

Example 10.2. Ritornello for "Fy Gar Rub."

Example 10.3. New version of the ritornello for "Fy Gar Rub."

Another example of Thomson's influence on the music of the arrangements is offered by the introduction to the song "Muirland Willy"[69] [Hob. XXXIa:242] (ex. 10.4). The editor praised the accompaniment, but complained that the introduction was too short and its third measure too difficult to play.[70] He asked Haydn to make the necessary changes, and accordingly the composer furnished a new introduction, which is two measures longer and eliminates the left-hand run in the third measure[71] (ex. 10.5). However it seems that the joke was on Thomson, since the new introduction is just about as difficult to play as the old one.[72]

Example 10.4. Introduction to "Muirland Willy."

---

[69] Th. 1805, v. 4/177; O. 98, G. 248.

[70] The song is to be found in London, British Library, Add. Ms. 35273, f. 47.

[71] The correction is in London, British Library, Add. Ms. 35272, f. 22b, and completely autograph.

[72] In some instances Thomson's demands were really justified. To no less than four airs Haydn had forgotten to write postludes and did so only after being reminded by Thomson. The publisher wrote for Haydn's information in each case the beginning of the instrumental introduction and the last measures of the vocal section. The composer added in his own hand the postludes. See ibid., f. 21b.

Example 10.5. New version of introduction to "Muirland Willy."

The editor did not always bother to communicate with his arranger if he wanted alterations in the music; and besides, Haydn was too old and weak to engage in such work after 1805, whereas the publication even of hitherto unprinted songs went on for many years after his death.[73] We therefore find that the printed editions deviate in many instances from the manuscripts. Among the minor changes are countless modifications of Haydn's indications of the tempo. Transpositions are not infrequent, as for instance in the song "The Bonnie Wee Thing"[74] [Hob. XXXIa:102], first printed in Haydn's key of A major and then in the edition of 1831 in G major. This song, incidentally, is presented in the first volume of the octavo edition of 1822 as a solo, according to the manuscript, but subsequently in the sixth volume of the same edition, published two years afterwards, as a vocal trio. The editor adds rather naïvely to the title of the trio "by Haydn—1824." Changes of solo songs into duets and vice versa are quite frequently to be found. Since the accompaniments were mainly of a harmonic nature and the different voices rhythmically alike, such a procedure presented no great difficulties. In "The Birks of Invermay" [Hob. XXXIa:187] the editor went so far as to add a measure[75] that is not to be found in Haydn's manuscript. Thomson's arbitrary attitude did not stop at tampering with the work of his arranger. He felt no compunctions at using Welsh instrumental tunes, mainly intended for performance on the harp, as vocal pieces, and he again and again changed the texts to his songs, so that three different poems were frequently associated with one and the same air.

Haydn had a certain understanding of, and respect for, an artistic despot like Thomson. At about the same period he had business relations with van Swieten, the librettist of *The Creation* [Hob. XXI:2] and *The Seasons* [Hob. XXI:3], who was endowed with a similarly dictatorial personality. The composer usually complied with van Swieten's recommendations regarding details in the composition of his oratorios, and in the same way he respected the demands of Thomson and did not altogether mind the editor's interference with his work.[76]

Whatever may be the verdict of our time with regard to Thomson's attitude, it cannot be denied that the secretary of the Board of Trade in Edinburgh succeeded in stimulating Haydn to apply his genius to the field of folksong. It seems almost as though the Napier songs were a preparation for, and the Whyte songs an imitation of, the more than 200 airs that Haydn adapted for Thomson.

There is a striking variety of expression in Haydn's different arrangements. "Roslin Castle"[77] [Hob. XXX1a:191] (ex. 10.6) has a bass of Baroque grandeur, which is in sharp contrast to the simplicity to be found in the Scottish duet "Cauld Kail in Aberdeen"[78] [Hob. XXXIa:55bis] (ex. 10.7), for example. Sudden harmonic changes from major to minor or vice versa add an unexpected flavor, as the following example (ex. 10.8) from "The Birks of Invermay" may show.[79] A principal attraction of these arrangements lies in their treatment of the string parts. Judging from the small number of copies of these parts which have been preserved,[80] it seems that in Haydn's time only a few

---

[73] Sixty-five of Haydn's arrangements were printed by Thomson for the first time in the year of the composer's death or afterwards.

[74] Th. 1822, v. 1/22; O. 131, G. 324.

[75] It is the thirteenth measure from the beginning. Cf. Th. 1804, v. 1/1 with Add. Ms. 35273, f. 63.

[76] On 5 August 1812, Thomson wrote to Beethoven: "Your great predecessor Haydn invited me to point out frankly everything which was likely not to please the national taste, and he very readily altered all those to which I took exception." Cf. Hadden, 323.

[77] Th. 1804, v. 1/14; O. 55; G. 205.

[78] Th. 1804, v. 1/31; O. 58; G. 208.

[79] Cf. also the Napier arrangement of "The Birks of Abergeldie," Na. II/59, G. 58.

[80] The writer of this article sent questionnaires regarding the Scottish songs to the leading music libraries of the U.S. and found that while most of them had several editions of the piano parts, hardly any string parts could be found.

Example 10.6. "Roslin Castle."

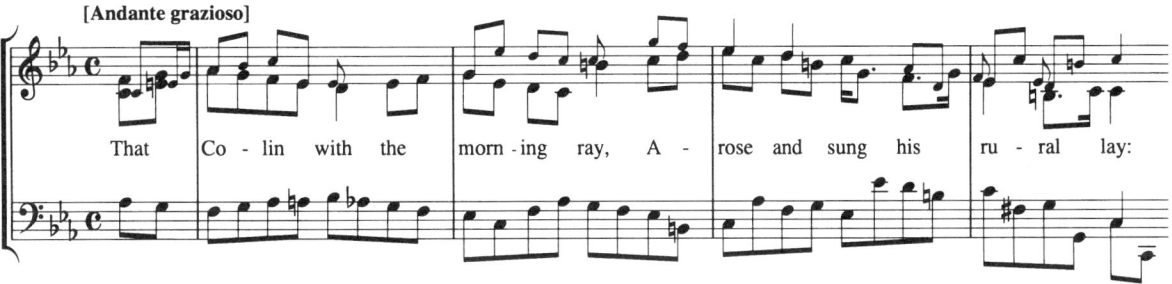

Example 10.7. "Cauld Kail in Aberdeen."

Example 10.8. "The Birks of Invermay."

musicians used them. In most cases the performers were satisfied with the piano and voice parts and did not want to complicate the performance by the inclusion of strings. As we have seen, Thomson's octavo edition of 1822-24 omits the string parts altogether. It is true that the violin and cello parts were *ad libitum*, but to omit them in performance is just as wrong as the omission of the violin and cello parts in one of Haydn's last piano trios would be. The strings are most important for adding color and with their countermelodies they contribute greatly to the charm of the arrangements. To the simple introduction reproduced in ex. 10.3 the violin part lends a very pleasing note. Similarly the duet "Robin Adair"[81] [Hob. XXXIa:202] is greatly enriched by the figurations of the violin (ex. 10.9).

Example 10.9. "Robin Adair."

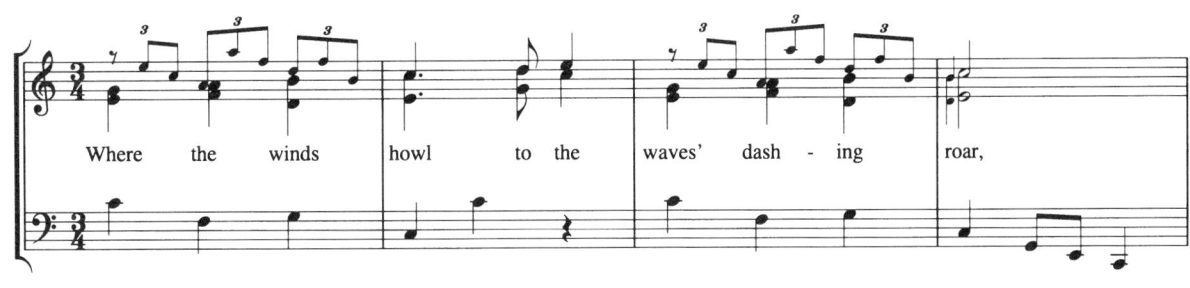

Continued

---
[81] Th. 1804, v. 2/92; O. 70; G. 220.

Example 10.9.—*Continued*

Even in the Napier arrangements some attractive violin parts can be found, as the following example from "The Bonnie Wee Thing"[82] can show (ex. 10.10):

Example 10.10. "The Bonnie Wee Thing."

The role of the cello is not so prominent, but even this instrument contributes to the greater variety of the bass and occasionally to the middle parts.

Some of the most important of Haydn's arrangements were not included in any of Thomson's collections. They are preserved in Add. Ms. 35275 of the British Library, mentioned before, and are dated by the master himself 6 February 1805. The themes for these *6 Airs with Variations*, "The Blue Bells of Scotland," "My Love Is But a Lassie Yet" [Hob. XXXIa:194], "Bannocks o'Barley Meal" [Hob. XXXIa:171], "Saw Ye My Father?" [Hob. XXXIa:5], "Maggie Lauder" [Hob. XXXIa:35], "Kilicrankie" [Hob. XXXIa:169]—are among the most popular tunes. Haydn's technique in each piece is to assign variations to the three instruments while the air itself remains unchanged in the voice part. In this way he develops a new type of folksong arrangement in which the accompaniment changes from stanza to stanza.[83] The piano part in particular exhibits a liveliness that contributes greatly to making this unusual type of vocal chamber music attractive.

---

[82] Napier III/3, G. 102. Haydn arranged the song also for Thomson (1822, I/22; O. 131, G. 234).

[83] The relation of this technique of that of the "Emperor" variations in Haydn's String Quartet op. 76, no. 3 is obvious.

Fig. 10.2. Illustration for Haydn's arrangement of "On Ettrick Banks," Hob. XXXIa:151, from Thomson's collection of Scottish airs of 1826, vol. 3

As has been mentioned, Haydn did his work without knowing what words would be sung to his music. Thomson, after he got the arrangements from Haydn, added the texts, which were chosen in such a way as not to be "inimical to the most virtuous and delicate feeling," so that the editor "would not hesitate to put [them] into the hands of his own daughters."[84] The result was an occasional discrepancy between the words and the music. In the song "Saw Ye My Father?,"[85] for instance, the gay and marchlike composition seems hardly to fit the elegiac character of Burns's poem "Where are the joys I have met in the morning." Such cases, however, are more or less exceptional, and on the whole text and music form a surprisingly harmonious combination.

Haydn was not a scholar, and his attitude towards the folksong was not the reverent one of a later generation. What mattered to him was the production of arrangements which, in the words of his publisher William Whyte, "can hardly fail to give pleasure to the classic ear."[86] That he succeeded in this aim is obvious. But, in addition, the close ties that bind Haydn's artistic personality to the folklore of all nations enabled him to grasp the spirit alive in the folksongs of the British Isles, no mean accomplishment for an Austrian musician, working in Vienna with bare tunes without words. Haydn's settings of these pleasant songs might occasionally be almost too elaborate, but they are always in perfect taste and full of charm.

---

[84] From the introduction to Thomson's edition of 1822.

[85] Th. 1802, v. 3/2; O. 2; G. 152.

[86] Preface to the first volume of Whyte's collection.

11

Haydn: The London Symphonies

Reprinted from the liner-notes booklet for *Joseph Haydn: London Symphonies*, Vienna Symphony and Vienna State Orchestras, cond. Hermann Scherchen (Westminster WN 6601 [1955]) with permission of MCA Music Entertainment Group.

Great men's life-stories seem to follow a certain pattern. Creative ability increases up to the age of forty when a peak of achievement is reached, whereupon the productive process gradually slows up until a stagnation point is reached in the late fifties. At times, however, fascinating exceptions occur to this rule. Mendelssohn wrote one of his finest works, the *Midsummer Night's Dream Overture*, when seventeen years old; Schubert at the same age created some of his most outstanding Goethe songs. While such precociousness is usually balanced by a premature death, there are other "law-breakers" among the great composers whose long careers seem almost miraculous. Verdi was seventy-four when he wrote his immortal opera *Othello*, seventy-nine when he produced his glorious *Falstaff*. Joseph Haydn belongs to a similar category. He wrote the *London Symphonies*, those masterworks which even obscured his former great contributions, between his fifty-ninth and sixty-third years of age, and he did so while embarking on an entirely new way of life.

Haydn had developed very slowly. For almost thirty years he resided in remote Hungarian castles, serving the wealthy magnate Prince Esterházy as conductor and court-composer. A semi-exile of this kind would have seemed intolerable to most men of genius. For Haydn it was a blessing and what to others would have been monotonous routine, became an exciting adventure to his vigorous spirit. Serving the Esterházys, he slowly and gropingly found a way toward expression of his own true self. He could work regularly with a group of well-trained singers and instrumentalists he had chosen himself; he studied at the closest range the possibilities of each instrument, and with his fine musicians the self-taught composer was able to experiment to his heart's desire until he developed a style of classical perfection. Moreover he had the enviable opportunity to hear each new composition the moment it was on paper. Thus Haydn wrote within a quarter of a century eighty symphonies, gradually solving all problems involved.

Any steady growth eventually leads to full maturity. When this phase was reached, Haydn began to look with new eyes on his official duties. The restrictions he had easily taken in his stride started to irk him. He was no longer satisfied to create his compositions for a tiny circle of connoisseurs and to submit to the verdict of his patron alone. Thus it was a relief to receive in 1784 a commission for symphonies from Paris, and significantly enough these works mark a decided progress over his previous output in the symphonic field. However the important element of personal contact with performers and audience in a musical center was still missing, as Haydn was unable to travel to Paris. Quite a different situation was created when the master, after his patron's death, accepted an invitation to London, entering British soil on New Year's Day 1791. The date of his landing may justly be termed as symbolic. A new life was starting for the man who in the fifty-eight preceding years had never left his native land or seen a town as vast as London, whose "various beauties and marvels caused me," as he wrote, "the most profound astonishment." He had concluded a contract with J. P. Salomon, distinguished violinist and concert-manager, to conduct the latter's subscription series and to present six new symphonies as well as twenty smaller compositions of his own. Haydn's success in the first two seasons he spent in London was so dazzling that he decided to follow a similar invitation to the British capital in 1794-95. To these two visits the musical world owes one of its greatest treasures, the twelve *London Symphonies.*

Musical conditions in eighteenth-century England have justly been compared to those in the United States of our days. To London flocked everybody who had gained acclaim in the field of music, for there the artist was sure to find audiences hungry for musical experience and willing munificently to reward successful virtuosos. Salomon's orchestra was far better equipped than Haydn's own group in Hungary. The audience used to highest standards in musical performance offered an electrifying challenge to the composer, and he nobly rose to the occasion, delighting in the enthusiastic acclaim that was showered upon him and repaying his gracious hosts a thousand times by the unending stream of his inspiration.

In the *London Symphonies* instrumental music reached a peak hardly surpassed in eighteenth-century art. Here Haydn managed, as Paul Lang expressed it, to achieve "the ideal balance of homophony and a specific modern polyphony. What a fantastic cavorting of melodies, rhythms, syncopations, dynamic contrasts, general pauses, hesitations, sudden explosions, distortions!" The very difference between a melody and its accompaniment is obscured in these works, as the composer endows all voices with thematic material, thus abolishing the last remnants of the Baroque distinction between leading and supporting parts. With inexorable logic he develops his themes, splitting them into minute motives and reassembling them in a dazzling array of new shapes. This process is by no means confined to the so-called development section in the middle of the movement. Haydn starts with it almost as soon as he has presented this thematic material and continues along these lines up to the last measures. In this respect he exercised a decisive influence on subsequent generations of symphonic composers. Far-reaching was also the effect of his selection of instruments for the *London Symphonies*, and the "Haydn orchestra" for almost a century was considered as the basis for symphonic writing.

The first four *London Symphonies* (nos. 93-96 of the collected edition) were all written in the year 1791, and their exact order is not known. According to recent research by H. C. Robbins Landon it appears that no. 96 was the first and no. 95 the second work of the set.

* * * *

SYMPHONY NO. 93 IN D MAJOR

I. *Adagio—Allegro assai*
II. *Largo cantabile*
III. *Minuetto: Allegretto*
IV. *Finale: Presto ma non troppo*

Here we have a slow introduction of lofty grandeur enhanced in dramatic impact by frequent pauses. The second movement seems to utter hesitating questions; its expressive theme may have been in Beethoven's mind when he wrote the hymnic finale of his *Pastorale* symphony. It is significant that Haydn near the end quite intentionally destroys the magic mood by allowing the bassoon to break in with a vulgar statement. The sparkling, delicately chiselled finale once more displays the composer's sense of humor, and we are as much delighted as we are filled with admiration by the masterly combination of rondo and sonata forms manifest in this movement.

* * * *

SYMPHONY NO. 94 IN G MAJOR

I. *Adagio cantabile—Vivace assai*
II. *Andante*
III. *Minuetto: Allegro molto*
IV. *Finale: Allegro molto*

Haydn: The London Symphonies 127

This symphony is generally known as the "Surprise," as in the Andante a sudden *fortissimo* chord is sounded after a *pianissimo* passage. It has been alleged that Haydn used this device to punish some somnolent members of the audience and we even hear of ladies fainting away at the concert. The movement uses as the basis for four variations a folksong-like, delightfully naïve tune which became popular so quickly that Haydn felt justified in quoting it in his oratorio *The Seasons* [Hob. XXI:3] when depicting the merry husbandman whistling while working in the field. In the symphony the original character is not maintained throughout the movement, for in the coda, with the help of harmonic alterations, a strangely oppressive atmosphere is created which is far removed from the simple gaiety of the beginning. Another surprise effect is to be found in the Minuetto where, at the end of the second part, a ridiculous snort and groan in the bassoons and violoncellos leads us back to the beginning of the main tune. As a matter of fact, humor and wit reign supreme throughout this masterwork. The personality of Haydn, so richly expressed in the sounds of the music, is also reflected in the autograph of the symphony whose first page is reproduced below.

Fig. 11.1. Beginning of Symphony no. 94, "Surprise" (1791)

Courtesy of Staatsbibliothek zu Berlin – Preußischer Kulturbesitz,
Musikabteilung mit Mendelssohn-Archiv

* * * *

SYMPHONY NO. 95 IN C MINOR

    I. *Allegro*
   II. *Andante cantabile*
  III. *Minuetto*
  IV. *Finale: Vivace*

Composed in 1791, this work is the only symphony of the set dispensing with a slow introduction to the first movement, which seemed unnecessary to Haydn, as the grave and solemn first subject displays the very qualities usually to be found in the introductory adagios. The gay and amiable second subject supplies all the contrast needed, creating the habitual spirit of the fast first movement. The powerful Minuetto is unusual in mood, its tempestuousness being far removed from the traditional dance character. The gently swaying trio consists of a delightful cello solo and we like to imagine that it was entrusted to an accomplished player like the cellist Menel who, after working under the master in London, was to carry the Haydn tradition to the United States.

* * * *

SYMPHONY NO. 96 IN D MAJOR

    I. *Adagio—Allegro*
   II. *Andante*
  III. *Minuetto: Allegretto*
  IV. *Finale: Vivace assai*

Known as "The Miracle," the nickname is not due to esthetic qualities (well-deserved though it would be), but rather to a story told about the first performance. At the end of the concert the applauding crowd rushed forward toward the platform to have a better view of the composer. At this moment a chandelier in the rear crashed down, and thanks to the enthusiasm the audience had shown, nobody was hurt, exclamations being heard that a miracle had happened.

    The forward-looking character of the set is manifested already in the very first movement. In the development Haydn concludes a section in F♯ major, and after a pause unexpectedly starts a half-tone higher with the chord of G, a truly Beethovenian effect. The slow movement, on the other hand, seems to recapture the very best spirits of Rococo art, and its dainty charm and exquisitely soft pastel coloring bring Watteau's masterpieces to mind. The finale presents a *perpetuum mobile*, allowing Haydn to display his uncanny resourcefulness in achieving a variety of humorous effects in spite of obstinately clinging to the same rhythm.

* * * *

SYMPHONY NO. 97 IN C MAJOR

    I. *Adagio—Vivace*
   II. *Adagio ma non troppo*
  III. *Minuetto: Allegretto*
  IV. *Finale: Presto assai*

The first movement of this symphony written in 1791 impresses us as a study for the magnificent "Drum Roll" symphony [no. 103]. In both works a close relationship is established between the slow introduction and the following Allegro section, and either uses a waltz-like second subject. In the following variation movement the unexpected *forte* entrance of trumpets and timpani in the second variation is particularly stirring. A gem outstanding even in this set of masterpieces is the Minuetto, in which Haydn displays his magical touch in orchestration.

The trio, a typical Austrian *Ländler*, captivates our hearts, and we are entranced when we hear the cumbrous horns provide the most delicate accompaniment, swaying in the prescribed dance rhythm and near the end even venturing the play the short grace notes the *Ländler* calls for.

* * * *

SYMPHONY NO. 98 IN B♭ MAJOR

I. *Adagio—Allegro*
II. *Adagio cantabile*
III. *Minuetto: Allegro*
IV. *Finale: Presto*

Composed in 1792, the first two movements of this symphony strike a somewhat unusual note. They place decided emphasis on strict contrapuntal elaboration and are uncommonly serious in mood. We may assume that they reflect Haydn's feelings after he learned of the recent tragic death of his beloved young friend, Mozart. There is a hymnic fervor in the tender Adagio cantabile in which Haydn anticipates both melodically and emotionally the prayer "Sei nun gnädig" in his oratorio *The Seasons*. Gaiety reigns in the second half of this symphony, and the Finale conjures up a hilarious operatic scene which achieves a particularly funny effect by surprisingly slowing up the brisk motion towards the end.

* * * *

SYMPHONY NO. 99 IN E♭ MAJOR

I. *Adagio—Vivace assai*
II. *Adagio*
III. *Minuetto: Allegretto*
IV. *Finale: Vivace*

Written between the two visits to England, in 1793-94, this work shows Haydn attempting musical innovations in various respects. For the first time he employs in a symphony the clarinet, revealing a fine understanding for its coloristic possibilities. In the fast section of the first movement Haydn teases his audience by introducing the second subject at so late a point that one has almost stopped expecting it; henceforth, however, he favors it to an extent as to give it preponderance over the first subject. The slow movement has shed the last remnants of Rococo's easy grace; it is a lofty piece stirring our souls like Beethoven's Adagios. The Minuetto and following trio are built on related melodic material, and the necessary contrast is mainly achieved through alterations of tonality (E♭ against C major) and orchestration. Thus Haydn could count on pleasing the novelty-hungry Londoners with the first symphony he was going to present after his absence.

* * * *

SYMPHONY NO. 100 IN G MAJOR

I. *Adagio—Allegro*
II. *Allegretto*
III. *Minuetto: Moderato*
IV. *Finale: Presto*

Composed in 1794, this work is usually known as the "Military Symphony" because in the second and last movements such military instruments as the triangle, cymbals, and big bass drum are employed. The melody of the Allegretto is an old favorite of the composer's; it is taken from the French romance "La gentille et jeune Lisette" which Haydn had used previously in his symphony "La Reine" [Hob. I:85] and in one of his hurdy-gurdy concertos [Hob. VIIh:3*]. The finale of the symphony begins, as Tovey remarks, "with one of those themes which we are apt to take for a kitten until Haydn shows that it is a promising young tiger." In this movement, the composer again inserts a surprise effect produced by the sudden *fortissimo* entrance of the kettledrums following on the heels of a diminuendo ending in *pianissimo*. The amiable work seems to reflect the glamor which parades and other peace-time occupations of the soldier held for the civilians.

*   *   *   *

SYMPHONY NO. 101 IN D MAJOR

I. *Adagio—Presto*
II. *Andante*
III. *Minuetto: Allegretto*
IV. *Finale: Vivace*

This work, composed in 1794, has the nickname "The Clock" in view of the tick-tock sounds produced in the slow movement by the accompanying bassoons and strings. The charmingly graceful piece displays the mixture of rondo and variation forms Haydn handled so masterfully in his mature works. He states his main idea three times, presenting it at each repetition in a new guise, and he interpolates two contrasting episodes, one of which quotes teasingly the beginning of the movement. So pleased was the composer with the results there achieved that he employed a similar form in the Finale. In spite of its gay and witty character this movement is very solidly constructed. The first three notes of the main theme are used throughout the piece and the second variation assumes features of the double fugue. Here supreme artistry is meted out with a light touch granted only to the greatest masters.

*   *   *   *

SYMPHONY NO. 102 IN B♭ MAJOR

I. *Largo—Allegro vivace*
II. *Adagio*
III. *Minuetto: Allegro*
IV. *Finale: Presto*

A strikingly unconventional attitude is revealed in the subsidiary subject of the first movement, which mixes *fortissimo* outcries with sections in *piano*, separating them by dramatic grand pauses. In the heart-stirring Adagio Haydn prescribes muted trumpets and muffled kettledrums; thus, instruments generally meant for blaring and noisy effects are used here to enhance a mysteriously solemn mood. It is not surprising that the lofty piece subsequently was used as an anthem. The Finale again displays dazzling wit and brilliance. Near its end the first violin suddenly begins to stutter and seems unable to produce more than the first few notes of the main theme. Ultimately the full orchestra breaks in, and a hilarious uproar concludes the movement.

*   *   *   *

SYMPHONY NO. 103 IN E♭ MAJOR

I. *Adagio—Allegro con spirito*
II. *Andante*
III. *Minuetto*
IV. *Finale: Allegro con spirito*

The work known as the "Drum Roll" owes its name to the very first measure of the symphony. Here Haydn boldly prescribes a solo for the timpani and thus transports the listener into a weirdly exciting atmosphere. There ensues a poignant melody intoned in unison by bassoons, cellos, and double basses, and the whole stirring episode reappears in the imaginative coda. The Andante offers one of the most exquisite examples of Haydn's treatment of the variation form. He uses first a theme in C minor which is followed by a second idea in C major somewhat related to the first. Thereupon the composer presents alternately variations on each of the two themes, displaying an inexhaustible wealth of imagination. Of the countless superb details in this movement the second variation in C major should be mentioned, which presents the theme in the oboes while the bassoons pompously accompany and the flutes chime in like tiny bells. The beginning of the Finale is as daring as that of the first movement. It starts with a horn-signal which presently reveals itself as the accompaniment to the main subject. This is a piece abounding in contrapuntal features, and as the composer develops it from one single germ-cell, the Finale is of a conciseness and unity rare even in these masterworks.

*   *   *   *

SYMPHONY NO. 104 IN D MAJOR

I. *Adagio—Allegro*
II. *Andante*
III. *Minuetto: Allegro*
IV. *Allegro spiritoso*

When Haydn wrote this symphony in 1795 he may have felt that this was not only the last destined for England but also the very ultimate one he was ever to compose. At that time the master was keenly aware of his artistic responsibility towards the future, and this induced him to give in this symphony even more than in the preceding ones. There is grandeur and breadth of vision in the first movement starting with a majestic D-minor introduction which gives way to an enchanting Allegro imbued with Mozartian warmth. The deeply felt Andante has dramatic episodes which create a mood removed from the customary serenity of Haydn's slow movements. In the Minuetto the accents on the last beat and the grand pause near the end followed by an orchestra trill anticipate Beethoven's scherzos. In the Finale we seem to hear in the distance bagpipes sounding at a rustic dance. It is a movement revealing a truly Romantic spirit and pointing to future developments of the symphonic form.

*   *   *   *

Looking at the whole set of the *London Symphonies* we are overwhelmed by the steady artistic growth to be noticed here. Stimulated by the new experiences gained during his first visit to the British capital, Haydn produced works of genius surpassing his former great contributions. He won tremendous acclaim, and yet the sexagenarian was not inclined merely to continue in the same vein. With youthful zest he carried out new experiments in the second set and achieved, especially in the last three numbers, masterworks outdistancing even the superb first six London symphonies.

12

The Complete String Quartets of Joseph Haydn

Reprinted from the analytical notes in brochures for *The Complete String Quartets of Joseph Haydn*, Schneider Quartet (Haydn Society, Boston, HSQ-A, E-H, L-M [1952-54]), with permission of Music and Arts Programs of America, Inc., who plan to reissue the recordings on compact discs. Geiringer collaborated with other scholars such as Marian Scott (for op. 1) in contributing notes to this set.

> [Robbins Landon] *founded the Boston Haydn Society, which had the aim of continuing the publication of the composer's complete works, started by Mandyczewski in Vienna but discontinued after the scholar's death. Landon's idea was to finance this ambitious enterprise through the sale of recordings of generally unknown Haydn music. I helped as much as I could and also provided jacket notes for some of the records. These records were, incidentally, mostly produced in Vienna, as the cost of hiring union members in this country was prohibitively high. The expected financial success of the venture unfortunately did not materialize. The musical public seemed to prefer buying the tenth recording of Beethoven's Fifth Symphony, or Handel's* Messiah, *to the acquisition of unknown Haydn works. After the publication of only four volumes, Landon's collected edition had to be discontinued and the Boston Haydn Society was eventually dissolved.*—This I Remember, *99.*

Opus 2

To young Haydn the invitation to the castle of Weinzierl in Lower Austria may have seemed like a miraculous stroke of good luck. In 1749, at the age of seventeen he had been expelled from the choristers' school at St. Stephen's in Vienna with three ragged shirts and a worn coat as his sole possessions. Henceforth he had to fight for his very existence by teaching, going *"gassatim"* (which meant playing open-air music at night), and doing any odd musical work chance presented to him. He had at first been allowed to share the garret occupied by the family of a fellow-musician, but even this proved impossible when the arrival of a baby increased the number of inhabitants. It was indeed a hand-to-mouth existence and a life of drudgery that Haydn led. When Karl Joseph von Fürnberg asked the young musician to his little castle at Weinzierl, Haydn could not but feel overjoyed. The castle was charmingly situated in a plain, offering a splendid view of a range of mountains 6,000 feet high. Haydn, so keenly responsive to natural beauty, must have revelled in it. (So, incidentally, did Emperor Francis II, who purchased Weinzierl in 1795 and liked to stay there for extensive visits.) Even more important, of course, were the artistic opportunities. Von Fürnberg, like so many members of the Austrian aristocracy, was an ardent music-lover, and he invited Haydn to the castle to take part in chamber music performances by the host's steward, the village priest, and other local musicians. Haydn not only played in this group but composed for it. Here he enjoyed the chance to have each new work played at once and to have these works performed and criticized by congenial friends. Under such happy conditions his music blossomed, and at Weinzierl he composed a great number of exquisite chamber works in rapid succession.

At that time, the make-up of what we know as the string quartet—two violins, viola, and cello—was not quite so firmly fixed as the standard combination. But before long, Haydn's new works for these four instruments became the favorites of the Fürnberg group, and we may say that the months spent by Haydn at the hospitable castle marked a momentous event in the history of the string quartet. However, this combination was not used exclusively. It is probable that trios for two violins and bass were also performed, and the harpsichord may occasionally have reinforced the cello, as well as filled a middle part. (This seems to be indicated by the somewhat thin texture in certain quartets and by the numbers to be found in the bass parts of old prints.) Horns at times also joined the group to increase both the volume and the variety of musical color.

The quartets opus 1 as well as opus 2 are products of these chamber music sessions at Weinzierl. Opus 2 shows a most attractive variety, as it contains two works (nos. 3 and 5) adding two horns to the string quartet. In later editions the horns were omitted; our recording is based on the original version.

The mood of opus 2 is light and gay, reflecting the young composer's happy state of mind at Weinzierl. These works clearly show the influence of the suite of dances of older times. Each of the six compositions is in a major key and contains two minuets, achieving a very symmetrical arrangement of movements (fast-minuet-slow-minuet-fast). In every work the main key is preserved throughout most of the movements. Within this rigid scheme, however, Haydn displays a surprising variety of details. They reveal the richness of his imagination even in their technical immaturity.

* * * *

QUARTET IN A MAJOR, NO. 1

The Allegro (A major, $\frac{2}{4}$) is a gay, whimsical piece in which Haydn at once shows a true grasp of the quartet style. Not only the dominant first violin but also the second violin and the viola are entrusted with significant material. At the beginning of the development section Haydn tries his hand at imitation work and achieves a texture of beautiful transparency (ex. 12.1). The following robust Menuet (A major, $\frac{3}{4}$) frequently allots the same notes to viola and cello: here the help of a harpsichord might have been welcome. The trio in A minor conjures the atmosphere of a serenade—a nocturnal music performance in honor of a lady, and highly fashionable in eighteenth-century Vienna. Viola and cello pluck the strings, imitating a guitar-effect, while the first violin plays an expressive melody endowed with frequent dynamic contrasts. The third movement, Adagio (D major, $\frac{2}{4}$), entrusts to the first violin a broadly contoured cantilena supported by a triplet motion in the other parts. At times a simultaneous use of different rhythmic patterns (two against three notes) adds an element of piquancy. The sprightly second Menuet (A major, $\frac{3}{4}$) leads to the finale, Allegro molto (A major, $\frac{2}{4}$). This dashing movement with its interchange of timid questions and blustering answers seems like a scene in a comic opera. It is well known that Haydn tried his hand at work of this kind while collaborating with the Viennese comedian Joseph Kurz-Bernardon. Some of the finales of opus 2 give us an idea what Haydn's first comic opera—*The Limping Devil* [Hob. XXIXb:1a], lost to posterity—may have been like.

Example 12.1. String Quartet in A major, op. 2, no. 1, movement 1, meas. 37-41.

QUARTET IN E MAJOR, NO. 2

This is the first among Haydn's early quartets to venture in its key signature beyond the limit of three flats or sharps. The initial Allegro molto (E major, $\frac{2}{4}$) is amiable rather than exuberant. The first violin starts all by itself, whereupon the other instruments utter the second half of the phrase, and a delightful conversation is achieved between the leading instrument and its three partners. The lilting Menuet (E major, $\frac{3}{4}$) contains a trio section in E minor, a highly expressive piece in which the combination of long-held notes with a staccato accompaniment produces a strangely ambivalent character. The following Adagio (A major, $\frac{4}{4}$) at times displays features to be found in a concerto. While at the beginning the two violins are engaged in an exchange of ideas, the first violin is subsequently given double stops and difficult passages which we would not expect in a chamber music work. Near the end provision is even made for the inclusion of a cadenza. Possibly Haydn felt tempted to display his skill on the violin to his host, and the viewpoint of the performer somewhat obscured that of the composer. The ensuing Menuet (E major, $\frac{3}{4}$) uses an effect which Haydn was to employ some thirty years later with great mastery in the finale of his Quartet, op. 50, no. 6, known as "The Frog." In opus 2, no. 2 the same notes are played by the second violin alternately on two neighboring strings, producing a very amusing croaking sound. In the trio (E minor) the first violin plays rapid passages which keep returning to the same note, thus creating a pedal-point effect which we would rather expect to find in the work of a contemporary of J. S. Bach. The austere character of this piece brings into full relief the gay comedy mood of the finale (Presto, E major, $\frac{2}{4}$). Particularly funny is the episode here when the first violin produces a sound that might almost be likened to the braying of a donkey (ex. 12.2).

Example 12.2. String Quartet in E major, op. 2, no. 2, Finale, meas. 36-43.

QUARTET IN E♭ MAJOR, NO. 3

This is the first of the two compositions Haydn originally conceived for string quartet and two horns. As a rule the brass instruments are just used for reinforcement, but occasionally they are entrusted with brief, though idiomatic, solo episodes.

The first movement (Allegro moderato, E♭ major, $\frac{2}{4}$) is a robust and vigorous piece in a very compact form. In the development a rather insignificant transitory motive is given a thorough work-out. Such a technique, used here in its simplest form, was later raised by the composer to a peak of perfection and eventually became one of the main tools employed by Beethoven. It is noteworthy that Haydn's original tempo indication "Allegro moderato" for this movement was changed in later editions to "Allegro molto" with the result of too fast an execution of this piece. The Menuet (E♭ major, $\frac{3}{4}$) divides the string instruments into two groups, the lower of which at times imitates the higher. The Haydn student will be pleased to find here features forecasting the "witches' minuet" which the composer included more than forty years later in his String Quartet, op. 76, no. 2. The trio offers in its second part an opportunity to the horns to display their technical skill. Such solos sound so well that the listener cannot help feeling regret for their subsequent omission when the work was adapted for string quartet. The situation is different in the Adagio cantabile (B♭ major, $\frac{4}{4}$), which, according to the custom of the time, did not provide brass instruments in the original version. This is a tender and delicate character-piece, achieving unusual coloristic effects through the employment of mutes in all four instruments and of pizzicato in the cello. The ensuing Menuet (Poco allegro, E♭ major, $\frac{3}{4}$) reveals a rather unusual feature: a trio followed by three free variations. These are really five dances loosely strung together, each of which, in true divertimento-manner, is dominated by different instruments. After the third variation the minuet is played again, thus giving a firmer cohesion to the sequence of dances. The finale (Allegro, E♭ major, $\frac{2}{4}$) starts with a vigorous unison of the six instruments. It is followed by gay fanfares of the horns conjuring the picture of a hunting scene (ex. 12.3). Apparently even in his young years Haydn was attracted by this rural pastime which later so often inspired him in his creative output.

Example 12.3. String Quartet in E♭ major, op. 2, no. 3, Finale, meas. 1-6.

QUARTET IN F MAJOR, NO. 4

The first movement (Presto, F major, $\frac{6}{8}$) is one of the most mature compositions Haydn produced at Weinzierl. It starts with a melody of four measures, delightful in its simplicity, and is built up in the exposition towards a powerful climax. In the development section we find a feature which was to assume great significance in subsequent works of the Viennese Classical masters: an energetic cadence in D major is followed by a grand pause after which, without any modulation or transition, the composition is resumed in B♭ major. The sequence of unexpected tonalities is continued with the appearance of chords in the key of E♭ minor abruptly replaced by G major (ex. 12.4). The players at Weinzierl may have been startled indeed by so bold a stroke. Much more conventional is the ensuing Menuet (F major, $\frac{3}{4}$), a gay and lively piece, enclosing a sprightly trio in B♭ major. The Adagio (F minor, $\frac{3}{4}$) is one of the earliest movements in a minor key written by Haydn. Here we may discern an influence which was to gain in power through the following years. The piece reveals traces of *Empfindsamkeit*, the passionately subjective idiom, with which Haydn had become acquainted through avidly absorbing the works of Carl Philipp Emanuel Bach. The second Menuet (Allegretto, F major, $\frac{3}{4}$) displays in its trio attractive alternations of $\frac{2}{4}$ and $\frac{3}{4}$ rhythms, such as Haydn was to use often in his mature works. In the sparkling final Presto (F major, $\frac{2}{4}$) the main melody exhibits a faintly Hungarian flavor.

Example 12.4. String Quartet in F major, op. 2, no. 4, movement 1, meas. 50-57.

QUARTET IN D MAJOR, NO. 5

Like no. 3, this work was originally written with two horns and is presented here in this version. In Haydn's time the horn was not equipped with valves; most of the changes in pitch were achieved with the lips, and consequently the composer had to confine himself to using only a limited number of notes.

The first movement (Presto, D major, $\frac{3}{8}$) is based on a gaily skipping motive (ex. 12.5), which is introduced in the very first measures and used throughout the piece. Haydn's love for surprises is revealed in the strange interpolation of three measures in Adagio tempo before the beginning of the coda. The buoyant Menuet (D major, $\frac{3}{4}$) has an amiable trio in D minor, to which the syncopations of the violins add a touch of piquancy. At times each of the instruments is given a significant part, whereby a texture of unusual intricacy is achieved. The following Largo cantabile (G major, *alla breve*) not only stands in the center of the work, but is obviously its most important movement. The horns keep silent and the lovely cantilena is carried by the first violin, while the other instruments provide the harmonic foundation. Syncopations are used for the accompaniment; this time, however, they create a dreamy atmosphere, as they seem to soften all edges and contours. At times there occur truly Romantic modulations in this movement. In the second subject we expect a cadence in D and are first led through a magic maze of B♭ major and E♭ major before the anticipated key finally appears. The second Menuet (D major, $\frac{3}{4}$) has the typical joyous character inspired by Austrian folk dances which Haydn liked to use in such movements. A contrast in color is offered in the trio where significant solos of the horns alternate with gay triplets of the first violin. The finale (Presto, D major, $\frac{2}{4}$) is one of the shortest concluding movements Haydn wrote and its two sections comprise $\frac{3}{4}$ measures only. Its constant fast motion produces the character of a *perpetuum mobile* such as the composer was to present with superior artistry in the finale of his Quartet, op. 64, no. 5, known as "The Lark."

Example 12.5. String Quartet in D major, op. 2, no. 5, movement 1, meas. 1.

QUARTET IN B♭ MAJOR, NO. 6

This work deviates somewhat from the structural plan generally used in this set. The first and third movements seem to have exchanged places so that a slow piece forms the beginning and a fast one the center of the work. The initial Adagio (B♭ major, $\frac{2}{4}$) consists of a theme with four variations, of a purely ornamental character; the bass of the theme remains unchanged and a strict technique is used which differs considerably from that to be found in no. 3 of the set. This introductory movement is imbued with gentle charm and typical Rococo grace. The gay effect of the following Menuet (B♭ major, $\frac{3}{4}$) is heightened in the amiably bustling trio (E♭ major). The center-piece (Presto, E♭ major, $\frac{2}{4}$) has the character of an exuberant finale, but in its construction it displays the da capo form with a middle section in a contrasting key, generally used by Haydn in his minuets. The first violin is entrusted with double stops (ex. 12.6) which add brilliance to the movement. In the ensuing Menuet (B♭ major, $\frac{3}{4}$) Haydn once more divides the four instruments into two groups; the two violins progress in octaves while viola and cello are mostly used in unison. An attractive feature is provided here by Haydn's attempt to have the lower group imitate the upper in a kind of contrary motion. The trio is in the key of B♭ minor, but the composer is obviously reluctant to use the complicated signature of five flats. He achieves his purpose by adding the flats to the notes wherever they are required. The Presto (B♭ major, $\frac{3}{8}$) is one of those light finales of the time which only aim at providing a carefree and pleasant conclusion. Movements of this kind make it difficult for the scholar to distinguish between Haydn's early output and the products of his contemporaries.

Example 12.6. String Quartet in B♭ major, op. 2, no. 6, movement 3, meas. 12-16.

Opus 20, "The Sun Quartets"

The year 1772, in which Haydn's six string quartets opus 20 were written, belongs to one of the most significant periods in the history of art. A movement which had been promoted for many years by a small group of North-German composers was now swaying the minds of the greatest artists far beyond the territory of its origin. Carl Philipp Emanuel Bach, Johann Sebastian's second son, while serving as court cembalist to King Frederick the Great of Prussia, had formulated a musical idiom of highly individual expression, imbuing instrumental music with the emotional fervor and passion hitherto only found in vocal composition. When Haydn was still an unknown and struggling young musician, he had pored over the clavier works of the "Berlin Bach" with the greatest fascination, but it took him a long time until he was ready to draw the ultimate consequences from these studies. Turning his back on the light charm and merry grace of his earlier works, he began in the 1770s systematically to explore the possibilities of an expressive musical language meant to stir heart and soul rather than to gratify the senses. He was encouraged towards experiments of this kind by a general trend of emotionalism manifest at that time in various fields, a trend which was given tremendous impetus by Goethe's epoch-making novel *The Sorrows of Young Werther*.

The six quartets of opus 20 are clearly a product of this "Storm and Stress" phase in Haydn's development. Attempts towards a Romantic subjectivism to be found in his earlier works are now vastly intensified, but while a wider emotional range is covered, the technical aspects are by no means neglected, and the more profound content is matched by superior workmanship. The thematic material is developed with a thoroughness not achieved in preceding compositions. The four instruments, in particular the cello, are granted an almost concertizing character; yet this is chamber music at its best in which each part is superbly integrated into the overall construction.

The fact that three of these quartets use fugues as finales has always puzzled research students, for the strict fugal form would at first sight appear like a foreign body in a highly emotional work. The composer apparently includes fugues to stress his independence from the light and uncomplicated *style galant*, but the venerable old form, in keeping with the general spirit of the time, assumes here new, almost Romantic aspects.

It is not surprising that contemporaries called these "die grossen Quartette," which means both the big and the great quartets. The rising sun shown on the frontispiece of an early edition was interpreted in a symbolic manner as signifying Haydn's rising genius. Young Mozart, then seventeen, was so deeply impressed by the *Sun Quartets* that he wrote six quartets (K. 168 to K. 173) in the same vein.

QUARTET IN E♭ MAJOR, NO. 1

The Allegro moderato (E♭ major, $\frac{4}{4}$) which serves as an introductory movement to the first string quartet is an unconventional piece, full of gay surprises. In the beginning the first violin intones the main theme, whereupon the second violin takes over, stating it a fifth higher, a procedure more common in a fugue than in the ordinary sonata form. Early in the development the main theme reappears for a moment in the tonic key; the listener gains the impression that the movement is starting over again, and he is thus subjected to one of those little jokes which Haydn enjoyed so much. The second movement, a minuet (Un poco allegretto, E♭ major, $\frac{3}{4}$) makes use of the simple, but effective contrast of high notes played *forte* and low ones played *piano*. The sweet and unassuming trio with its delicate pastel hues is the kind of music which seems to have greatly impressed Johannes Brahms, an ardent student of Haydn's chamber music, who included similar coloristic episodes in his own quartets. The third movement, Affettuoso e sostenuto (A♭ major, $\frac{3}{4}$), uses a heading typical of the period of *Empfindsamkeit* (sensibility). The prevailing dynamic sign is *mezza voce* (with half the volume of tone), giving a Romantic twilight character to this lofty, deeply serious piece. The finale (Presto, E♭ major, $\frac{2}{4}$), on the other hand, is very gay and carefree. In this piece full of piquant syncopations and amusing pauses Haydn likes to divide the quartet into a lower and a higher group of two instruments which answer or contradict each other, and he thus creates a scene of pure comedy.

QUARTET IN C MAJOR, NO. 2

At the opening of the first movement (Moderato, C major, $\frac{4}{4}$) of this brilliant quartet the cello presents in its high tenor register the triumphant main theme (ex.12.7), with viola and second violin providing bass foundation and middle parts respectively—a rather revolutionary departure from the traditional beginning of a quartet. A few measures later the cello again attracts our attention. This time it merely accompanies, but its arpeggios lead in quick 16ths motion from the majestic lowest string to the sweetly resonant upper range. At the beginning of the development the movement assumes real concerto character, when first violin and cello are engaged in a spirited dialogue, while arpeggios of quite sizable difficulty are entrusted to the second violin. Haydn, who never does the obvious, closes this high-spirited piece quietly in mysterious *pianissimo*. The second movement (Adagio, C minor, $\frac{4}{4}$) starts with a powerful unison of the four instruments sounding like a Baroque ritornello. To indicate the unconventional, fantasia-like character of this piece, in which the style of earlier Austrian composers like Fux and Caldara is revived, Haydn gave it the title capriccio. The Adagio reaches its climax in the middle, when the shadows of the oppressive C minor suddenly lift and the first violin in radiant E♭ major intones a song of gratitude and bliss. More than a decade later Haydn was to use in his *Seven Last Words* a similar modulation to conjure the wonders of Paradise. A gentle minuet (Allegretto, C major, $\frac{3}{4}$) in the veiled and subdued character of a ninteenth-century intermezzo, interrupted by a darkly threatening trio, leads to the finale, an Allegro (C major, $\frac{6}{8}$) which Haydn designates as "Fuga a 4^{tro} soggetti" (fugue with one main subject and three countersubjects). Here it is not the player but the composer who displays his technical skill. With an almost naïve pride in his achievements Haydn indicates in the original score the inversion of the main theme with the remark "al roverscio." However, he does not take this exhibition of contrapuntal fireworks too seriously. At the end of the original manuscript we find the ironical remark "sic fugit amicus amicum" (thus friend runs away from friend), which seems to anticipate the current joke that a fugue is a form of composition in which each voice runs away from the others, and the listener from all of them.

Example 12.7. String Quartet in C major, op. 20, no. 2, movement 1, meas. 1-7.

QUARTET IN C MINOR, NO. 3

The third quartet is in the minor mode which Haydn had only rarely used in previous works. The first movement (Allegro con spirito, G minor, $\frac{2}{4}$) displays a serious, in places quite mysterious, character. As a faithful disciple of Emanuel Bach, the composer reveals permanently new sides of the same idea, displaying the first subject in quick succession in G minor and in the parallel key of B♭ major. Even more sombre is the following minuet (Allegretto, G minor, $\frac{3}{4}$), a character-piece completely removed from the traditional graceful vein of the French dance. Its oppressive mood is only relieved in the gently rocking trio in E♭ major with its delightfully sweet and tender modulation at the end. Broadly conceived is the Poco adagio (G major, $\frac{3}{4}$), whose lovely cantilena (ex. 12.8) is explored by the composer in all its potentialities. The last movement (Allegro di molto, G minor, $\frac{4}{4}$) is particularly transparent in texture. Although again in G minor, it is not lacking in gay and whimsical episodes, and when the *pianissimo* of the end is reached, the listener has the impression of having witnessed an eerie procession of gnomes and ghosts.

Example 12.8. String Quartet in G minor, op. 20, no. 3, movement 3, meas. 1-8.

QUARTET IN D MAJOR, NO. 4

This is probably the most ingratiating of the "Sun Quartets" and the easiest to understand. The initial gay and witty Allegro di molto (D major, $\frac{3}{4}$) is followed by a set of variations in D minor, inscribed Un poco adagio e affettuoso ($\frac{2}{4}$). The passionate character of the theme is lightened through the paraphrases and ornamentations required by the variation technique. In the ensuing Menuet alla zingarese (Allegretto, D major, $\frac{3}{4}$) the composer gladly follows a trend of the time. The study of different nations' folksongs had become highly fashionable and Haydn, who spent the greater part of his life in the Hungarian countryside, received great stimulation from the music of the Hungarian Gypsies, which he immortalized in compositions like this minuet, with its obstinate, syncopated rhythms. The following Presto e scherzando (D major, $\frac{4}{4}$) is written in a similar vein. Towards the end of the exposition the listener witnesses a Hungarian peasant festivity at which the cracks of the whip produced by the second violin add excitement to the general merry-making (ex. 12.9).

Example 12.9. String Quartet in D major, op. 20, no. 4, movement 4, meas. 40-45.

Example 12.9.—*Continued*

QUARTET IN F MINOR, NO. 5

This work is as dark and brooding in its mood as the preceding composition is light and gay. The tragic Moderato serving as first movement (F minor, 4/4) is conceived on a large scale and equipped with an impressive coda. A characteristic detail ought to be mentioned in this connection. Donald Tovey in his valuable analysis of Haydn's quartets points to this coda's "*ff* climax . . . followed by a pathetic collapse." The great English musicologist did not have access to Haydn's original manuscript and based his study on nineteenth-century editions which sentimentalized the composer's intentions by adding a *ff* and two *decrescendi* not to be found in the autograph. There follows a nostalgic minuet (F minor, 3/4) leading to a kind of *siciliano* (Adagio, F major, 6/8), in which an interesting effect is achieved through the combination of a singing cantilena in the first violin with a sharp staccato accompaniment of the other instruments. At the end of the middle section (meas. 54 to 56) the autograph has in the composer's own hand the curious remark "per figuram redartationis" (*sic*!). Haydn's faulty Latin apparently indicated that the figuration in the first violin makes a somewhat delayed appearance; the leading instrument plays dissonant notes on the accented beats with the resolution coming haltingly afterwards. The finale (F minor, 2/2) is once more a fugue, this time "a 2 soggetti," by which remark Haydn implies that besides the main subject an obbligato countersubject is introduced. With its strettos, inversions and canonic treatments of the theme this movement belongs to the finest fugue compositions written at that time. Remarkable is the almost complete absence of expression marks in this as well as the other fugues of the set. At the beginning of the F minor fugue Haydn prescribes "Sempre sotto voce" (always with a subdued tone), and no other indicaton is given for 160 measures. A highly Romantic picture of spectral figures swiftly gliding to and fro is thus achieved.

QUARTET IN A MAJOR, NO. 6

The first movement of the Quartet no. 6 is inscribed Allegro di molto e scherzando (A major, 6/8). This high-spirited, humorous piece is followed by an Adagio (E major, 2/2), again revealing the admiration Haydn felt for the work of Emanuel Bach. As in the latter's *Sonaten mit veränderten Reprisen*, Haydn states the exposition twice, the second time subtly changing it and surrounding the melody with delicate figurations. The graceful minuet (A major, 3/4; ex. 12.10) introduces a trio, this time really written for three instruments, as it does not employ the second violin. All three instruments are, according to a note in the autograph, to play "sopra una corda"—on the lowest string only—which produces a most attractive coloristic effect. The finale (Allegro, A major, 4/4) is once more a fugue, this time "con 3 soggetti," introducing two countersubjects apart from the main theme. In spite of the strictness of the contrapuntal design the mood of the movement conforms with the playful and humorous character of the whole quartet. It seems of symbolic significance that the "Sun Quartets" stressing equal rights for all four instruments thus end with a form of composition in which this principle is a postulate of the highest order.

Example 12.10. String Quartet in A major, op. 20, no. 6, movement 3, meas. 1-8.

THE SOURCES

The autographs of the quartets of opus 20 are manuscripts of extreme beauty. They are written in a very fine and speedy hand which remains always completely legible and is free of corrections or errors. Each of the six quartets has the same heading. In the top left corner it reads "Divertimento a quattro" (a term frequently used for Haydn's quartets). In the middle of the page the deeply religious composer writes: "In Nomine Domini" ("in the name of the Lord") and in the right top corner we read: "Di me Giuseppe Haydn [manu pro]pria 772" ("By me, Joseph Haydn, in my own hand, 1772"). At the end of each quartet we find such expressions of gratitude: "Laus omnipotenti Deo" ("Praise to the Almighty God"), or "Gloria in excelsis Deo" ("Glory to God in the highest").

The six autographs were formerly in the possession of Johannes Brahms and were bequeathed by him to the Society of Friends of Music in Vienna, the institution which also owns the autographs of opus 17. Brahms, who was a great admirer of Haydn's quartets, was very fond of this manuscript. He studied it thoroughly and marked in his printed miniature scores the numerous deviations from the original. We like to think that Brahms would have approved of the present recording which goes back to the original source, eliminating all later additions.

Opus 33, "The Russian Quartets"

In November 1781 the imperial court of Vienna celebrated the visit of some august guests. Grand Duke Paul of Russia (subsequently Czar Paul II) and Duke Franz Eugen of Württemberg had arrived with their wives for a stay of several weeks, and, as they were intensely interested in music, Vienna proudly exhibited to them its greatest attractions in this field. The visitors attended performances of two Gluck operas, a contest on the piano between Mozart and Clementi, and a concert in which, as the *Wiener Zeitung* reports, works by the "famous Joseph Haydn" were played. While we do not know whether it was Mozart or Clementi who impressed the Russian guests most favorably, there is no doubt that Haydn's music delighted them. After the concert the composer was presented with a magnificent golden box studded with diamonds, and the Grand Duchess asked him to give her lessons on the piano while she stayed in Vienna. A program of the works performed at this occasion has not been preserved, but we know that quartets were played, and, as soon afterwards Haydn's new set of string quartets opus 33 was dedicated to Grand Duke Paul, we may assume that these were the compositions which so greatly impressed the exaulted visitors.

A few days after the concert Haydn wrote about the same quartets to Prince Ernst of Oettingen-Wallerstein, a stanch admirer of his music; in this letter the composer claimed that the works were "written in an entirely new and original manner." Haydn was an excellent businessman and the descriptions he gave of his own compositions to publishers or august patrons were not exactly of a self-deprecatory nature. In this particular case, however, we may take his words quite literally, for he had indeed written these quartets in an "entirely new manner."

It is most significant that no less than nine years separate the completion of opus 33 from that of the preceding quartets, opus 20. Although these nine years were a period of intense creative activity, during which Haydn wrote several operas, a large oratorio, and many symphonies, he avoided his favorite form of chamber music composition. When he finally returned to the string quartet, the character of the works had undergone a change. While the quartets of opus 20 had revealed a highly subjective and passionate mood, Haydn gave reign to his sense of humor in opus 33, which contains some of the wittiest comedy scenes he wrote in the form of the string quartet. The nickname "Gli scherzi," often given to this set, therefore assumes a deeper significance, although it primarily refers to the fact that in these "Russian Quartets" Haydn designates the minuet movement as "Scherzo" or "Scherzando." Even more important is the difference in form between the quartets of opus 20 and opus 33. Three quartets of the earlier set ended with fugues, thus achieving a strong concentration both in structure and content. Later this seemed too old-fashioned and rigid a solution to the composer, and he strove to achieve unification in his own way. Thoroughly and steadfastly, as was his custom, he wrestled with the problem for many years until he felt ready to submit his method of "thematic development" to the scrutiny of the musical world. What had been haphazardly attempted in earlier works became the guiding principle of the opus 33 quartets, particularly in the development sections of the first movements. Haydn dissected the subjects of the exposition and developed and reassembled the resulting fragments in the most variegated ways, making at the same time ample use of modulations. Even the accompanying and purely filling parts were often based on motives derived from the main subjects, and thus all four instruments were given an important share in the thematic elaboration.

It may well be doubted whether Haydn's contemporaries realized the technical and intellectual work that went into the composition of these quartets. Nevertheless music lovers were captivated by their obvious beauty and wit. The Hamburg critic Carl Friedrich Cramer wrote one year after the publication of the set: "These works are praised, and cannot be praised enough, in view of their highly original character and the most vivacious and pleasant wit manifest in them."

* * * *

QUARTET IN B MINOR, NO. 1

This is the only quartet of the set in a minor key, and its general mood somewhat differs from that prevailing in the other works. In this composition Haydn is so anxious to demonstrate the possibilities of the newly adopted "thematic development" that he uses the sonata form, offering the best medium for this device, in no less than three out of four movements. The dark-hued first movement (Allegro moderato, B minor, $\frac{4}{4}$) mystifies the listener by starting with the D-major chord and only subsequently revealing its true tonality. It is interesting to note that the composer used the same procedure in another B-minor quartet, op. 64, no. 2, and that Brahms, who was a very enthusiastic student of Haydn's chamber music, did likewise in his Clarinet Quintet in B minor. The whole first movement of opus 33, no. 1 seems to be dominated by a single subject, as the second idea is really a rhythmic variation of the first. Haydn is indefatigable in exploring all its potentialities, and features of the development technique are to be found even in the recapitulation, when all four instruments present the second idea in an imitative style (ex. 12.11). The following movement (Allegro, B minor, $\frac{3}{4}$) has the heading scherzando. Four of the six quartets of this set have moderately fast first movements and accordingly, by way of contrast, a lively piece ensues instead of a slow one. Our scherzando, though fast-moving, is not a gay piece. Its simple melody wanders from the first violin to the second, to end up in the cello. An interesting coloristic effect is achieved through the intonation of the same note on two neighboring strings, a device Haydn was to give much wider use in his quartet "The Frog," op. 50, no. 6, written a few years later. The trio, in the unusual key of B major, presents with great logic a stepwise ascending motive as well as its inversion. The third movement (Andante, D major, $\frac{6}{8}$) is the only piece in a major key in this quartet. Yet its character is at times grave and contemplative; sharp dissonances and bold chromaticism introduced in the subsidiary subject create a curiously ambivalent mood. The last movement (Presto, B minor, $\frac{2}{4}$) radiates zest and vigor. The ending, with its sudden dynamic changes and unexpected hold, uses a surprise effect Haydn was very fond of and thus adds a touch of lightness to this rather serious-minded work.

Example 12.11. String Quartet in B minor, op. 33, no. 1, movement 1, meas. 78-79.

QUARTET IN E♭ MAJOR, NO. 2

The first movement (Allegro moderato cantabile, E♭ major, $\frac{4}{4}$) is in a gentle and amiable mood. Technically it reveals the same superb artistry as the preceding work, and the simple, rhythmic motive of an 8th-note preceded by two 16ths, presented at the beginning, assumes ever new and surprising aspects. The following scherzando

(E♭ major, 3/4) is a robust and energetic piece. Haydn in this, as in the subsequent movements of this type in opus 33, simplifies the form by keeping the first section in the tonic key throughout, which enables him to repeat it literally as a third section. Thus the same tune is played rather stubbornly over and over again, as a means of enhancing comical effects. The trio belongs to those delightfully catching dance melodies in which Austrian musicians have excelled from the eighteenth century up to our own time. The third movement (Largo sostenuto, B♭ major, 3/4) is written in a kind of free variation form. The solemn theme is first presented by viola and cello (ex. 12.12), then the first and the second violin take it over, and gradually it is surrounded by the loveliest melodic arabesques. During the episodes separating the entrances of the main idea a multitude of dynamic signs is displayed ranging from *pianissimo* to *forte* and including numerous *sforzandi*. We know that Haydn himself did not perform in the gala concert for the Russian guests when these quartets were presented—the executants being Tomasini, Asplmayer, Huber, and Weigl—and he may therefore have felt the need to guide the players with the help of dynamic signs. In his eagerness he almost overdid it, supplying in meas. 21 to 24 for eighteen successive notes no less than twelve expression marks. The finale (Presto, E♭ major, 6/8) is generally referred to as "The Joke." This is a rondo using a rather undistinguished gayly prattling theme. The real joke develops in the coda, when the effervescent Presto is quite unexpectedly interrupted by a solemn Adagio. After three measures Haydn resumes the initial tempo; he splits the main theme into four sections and between each utterance of one of the fragments a rest of two full measures is inserted. When the whole theme has been played Haydn doubles his rest and then, to the acute discomfort of the audience, starts all over with the prattling melody. This time, however, he does not proceed; after two measures the unfinished tune remains suspended in midair, and the listener is left both puzzled and amused.

Example 12.12. String Quartet in E♭ major, op. 33, no. 2, movement 3, meas. 1-8.

QUARTET IN C MAJOR, NO. 3

The reason for the name "The Bird" usually given to this quartet is already apparent in the initial movement (Allegro moderato, C major, 4/4). Here the twittering grace-notes characterizing both the first and the second subjects conjure up pictures of those feathered friends Haydn loved to watch on his early morning walks in the country. With the help of the newly mastered technique, the composer displays charming rural scenes in which nature's winged creatures seem to unite in praise of their Maker. In the following Allegretto (C major, 3/4), the heading "Scherzando" seems rather incongruous. The trio uses two violins only, and here the jolly aviary of the first movement is heard again (ex. 12.13). The third movement (Adagio, F major, 3/4) is a lofty and tender piece, in modified sonata form. The exposition, which introduces a heart-stirring second subject, is presented twice, the second time in a more ornamented version (a device often used by Philipp Emanuel Bach, whose compositions Haydn admired so much). After a passionate, strongly modulating middle section there follows a recapitulation of the main part, again delightfully varied. The finale (Rondo presto, C major, 2/4) begins with merry cuckoo-calls of the first violin supported by a 6/4 chord of the other instruments. A fiery episode in A minor in the character of Hungarian Gypsy music follows. Haydn's wit is most clearly revealed in the enchanting little surprises he offers in the bridge passages to the re-entrance of the theme.

"The Bird" was a favorite with the Joachim Quartet, and this may partly account for the fact that in concert performances it is given preference over the other numbers of the set. The present recording will, it is hoped, prove to listeners that the five other "Russian Quartets" are by no means inferior in quality.

Example 12.13. String Quartet in C major, op. 33, no. 3, movement 2, meas. 35-42.

QUARTET IN B♭ MAJOR, NO. 4

The first movement (Allegro moderato, B♭ major, 4/4) starts boldly with an inverted seventh chord (ex. 12.14), a device used to accentuate the humorous character of the piece, revealed also in the unexpected rests and the puckish little coda. The following scherzo (Allegretto, B♭ major, 3/4) presents a lilting tune, very Austrian in character, which is effectively contrasted with the sighs of the trio ("minore") in the unusual key of B♭ minor. The third movement (Largo, E♭ major, 3/4) is a solemn piece in ternary form, imbued with hymnic fervor. Although the lead is entrusted to the first violin which soars up to the highest range, the other instruments, in particular the cello, most significantly enrich the musical texture. In the final rondo (Presto, B♭ major, 2/4), the delightfully jocular theme, sounding like a clever paraphrase of a folksong, is presented in ever new disguises. Haydn's infectious good humor appears to be inexhaustible, and when the merry tune is offered for the last time in piquant pizzicato chords, nobody can help feeling regret that the fun is over.

Example 12.14. String Quartet in B♭ major, op. 33, no. 4, movement 1, meas. 1-3.

QUARTET IN G MAJOR, NO. 5

The first movement (Vivace assai, G major, 2/4) starts with a kind of motto which is frequently employed throughout the piece. It is in the nature of a greeting, and Walter Wilson Cobbett, famous British chamber music enthusiast and lexicographer, liked to point out that it could be sung to the words "How do you do." This gay, unusually extensive movement introduces three subjects, each of which is given a thorough elaboration radiating wit and grace. In the second movement (Largo cantabile, G minor, 4/4), the atmosphere of Gluck's operas is recaptured, the noble serenity of the Elysian fields in *Orfeo ed Euridice*, as well as the more tragic accents of *Iphigénie en Aulide*. The expressive cantilena of the first violin, dramatically supported by the utterance of its partners, conjures a stirring dramatic scene. A most effective contrast is offered by the following scherzo (Allegro, G major, 3/4). This movement has completely shed the character of a dance; with its rapid rhythmic changes, its *sforzando* accents on weak beats, its blustering exclamations which, after a sudden rest, are timidly concluded (ex. 12.15), it comes closer to the spirit of a Beethoven scherzo than anything Haydn had written up to that time. The finale (Allegretto, G major, 6/8) is an entracing *siciliano* dance, with three variations in which viola and cello are given ample opportunities to display their technical skill. A short Presto coda merrily concludes the captivating piece. Mozart was deeply impressed by this unusual quartet finale, and he paid the older master the compliment of including into his own Quartet in D minor, written two years later, a last movement obviously inspired by Haydn's piece. To avoid any misunderstanding, Mozart inscribed the work to his "beloved friend Haydn."

Example 12.15. String Quartet in G major, op. 33, no. 5, movement 1, meas. 1-10.

QUARTET IN D MAJOR, NO. 6

The first movement (Vivace assai, D major, $^6_8$) is imbued with the merry mood usually reserved for a finale. Its development section is brief, but harmonically interesting, and to make up for the terseness of the middle part the composer continues in his recapitulation to elaborate thoroughly on his themes. In the second movement (Andante, D minor, $^4_4$) the melody is repeatedly entrusted to second violin and viola, while the first violin holds a high note like an organ point (ex. 12.16). This is a truly Romantic, passionate piece, reminiscent in its expressive power of Haydn's previous set of quartets, opus 20. The third movement (Scherzo, Allegro, D major, $^3_4$) consists of two sections which, contrary to custom, are not contrasting in mood, but rather supplement each other. In the scherzo proper the boorish *sforzandi* on the last beat achieve a highly humorous effect. Even funnier is the uncouth trio with its cello solo and canonic imitations. The finale (Allegretto, D major, $^2_4$) uses a device which Haydn was to grow very fond of in later years. It introduces first a theme in major which sounds like a merry tune in a Singspiel, then a contrasting idea in the minor mode; variations on these two ideas are offered, and finally, as a conclusion, a modified statement of the theme in major. While the form of this movement recurs in many of Haydn's subsequent works (best known is probably the slow movement of the Symphony no. 103 "with the drum roll"), the main melody seems to anticipate the folksong-like aria "An honest country girl" from Haydn's *The Seasons* [Hob. XXI:3], written some twenty years later. This utterly enchanting piece, the structural pattern of which was to assume significance in the works of Beethoven, too, offers a suitable ending to one of Haydn's most important sets of string quartets.

Example 12.16. String Quartet in D major, op. 33, no. 6, movement 2, meas. 1-5.

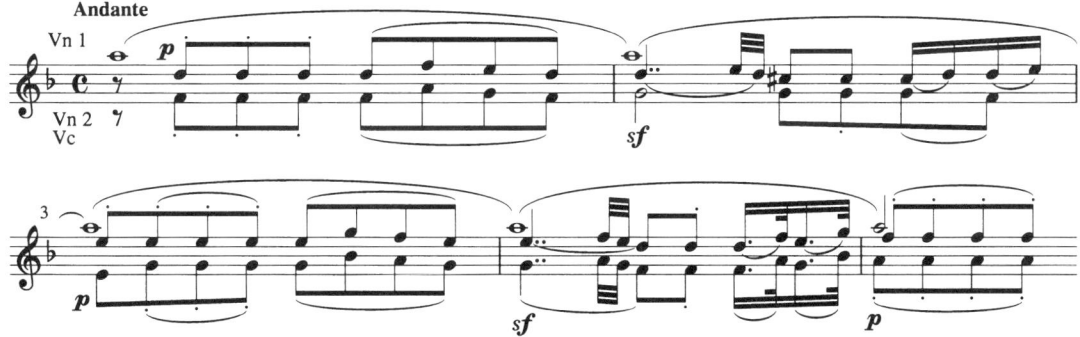

Opus 50

Haydn's six quartets, opus 50, were composed in the years 1784 to 1787 and printed by his favorite publisher Artaria in Vienna, with a dedication to Frederick William II, King of Prussia. This monarch continued the artistic traditions established by his uncle and predecessor on the throne, Frederick the Great. King William was a very fine cello player and a passionate devotee of chamber music. He took an active interest in the art of his time, and the list of great composers who dedicated music to him included, in addition to Haydn, Carl Philipp Emanuel Bach, Boccherini, Mozart, and Beethoven. It may safely be assumed that none of these works appealed more to the king than Haydn's six quartets. The monarch acknowledged their receipt with a most gracious letter and a beautiful ring which Haydn treasured above other tokens of favor bestowed upon him, and liked to wear when engaged in creative work. The letter accompanied him to his trips to England, and he was able to show it proudly to some Prussian officers who doubted that the homely little man they met in an inn was the world-famous composer.

The quartets opus 50 belong to those works which clearly reflect the spirit of give-and-take which prevailed in the unique relationship between Austria's two greatest composers of the time. Haydn's six "Sun Quartets," op. 20, of 1772 inspired Mozart to write in the following year six quartets, K. 168-173, on somewhat similar lines. Haydn let a period of nine years elapse before he turned again to the string quartet. Mozart acted in the same way and only after the older composer had published in 1781 his six quartets, op. 33, did the young genius produce his set known as opus X, K. 387, 421, 428, 458, 464, 465, which he inscribed with heartfelt words of homage to his "beloved friend Haydn." We know that the dedicatee took part in their performance, while they were still in manuscript, and that he remarked at this occasion to Mozart's father: "In the face of God and as an honest man I tell you your son is the greatest composer known to me." This admiration is evident in the quartets opus 50, which Haydn was composing at that time. A glance at the first movement of no. 4, notably its subsidiary subject, is sufficient to reveal the deep impression the young composer's style had made on the mature artist. Mozart, on the other hand, preserved his habit of following in his friend's footsteps and two years after Haydn's opus 50, he produced three quartets, K. 575, 589, 590, the last he was fated to write, which he also dedicated to King Frederick William II.

Haydn's opus 50 shows features significant for the works written in the 1780s. The texture is of Classical lightness and transparency, the treatment of the musical form superbly balanced. The composer explores all possibilities of thematic elaboration, dissecting his themes and reassembling the fragments with inexhaustible imagination. The four instruments are allotted highly individual utterances, but they cooperate in the task of discussing each subject thoroughly so as to cast full light upon all its potentialities. In his zest for achieving the greatest possible development or variation of themes Haydn sometimes dispenses with a contrasting second subject, thus letting a whole movement unfold out of a single germ cell.

QUARTET IN B♭ MAJOR, NO. 1

The first movement (Allegro, B♭ major, $\frac{2}{2}$) begins with two introductory measures played by the cello only, as if Haydn wanted to give to the royal player a chance to precede his musicians. The main theme which presently ensues is of unusual simplicity; apparently the composer was anxious to show that out of the humblest clay artistic edifices of greatest magnificence might be erected. Beethoven followed Haydn along these lines and it is characteristic that the opening theme of Beethoven's first quartet, op. 18, no. 1, shows a certain resemblance to that of Haydn's op. 50, no. 1. The second movement (E♭ major, $\frac{6}{8}$) has the rather unusual tempo indication Adagio non lento, which we might freely translate as "comfortably slow, but not dragging." It consists of a charming and whimsical little song made up of two groups of six measures each, which the composer presents together with three variations. Haydn, after showing in the first movement how to build up and develop a musical idea, now displays his art in subtly veiling and disguising a theme. In particular the second variation written in the minor mode exhibits an enticing exotic quality. Gay and graceful also is the third movement (Poco allegretto, B♭ major, $\frac{3}{4}$). Near the end of its trio section Haydn achieves a delightful joke by merely breaking up the notes of a descending chord (ex. 12.17). The finale (Vivace, B♭ major, $\frac{2}{4}$) combines in its structure both elements of sonata and of rondo form. The witty manner in which a cadenza of the solo violin and, later, a grand pause precedes the re-entrance of the main theme again shows Haydn's familiarity with similar works of Mozart.

Example 12.17. String Quartet in B♭ major, op. 50, no. 1, movement 3, meas. 56-60.

QUARTET IN C MAJOR, NO. 2

In the initial movement (Vivace, C major, 3/4) the composer deviates slightly from the traditional relationship of the main ideas. He stresses the significance of the second subject (ex. 12.18) at the expense of the first, whereby the piece achieves a somewhat feminine elegance. Similar features can frequently be detected in Romantic music of the nineteenth century. In the following Adagio cantabile (F major, 4/4), a fantasia-like movement offering rich opportunities for the display of technical skill, the second violin utters the initial statement of the main theme. The Menuetto (Allegro, C major, 3/4) starts with a skip of an octave which is presently extended to a ninth and eventually to an uncouth tenth, whereby an atmosphere of robust jocularity is produced. A similar spirit prevails in the finale (Vivace assai, C major, 2/4), a movement which, despite the iron logic determining the unfolding of the opening theme in its most variegated aspects, seems to the listener to be as lightly constructed as a playful improvisation.

Example 12.18. String Quartet in C major, op. 50, no. 2, movement 1, meas. 43-51.

QUARTET IN E♭ MAJOR, NO. 3

The first movement (Allegro con brio, E♭ major, 6/8) deceptively displays at the beginning the simple character of a minuet; yet its construction based on a single idea (ex. 12.19) reveals a degree of artistry commensurate with the importance of an introductory movement in a large instrumental form. The following Andante più tosto allegretto (B♭ major, 2/4) is, as in the first quartet of the set, a theme with three variations, one of which is in the minor mode. An important part is assigned to the royal instrument, the violoncello, which frequently plays the melody in its high tenor register, the viola assuming the unfamiliar role of a supporting bass instrument. The Menuetto (Allegretto, E♭ major, 3/4) is a vigorous piece. Its extensive second part introduces interesting modulations, and in a little coda near the end two unexpected holds add an element of dramatic tension. It is significant that the busily moving trio uses a theme somewhat related to that of the minuet, which again demonstrates Haydn's joy in revealing all the facets of a musical idea. A similar tendency is evident in the buoyant finale (Presto, E♭ major, 2/4), to which the composer gives a surprise ending in mysterious *pianissimo*.

Example 12.19. String Quartet in E♭ major, op. 50, no. 3, movement 1, meas. 1-8.

QUARTET IN F♯ MINOR, NO. 4

This is the only quartet in a minor mode in this opus and a work of highly unusual character. The first movement (Allegro spirituoso, F♯ minor, 3/4) begins with an upbeat of three 8th notes (ex. 12.20), a rhythmic pattern subsequently immortalized in Beethoven's Fifth Symphony. This figure occurs also in the second subject which captivates by a luxuriant singing quality. The recapitulation turns from F♯ minor to F♯ major, thus changing the initial sadness to a mood of quiet confidence. In the second movement (Andante, A major, 2/4) we find the mixture of rondo and variation form which Haydn used in many of his mature works, among them the Symphony no. 103 ("Drum Roll"). A serene theme in major is followed by a contrasting plaintive episode in minor. There ensues one variation each on the major and the minor sections, and the piece is concluded by another variation of the main subject. A modern musicologist objected to this ending without any specific coda, claiming that it left the impression of perfunctoriness. Such a criticism does not seem justified; Haydn avoided too meaningful a conclusion in order to lead the listener gently toward the next movement. The Menuetto (Poco allegretto, F♯ major, 3/4) reverts to the luminous key used at the end of the first movement. An upbeat of four 16th notes marking its beginning is also used throughout the trio. The finale (Fuga: Allegro moderato, F♯ minor, 6/8) holds a position of its own in this set. Here we have the only fugue within this opus and, at the same time, the only final movement which maintains a mood of sadness and pathos to the very end. In this mature work Haydn uses a form employed in his opus 20, and he recaptures the spirit of emotional intensity of the earlier composition.

Example 12.20. String Quartet in F♯ minor, op. 50, no. 4, movement 1, meas. 1.

QUARTET IN F MAJOR, NO. 5

This work is as different in character from the preceding quartet as two compositions written in close succession can possibly be. The ancient Greeks used to have the performance of a tragedy followed by that of a comedy. Haydn, prompted by similar considerations, contrasts the darkness of the F♯ minor Quartet with the light-hearted joyousness of the F-major quartet. The first movement (Allegro moderato, F major, 2/4) appears like a carefree finale. Here we find for once the spirit of childlike naïveté which has so often been unjustly ascribed to the works of "Old Papa Haydn." The brief second movement (Poco adagio, B♭ major, 3/4), with its mysterious middle voices, has an ethereal quality which was responsible for the nickname "The Dream" given to it. The Menuetto (Allegretto, F major, 3/4) begins with an energetic idea (ex. 12.21), the first motive of which is upheld throughout the whole piece; even the trio in F minor is based on it. The finale (Vivace, F major, 6/8) displays more of a dance character than the Menuetto. Its main theme shows a certain relationship to that of the last movement in Mozart's Quartet in D minor dedicated to Haydn. An interesting coloristic effect is achieved here, as Haydn has most of the widely contoured melody played on a single string. The unusual tone quality thus produced fits in very well with the general merriment of this folk scene.

Example 12.21. String Quartet in F major, op. 50, no. 5, movement 3, meas. 1-5.

QUARTET IN D MAJOR, NO. 6

In this composition Haydn, the great lover of the outdoors, delights in including the voices of some of his animal friends. The beginning of the first movement (Allegro, D major, 4/4) was interpreted by Wilhelm Altmann, the great expert on chamber music, as an imitation of the flight of birds and the voices of quails. The piece is full of delightful humorous episodes such as the disguise of the first notes in the development as a repetition of the exposition. However, when the boisterous movement near the end fades out in dreamy *pianissimo*, this is not to be considered as a funny "surprise," but rather as a preparation for the ensuing second movement (Poco adagio, D minor, $\frac{6}{8}$), which is of a remarkably progressive nature. The Romantic glow of its melodic language, the rich texture and the bold modulations reaching a climax in the change to D major in the coda make us think of Franz Schubert's heart-stirring musical language. The Menuetto (Allegretto, D major, $\frac{3}{4}$) is a forceful and virile piece, effectively contrasted with the timid, hesitant trio, whose flow is interrupted twice by unduly elongated pauses of the whole group. The finale (Allegro con spirito, D major, $\frac{2}{4}$) gave the quartet its name "The Frog." We hear funny croaking sounds as the same notes are being played alternately on two neighboring strings (ex. 12.22). Haydn had used a similar device of *barriolage* in earlier quartets (op. 17, no. 6; op. 33, no. 1), but not with the same obstinate perseverance, and the results he achieves here are highly amusing.

Example 12.22. String Quartet in D major, op. 50, no. 6, movement 4, meas. 1-2.

The historian is inclined to consider the quartets of opus 50 as manifestations of the Classical perfection which Haydn had reached after a long and arduous struggle. Yet it would be wrong to expect so dynamic an artist ever to stand still, even if it were on the peak of excellence. In countless details Haydn was constantly experimenting and exploring new possibilities which were to bear rich fruit in the music of coming generations.

Opus 51, The Seven Last Words of the Savior on the Cross

Haydn's *Seven Last Words* owes its existence to the great admiration the composer's works enjoyed in Spain. Although he led a secluded life in a remote Hungarian castle, his music spread all over Europe. As early as 1779, at a time when barely a single one of those works was written on which Haydn's fame is based in our time, the Spanish author Yriarte praised him enthusiastically in a poem entitled "La Musica." Two years later King Charles of Spain had the secretary of his Legation in Vienna travel to Hungary in order to pay a formal call on Haydn and present him with a golden snuffbox set with diamonds. In 1785 the composer received a commission from Spain, about which he reports as follows in the preface to a score published by Breitkopf & Härtel in 1801:

> About fifteen years ago I was requested by a canon of Cádiz to compose instrumental music on *The Seven Last Words of the Savior on the Cross*. It was customary at the Cathedral of Cádiz to produce an oratorio every year during Lent, the effect of the performance being not a little enhanced by the following circumstances. The walls, windows, and pillars of the church were hung with black cloth, and only one large lamp hanging from the center of the roof broke the solemn obscurity. At midday the doors were closed and the ceremony began. After a short service the bishop ascended the pulpit, pronounced the first of the *Seven Words* and delivered a discourse thereon. This ended, he left the pulpit and prostrated himself before the altar. The pause was filled by music. The bishop then in like manner ascended and descended a second and a third time, and so on, the orchestra following on the conclusion of each discourse. My composition was subject to these conditions, and it was no easy matter to compose seven Adagios to last ten minutes each and succeed one another without fatiguing the listeners.

Haydn certainly succeeded in overcoming these difficulties. The Spanish clergyman was delighted and had a handsome honorarium of gold pieces sent to Haydn, hidden, for the sake of safety, within a chocolate cake. Before long the composition enjoyed tremendous popularity—in the United States it was performed for the first time as early as 1793—and it was presented in different versions for full orchestra, for string quartet, and for piano. Nor was the composer the only one to arrange the work for different media. On his way to England in 1794, while passing through Passau in southern Germany, Haydn happened to hear an oratorio by a certain Joseph Frieberth based on the original instrumental setting of the *Seven Last Words*. Haydn was intrigued by the idea, and, with the help of Baron van Swieten, he made his own vocal adaptation which again won greatest success. The composer liked to conduct it, and it is significant that this oratorio was the last work the seventy-one-year-old Haydn directed in public.

Although the original composition was written for full orchestra, Haydn may not have known which instruments would actually be available for the performance in Cádiz. He therefore concentrated the melodic life in the string parts, using the wind instruments for doubling and reinforcing. Thus it required only minor changes to fashion the work into a string quartet. The words of Jesus were printed in Latin into the first violin part at the beginning of each piece to convey to the executants the programmatic meaning of the music. In this form the work was before long accepted as an integral part of the composer's chamber music, and it was included in Pleyel's list of Haydn's string quartets, which appeared around 1801, "with the approval of the author."

INTRODUCTION (Maestoso ed adagio, D minor, 4/4). This piece strikes a fundamental note of tragedy and pathos conjured up by the picture of the crucifixion. The sudden changes of *forte* and *piano* and the frequent *sforzandi* provide it with an element of Beethovenian dramatic tension. On the other hand, there is a certain Baroque aspect due to Haydn's employment of the dotted rhythms used in the French overture of earlier generations.

1. SONATA NO. 1 (Largo, B♭ major, 3/4) on "Dimitte illis, non enim sciunt quod faciunt" ("Father forgive them, for they know not what they do"—Luke 23:34). This movement, like the following six sonatas, is written in a kind of free sonata form and is built on one motive (ex. 12.23). Here we have a gentle and sweet prayer in which the Savior interceded for sinning mankind. No bitterness is expressed, no resistance against the agony suffered, only a wealth of love and compassion.

Example 12.23. Sonata, op. 51, no. 1, meas. 2.

2. SONATA NO. 2 (Grave e cantabile, C minor, 4/4) on "Amen dico tibi: hodie mecum eris in paradiso" ("Verily I say unto thee, today shalt thou be with Me in Paradise"—Luke 23:43). This piece again grows out of a single germ-cell (ex. 12.24). The motive appears timidly at first in the minor key, as though the poor malefactor dared not believe in his own good fortune. Later it is transposed into E♭ major, appearing as a radiant cantilena which expresses the tormented man's happiness about God's mercy. In the development section the shadows of death seem to loom up again, until the return of the cantilena, this time in C major, conjures up all the wonders of paradise.

Example 12.24. Sonata, op. 51, no. 2, meas. 1-2.

3. SONATA NO. 3 (Grave, E major, 4/4) on "Mulier, ecce filius tuus, et tu, ecce mater tua!" ("Woman, behold thy son—son, behold thy mother"—John 19:26-27). Jesus brings his beloved disciple and his mother together and accordingly the beginning of the piece (ex. 12.25) is imbued with beauty and love. However, anguish and despair fill the hearts of the two persons closest to the Savior and presently the main motive ("a") played by the cello assumes the aspect of a nightmare.

Example 12.25. Sonata, op. 51, no. 3, meas. 3-6.

4. SONATA NO. 4 (Largo, F minor, 3/4) on "Eli, Eli, Lama sabachthani" ("My God, my God, why hast Thou forsaken me?"—Matthew 26:46). Here Haydn does not really describe revolt but rather the terrible loneliness of a dying man. Sighs are uttered by the first violin which repeatedly plays phrases with barely any accompaniment, and poignant exclamations sound forth from the quartet (ex. 12.26).

Example 12.26. Sonata, op. 51, no. 4, meas. 43-46.

5. SONATA NO. 5 (Adagio, A major, 4/4) on "Sitio" ("I thirst"—John 19:28). This movement has a strangely idyllic character. It is based on the motive of no. 3, which was meant to describe a mother's love for her son. In His agony the Savior has visions of his mother soothing his discomforts when he was a child; but again and again these peaceful pictures are interrupted by awareness of his actual suffering (ex. 12.27).

Example 12.27. Sonata, op. 51, no. 5, meas. 18-21.

6. SONATA NO. 6 (Lento, G minor, 4/4) on "Consummatum est" ("It is finished"—John 19:30). The piece starts on five solemn notes played in unison by the quartet which appear like a setting of Jesus' words (ex. 12.28). The composer does not, however, dwell on the Savior's terrestrial experience but turns to picture the blissful life to come, changing from the initial minor to a major mode.

Example 12.28. Sonata, op. 51, no. 6, meas. 1-3.

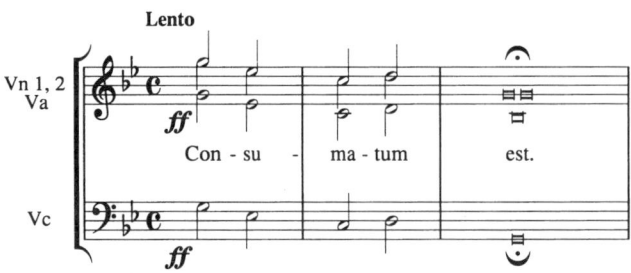

7. SONATA NO. 7 (Largo, E♭ major, 3/4) on "Pater, in manus suas commendo spiritum meum" ("Father into Thy hands I commend My spirit"—Luke 23:46). In this delicate piece, played throughout with mutes, the last remnants of sadness are shed. Jesus' spirit enters paradise, and mankind rejoices the redemption brought about through His sacrifice. Suddenly, however, we return to earth when the final number starts which, according to Haydn's instruction, is to follow the seventh sonata without any break.

"IL TERREMOTO" (The earthquake) (Presto con tuta la forza, C minor, 3/4). This short and very realistic piece which Haydn wants to have played "quickly and with full force" portrays the upheaval in Nature accompanying the passing of Jesus. Apparently the composer felt it to be necessary after eight Adagios to conclude with a forceful and fast finale. It may be wondered, however, whether this slightly conventional number does not constitute an anticlimax.

Even without the finale the *Seven Last Words* is by no means monotonous. A regular interchange of movements in effectively contrasting major and minor modes, one tone or a major third apart, supplies variety, and new musical pictures are presented again and again, conveying both the drama of the Passion and the miracle of Salvation. The simplicity of form and the freshness of invention secure to this composition the effect Beethoven desired for his *Missa solemnis*: "From the heart—to the heart."

Opus 76

In 1796 Ludwig van Beethoven dedicated to his former teacher Joseph Haydn his first three piano sonatas, op. 2. Soon afterwards the old master started to write a set of six string quartets known as his opus 76, which he dedicated to the Hungarian Count, Joseph Erdödy. They were completed and published in 1799, the significant year in which the first performance of *The Creation* won the master, aged sixty-seven, an overwhelming success in a new field.

We like to think that there is some subtle connection between Beethoven's homage and the composition of the opus 76. Beethoven's bold departure from tradition may have strengthened Haydn's urge for experimentations of his own. These quartets do not reflect the personality of an old master pursuing the path of former successes; there is a youthful quality in them, a zest for the conquest of new realms of expression, which reminds us of the music Haydn wrote at a much earlier date. If anything, the old Haydn is more enterprising and unconventional than the young composer dared to be. But there is no groping, no technical uncertainty in these quartets. Haydn, who, after winning unparalleled triumphs in England, was recognized as the world's greatest living composer, felt constantly aware of the tremendous responsibility his exalted position imposed on him. Every note he wrote was mentally submitted to the pitiless scrutiny of posterity, and thus no other set of his quartets contains a larger number of immortal masterpieces than the opus 76.

QUARTET IN G MAJOR, NO. 1

The first movement (Allegro con spirito, G major, 2/2) begins in a symphonic manner with three powerful chords of the whole ensemble. Immediately afterwards, however, the chamber music character of the composition asserts itself as, starting with the cello, one instrument after the other presents the main subject. Haydn's artistry is revealed at the beginning of the recapitulation, when the composer, instead of literally repeating his exposition, first introduces the main subject accompanied by a playful new countermelody and subsequently tosses in with perfect ease a little canon derived from the principal idea (ex. 12.29). The second movement (Adagio sostenuto, C major, 2/4) is marked *mezza voce* (with half-voice), which reminds us of similar indications in Haydn's "Sun Quartets," op. 20. Also the mood of this beautiful and deeply-felt piece is related to the passionately Romantic character of the early set. The fast-moving Menuetto (Presto, G major, 3/4) shows a decided approach to the robust gaiety of Beethoven's scherzos. A dance character is only apparent in the ensuing trio; here the first violin plays the melody, while the three other instruments confine themselves to a pizzicato accompaniment. After three movements in the major mode, the finale (Allegro ma non troppo, 2/2) begins with a dramatic unison of all the four instruments in G minor. Nevertheless the prevailing mood is anything but serious, and in the recapitulation the radiant G major breaks through, bringing the quartet to a triumphant close.

Example 12.29. String Quartet in G major, op. 76, no. 1, movement 1, meas. 144-47.

QUARTET IN D MINOR, NO. 2

This work starts with an Allegro (D minor, 4/4) based on powerful motives of falling fifths (ex. 12.30). The constant reappearance of this idea or its inversion and rhythmic syncopations presented by the whole ensemble provide the piece with unusual *élan* and drive. The second movement (Andante o più tosto allegretto, D major, 6/8) is one of those deceptively simple and transparent pieces Haydn liked to write. It abounds in delightful details, revealing ever new aspects of the ingratiating main theme. Interesting is a little cadenza near the end. Similar passages were improvised by eighteenth-century musicians, but Haydn may have preferred for once to give the performers some guidance. The third movement (Allegro ma non troppo, D minor, 3/4) is known as the "Witches' Menuet." Haydn returns here to the technique of his youth by leading the two violins in octaves. Their eerie melody is imitated by viola and cello, and thus a weird two-part canon is produced. In the finale (Vivace assai, D minor, 2/4) Haydn makes his obeisance to the country where he worked for more than thirty years. The augmented intervals and dashing rhythms create a buoyant Hungarian atmosphere irresistibly carrying the listener away.

Example 12.30. String Quartet in D minor, op. 76, no. 2, movement 1, meas. 1-2.

QUARTET IN C MAJOR, NO. 3

This composition, known as the "Emperor Quartet," is one of Haydn's most famous chamber music works. Yet, paradoxically enough, it is only rarely heard in its entirety, for the slow movement, to which the composition owes its name, enjoys such popularity that it is frequently played alone. It is true that in comparison to this piece the other movements seem somewhat to fade in significance. There is an energetic first movement (Allegro, C major, 4/4) with interesting modulations, a jocular and robust Menuetto (Allegro, C major, 3/4), and a serious finale (Presto,

C minor, 4/4), which only in the middle of its recapitulation makes the traditional change to the main key of C major. The climax of the quartet is reached in the Poco adagio cantabile (G major, 2/2), which comprises four variations on the Austrian national anthem "Gott erhalte Franz den Kaiser" ("God save our Emperor Franz") [Hob. XXVIa:43]. No other composition of Haydn's was given wider circulation than this anthem, and no other was as dear to his heart. Noticing the deep impression produced in England whenever "God save the King" was played, Haydn felt that in the distressed times of the Napoleonic Wars Austria also needed a patriotic song. In January 1797 he wrote the anthem and on February 12, the Emperor's birthday, it was introduced to the population, being sung in all the theaters of Austria. Haydn was deeply moved by his own tune, and it was the very last music he played before he died, repeating it three times and achieving, as his faithful friend and servant Elssler reported, "an expressiveness that surprised even himself." Up to the present the hymn has maintained its popularity. It was used with various texts as the anthem of the Austro-Hungarian monarchy, as the patriotic song "Deutschland, Deutschland über alles" in Germany, and as a church hymn in English-speaking countries.

In the quartet the composer does not attempt greatly to change the original tune. He entrusts the immortal melody in each variation to a different member of the ensemble, surrounding it with ornaments or supporting it with lovely counter-melodies which blend into sonorities of soul-stirring loftiness. With this movement Haydn set the pattern for many similar sets of variations in Schubert's chamber music.

QUARTET IN B♭ MAJOR, NO. 4

This work, known as the "Sunrise Quartet," derives its nickname from the main theme of the first movement (Allegro con spirito, B♭ major, 4/4). Out of sustained harmonies played by the three lower instruments, the poignant song of the first violin rises like the sun slowly emerging from a bank of clouds (ex. 12.31), and a feeling of growth and expansion permeates the whole movement. Those modern scholars who claim that Haydn neglected the viola in his quartets are contradicted by this piece containing highly difficult and at the same time most rewarding passages for the instrument. The fervent and religious Adagio (E♭ major, 3/4), conceived in a kind of abridged sonata form, radiates the depth of feeling we are wont to associate with similar pieces by Beethoven. A gay, highly rhythmical Menuetto (B♭ major, 3/4) leads to the finale (Allegro ma non troppo, B♭ major, 2/2), the mischievous and exuberant spirit of which is heightened by two increases in tempo.

Example 12.31. String Quartet in B♭ major, op. 76, no. 4, movement 1, meas. 1-6.

QUARTET IN D MAJOR, NO. 5

Here the slow second movement is once more the most famous, though it by no means excels the others which are equally superb. The initial Allegretto (D major, 6/8) belongs to those typically Haydnian movements which grow entirely out of a single melody (ex. 12.32). The only second idea that is introduced in the course of this extensive piece is a stepwise ascending or descending scale-motive. Haydn chose for this first movement a simple three-part construction, shunning the customary sonata form, and a delightful coda in faster tempo (Allegro) is attached to this graceful and tender composition. The following Largo, cantabile e mesto ("Singing and mournful," F♯ major, 2/2) shows a similar architecture. Decidedly bold is the use of F♯ major, which excludes the employment of any open strings by the four members of the quartet, whereby a tone quality of ethereal beauty is achieved. Felix Mendelssohn's sister Fanny once wrote to the composer Moscheles about this piece: "Do you remember how

Example 12.32. String Quartet in D major, op. 76, no. 5, movement 1, meas. 1-4.

Felix played to us the magnificent Adagio in F♯ major? Father had a predilection for Haydn. This piece was new to him and moved him deeply. He cried while listening and afterwards said that it was so immensely sad. This surprised Felix, for he, like the rest of us, felt it to be in a rather bright mood." The divergence of opinion between the Mendelssohns may well have been due to the difference in age. The Adagio reflects the serenity of old age contemplating the end of a rich and fruitful life. This seemed infinitely touching to old Abraham Mendelssohn, but it was beyond the grasp of his children. The piquant Menuetto (Allegro, D major, $\frac{3}{4}$), with its alternating $\frac{2}{4}$ and $\frac{3}{4}$ rhythms, is followed by a trio in which the obstinate repetition of a grumbling motive in the cello produces a highly humorous effect. In the finale (Presto, D major, $\frac{2}{4}$) we have a gay and turbulent folk scene to which the frequent open fifths in the accompaniment give the character of bagpipe music (ex. 12.33).

Example 12.33. String Quartet in D major, op. 76, no. 5, movement 4, meas. 7-12.

QUARTET IN E♭ MAJOR, NO. 6

The last quartet is perhaps the only one of the splendid set in which the composer's age occasionally makes itself felt through a slight decrease of creative imagination. The initial movement (Allegretto, E♭ major, $\frac{2}{4}$), again avoiding the sonata form, is a theme with simple variations ending in a gay Allegro. The following movement in the remote key of B major is inscribed "fantasia" (Adagio, $\frac{3}{4}$). This broadly contoured, freely constructed piece expresses, with the help of rich modulations, gentle smiles as well as serious emotions. The Menuet (Presto, E♭ major, $\frac{3}{4}$) is of the jocular scherzo type and it is followed by an "Alternativo," which, as the great musicologist Donald Tovey wrote, "consists wholly of the scale of E flat in iambic rhythm, descending and ascending with counterpoints as multitudinous and heavenly as the angels on Jacob's ladder." A froliscome Allegro spiritoso (E♭ major, $\frac{3}{4}$) introducing interesting rhythmic patterns serves as the finale.

The publishing house of Artaria in Vienna announced the first edition of opus 76 with this clarion call: "Nothing has yet been presented by us that could equal this publication." Probably they had in mind the physical appearance distinguished by very clear engraving and a frontispiece with the composer's portrait. However, in a purely artistic sense, their claim has been corroborated by the love and admiration of later generations.

Part 3
Haydn and His Contemporaries

A Birthday Cantata by
Pietro Metastasio and Leonardo Vinci

The piece is a methodological tour de force employing iconography, organology, diplomatic, musical analysis, manuscript study, and biography with telling effect. Its publication as "Eine Geburtstagkantate von Pietro Metastasio und Leonardo Vinci" in Alfred Einstein's prestigious *Zeitschrift für Musikwissenschaft* 9 (1927): 270-83 helped establish Geiringer's early career. An offprint preserved at the Gesellschaft der Musikfreunde in Vienna indicates that this article was presented "as a modest token of most sincere gratefulness and admiration" to Eusebius Mandyczewski, Geiringer's mentor and predecessor as curator of the library and archives at the Musikverein.

The identification of the date, place, and occasion depicted in the spectacular Pannini painting, to which Geiringer refers at the beginning of the article, has not always been agreed upon, as can be seen from Geiringer's characterizations made later in his memoirs (see below). Most recently (1992) the work has been relabeled by the department of documentation of the Louvre as a depiction of a performance ordered by Cardinal de Rochefoucauld at the Roman Teatro Argentina on 15 July 1747, the occasion of the second marriage of Louis, Dauphin and son of Louis XV, with Marie-Josèphe de Saxe. The relabeling could be made by identifying the coat of arms suspended from the upper balcony on the right in the painting—see *Exposition Pannini*, ed. Michael Kiene, Exposition Dossier du Département de Peintures, 41 (Paris: Musée du Louvre, 1992), 33ff. The painting is reproduced here with permission of the Musée du Louvre.

The passages from the *Mercure de France* quoted on pages 162-64 have been translated based upon Geiringer's German reading of the original. The essay is reprinted with permission of Breitkopf & Härtel, Wiesbaden-Leipzig.

> *My next study again concerned a work of art. In the Paris museum of the Louvre I saw a painting showing a group of both instrumentalists and singers on a stage performing for an elegant audience in a magnificent theater. I found out that the canvas depicted a festivity in honor of Louis Charles, son of King Louis XVI, becoming Dauphin in 1789* [sic]. *A special theater was built for this performance in the courtyard of the Louvre* [sic]. *The famous Italian composer, Leonardo Vinci (not a relative of the painter), provided the music based on a text by Pietro Metastasio, the leading librettist of the time. The respected Italian painter G. P. Pannini recorded the memorable event on canvas. To my pleasant surprise I found that the wonderfully rich library of the Gesellschaft der Musikfreunde in Vienna owned a hand-written copy of the score. Thus I was enabled to write a study both on the painting and the composition.*—This I Remember, *44.*

The collection of paintings in the Louvre includes one piece by the Roman architectural painter Giovanni Paolo Pannini (Panini, 1695-1768)[1] that is extremely interesting from the perspective of music history [see figs. 13.1 and 13.2]. It shows the interior of a splendidly appointed Baroque theater; in its parterre and balconies a radiant audience of clerical and lay dignitaries is present. Many of these people follow the plot with the libretto in hand. However, the gaze of the observer is drawn primarily to the rich decoration of the stage, which takes up the middle of the painting. In a high portico adorned in wreaths and surrounding four actors seated in the center, a chorus and mass orchestra of the thorough-bass era rest on a throne of clouds. The important continuo instruments occupy the foreground in two groups arranged symmetrically on either side of the actors. Only the keyboards of the two harpsichords nearest the singers are visible, while their cases are concealed behind clouds. The harpsichordist on the right side is absorbed in his playing. Apparently he is realizing the figured-bass. The player on the other

---

[1] No. 1409.

Fig. 13.1. "Concert, donné à Rome le 27 novembre 1729 à l'occasion de la naissance du Dauphin, fils de Louis XV [= Fête musicale donnée sur les ordres du cardinal de La Rochefoucauld au théâtre Argentina de Rome le 15 juillet 1747 à l'occasion du second mariage de Louis, Dauphin de France et fils de Louis XV avec Marie-Josèphe de Saxe]" by Giovanni Paolo Pannini

Reprinted by permission of the Louvre

Fig. 13.2. Same, detail

Reprinted by permission of the Louvre

side strikes the keys only with his left hand while conducting the strings and winds, seated in a raised position behind him, with his right. Clearly he is leading the entire ensemble from the harpsichord. Behind the keyboard instruments the string basses have positioned themselves—on each side a cello and two contra-basses (is the instrument nearer to the center intended to be only a half-sized bass?). A pair of drums stands on each of the two flanks. The remaining orchestral instruments as well as the chorus occupy a graduated, slightly circular concave podium. The first row is reserved for the continuo instruments, the second, third, and fourth for the ornamental instruments. On the lowest level two bassoons provide the link on both outer sides to the leading continuo instruments. Adjacent to them and towards the middle are two woodwind instruments—probably oboi da caccia— which likely supported the bassoons in the upper octaves and thus played *unisono* with the violas next to them. The second and third levels are occupied by violins. In their midst the concertmaster stands in an elevated place; like the other string players, his glance is turned toward the conductor at the harpsichord. The highest level is reserved for the winds. At their flanks the trumpets stand in their traditional separation from the rest of the orchestra. Towards the middle from here are the horns. The oboes occupy the center and thus stand directly behind the violins. The chorus is positioned in the wings; women to the left, men to the right. Notated music is visible only in the hands of the male singers. The other musicians likely have their parts before them concealed behind clouds.

Hence the painting shows a rich ensemble of singers and instrumentalists, the likes of which were only seldom commemorated in images during the thorough-bass era, particularly in Italy. A comparison of this ensemble's display with the arrangement of other large orchestras of the time attests to the correctness of the painter's observation.[2] With such large ensembles it was usual for a specific continuo player to be employed alongside the harpsichord conductor. Around these two keyboardists the bass instruments would gather. The ornamental

---

[2] Cf. material in Georg Schünemann's *Geschichte des Dirigierens*, Kleine Handbücher der Musikgeschichte nach Gattungen, 10, ed. Hermann Kretschmar (Leipzig: Breitkopf & Härtel, 1913), 161ff.

instruments were led by a special violin conductor, who was subordinate to the harpsichord conductor. Finally, the instrumental groups that were often led in *unisono* and therefore belonged together, such as string bass and bassoon, violin and oboe, trumpet and horn, were when possible seated next to each other. We can discover all of these characteristics reflected in the Pannini painting.

Yet the painting also shows interesting deviations from the usual style of presentation. Above all, it is striking that the concertmaster is not standing in the immediate vicinity of the harpsichord conductor, as was otherwise the norm, but is rather at quite a distance from him. It is also unusual to support the bassoons with smaller woodwinds. Finally, the separation of the trumpets from the percussion, as well as the division of the chorus from the orchestra, are only seldom found. However, as the material available to us for comparison is quite limited, we are not at liberty to decide if these deviations in the arrangement of orchestra and chorus were typical for Italy at the time or if they only occurred in the performance commemorated by Pannini.

But what was the work whose rendering featured a chorus and an orchestra adorned with wreaths and seated in clouds on the stage of a theater, and what was the occasion for this glorious performance?

Pannini's painting bears the title "Concert performed in Rome on 27 November 1729, on the occasion of the birth of the French crown prince, the son of Louis XV."[3] It was commissioned by Cardinal de Polignac[4] together with two other Pannini paintings, "Visit by Cardinal de Polignac in St. Peter's in Rome" and "Preparations for a Festival in the Piazza Navona, on the Occasion of the Birth of the French Crown Prince," and came into the possession of the Louvre during the reign of the citizen-king Louis Philippe.[5]

A contemporary source, *Mercure de France*, published a report in its December 1729 issue about the celebrations in honor of the Dauphin's birth,[6] which, along with other material, contains valuable information about the performance represented in Pannini's painting. We present below an excerpt from this article, in which we find not only a portrayal of the musical performance that corresponds closely to Pannini's painting but also several interesting details that offer an image of the love of ostentation characteristic of the Roman Baroque:

> Report on the Celebrations in Rome Arranged by Cardinal de Polignac, the Royal Envoy to the Court of His Holiness the Pope, Benedict XIII.[7]
>
> After receiving by special messenger the joyous news of the birth of His Highness the Dauphin on September 13 of this year, the Cardinal de Polignac's first concern was to set out without further ceremony for the French National Church of St. Louis, to thank God for the precious gift with which He had delighted France and all of Europe, and thereafter to inform the Pope, the Holy See, the Ministers, and the entire Roman court of the Dauphin's birth.
>
> Driven by his zeal to obey the instructions given to him and to arrange a splendid celebration worthy of the great occasion, he decided to give a festival that the entire city could attend. For this reason he postponed all festivities until after St. Martin's Day, at which time the cardinals, prelates, and aristocracy would return from the country. This was all the more convenient for him, as he wished to arrange especially glorious festivities and thus needed several days for the preparations. . . .

---

[3] "Concert, donné à Rome le 27 novembre 1729 à l'occasion de la naissance du Dauphin, fils de Louis XV."

[4] Melchior de Polignac (1661-1741) was the most famous member of one of the oldest and most esteemed aristocratic families in France. He studied theology at the Sorbonne, but was also active as a politician. In 1693 he was named *ambassador extraordinaire* to Poland and entered into the treaty of Gertruydenberg with the Dutch in 1710, the treaty of Utrecht in 1712. In the same year he was named cardinal and soon thereafter "Maître de la chapelle de Roi" by Pope Clemens XI. From 1724 to 1730 he remained in Rome. Melchior de Polignac was an honorary member of the Académie des Sciences and was among the forty members of the Académie Française. He was also a great advocate and patron of the arts. As a passionate collector, he arranged important excavations in Rome, including one leading to the discovery of Marius's villa and Caesar's palace at the Palatine. His main literary work was the significant *Anti-Lucretius* (Paris: Coignard, 1747). Cf. Louis Moreri, *Le Grand Dictionnaire historique de l'histoire*, 10 vols. (Paris: Drouet, 1759), and *Biographie universelle ancienne et moderne*, 55 vols. (Paris: Michaud, 1811-62), Polignac entries.

[5] Cf. Seymour de Ricci, *Description raisonée des peintures du Louvre* (Paris: Impr. de l'Art, 1913).

[6] The French Crown Prince Louis was born on 4 September 1729 to King Louis XV and Marie Leszinskas of Poland. He was exceedingly pious and conservative and opposed his father's extravagant lifestyle. Louis XVI was a product of Louis XV's (second) marriage to Maria Josepha of Saxony. Crown Prince Louis died in 1765, nine years earlier than his father. Cf. Henri Carré, *Le Regne de Louis XV [1715-1774]* (Paris: n.p., 1909), 136ff.

[7] "Rejouissances faites à Rome, par la Cardinal de Polignac, Ministre du Roi auprès de N.S.P. le Pape Benoît XIII."

Following this passage is a description of the festive *Te Deum* held in the French National Church of St. Louis on 18 November 1729 in the presence of eighty-eight prelates and the entire Roman aristocracy:

> Since the cardinal knew that the Roman people loved plays above all else and would be delighted to see a blend of antique and modern beauty, he decided to hold two horse races with prizes, present a cantata in a court of his palace that was converted into a theater, and finally hold a great fireworks show on the Piazza Navona that would preserve the ancient majesty of the Roman circus through modern decoration.

A description of the first race, as well as the reception for the nineteen cardinals of the Holy See in the Palace of the Académie de France in Rome, follows:

> After the race all of the spectators proceeded to the cardinal's palace where the lighting gave a wonderful impression. The windows were adorned with torches of white wax, the mouldings with artfully distributed Chinese lanterns. . . .
>
> The court, with its admirable architecture and proportions, had been transformed into a magnificent theater with the help of numerous chandeliers, which illuminated it, and an abundance of tasteful ornaments.[8] The ground floor was decorated with artful embroideries and many sconces, each holding several candles. Crimson damask interwoven with flowers ornamented the second floor windows on the right and left sides. The coats of arms of the king, queen, and Dauphin were hung above. A canopy in the form of a crown with curtains carried by two gilded Amors covered those escutcheons. Each pilaster was covered in a fabric dyed the color of Lapis Lazuli and decorated with golden lilies and dolphins, and each was illuminated by a chandelier of twelve candles. The base of each pilaster held two torches of white wax. Gilded Corinthian capitals served as crowning glory. The mouldings rested upon a frieze of crimson velvet, trimmed with braid and interwoven with flowers. Beneath the mouldings were the pilasters of the third floor, the bases of which were concealed behind large vases with the coat of arms of His Eminence, which gave the effect of porcelain and held orange trees with transparent fruits. Small vases of the same material stood next to these with lights that diffused a gentle brightness. The pilasters on the third floor were covered in red velvet with golden fringes, and the windows were adorned as on the second floor.

To this we add the description of the theatrical area represented in Pannini's painting, which implies that the painter transformed a temporal succession into a spatial co-existence insofar as he represents the ongoing performance on the stage in one part of the audience while representing a moment of pause in the other part. Moreover, Pannini allowed himself the artistic license to heighten the visual continuity of his own painting, occasionally at the cost of a completely faithful rendering of reality.

> The front side of the court was taken up by a stage suspended by clouds, on which an orchestra of 130 players of the most various instruments was placed, all dressed as genies and wearing laurel wreaths on their heads as well as black belts and armbands adorned with precious stones. The six musicians representing Jupiter, Apollo, Mars, Astrea, Pace, and Fortuna were costumed just as legends describe these divinities and invested with the corresponding attributes, and all sat on clouds.[9] The five colonnades[10] presented lovely views to as many galleries, at the ends of which one saw the golden statues of the five greatest French kings from whom the Dauphin was directly descended: namely, Hugo Capet, Philipp August, St. Louis, Henry IV, and Louis the Great.
>
> Above the stage was hung the Dauphin's coat of arms covered by a canopy in the form of a great crown; its curtains portrayed a silver coat worn by two gilded Amors and strewn with gilded lilies and blue dolphins. Above the cloud-shrouded ceiling one could see a rising sun steer its chariot, which was pulled by four horses and surrounded by rays of light that spread a bright radiance.[11] These

---

[8] The details described in this paragraph are not visible in Pannini's painting.

[9] In Pannini's painting only Mars, Astrea, Jupiter, and Apollo appear (right to left).

[10] Evidently this refers to the colonnades that open up behind the orchestra in Pannini's painting, where pillars borne by caryatids stand at their entrances.

[11] Diverging from this description, Pannini moves the sun's chariot to the central arched passage.

rays seemed to reflect back from the light-bathed clouds and surround the Earth,[12] upon which the following words were legible in brilliant script: "In commune bonum. . . ."

The gallery directly across from the stage was occupied by the Holy See, the prelates, and the nobility.[13] This area was furnished with such taste that it can hardly be expressed in words. . . .

In addition to the candles mounted in front of the pilasters, a chandelier with twenty-four candles hung in the center of each arched passage. The radiance produced by this abundance of lights was overwhelming when combined with the glittering of the gemstones adorning the princesses and noble ladies seated at the upper and lower windows of the chamber. . . .

As soon as everything was in its place, the curtain concealing the decorations was opened and all applauded, offering praise to the lovely play. The symphony began, and the cantata was performed at its best. Between the first and second parts a variety of refreshments was distributed to all spectators in great quantity. . . .[14] Thus the day ended without disorder or accident, despite the multitude of people attending the festival. Nearly three thousand people occupied the parterre and anterooms alone. The precaution had been taken to station soldiers along the streets leading to the palace, which maintained order among the approaching carriages. The most beautiful houses in the city as well as several less prominent ones were illuminated for much of the evening.

A description follows of the second race, which took place on November 30, and the fireworks set off on that same evening. At the end of the article the reporter details the work performed at the festival:

The Italian cantata mentioned in this context is a very beautiful composition. It could just as easily bear a name other than that of cantata, for as a consequence of the new form that its author has given it, it belongs to the dramatic genre, while the usual cantatas are epic. That is, the story is not told by the author but rather performed by actors. It is our belief that, in bringing the content of this composition to the attention of our readers, we offer them great pleasure.

The report by *Mercure de France* now begins a long-winded account of the plot with many poetic examples, which we do not reproduce due to its verbosity. Rather, we turn to the synopsis, which is necessary for our further examination.

The figures in the composition are Jupiter, Mars, Apollo, Astrea, Pace, and Fortuna. The scene takes place on Mt. Olympus.

First Part: A quarrel has broken out among the gods, for they refuse to reach an agreement about who among them will be entrusted with the upbringing of the newborn Dauphin of France. Jupiter seeks to put the argument right and challenges the others to name the traits that would qualify them for the position for which they all strive. Each of the gods presents his merits. But Jupiter is unable to come to a decision, as he has the impression that all candidates are equally worthy. Now the gods break out into passionate threats, and all proclaim the misfortune they are determined to inflict upon the prince if denied this position. Jupiter is frightened and attempts to restore the peace by challenging the gods to explain how they wish to educate the prince. The second part presents the exposition of the five gods' plans for the prince's upbringing, which leads Jupiter to the conviction that none of the gods alone can sufficiently instruct the royal prince. They are all necessary for the prince's upbringing, and thus the gods are to make their home in France now in order to fulfill this great responsibility under the guidance of Jupiter.

In the report by the *Mercure de France*, the account of the plot ends with these words: "The poetry is by Abbé Pietro Metastasio, the music by Leonardo Vinci."

We find the cantata discussed in the report by *Mercure de France* in the works of Metastasio under the title *La Contesa de' Numi* (The Gods' Quarrel).[15] The subtitle reads:

Festa teatrale scritta dall'Autore in Roma / l'anno 1729 ad istanza del Cardinale / di Polignac, allora ivi ministro della / corte Cristianissima; e sontuosamente rap- / presentata la prima volta con musica

---

[12] The Earth is not visible in Pannini's painting.

[13] For Pannini, the religious dignitaries sit in the parterre.

[14] In Pannini's painting, as already indicated above, refreshments are distributed during the performance of the cantata.

[15] *Opere del Sigr. Abate Pietro Metastasio / Poeta Cesareo* (Venice: Carlo Palese, [1781]), 9:1.

del / Vinci nell'ornatissimo cortile del palaz- / zo di sua Eminenza, per festeggiare la nascita del Real Delfino di Francia.

The same text was set to music by Gluck to celebrate the birth of the subsequent King Christian VIII of Denmark (b. 29 January 1749). The first performance of this composition took place on 9 April 1749 in Charlottenburg Palace.[16] In 1787 Metastasio's libretto was set for the third time by Paisiello.[17]

The Vinci setting of the cantata has been handed down in two manuscript scores,[18] one of which is located in Naples, while the other is the property of the archive of the Gesellschaft der Musikfreunde in Vienna.[19]

To our dismay we could not use the Neapolitan manuscript for the purposes of this project. Yet we still expected to accomplish this project just as well, since the Viennese manuscript apparently represents a true copy of the original. In addition to the stylistic correspondence with other text settings by the master—particularly the subsequent opera *Artaserse* of 1732—this opinion finds support in the use of Metastasio's entire text, which matches precisely with the libretto reproduced in the poet's collected works as well as the use of all orchestral instruments portrayed in Pannini's painting. The title of the Viennese score

> La Contesa de Numi / Cantata a sei voci con tutti / Stromenti da Fiato / Cantata In occasione Della Nascita / Del Real Delfino / Musica del Sig. Leonardo Vinci / Poesia del Sig. Pietro Metastasio / L'Anno 17.0.[20]

also reinforces the suspicion that the manuscript of the Gesellschaft der Musikfreunde is an exact copy of Leonardo Vinci's original composition. Before we turn to the question of why this copy was prepared, the music of the work merits a brief description.

The cantata is written for six solo singers, a chorus, and orchestra. The role of the main character Jupiter as well as that of Apollo fall to male sopranos. Astrea and Fortuna are sung by female sopranos, Mars by a tenor, Pace by a contralto. The orchestra consists mainly of those instruments presented in Pannini's painting, most of which—basses, bassoons, violas, violins, oboes, horns, trumpets, and timpani—are also named specifically in the score. The use of harpsichord arises from a remark that appears twice: "senza cembalo."[21] Furthermore, two flutes and one "Salterio" are assigned in Fortuna's aria in the second part.[22] In combining these instruments with two horns and a string quintet in pizzicato,[23] this passage has a particularly charming effect coloristically. The instrument designated here as "Salterio" is written in the treble clef and is used to carry out passages entirely idiomatic for strings. Double stops and even one chord consisting of four pitches (!) are required of it. The range of the instrument used here is $c\sharp'$ to d'''. It is always deployed soloistically and only accompanied by plucked strings. Whether this "Salterio" is actually a psalterium, a plucked dulcimer, cannot be established with any certainty. At the same time it is questionable if Vinci's salterio is identical with the instrument of the same name written into the "Licenza" of Johann Georg Reutter's *Magnanimità di Alessandro* in the same year.[24] The technique of the salterio of

---

[16] Cf. Alfred Wotquenne, *Thematisches Verzeichnis der Werke von Chr. W. v. Gluck* (Leipzig: Breitkopf & Härtel, 1904), 36-38. The manuscript is located at the Staatsbibliothek zu Berlin, under the incorrect title "Tetide." Robert Eitner, *Biographisch-bibliographisches Quellen-Lexikon der Musiker und Musikgelehrten der christlichen Zeitrechnung bis zur Mitte des XIX. Jahrhunderts*, vol. 4 (Leipzig: Breitkopf & Härtel, 1901), 28, and Hugo Riemann, *Opernhandbuch* (Leipzig: Koch, 1887), 55, also know the work only under this designation.

[17] Cf. Riemann, 83. The manuscript is located in Naples—cf. Eitner, vol. 7 (1902), 288.

[18] Cf. Eitner, vol. 10 (1904), 96.

[19] Call no. VI, 27 703. The score consists of two half-parchment volumes in oblong format, 27 x 21 cm, which each contain one part of the cantata. The manuscript was written rather quickly and shows numerous inkstains and erasures. It is interesting that in a particularly unclear passage (Fortuna's aria, part 1), four notes of the first violin have been written over with the letters "g a h [=b] c."

[20] The note "L'Anno 17.0" was added by another hand in darker ink. The third numeral of the year is completely illegible.

[21] Vol. 2, p. 1, V, and vol. 2, p. 7, V. The score is paginated continuously in the scribe's hand with arabic numerals on every other eighth page. We have identified the intervening unpaginated eight pages with Roman numerals.

[22] Vol. 2, p. 7, V.

[23] The bass system contains the following instruction: "senza cembalo pizzicando senza fagotto."

[24] Score, Vienna, Österreichische Nationalbibliothek, Musiksammlung, no. 18015.

the *Magnanimità* does not correspond to that of Vinci's instrument. In Reutter the instrument is written not only in treble but also in bass clef and mainly used for arpeggiating triads within the large range of *D* to *e´´*.

The double arrangement of the cantata's text is also expressed in its musical construction. Each part is preceded by an instrumental introduction, while a chorus ends each part. The instrumental introduction to part 1 is a French overture consisting of a two-part Grave and a rushing Allegro. Vinci used the same Allegro as the first movement of the Italian overture to his aforementioned opera *Artaserse*.[25] A simple minuet with an alternative movement introduces part 2 of the cantata. In the grandly developed final choruses the text is presented first by the soloists and only later taken over by the full four-part chorus. The finale of part 1 is particularly appealing through its frequently-used and always clearly-prescribed echo effects.

Between the two powerful cornerstones of the introductory instrumental movement and the final chorus in each part are six great da capo arias, offering the six performers the opportunity for solo interpretation. Each of these arias is preceded by long secco-recitatives that intensify to accompagnato-recitatives at more important junctures in the text. The abstract, undramatic text, filled with figures of speech and generalities, offered the composer little inspiration for creating characteristic musical images. Yet Vinci makes the best possible use of the libretto's restricted possibilities, whether through musical representations of a situation or simply through individual word painting. Hence, in Apollo's aria in part 1 the words "per sempre" are powerfully portrayed through elongated half notes.[26] In Pace's first aria the string quartet and continuo are at first only accompanied by oboes.[27] Before the words "bellicoso acciar," however, trumpets and horns are inserted.[28] From the standpoint of color, it is interesting that when the same passage is repeated in the second vocal solo, solo bassoons take over the trumpet fanfare. The accompagnato-recitative that precedes Mars' aria in part 2 is full of ingenious constructions.[29] In a simple string arrangement, gentle sleep ("placidi sonni"):

Example 13.1a-d. Vinci, *La Contesa de Numi*, part 2, accompanied recitative, Mars.

the sound of trumpets ("tuono de'cavi bronzi"):

merry jests ("scherzi"):

and bellicose exercises ("battaglie"):

---

[25] Manuscript, Vienna, Österreichische Nationalbibliothek, Musiksammlung, no. 14513.

[26] Vol. 1, p. 13, V.

[27] Vol. 1, p. 14, IV.

[28] Vol. 1, p. 13, VI.

[29] Vol. 2, p. 1, VII.

are portrayed. In the central part of the subsequent aria, the portrayal of stupefaction ("et agghiacciar si sente") with a series of partly diminished sevenths is most effective:

Example 13.2. Vinci, *La Contesa de Numi*, part 2, aria, Mars.

This piece is the only one in the composition that, referring back to the text's word "timida," is in a minor key; its mysterious quality is intensified even more through the direction "sotto voce." In the aforementioned aria of Fortuna with salterio obligato, the silence at the word "chete" is conveyed through a grand pause. The second accompagnato-recitative of this part, in which Jupiter makes his judgment known, also offers several striking interpretations of the text.[30] In this number the tonal figure used to characterize Fortuna is truly lovely:

Example 13.3. Vinci, *La Contesa de Numi*, part 2, accompanied recitative, Jupiter.

Nor is the text lacking in appealing melodic ideas, for example the opening theme of Fortuna's aria in part 1:[31]

Example 13.4. Vinci, *La Contesa de Numi*, part 1, aria, Fortuna.

and the interesting, imitatively arranged beginning of Astrea's aria in part 2:[32]

Example 13.5. Vinci, *La Contesa de Numi*, part 2, aria, Astrea.

Now we turn to the final question of our inquiry: For what purpose was the manuscript score now in the hands of the Gesellschaft der Musikfreunde in Vienna prepared? The manuscript itself offers us exhaustive information with regard to this question.

We note first of all that the text entered by the copyist, which, as already mentioned, corresponds precisely to the libretto of the cantata printed in Metastasio's collected works, has undergone some belated changes. Under individual passages, other phrases are entered in ink a handwriting that deviates from the copyist's.

---

[30] Vol. 2, p. 16, VIII.

[31] Vol. 1, p. 23, VIII.

[32] Vol. 2, p. 11, VII.

With these corrections, however, individual words were lost by the corrector, so that a third hand has undertaken several further changes in pencil. The type of correction, given in the following examples, is self-explanatory:

    Ink corrections under: [changed to:]

Ink corrections under:	[changed to:]
Giglio (vol. 1, p. 6, I):	*fiore,*
Le Regie sponde (vol. 1, p. 6, I):	*Le nostre sponde,*
germoglio real (vol. 1, p. 10, V):	*germoglio gentil,*
Regio infante (vol. 1, p. 10, VII):	*Sangue illustre,*
Galliche sponde (vol. 1, p. 10, VII):	*Germane sponde,*
ai Franchi Regi (vol. 1, p. 13, VIII):	*e in questo luogo,*
La tua Gallia o Giove onori (vol. 1, p. 20, IV):	*La Germania o Giove onori,*
del Regnante Luigi (vol. 1, p. 21, IV):	*Dell'Eccelso Signore,*
al Gallico monarco (vol. 1, p. 23, IV and V):	*al Genitor del figlio,*
Monarchi (vol. 1, p. 11, III):	*L'Eroi,*
Regio (vol. 1, p. 11, III):	*Stato,*
Lodovico (vol. 2, p. 14, V and VI):	*Questembergh.*
Pencil corrections under:	
della Senna (vol. 1, p. 6, II):	*dal Danubio,*
guerriera (vol. 2, p. 21, VII):	*maniera.*

The given examples demonstrate the correctors' efforts to transform the direct references in Metastasio's text to France, the French court, and the French king, made necessary by the original occasion for the stage festival, into remarks that refer to a German royal whose homeland was located somewhere in the Danube region. The name of this nobleman is given explicitly. The "grande, giusto, e pio Lodovico" of whom Apollo speaks in a recitative in part 2 is rechristened as "Questembergh."

Nevertheless, some references to France and its rulers were perpetuated through both text revisions. Thus, "Gigli d'oro" and "Gallici coturni" (vol. 1, p. 10, VIII), "Cigni della Senna" (vol. 1, p. 11, I), "Gallica industria" (vol. 1, p. 14, I), "Degl' invitti Borboni" (vol. 1, p. 21, II), "i Regi figli" (vol. 1, p. 21, III), "Re" (vol. 2, p. 5, VII), and "la Gallica Reggia" (vol. 2, p. 20, III and IV) remain unchanged. These words were likely modified during performances by the singers themselves in the mode of the other text changes.

The insights gained from the added textual corrections are complemented by the cast of characters that play a role in the cantata. It is located on the end-paper of the score and reads:

Giove	Sopr.:	Sig[a]:	Johanna M
Marte	Teno:	Sig:	Mitscha
Astrea	Sop:	Sig:	Elisabet: H:
Pace	Contralto:	Sig:	Antoni K (?):
Apollo	Sopr:	Sig[ra]:	Johana M
Fortuna	Sopr:	Sig[ra]:	Elisab: H:

Alongside the following appears in faded pencil:

    Elisab: Hawlinen,
    Antoni Kratochwil,
    Elisabetha Hawlin.[33]

In the performance in question, therefore, the four soprano roles were played by only two singers.

---

[33] Under the name Elisabetha Hawlin are several other very blurred and illegible letters.

The name Mitscha is known through the research of Vladimir Helfert.[34] Franz Mitscha (1694-1744) was the self-described "Valet and Musical Director" to Count Johann Adam Questenberg.[35] As a tenor he regularly took part in Questenberg's opera performances. His master, Count Johann Adam Questenberg (1678-1752), the grandson of the imperial commissar made famous by Schiller's Wallenstein, was a particular friend and patron of the fine arts and contributed considerably to their advancement in Moravia.[36] Above all he loved music, which he also practiced himself.[37] In 1706-11 he supported an orchestra in his Viennese palace on the Johannesgasse. At the same time he had his sovereignty's old castle Jaroměřice, located near Olmütz in Moravia, rebuilt in Baroque style. With this opportunity a theater was also added to the castle, in which comedies and operas were performed regularly from 1722 on, although the reconstruction was completed only in 1737. According to documentary evidence Count Questenberg had been in close contact with Italy since 1728, particularly with Naples, Venice, Parma, and also Rome. He sent for new operas from Italy to be performed at Jaroměřice.[38]

Count Questenberg may also have obtained *Contesa de'Numi* from Italy and brought it to the stage in Jaroměřice or possibly also in Vienna. A comparison of the *dramatis personae* of the Viennese score of Vinci's cantata with that of a dramatic composition by Mitscha makes this nearly certain.

The Austrian National Library in Vienna owns the manuscript of a score:

> L'Origine di Jaromeriz in Moravia. Drama per musica Fatto produrre a perpetua memoria di detta città da Sua Eccelenza, il signor Giovanni Adamo Conte di Questemberg. La poesia e di Nicodemo Blinoni, [la] Musica é del Signor Franceso Mitscha Patrizio e Maestro di Capella di Jaromeritz. Anno XXX (1730).

Under the register of performers we find:

Guateno:	Francesco Mitscha	Tenore,
Fridengildo:	Antonio Kratochwil	Tenore,
Draomira:	Signora Hawlin	Soprano.

Thus, three of the performers named in the Viennese score of *Contesa de'Numi* also appear in a composition intended for Count Questenberg to extol the history of his Jaroměřice castle. Only Johanna M., who played the roles of Jupiter and Apollo in Vinci's cantata, is not named as one of the performers of the "musical drama." Yet she also may have been a singer in the count's musical organization, since at any rate she is identical with the soprano Marie Johanna Mitscha, Franz Mitscha's niece, born in 1715.[39]

The point in time at which the cantata *La Contesa de'Numi* was performed in the court of Count Questenberg can also be established with some certainty. The singer of Pace, the tenor Antonio Kratochwil, was active in the count's band from 1728 to 1738.[40] If one considers the generally short life of occasional compositions in the Baroque age and remembers furthermore that the year entered on the title page of the Viennese score reads 17.0 (the third digit is illegible, cf. above, p. 165, n. 20), it becomes clear that Vinci's cantata reached the stage at the court of Count Questenberg in 1730, one year after its premiere in Rome. The performance thus took place in the same year as that of the musical drama *L'origine di Jaromeriz*.

---

[34] Cf. *Hudební barok na ceskych zámcich* (Baroque music at Bohemian castles) (Prague: Czech Academy of Sciences, 1916), and "Zur Entwicklungsgeschichte der Sonatenform," *Archiv für Musikwissenschaft* 7 (1925): 117-40. As *Hudební barok* is out of print and unavailable to me, Prof. Helfert kindly provided me with written information about the relevant questions.

[35] On the title page of his cantata *Abgesungene Betrachtungen über etwelche Geheimnüssen des büttern Leyden und Sterbens Jesu Khristi 11/4 1727*. Vienna, Österreichische Nationalbibliothek, Musiksammlung, Ms. no. 18145.

[36] Cf. Constant von Wurzbach, *Biographisches Lexikon des Kaiserthums Österreich*, vol. 24 (Vienna: k. k. Hof- und Staatsdruckerei, 1872), 147-51.

[37] In the portrait by C. Heckenauer he is shown holding a lute.

[38] Statements about the reconstruction and the interest in music at the count's court are based upon written information provided by Prof. Helfert.

[39] According to written information from Prof. Helfert.

[40] Ibid.

The suspicion would therefore be close at hand that Metastasio's birthday cantata was also performed in the home of Count Questenberg in celebration of the birth of a son. However, the birth dates of Count Questenberg's children show this assumption to be invalid. Count Johann Adam Questenberg's only son Karl Adam was born in 1711 and died already in 1714. Besides his son, the count had three daughters born in 1712, 1715, and 1717. The performance of the cantata *La Contesa de'Numi* in 1730 therefore may not have taken place at any particular occasion. It speaks as much for the count's love for art as for his love of splendor that he sent for the work from Italy without a particular public purpose and as a cheerful matter of course, transferred the flattery intended for the king of France to his own person.

Let us summarize the results of our examination: Upon hearing the news of the French crown prince's birth, the son of Louis XV, the French envoy to the papal court, Cardinal Melchior de Polignac, put on a grand festival in November 1729 in Rome, in which a musical stage play dealing with the subject of the young prince's upbringing, came to be performed. Metastasio was entrusted with drafting the text, Leonardo Vinci with the musical composition. The performance took place in the palace court of the French legation, which was splendidly decorated for this purpose. Two representations of different types portray this celebration for posterity. The Cardinal de Polignac commissioned the Roman architectural painter G. P. Pannini to preserve the glorious image of the performance in a painting, and the French state newspaper, *Mercure de France*, offered a portrait of the Roman festivities and with this opportunity also a detailed summary of Metastasio's poetry. The festival performance itself also did not sink into oblivion after the event for which it was intended. In 1730 an Austrian count brought the work to the stage in his castle, and several decades later Metastasio's text was passed on to none other than Gluck and Paisiello to be set to music.

Gluck and Haydn

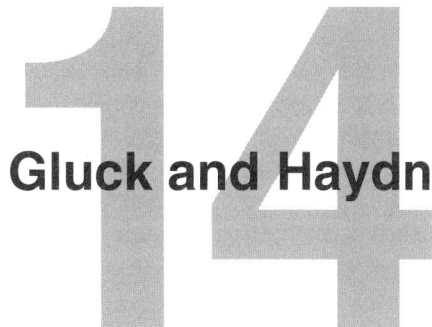

Originally published in German *Festschrift Otto Erich Deutsch zum 80. Geburtstag*, ed. Walter Gerstenberg, Jan LaRue, and Wolfgang Rehm (Kassel: Bärenreiter, 1963), 75-81. Reprinted with permission of Baerenreiter Music Corporation. Geiringer's familiarity with Haydn's operas led him early on to recognize the influence of Gluck on the Esterházy opera Kapellmeister (see the earlier essay 8 of 1939-40, p. 89). This recognition in turn led him quite naturally to explore Gluck further. The article below together with essays 15 and 16 are representative of his fine contribution to this area of eighteenth-century musical scholarship.

As a small contribution in honor of this well-deserved jubilee for musicological research on the eighteenth century, the following study attempts to sketch out in its essentials a relationship between artists of the time that has thus far garnered little attention. The resulting image is not free of internal contradictions, but rather becomes significant precisely through those contradictions.

It is not possible to establish with any certainty if Gluck and Haydn knew each other personally. At the start of the 1750s Gluck settled in Vienna and maintained his home in the city on the Danube, albeit with numerous interruptions, until his death. In the first years of his residence, as Dittersdorf reports in his autobiography, Gluck appeared frequently in the academies of Prince Joseph-Friedrich of Sachsen-Hildburghausen.[1] The young Haydn, who was at that time still in the service of Nicola Porpora, occasionally accompanied singers at the same concerts, and thus it is possible that Gluck met him at that time. Later, when Haydn himself had achieved fame, opportunities for a meeting between the two men arose time and again. When the Russian Grand Duke Paul and his wife, Maria Feodorovna, paid a visit to the Viennese court in 1781, for example, Gluck as well as Haydn contributed to the entertainment of those illustrious guests.[2] Also noteworthy is a report by Burney that during a visit in Gluck's home in Vienna in 1772, he heard quartets by Haydn performed by Starzer, Ordoñez, Count Brühl, and Weigl.[3]

There can thus be no doubt that Gluck was familiar with works by Haydn. It is also almost certain that the younger artist had heard compositions by the great opera dramatist. By 1790 more than twenty stage works by Gluck—including ballet, French and Italian opera—had been performed in Vienna,[4] and it is unimaginable that Haydn, who often came to Vienna and was actively interested in new music, would not have attended at least several of these performances. One strong indication of this can be found in the first movement of Haydn's Trio no. 5 for baryton [Hob. XI:5], written around 1765. It begins with the following melody:[5]

---

[1] *Karl Ditters von Dittersdorfs Lebensbeschreibung* (Leipzig: Breitkopf und Härtel, 1801; reprint, ed. Bruno Loets, Leipzig: Staackmann, 1940), 44.

[2] Cf. Carl Ferdinand Pohl, *Joseph Haydn*, 2 vols. (Leipzig: Breitkopf & Härtel, 1878-82), 1:175, and 2:183ff.

[3] Charles Burney, *The Present State of Music in Germany, the Netherlands, and United Provinces*, 2 vols. (London: Becket, Robson, and Robinson, 1773), 1:290.

[4] Alfred Loewenberg, *Annals of Opera 1597-1940* (Cambridge: W. Heffer & Sons, 1943), and Alfred Wotquenne, *Thematisches Verzeichnis der Werke von Chr. W. v. Gluck* (Leipzig: Breitkopf & Härtel, 1904).

[5] The work has been authenticated beyond a doubt by an autograph entry in Haydn's Draft Catalog (p. 7) and by the listing in the *Haydn-Verzeichnis* of 1805 (p. 7). It survives in a copy as a "Divertimento a due violini e basso" (G major) in the West German Library in Marburg (Mus. ms. 10 043).

Example 14.1. Haydn, Baryton Trio no. 5, movement 1, principal theme, meas. 1-6.

We know that after its Vienna premiere in 1762 Gluck's *Orfeo ed Euridice* was repeated several times. Haydn may well have visited one such performance with the prince and interwoven the immortal tones of "Che farò senza Euridice" into a new chamber music piece in order to remind his illustrious patron of their shared experience.[6] Yet Prince Esterházy's attitude seems later to have changed fundamentally. The comprehensive studies presented by Bartha, Somfai, and Harich on the opera performances at Esterháza demonstrate that, of the many Italian operas brought to the stage under Haydn's leadership in the palace, Gluck's operas are entirely absent.[7] Still, it is not justified to draw conclusions about Haydn's own attitude. We know that he held the greatest admiration for Mozart's operas.[8] Regardless, however, no performance of a Mozart opera took place at Esterháza, since the prince's taste was decisive for the choice of works to be rendered.

In any case, the conservative attitude of the Prince did not prevent his Kapellmeister from paying homage in his own compositions to the major musical and dramatic developments of the time, most strongly expressed in Gluck's works. An examination of Haydn's production for the stage shows that, with the exception of *Acide* [Hob. XXVIII:1], which emerged in the same year as Gluck's *Orfeo ed Euridice*, all serious operas by the master take Gluck's accomplishments into account in some sense. It is also worth emphasizing that three of these operas employ material that Gluck had already adapted earlier.

Moreover, Haydn wrote a comic opera that employs not only the same material, but even the same libretto. To be sure the conditions under which Gluck and Haydn began their compositions were so utterly different that the final products hardly resemble one another. Gluck's *La rencontre imprévue* was performed at the Viennese court in 1764. Eleven years later *L'incontro improvviso* [Hob. XXVIII:6], an Italian adaptation of the same libretto, which the singer Carl Friberth had acquired, came to the stage at Esterháza with Haydn's music.[9] In consideration of the unavoidable space limitations in the small palace theater, in the later work the number of singers is reduced and the text shortened. In a musical sense, however, the Haydn opera is written on a more generous scale than Gluck's composition. It employs carefully designed recitatives as well as arias with occasional coloraturas. On the other hand, the older work uses spoken dialogue and demonstrates a preference for simple folksong forms and syllabic declamation. Despite all of their approximations of German and Viennese contemporary tastes, Gluck's opera is essentially a French *opéra comique*, Haydn's an Italian *opera buffa*. Their textual relation only helps to illuminate the fundamental differences between the two works.

A different state of affairs presents itself with respect to the serious works of Haydn and Gluck that treat the same material. In August 1769 Gluck presented *Le feste d'Apollo*, consisting of a prologue and three one-act operas, at the court theater in Parma on the occasion of the Infante's engagement to an Austrian archduchess. The

---

[6] Similarly, in the first movement of the Trio no. 29 for baryton, a quote from the aria "Che visino delicato" can be found from Haydn's own opera *La canterina*. Cf. *Joseph Haydn: Thematisch-bibliographisches Werkverzeichnis*, comp. Anthony van Hoboken, vol. 1 (Mainz: Schott, 1957), 608.

[7] Dénes Bartha and László Somfai, *Haydn als Opernkapellmeister* (Budapest: Hungarian Academy of Sciences, 1960); János Hárich, *Esterházy-Musikgeschichte im Spiegel der zeitgenössischen Textbücher* (Eisenstadt: Burgenländisches Landesarchiv, 1959), and "Das Repertoire des Opernkapellmeisters Joseph Haydn in Esterháza (1780-1790)," *Haydn Yearbook* 1 (1962): 9-110.

[8] Cf., for example, Haydn's famous letter from December 1787 to the senior administrator of provisions in Prague, Franz Rott, first printed in Franz Xaver Niemetschek, *Leben des K. K. Kapellmeisters Wolfgang Gottlieb Mozart* (Prague: Herrlische Buchhandlung, 1798), 51f.; or see the charming letter of 9 February 1790 to Frau von Genziger, in which he describes how he dreamed of *Le nozze di Figaro*, first printed in Theodor von Karajan, *Joseph Haydn in London, 1791 und 1792* (Vienna: Gerolds, 1861), 66ff.

[9] Gluck's opera (better known under its German title *Die Pilgrime von Mekka*) was edited by Max Arend in the first volume of the original Gluck edition (Leipzig: Verlag der Gluckgesellschaft, 1910), likewise by Harold Heckmann in *Gluck, Sämtliche Werke*, part 4, vol. 7 (Kassel: Bärenreiter, [in progress]), while Haydn's work was published as *Unverhofftes Begegnen* by Helmut Schultz (Leipzig: Musikwissenschaftliches Verlag, 1939). Helmut Wirth has undertaken a thorough comparison of the two works in *Joseph Haydn als Dramatiker*, Kieler Beträge zur Musikwissenschaft, 7 (Wolfenbüttel: Kallmeyer, 1940), 47ff. See also Hans Joachim Moser, *Christoph Willibald Gluck* (Stuttgart: Cotta, 1940), 130ff.

first of these works bears the title *Atto di Bauci e Filemone*.[10] To commemorate the visit of the Empress Maria Theresa to Esterháza in 1773 Haydn composed a puppet opera, *Philemon und Baucis* [Hob. XXIXa:1, 1a], which was reworked several years later as a Singspiel, in which form it survives.[11] Gluck's composition requires three singers—two sopranos for the roles of the old couple and one tenor for that of Jupiter—as well as a chorus of shepherds and shepherdesses. In Haydn's work Jupiter is accompanied by Mercury, and the two gods are given speaking roles, while the humans are played by singers. Two sopranos and two tenors are engaged here, since in Haydn's work the intimate bond between Philemon's son Aret and his wife Narcissa is portrayed as counterpart to the enduring love between Philemon and Baucis. A chorus of peasants is also employed here. Haydn's overture, which is especially generously endowed with dynamic markings, bears a programmatic character much like the overtures of Gluck's reform operas. The first part portrays the majesty of the gods and their anger at human depravity, the second the idyll of the loving couples. The place of a finale is taken by the introductory chorus of the Singspiel in which the threatening character of the overture's beginning is rendered in the form of a thunderstorm, until the gods' anger is stilled through the intervention of the virtuous couples. The music of the entire Singspiel shows that Haydn's musical language at the beginning of the 1770s approaches Gluck's expressive world in its dignity and noble warmth.[12] This is apparent in Aret's aria no. 7 in G minor, in which he is awakened from death by Jupiter. With its chaste oboe solo, strings pizzicato and muted arpeggios of the second violin, the piece leads us into an atmosphere of dreamlike transfiguration in the spirit of Gluck. It is noteworthy that at the end of the Singspiel version of Haydn's work, elements of the ballet music to Gluck's *Paride ed Elena* are interwoven without a noticeable stylistic break. The recognition that an intellectual relation existed between the works of Haydn's *Sturm und Drang* period and Gluck's compositions has also led to a curious combination in a manuscript of the Regensburg library. Here, in the first movement of Haydn's Symphony no. 49 ("La Passione"), a gavotte from Gluck's *Paride ed Elena* is attached in the place of the coda—the same piece, incidentally, that was also incorporated in a somewhat different form into Haydn's *Philemon und Baucis*.[13]

Before we turn to the next opera, which also employs material used by Gluck, Haydn's *L'isola disabitata* [Hob. XXVIII:9] ought to be mentioned, a work that was performed in Esterháza in 1779. In this *azione teatrale*, a distinct inclination towards Gluck's ideals can be observed.[14] As in *Orfeo*, which bears the same subtitle, true conjugal love is tested by fate. The plot is limited to a minimum and is contested by only four figures. The overture prepares the way for the opera by appealing to the emotions; secco recitatives are entirely absent and are replaced by accompanied recitatives and ariosos. Moreover, Haydn strives to unite scenes and construct larger forms with the repetition of material motives.

While *L'isola disabitata* is regarded as something of a chamber opera—likely due to the destruction of the Esterháza palace theater by fire and the subsequent lack of an appropriate performance space—Haydn's reestablishment of a grand style is evident in *Armida* [Hob. XXVIII:12] of 1784, his most successful stage work. A comparison of the opera with Gluck's *Armide*[15] distinctly illuminates the dissimilarity and yet also the correspondence in the perspectives of the two artists. Gluck's work still uses Quinault's text, which Lully had already set to music; it portrays Armide as a demonic sorceress who transforms herself only slowly into a loving woman. Her powerful and passionate personality stands at the forefront of the work and places the feeble character of Rinaldo entirely in her shadow. The crucial change in the knight's attitude, the reawakening of a sense of duty, and the renunciation of sensual pleasure, is barely motivated and occurs at lightning speed towards the end of the opera. In Haydn's work the human element is more strongly emphasized and the opera takes on a more dualistic character in that

---

[10] The second is entitled *Atto d'Aristeo*, the third *Atto d'Orfeo* (a shorter version of *Orfeo ed Euridice*). A copy of the beautifully printed libretto, with four engravings, can be found at the Library of Congress in Washington, and a manuscript score in London (British Library, RCM 216).

[11] The manuscript score of the Singspiel is preserved at the Conservatoire National de Musique, Paris.

[12] Cf. H. C. Robbins Landon, *The Symphonies of Joseph Haydn* (London: Universal Edition, Rockliff, 1955), 276 and 315. Landon's claim that the Adagios in Haydn's symphonies of 1772 reflect the strong influence of Gluck's *Orfeo* and *Alceste* may, however, go a bit too far.

[13] Cf. Hoboken, 61. As is well known, Brahms adapted the same gavotte for piano.

[14] The opera was first published in a piano reduction by Welleminsky, Edition Moderna, 4 (Vienna: Nickau u. Welleminsky, 1909).

[15] Gluck's opera is accessible in various printed editions. The (incomplete) autograph of Haydn's *Armida* can be found at the Royal College of Music, London, while a fragment is in the Harvard University Library. (Copies of the score of this work, which was frequently staged in the eighteenth century, can be found in many libraries.)

the two lovers are given a roughly equal status. The change in Rinaldo's character appears more believable, and since he is introduced earlier in the drama, greater opportunity arises for the knight to prove his steadfastness in the face of Armida's seductive crafts. The magical forest, which contributed to Rinaldo's entrapment and to which Lully's and Gluck's versions refer only episodically, is lovingly portrayed by this Austrian composer, who was so inspired by his strong sense of nature. Haydn returns in *Armida* to secco recitative, and in his ensembles we notice a structure occasionally determined more musically than dramatically. Regardless, Haydn's *Armida* is permeated by the spirit of Gluck, both in its monumental simplicity and in its dispensation with unimportant details. The artistic relation also reveals itself again in the great scenes that Haydn constructs, in which he allows recitative, arioso, and aria to merge with one another, and particularly in the programmatic overture.[16] Haydn's prelude, which this author has discussed in detail elsewhere,[17] fits the famous words that we find in the foreword to Gluck's *Alceste*: "Ho imaginato che la Sinfonia debba prevenir gli spettatori dell'azione, che ha da rappresentarsi e formarne per dir così l'argomento."

Haydn's last opera, *L'anima del filosofo (Orfeo ed Euridice)* [Hob. XXVIII:13],[18] demonstrates anew the ambivalent attitude of the composer. Justifiably he wrote to Prince Esterházy from London that his libretto was completely different from Gluck's text.[19] The libretto, originally five acts but later condensed into four, begins previous to the marriage of Euridice and portrays the death of Orpheus after the second passing of his wife and even the fall of the Bacchantes who had offered him poison. In this work the overture does not really prepare the way for the subsequent drama, nor does it appear certain that it was originally intended for this opera at all.[20] The traditional Italian opera style makes itself evident in the coloratura-rich role of the "genio" and also in Euridice's arias. On the other hand, however, the chorus is given an unusual significance; sometimes it engages in the action, sometimes it offers commentary in the spirit of an antique chorus. It plays a role in every act of the work, and, save for secco recitatives, the last act consists almost exclusively of choral numbers. It seems almost as if Haydn wanted to compensate here for having to forgo this dramatic device in his earlier operas due to the limited space at Esterháza. Solo passages and choral numbers alternate with one another in free dramatic exchange, sometimes in almost rondo-like arrangements, creating episodes filled with powerful tragic expression. This includes the C-minor passage in the first act, where Euridice is warned by the chorus about a momentous step, or the sorrowful manner of the shadow that wanders the banks of the Lethe river at the beginning of the final act. In a sense Haydn's *Orfeo* follows the reform ideas of the time even more than Gluck's opera, since the opera ends tragically. In Haydn's work all of the figures perish, and even the ship carrying the dead body of the singer sinks into the waves during a storm, as if it were the twilight of the gods.

To summarize, it may be said that Haydn was by no means indifferent to the notions of reforming serious opera as expressed in Diderot, Algarotti, and Calzabigi, as well as partly in the compositions of Hasse, Jommelli, and Traetta. In particular, he certainly knew the operatic work of Gluck, in which the movement reached its climax. He followed the ideas of the reform faction repeatedly, yet lacked Gluck's combative spirit. Also, as a true Austrian, he felt less strongly attracted to a dramatic style that mirrored French aesthetic ideals in so many ways. Joy at new experimentation flowed in his blood, but, like many of his contemporaries, he was also readily willing to fall back upon traditional modes of expression. Strictly speaking, *opera seria* was not the focal point of his interest, and in his stage work he favored the mixed genre of the "dramma giocoso" or "dramma eroicomico."

In any case, it is noteworthy for the power of dramatic reform ideas in the eighteenth century that even a great artist who by nature faced these currents with a certain reserve would in no way shut himself off from their effects.

---

[16] Newly edited by Hans Gál (London: Augener, 1939).

[17] With Irene Geiringer, *Joseph Haydn* (Mainz: Schott, 1959), 242ff.

[18] The incomplete autograph of the work can be found in the West German Library in Marburg, a copy of the score, an important one as far as the sources are concerned, is in the Országos Széchényi Könyvtár, Budapest. A fragment consisting of eleven numbers appeared in 1805 as a score and piano reduction at Breitkopf and Härtel, Leipzig, under the title *Orfeo e Euridice*. In 1951 a recording of the work was produced by the Haydn Society, together with a booklet containing excellent studies by Helmut Wirth and H. C. Robbins Landon.

[19] Cf. Arisztid Valkó, "Haydn magyarországi müködése a levéltári akták tükrében" (Haydn's activities in Hungary as reflected in archival documents), in *Kodály Zoltán 75. születésnapjára*, ed. Bence Szabolcsi and Dénes Bartha, Zenetudományi tanulmányok, 6 (Budapest: Akadémiai Kiadó, 1957), 658.

[20] Cf. Hoboken, 279.

Concepts of the Enlightenment as Reflected in Gluck's Italian Reform Opera

Originally read as a paper at the Third International Congress on the Enlightenment held at Nancy in July 1971, and subsequently published in *Studies on Voltaire and the Eighteenth Century* (Voltaire Foundation, Oxford, U.K.) 88 (1972): 567-76. Reprinted with permission of the Voltaire Foundation, Ltd.

The age of reason witnessed a reassessment of all artistic forms, eminent theorists outlining the principles and goals of artistic expression. A favorite target of their criticism was the grand Italian opera which reigned supreme through large parts of Europe. Since the first tentative experiments in the field of dramatic music, made at the end of the sixteenth century, this form had developed in an unexpected way, quite divergent from the original concepts. Opera had been conceived as an attempt at reviving the ancient Greek drama. At this stage it was a restrained and dignified form in which the music was subservient to the text. However, in the course of the seventeenth century a decisive transformation took place. The musical composition, the overwhelming contributions of vocal virtuosos, of theatrical architects and engineers, more and more overshadowed the drama. The librettos became increasingly irrational and chaotic, interspersing tragic action wth comic episodes which lacked any connection with the main plot.

A reaction against these excesses came from various quarters. Early in the eighteenth century the Accademia degli Arcadi in Rome postulated a more rational and concise libretto. Similarly, Joseph Addison, exasperated by the lack of logic in contemporary opera, wrote in 1711 in the *Spectator* that an opera's "only design is to gratify the senses" and continued: "Nothing is capable of being well set to Musick that is not Nonsense." Particularly violent were the attacks made by a man who was a composer of Italian operas himself. His criticism was directed primarily against the autocracy of the singers and the abuses to which their tremendous powers led. As his pamphlet assumed the form of a bitter satire, it was particularly effective. Allow me to present to you a few tidbits from Benedetto Marcello's literary masterwork *Il teatro alla moda*, published in 1720. The author wrote it in the form of advice given to librettists, opera composers, and the personnel employed for the production of an opera.[1]

> The librettist should write the whole opera without any preconceived plan but rather proceed verse by verse. For if the audience never understands the plot their attentiveness to the very end of the opera will be insured. If the work should be such that certain characters have little to do or to sing he should immediately comply with the requests of these singers to add to their parts. He should always keep at hand a supply of a few hundred arias, in case alterations or additions should be wanted.
>
> The librettist might notice that the singers pronounce their words indistinctly, in which case he must not correct them. If the virtuosos should . . . enunciate clearly, the sale of the libretto might be seriously impaired. The librettist should pay frequent social calls to the prima donna since the success of the opera generally depends upon her. He should change his drama as her artistic genius may order him to do. . . . But he must be on guard not to reveal to her anything about the opera's plot—the modern virtuosa is not supposed to know anything about that.

---

[1] Cf. Reinhard G. Pauly, "Benedetto Marcello's Satire on Early 18th-Century Opera," *Musical Quarterly* 34 (1948): 222-33.

> The composer should speed up or slow down the tempo of the arias according to every whim of the singer and he should swallow all their impertinences, remembering that his own honor, esteem and future are at their mercy.
>
> The composer-conductor must see to it that the best arias are always given to the prima donna. In the event that some cuts in the opera become necessary these must never be made in her arias or ritornelli.
>
> To become a virtuoso a singer need not be able to read or write ... nor does he have to understand the text. He must be an expert, however, at disregarding sense and at mixing up letters and syllables in order to show off flashy passages and trills.... When addressed by another character or while the latter might have to sing an arietta, he should wave greetings to some masked lady-friend in one of the boxes or smile sweetly to someone in the orchestra.... In that way it will be made quite clear to the audience that he is Alipio Forconi, the famous singer, and not Prince Zoroaster whose part he is playing.
>
> When he reaches the repeat in the da capo aria he should change it completely in any way he pleases, regardless of whether or not these changes will go with the accompaniment of bass or violins and whether they will distort the tempo entirely.
>
> As soon as the virtuosa receives her part for a new opera she should send the arias to her voice teacher so that he can add for her the usual coloraturas, variations and embellishments. She should do this right away and not waste any time on having the accompaniment copied. Then maestro Crica can write underneath the voice part ... any embellishments he happens to think of ... , the more the merrier, though he does not have the faintest idea about the composer's intentions regarding the tempo of the arias or the accompaniment.

I believe these few excerpts will give you an idea of Marcello's rather poisonous wit.

At the time this pamphlet was written, attempts towards opera reform were already under way. They originated with two Italian poets, both of whom were connected with the Austrian capital. Apostolo Zeno (1668-1750) was court poet of Charles VI in Vienna. When the poet returned to his native city of Venice in 1729, Pietro Metastasio (1698-1782) became his successor and remained in Vienna for more than fifty years. These two men mitigated the coarseness of the Italian opera libretto, providing it, partly under the influence of the French drama, with a noble classicistic character. Metastasio's dramas were based on the conflict between passion and duty. Highly principled virtuous persons were opposed by ruthless villains. The well balanced form of his librettos conformed to the dictates of rationalism. He showed decided preference for the three-act opera with six characters and two pairs of lovers who had to overcome countless adversities of fate before they were eventually united. The texts consisted of dialogues, to be treated by the composer as recitatives, and da capo arias in which the singer expressed his feelings—often in the form of a parable—while the action came to a full stop. The number of arias allotted to each singer was strictly regulated, and ensemble numbers—even duets—were extremely rare.

This unnatural highly stylized form found greatest acclaim with composers. Some of Metastasio's librettos were set to music as often as seventy times, and not only Handel, Haydn, and Mozart, but even Beethoven and Schubert turned to Metastasio's texts. Critics, however, were still far from satisfied and kept raising their voices against the weaknesses of the opera. Their spiritual leader was Diderot, who was mainly concerned with the representation of truth in his dramas. When Rousseau complained in *La Nouvelle Héloïse* (II.xvii) that the actors' main concern was to shine, he must have entertained similar objections against the shortcoming of the Italian opera in which the display of virtuosity and brilliant technique seemed a main aim. The German theorists reacted in the same way. Johann Christoph Gottsched (1700-66) remarked: "Opera should strive more toward noble simplicity, than toward the shapeless excesses of the Italians"[2] and he went so far as to describe the opera of his time as "the most absurd thing human intelligence has ever invented."

Other German writers like Christian Gottfried Krause (1719-70) and Johann Anton Scheibe (1708-76) expressed themselves less aggressively, but they also advocated naturalness and simplicity in opera.

In 1755 the various criticism and attacks were summed up in a most telling way by Count Francesco Algarotti (1712-65). His critical masterpiece *Saggio sopra l'opera in musica* eloquently expounds the esthetic creed of the time.[3] Algarotti, looking back at the origin of opera in the sixteenth century, states it has meanwhile "fallen from

---

[2] *Bayträge zur critischen Historie der deutschen Sprache, Poesie und Beredsamkeit* (Leipzig: Breitkopf, 1734-35), 312.

[3] The work appeared anonymously in England in 1768, and this version is used for the following quotations.

heaven upon the earth" and pleads to revert once more to mythological characters rather than historical figures. "For who can be brought to think that the trillings of an air flow so justifiably from the mouth of a Julius Caesar or Cato as from the lips of Venus or Apollo?" As a true son of the era of Enlightenment he wants the poet to "rouse up and affect the hearts of an audience, without the risk of sinning against reason or common sense." Regarding the recitative he remarks "What a kindly warmth might be communicated to the recitative if, where a passion exerts itself, it were to be enforced by the united orchestra [instead of by harpsichord and basses only]. By so doing the heart and mind at once would be stormed, as it were, by all the powers of music." In his opinion the arias likewise require reform:

> [They are] now whelmed under and disfigured by crowded ornaments with which unnatural method the rage of novelty labors to embellish them. How tediously prolix are those [instrumental] *ritornelli* that precede them; nay, and are often superfluous! For can anything be more improbable than that, in an air expressive of wrath, an actor should calmly wait with his hand stuck in his sword-belt until the *ritornello* be over to give vent to a passion that is supposed to be boiling in his breast.

Another aspect of the arias also provokes his biting criticism:

> The repeating of words, and these chiming encounters that are made for the sake of sound merely and are devoid of meaning, prove intolerable to a judicious ear. Words are to be treated in no other manner, but according as the passion dictates; and when the sense of an air is finished, the first part of it ought never to be sung over again, which is . . . quite repugnant to the natural process of our speech and passions, that are not accustomed to thus turn about and recoil upon themselves.

The principles laid down in Algarotti's impassioned discourse were presently to be applied to the ballets and operas of Christoph Willibald Gluck (1714-87). The composer's "opera reform," as it is commonly called, originated once more in the imperial capital. Nevertheless it would be wrong to consider Vienna as particularly progressive in artistic matters. The important advances achieved in this case resulted from the collaboration of four energetic and inspired men. Count Giacomo Durazzo (1717-94), general director of the imperial theaters, provided unfailing understanding and support for the new ideas; Raniero Calzabigi (1714-95), a follower of Rousseau and the Encyclopedists, served as the librettist and theoretician of the movement; Gasparo Angiolini (1731-1803), imperial ballet master, took care of the dance scenes until he left for St. Petersburg in 1766; his place as helper in the composer's later operas was taken by Georges Noverre (1727-1810), author of the highly successful *Lettres sur la danse et sur les ballets* (1760). The group's natural leader was Gluck himself, a man of unflagging energy and resourcefulness, whose genius provided ever new inspiration.

Although the two dancing-masters had their disagreements about certain points, both were convinced that the traditional ballet had to undergo decisive changes. *Danza pura* should be replaced by *danza parlante*, or pantomime; "beautiful simplicity" and "imitation of nature" should be the goal. As Noverre remarked: "Il est honteux que la Danse renonce à l'empire qu'elle peut avoir sur l'âme et qu'elle ne s'attache qu'à plaire aux yeux." The first result of the reformatory efforts was the ballet *Don Juan* of 1761, for which Angiolini wrote the scenario and Gluck composed the music. It is a true masterwork which, incidentally, made a profound impression on Mozart. In the typical enlightened manner a preface appeared in the score[4] which explained that in this ballet the ancient pantomime was brought to life again, and added: "The music is an essential part of the pantomime: it speaks, we make gestures like the old players of Tragedy and Comedy, who confined themselves to dumb show while others recited the verses."[5] In this work a real unity between choreography and music was achieved. Especially notable was the tremendous final number, the dance of the furies.

Four years later Angiolini and Gluck collaborated in another ballet, *Semiramide*, based on Voltaire's tragedy. Here again they adopted progressive ideas by presenting a shattering dramatic story as ballet, and Angiolini contributed, in traditional manner, a *Dissertation sur les ballets pantomimes des anciens . . . pour servir de programme au ballet pantomime tragique de Semiramide*.[6] In between, Gluck had also carried out a most significant reform

---

[4] Christoph Willibald Gluck, *Sämtliche Werke*, sec. 2, vol. 1, ed. Richard Engländer (Kassel: Bärenreiter, 1966), foreword, xxiv-xxvii.

[5] Cf. Martin Cooper, *Gluck* (London: Chatto & Windus, 1935), 82.

[6] Copy of the print in the New York Public Library, Collection Cia Fornaroli. Facsimile, ed. Walter Toscanini (Milan: Dalle Nogare e Armetti, 1956).

in an opera. His *Orfeo ed Euridice* was presented in Vienna on 5 October 1762, a date that constitutes a milestone in the history of opera. Here, as Calzabigi, the author of the libretto, put it,[7] "all the Gothic barbarous and extravagant things that had been introduced into our music" were banished.

It is characteristic that Calzabigi's libretto—unlike the dramas of Metastasio—was specifically written for Gluck, and, with a single exception,[8] never set to music afterwards. The subject of *Orfeo ed Euridice* may have been chosen to point to the inner relationship between this new beginning and the earliest operas written on the same topic by Peri, Caccini, and Monteverdi more than 150 years earlier. As Algarotti had demanded it, Calzabigi and Gluck treat a mythological plot instead of a historical subject with its web of intrigues. Their opera uses only three solo singers and presents a simple, concise action of deep human interest. The *recitativo secco* with harpsichord and bass is replaced by the *recitativo accompagnato* imbued with dramatic power and exhibiting profound psychological insight. Coloratura arias in da capo form and virtuoso display are avoided, but chorus and ballet are meaningfully used; combined with solo numbers they are presented in large blocks of scenes. What a difference from the monotonous sequence of recitatives and arias in the traditional Italian opera! In Gluck's noble and stirring work the ideas of forward-looking theorists and artists had come to a magnificent fruition.

Gluck continued along similar lines. On 16 December 1767 Vienna witnessed the premiere of his *Alceste, dramma per musica*, again with a libretto by Calzabigi, while this time the choreography was entrusted to Noverre. The score of the opera, which is stylistically closely related to *Orfeo ed Euridice*, contains in its dedicatory preface, addressed to the grand duke of Tuscany, the manifesto (written by Calzabigi, but signed by Gluck) which clearly delineates the two men's artistic aims. I am going to read to you a sizeable portion of this preface as it is, once more, a true document of the spirit of the time.

> When I undertook to write the music for *Alceste,* I resolved to divest it entirely of all those abuses, introduced into it either by the mistaken vanity of singers or by the too great complaisance of composers, which have so long disfigured Italian opera and made of the most splendid and most beautiful of spectacles the most ridiculous and wearisome. I have striven to restrict music to its true office of serving poetry by means of expression and by following the situations of the story, without interrupting the action or stifling it with a useless superfluity of ornaments; and I believed that it should do this in the same way as telling colors affect a correct and well-ordered drawing, by a well-assorted contrast of light and shade, which serves to animate the figures without altering their contours. Thus I did not wish to arrest an actor in the greatest heat of dialogue in order to wait for a tiresome *ritornello*, nor to hold him up in the middle of a word on a vowel favorable to his voice, nor to make display of the agility of his fine voice in some long-drawn passage, nor to wait while the orchestra gives him time to recover his breath for a cadenza. I did not think it my duty to pass quickly over the second section of an aria of which the words are perhaps the most impassioned and important, in order to repeat regularly four times over those of the first part, and to finish the aria where its sense may perhaps not end for the convenience of the singer who wishes to show that he can capriciously vary a passage in a number of guises; in short, I have sought to abolish all the abuses against which good sense and reason have long cried out in vain.
>
> I have felt that the overture ought to apprise the spectators of the nature of the action that is to be represented and to form, so to speak, its argument; that the concerted instruments should be introduced in proportion to the interest and the intensity of the words, and not leave that sharp contrast between the aria and the recitative in the dialogue, so as not to break a period unreasonably nor wantonly disturb the force and heat of the action.
>
> Furthermore, I believed that my greatest labor should be devoted to seeking a beautiful simplicity, and I have avoided making displays of difficulty at the expense of clearness. . . .
>
> Such are my principles. By good fortune my designs were wonderfully furthered by the libretto, in which the celebrated author, devising a new dramatic scheme, had substituted for florid descriptions, unnatural paragons and sententious, cold morality, heartfelt language, strong passions, interesting situations and an endlessly varied spectacle. . . . It [is] clearly evident that simplicity, truth and naturalness are the great principles of beauty in all artistic manifestations.[9]

---

[7] Cf. his letter to the *Mercure de France*, 25 June 1784.

[8] Fernando Giuseppe Bertoni's *Orfeo* of 1776.

[9] Translation by Eric Blom in Alfred Einstein, *Gluck*, 2nd ed. (London: Dent, 1964), 98-99.

Persuasive though these ideas seem to the modern reader, it may be doubted whether they achieved in Gluck's time the full result the composer had anticipated. Applause for the new operas was by no means unanimous. It is true that the Austrian empress presented Gluck after the third performance of *Orfeo* with a snuffbox filled with ducats. But to others the new works seemed too strange, too different from the customary fare. There may have been many Viennese who shared Metastasio's opinion that Gluck was *pazzo* (crazy).[10]

The composer himself was keenly aware of the situation. When he offered, in 1770, his third opera in the new style, *Paride ed Elena*, using again a book by Calzabigi, he felt it necessary to refer in the dedicatory preface to the attacks his works had suffered. He attempted to clear up some misunderstandings and once more to explain his principles. The following statement again emphasizes the close relation between music and text: "In attempting truthful expression one has to adjust the artistic means employed to the nature of the subject. The most beautiful melodies and harmonies turn into faults and flaws if they are used in the wrong place."[11]

However, *Paride ed Elena* was again a disappointment for the composer. It appealed less to the operatic audience than *Orfeo* or *Alceste*. Thereupon Gluck gave up the struggle and decided henceforth to forego composing Italian operas. France, the home of enlightened thinking, a country where, moreover, stylistic concepts in the field of opera were more closely related to his own artistic ideals, exercised a strong attraction upon him. Thus a new chapter in his life and work started, a chapter that need not concern us here as Gluck was no longer striving for reform of the Italian opera.

---

[10] In the foreword quoted above Gluck indicated that his work met with "universal approbation" in the "enlightened city" of Florence. This may have been intended as a compliment to the grand duke of Tuscany, rather than as a statement of fact.

[11] Cf. *Sämtliche Werke*, sec. 1, vol. 4, ed. Rudolph Gerber, foreword, xiii.

Gluck's *Telemaco*

Originally published in German as the foreword to Geiringer's edition of Christoph Willibald Gluck, *Sämtliche Werke*, sec. 1, vol. 2: *Telemaco* (Kassel: Bärenreiter, 1972), vi-xi, henceforth given as NA. Reprinted by permission. An abridged version in English was read as a paper entitled "Gluck's Treasure Chest: The Opera *Telemaco*" at the thirty-fifth annual meeting of the American Musicological Society, St. Louis, Missouri, 27-29 December 1969. Geiringer's introduction goes well beyond a mere recounting of the circumstances leading to the work's first performance and its eighteenth- and nineteenth-century reception history, to dispelling widely held views concerning the intended finale and previously existing forms of the opera, and evolves ultimately into a penetrating study of Gluck's compositional processes. The quotations from the *Supplément à la Gazette de Vienne* and Berlioz's critiques in the *Gazette musicale de Paris* have been translated from the French by Peter Moscatelli.

> In Budapest I also met Professor Rudolf Gerber, who had recently started the publication of a collected edition of Gluck's compositions. I told him that Guido Adler long ago had asked me to edit in the Österreichische Denkmäler Gluck's opera Telemaco, written for Vienna, but that somehow this plan had never materialized. Gerber was interested, and we agreed to keep the matter alive, which later led to very interesting work for me. . . . In . . . 1972 Gluck's opera Telemaco also appeared in print as a part of the Gluck collected edition. The work on the Gluck opera had been particularly difficult. No less than ten different manuscripts had to be consulted. They were mostly from the eighteenth century, but all of them deviated in details from one another. Only eight pages of the score in Gluck's own hand have survived; thus there was comparatively little secure evidence. In editing a score which, in printed form, filled 370 large pages, I had again and again to make difficult choices between versions of certain passages. I can only hope that I did not err too often in my attempt to reconstruct Gluck's masterwork.—This I Remember, 130-31, 158.

The opera *Il Telemaco / o sia / L'isola di Circe* belongs to the group of works that Gluck composed while in the service of the imperial house of Habsburg in Vienna. He had already written the serenade *Tetide* for the first wedding of the crown prince, later Emperor Joseph II, in 1760. When Joseph's young wife, Isabella of Parma, succumbed to smallpox only three years later, the widower felt compelled to remarry and chose Princess Maria Josepha of Bavaria. Gluck, who shortly before (at the end of March 1764) had successfully presented a new coloratura aria for Joseph's coronation in Frankfurt,[1] was now commissioned to deliver no less than three new works for the wedding celebration. On 24 January 1765 at Schönbrunn Palace, the immediate family of the imperial house heard his minor festival piece *Il Parnaso confuso*, which was sung by the four Archduchesses Amalia, Elisabeth, Josepha, and Charlotte, while Archduke Leopold conducted from the harpischord.[2] On January 30 his

---

[1] This was later adopted into the Paris version of *Orfeo*. Cf. Christoph Willibald Gluck, *Sämtliche Werke*, sec. 1, vol. 6: *Orphée et Euridice*, Paris version of 1774, ed. Ludwig Finscher (Kassel: Bärenreiter, 1967), foreword, viii f. and xviii f.

[2] References to these events can be found in the diary of Prince Johann Josef Khevenhüller-Metsch, *Aus der Zeit Maria Theresia*, ed. Rudolf Graf Khevenhüller-Metsch and Hanns Schlittler, vols. 1764-67 (Vienna: Holzhauser; Leipzig and Berlin: Engelmann, 1917), 78, as well as in *Wienerisches Diarium*, no. 9 (30 January 1765). Details of the production and performance of this *festa teatrale*, written by Metastasio, can be found in Gluck, *Sämtliche Werke*, sec. 3, vol. 25: *Il Parnaso confuso*, ed. Bernd Baselt (Kassel: Bärenreiter, 1970).

new opera *Telemaco* resounded in the Burgtheater, and on the following day his ballet *Semiramis* was presented.[3] A repeat performance of *Telemaco* took place on 2 February 1765.[4] There is no mention of other performances of *Telemaco* in the reports of the time. Moreover, only very few remarks about Gluck's new opera can be found in the diaries and newspapers of the time. Prince Khevenhüller-Metsch writes:

> Abends gienge mann in mezzo publico zur neuen Opera: *Telemaco* genant, della compositione del signore Coltellini, colla musica del cavaliere Gluck—ohne neuen Ballet, so die Spectateurs nicht wenig choquiret hat.[5]

The report by the *Gazette de Vienne* takes a friendlier tone:

> Les paroles de cet Opera sont de Mr. Coltellini déjà connu avantageuesement par d'autres ouvrages Dramatiques. Le Chevalier Gluck en a fait la musique; ele a été trouvée très savante & ne dement point la juste reputation que ce compositeur s'est acquise.[6]

On the other hand, Count Zinzendorf reports in his diary only that he attended the opera on January 30 but does not once mention the title of the new work.[7]

Regardless of what the reception of *Telemaco* may have been, however, it is certain that a group of artists were enlisted who seemed to guarantee a rendering of high quality.[8] Gaetano Guadagni (1725-92)[9] sang the role of Telemaco, and surely Gluck had the particular artistry of this important singer in mind when conceiving the castrato part. The composer's high regard for Guadagni is also evident in that Gluck entrusted him with the role of Orfeo in the Viennese première in 1762 and had him perform the newly composed aria at the coronation in Frankfurt. The singer was also an outstanding performer, having studied with the great actor David Garrick. Charles Burney, who reports extensively on the artist in his *General History of Music*, was particularly impressed by Guadagni's appearance:

> His figure was uncommonly elegant and noble; his countenance replete with beauty, intelligence, and dignity; and his attitude and gestures were so full of grace and propriety that they would have been excellent studies for a statuary.[10]

As Burney relates, Guadagni refused to take a bow at the end of an aria or even to repeat it, an attitude that was often perceived by listeners as animosity.[11] What must have pleased Gluck especially was Guadagni's avoidance of all ornamentations and additions in his part;[12] his primary aim was to be in full and complete accordance with the composer's intentions.

---

[3] Cf. the new edition in Gluck, *Sämtliche Werke*, sec. 2, vol. 1: *Don Juan, Semiramis*, ed. Richard Engländer (Kassel: Bärenreiter, 1966).

[4] Cf. *Supplément à la Gazette de Vienne*, no. 11 (6 February 1765).

[5] Khevenhüller-Metsch, 80.

[6] Cf. *Supplément*, no. 11 (6 February 1765).

[7] Vienna, Haus-, Hof- und Staatsarchiv. The Count mentions that he tried to meet a nobleman there and continues: "Je le suivi a l'opera et allors au Parterre. . . ."

[8] In a letter to Prince Kaunitz from 6 March 1767, however, Ranieri de Calzabigi wrote disparagingly of Guadagni's performance and that of the two female leads in *Telemaco*. Cf. Vladimír Helfert in *Musikologie* 1 (1938): 114-22, and Hans Hammelmann and Michael Rose, "New Light on Calzabigi and Gluck," *Musical Times* 110 (1969): 609-11. Yet his spiteful remarks are hardly to be taken seriously, as Calzabigi is attempting in the letter to praise not only himself but also his pupil Coltellini and naturally Gluck, and thus feels obligated to place the blame for the minimal success of *Telemaco* with the singers. Characteristic of Calzabigi in this context is that in two consecutive sentences he praises Guadagni as Orfeo, and then dismisses his performance as Telemaco with an insult (he calls him "un birbante").

[9] Cf. the article by Hans Kühner "Guadagni, Gaetano," *MGG*, 5 (1956), cols. 991-93.

[10] *A General History of Music*, 4 vols. (1776-89); ed. Frank Mercer, 2 vols. (New York: Dover, 1957), 2:876.

[11] Ibid., 877.

[12] This is also evident in an edition by Domenico Corri, *A Select Collection of the Most Admired Songs* (Edinburgh, 1788; [reprint, New York: Garland, 1993]), which reproduces pieces sung by Guadagni in *Orfeo* with notably few ornamentations. Cf. Daniel Heartz, "From Garrick to Gluck: The Reform of Theatre and Opera in the Mid-18th Century," *Proceedings of the Royal Musical Association* 94 (1967-68): 124.

The part of Ulysses was likewise entrusted to an outstanding artist, the tenor Giuseppe Luigi Tibaldi (1729-after 1790?), who so satisfied Gluck that the master conferred upon him the role of Admet in the première of *Alceste* in 1767.[13] He often performed with his wife Rosa Tartaglini, who took on the role of Asteria in the performance of *Telemaco*. The crucial part of Circe was sung by the only Austrian woman in the ensemble, Elisabeth Teyber (1744-1816), who as a pupil of Johann Adolf Hasse and Vittoria Tesi-Tramontini was fully acquainted with the Italian style of opera and was beginning a successful artistic career.

That the performance reached a high level is evident in the finale remarks of the *Gazette de Vienne*:

> Les Ballets liés à la piéce sont du Sr. Gaspar Angiolini et ont fort bien rendu les differentes situations qu'ils devoient exprimer. Les Decorations sont des Srs. Quaglio père et fils. On les a trouvé très bien entenduës & enfin le Sr. George Speck a mis dans les habits toute l'elegance et toute la magnificence qu'on pouvoit s'en promettre.[14]

The Telemaco theme enjoyed a certain popularity in the eighteenth century. Since the publication of the novel *Les Aventures de Télémaque* by François de Salignac de la Mothe Fénelon in 1694, opera librettists had recognized a suitable topic in the experiences of Odysseus' son. To be sure, Fénelon himself had not expected this turn of events. With his work he had pursued a didactic aim; it was his aspiration to teach his royal pupil, the Duke of Burgundy and grandson of Louis XIV, the fundamental features of a wise government in an easily accessible way. However, the French court saw the work as a *roman à clef* in which a whole series of prominent personalities and even the king himself were portrayed in unflattering terms. The novel was banned and the author was denied entrance to the royal court. Outside of France, Fénelon's work was seen as an engaging adventure story, with a relation to the French royal house that was quite *risqué*. Readers felt compassion for noble Telemachus, who is exposed to all kinds of temptations during his search for his long-absent father (beginning with the wooing of the nymph Calypso, who had of course also already held Odysseus under her spell), endures them heroically, and finally, after much wandering-about, meets his father. In this tale was real operatic material, even more so in that the introduction of the magically-gifted Calypso permitted the possibility, so popular at that time, of bringing fantastic events to the stage.

Already in 1706 the German Georg Caspar Schürmann (1672 or 73-1751) staged an opera entitled *Telemaque* in Naumburg.[15] In 171 he revised the work for a repeat performance in Braunschweig and gave it the title *Telemachus und Calypso*. In London Johann Ernst Galliard (ca. 1680-1749) set a libretto by J. Hughes to music with the title *Calypso and Telemachus* for the Queen's Theatre in 1712. In 1718 the opera *Telemaco* by Alessandro Scarlatti (1660-1725), with libretto by Carlo Sigismondo Capeci, resounded in Rome. Gluck followed in 1765, using a text by Marco Coltellini (ca. 1740-75), a pupil of Calzabigi and the poet's successor at the Viennese imperial court.[16] After Gluck, still more operas based on the Telemaco material have been identified. In 1795 Franz Anton Hoffmeister (1754-1812) set a libretto by Emanuel Schikaneder with the title *Der Königssohn aus Ithaka*, a work that after multiple revisions remained for many years in the repertory of various theaters. In 1796 Jean François Le Sueur (1760-1837)[17] composed a text by Dercy, *Télémaque dans l'ile de Calypso*, and François-Adrien Boieldieu (1775-1834) used the same libretto for the opera *Télémaque*, which was performed in St. Petersburg in 1807. Capeci's libretto was also set to music again. In 1797 it served the Spanish guitarist Ferdinand Sor (1778-1839) as a basis for his opera *Telemaco nella Isola di Calipso*.

---

[13] Calzabigi engaged him again in 1778 for a repeat performance of *Alceste* in Bologna. Cf. the article by Pierluigi Petrobelli, "Tibaldi, Giuseppe Luigi," *MGG*, 13 (1966), col. 384.

[14] *Supplément*, no. 11 (6 February 1765).

[15] To this and subsequent enumerations of settings of the Telemaco material, cf. Alfred Loewenberg, *Annals of Opera 1597-1940*, 2nd ed., ed. Frank Walker (Geneva: Societas Bibliographica, 1966), 117, 126, 520, 534, 599.

[16] Already in 1763 a libretto written by Coltellini (*Ifigenia in Tauride*, with music by Traetta) was performed in the imperial palace at Schönbrunn; cf. Loewenberg, 272. In the letter to Prince Kaunitz mentioned above, Calzabigi accords a place of honor among the reform operas to this Coltellini-Traetta version of *Ifigenia*.

[17] Cf. the article by Georges Favre "Le Sueur, Jean-François," *MGG*, 8 (1960), cols. 570-72.

A brief synopsis of Coltellini's text is found at the beginning of the Italian-German libretto printed for the première (cf. facsimile, fig. on opposite page). Far more extensive is the summary of the French plot, given in the already-cited, valuable report in the *Supplément à la Gazette de Vienne* and presented here in excerpted form:[18]

> At the opening of the scene the stage shows a temple devoted to Amor [Love]. Circe, Asteria, and Telemachus, along with a choir of nymphs and shepherds, plead for the intercession of this deity, and are begging him to descend among them. His image shines with a fresh gleam, and an oracle announces to Circe that Love disdains tyranny: that she must not expect any sympathy at all. . . . Telemachus and Asteria urge her on his part to take her leave, and on her part to clear up the mystery of her birth, which she alone knows. Circe promises them that they will both be satisfied. . . .
>
> Telemachus and Asteria remain alone, the son of Ulysses asking him just which lover it is for whom Circe weeps; she informs him that a vessel had been driven to their shore by shipwreck about seven years ago, that it was carrying warriors, that Circe was inflamed with passion for one of them and that a strict prohibition of the sorceress had prevented them from doing any more about it. . . . At these words Telemachus suspected that this warrior could be Ulysses. . . .
>
> Merion arrives hurriedly and tells them to flee these surroundings, where there is nothing but dread and horror. "I used to be," he added, "alone and pensive in a wood where the ancient trees inspired something like fear; in my distraction I broke off a branch from one of those trees; I saw living blood spurt out of it and I suddenly heard a pitiful voice: "Why tear me so cruelly? Let me use up in peace the sad remains of an unhappy life. . . . This forest hides the mortal conquerors of Troy, and might also enclose the wise Ulysses."
>
> Telemachus urges his friend to lead him towards this terrible forest. . . . He leaves with Merion; the sad Asteria laments her troubles and recalls with feeling the moment when she had gathered Telemachus onto the shore, pale and dying. "Alas," she says, "I saw him and I loved him. . . ."
>
> The stage next shows the forest that had been talked about. Ulysses appears there first with Circe; she is asking him why she finds him in this abode of horror, and she reproaches him with misuse of his gifts. "What I owe you," he tells her, ". . . You flatter me and deceive me every day. Here are your deserts." Circe promises him that he will be satisfied on that very day; she swears to him on the Styx and asks nothing of him but a few moments. . . .
>
> Ulysses follows her in the interior of the forest. Telemachus arrives meanwhile with Merion; the invisible companions of Ulysses address these words to him: "Misfortunate one, flee far from this forest; it is the abode of death and of pain." Telemachus asks them where his father is, and he finds out from them that he too has lost his life and his liberty. Overcome by this blow, he stays motionless and Merion urges him in vain to leave these sad precincts. . . .
>
> Circe drops in with Ulysses. Telemachus flies into his arms; all are swept by the most lively joy, and Ulysses is ready to depart with his son, at which point he is interrupted by the cries of his invisible companions, who reproach him for abandoning them to the tribulations of their fate. Ulysses begs the sorceress to take pity on those unfortunates; being unable to refuse him anything, she then makes the trees vanish and produces before his eyes his companions from their travails. They celebrate this happy moment together with the nymphs of the island with the songs and the dances that bring the first act to a close.
>
> Act 2
>
> The scene shows a lighted room during the night. Ulysses is there with Merion. He informs that prince of the ties of friendship that bind him to his father Idomeneus, and asks if he had not recovered any trace of his daughter who had been intended to be the bride of Telemachus. Merion tells him that he has been looking for her, and free as he thus henceforth will be, that he is going to search with renewed vigor. Ulysses additionally relates to him that Circe has been shirking her oaths, that she refuses to do anything that could assist in their departure; he adds, however, that he has given orders for his comrades to reassemble, as soon as night should begin to fall, anything that might remain of the vessels on which they were beached after the shipwreck; but that he trembles to think of the insidious love of the enchantress and of the small number of warriors that he has with him. . . .

---

[18] Nos. 10 and 11 (2 and 6 February 1765).

ARGOMENTO.

Dopo l'impresa di Troja sono abbastanza noti i lunghi errori di Ulisse. Penelope impaziente del di lui ritorno, mentre deludeva con una frode innocente le istanze de' Principi, che aspiravano alle sue nozze, ed al regno, spedì il figlio Telemaco in traccia del padre. Delle di lui avventure non ci han lasciato nulla i Mitologi, e han dato luogo al celebre o Romanzo, o Poema del Signore di Fenelon. Mi son creduto in diritto ancor io di fingere su di esse a mio talento, e lo fo giungere nella famosa isola di Circe, in tempo che Ulisse vi era colla massima gelosia custodito da quella innamorata incantatrice, figlia del sole. Le di lei inquietudini, e inganni, gli amori di Telemaco, e d'Asteria, che si scuopre alla fine per la figlia d'Idomenéo Rè di Creta, la riconoscenza di lei col fratello, e di Telemaco col padre formano tutto l'intreccio del presente Dramma, e ne fanno lo scioglimento la disperazione della maga, le nozze di Telemaco, e la di lui partenza col padre, colla sposa, e coll'amico dall' Isola d'Enaria, in cui si finge la Scena.

Vorbericht.

Daß Ulysses nach der Verheerung der Stadt Troja viele Jahre in der Welt herumgeirret, ist eine bereits weltkündige Sache. Die über das zulange Außbleiben ihres Gemahls ungeduldig gewordene Penelope, so inzwischen viele, um ihre Person und ihr Reich sich äusserst bewerbende Fürsten mit einer unschuldigen List beständig zu äffen wuste, schickte endlich ihren Sohn Telemach aus, seinen Vater aufzusuchen. Was ferner mit diesem Telemach geschehen, davon haben uns die Verfasser der fabelhaften Geschichten keine Spure unterlassen, hiedurch aber dem Herrn von Fenelon Gelegenheit gegeben, ein so schön als berühmtes Heldengedicht von diesem Telemach zu schreiben. Auch ich glaube gewisser massen berechtiget zu seyn, in dieser Geschichte nach meinem Gutdunken weiter zu dichten, und lasse derohalben den Helden eben zur Zeit in das berüchtigte Eyland der Circe kommen, als sein Vater Ulysses mit grösster Sorgfalt, und Eifersucht von dieser verliebten Zauberinn, so für eine Tochter der Sonne ausgegeben wird, daselbst verwahret wurde. Die Unruhen der Zauberinn, und ihre manigfältige Ränke, die Liebe des Telemach und Asteria, welche zuletzt für die Tochter des Jdomeneus, Königs in Creta, erkannt wird, und der Zufall, daß diese ihren Bruder, Telemach aber seinen Vater wieder findet, ist eigentlich der Knoten des gegenwärtigen Singspiels; die Verzweifung der Circe, die Vermählung des Telemach, und dessen Abreise mit seinem Vater, seiner Braut, und seinem Freunde, dienen der ganzen Handlung, so auf dem Eyland Enaria vorzugehen gedichtet wird, zur Entwickelung.

INTERLOCUTORI.

ULISSE, Rè d'Itaca. *Sig. Giuseppe Tibaldi.*

TELEMACO, suo figlio. *Sig. Gaetano Guadagni.*

MERIONE, Figlio d'Idomenèo Rè di Creta, compagno di Telemaco. *Sig. Luca Fabris.*

ASTERIA, Seguace di Circe, e riconosciuta Sorella di Merione. *Siga. Rosa Tibaldi Tartaglini.*

CIRCE, Figlia del Sole, Amante d'Ulisse. *Siga. Elisabetta Teyberin.*

Una voce d'Oracolo.

CORI.

Coro di Ninfe e Pastori.

Coro de' Campagni d'Ulisse.

Coro di Sogni.

La Poesia è del Sig. Marco Coltellini.

La Musica è del celebre Sig. Cavalier Gluck.

Le Decorazioni sono dè Sig.ri Quaglio Padre e Figliolo.

Gli abiti del Sig. Giorgio Speck.

Auftrettende Personen.

Ulysses König von Ithaca.
   Herr Joseph Tibaldi.

Telemach, dessen Sohn.
   Herr Cajetan Guadagni.

Merion, ein Sohn Jdomeneens Königs von Creta, Gefährde des Telemach.
   Herr Lucas Fabris.

Asteria, eine aus dem Gefolge der Circe, nach der Hand erkannte Schwester des Merion.
   Frau Rosa Tibaldi Tartaglini.

Circe, eine Tochter der Sonne, verliebt in Ulyssen.
   Jungfrau Elisabetha Teyberin.

Eine Orackelstimme.

Chöre

Von Nymphen und Schäfern.
Von Gefährden Ulyssens.
Von Traumgeistern.

Die Worte sind von dem Herrn Marx Coltellini.

Die Musick ist von dem berühmten Herrn Chevalier Gluck.

Die Auszierungen sind von der Erfindung der Herren Quaglio dem Vater und dem Sohn.

Die Kleidungen vom Herrn Georg Speck.

Fig. 16.1. *Telemaco*, Italian-German synopsis, printed textbook, Vienna 1765

Courtesy of Washington, Library of Congress

They separate after this conversation, and the scene shows another spacious [room] devoted to the superstitious practices of Circe. She arrives there; she seats herself upon a tripod; she evokes the phantoms, the glowworms and the dreams; "Hideous and deceitful spirits," she says, "seduce the son of my perfidy." . . .

The spirits melt away in order to obey Circe, and the grotesquerie [*Grote*] takes place in a large drawing-room, dimly lit by several lamps, where Telemachus is seen, fallen asleep. The spirits perform a ballet which represents the death of Penelope. Ulysses arrives after this ballet; Telemachus wakes up, looks everywhere for his mother, and hugging the King of Ithaca in his arms, he tells him that her days have come to an end. . . . Ulysses . . . is for a moment pierced by horror; nevertheless he soon reassures himself on the faith of the oracles he has consulted. Merion, who arrives, builds up his hopes yet further; he informs him that the love of freedom has given his comrades an uncommon courage and strength, that at the rising of dawn everything will be ready for their departure. . . .

Telemachus, who sees himself on the brink of being separated from Asteria, tries to bring about obstacles. He admits that he is infatuated by a nymph worthy of the love of a very god, that he owes his life to her, and that he has promised her to sunder the fetters in which Circe has kept her. Ulysses explains to his son that the passion he was telling him about was nothing but a deceptive allurement that the sorceress offers him towards his loss and that she will make use of to find new pretexts for keeping them there. He then goes to hurry along the preparations for departure. Telemachus gives vent to the full bitterness of his fate. . . .

Asteria appears and comes to exhort him to fulfill his promises; the silence that he keeps enlightens her of his unhappiness. . . . In despair, Telemachus indicts the heavens, asks for death, and goes away from Asteria. Circe arrives and Asteria begs for her pity. "What," says Circe, "you are speaking of pity when nothing is to be thought of but vengeance. The ingrate Ulysses is ready to abandon me. . . . Run along with your companions the nymphs; bring all the flame into the vessels of the ingrate."

The scene shows the seacoast following this. Ulysses and his companions Telemachus and Merion are ready to set sail, until Asteria arrives and, in desperation, deplores Telemachus for his ingratitude and Ulysses for his cruelty. In order to console her, Ulysses explains to her that once distanced from Circe, who is the only one capable of illuminating her destiny, it would be in vain for her to try to find it out, and upon this Asteria, showing him a node of gemstones, tells him that this precious token could perhaps be of use to him in solving the mystery. Upon seeing in this node an ornament sacred to the King of Crete, Merion then realizes that Asteria must be his sister. Suffused by the most vivid joy, Ulysses consents with pleasure to Telemachus giving her his hand, and everybody disembarks together with the utmost satisfaction.

Scarcely have the vessels unfurled their sails, when the nymphs of Circe appear with torches in their hands; the sorceress is inciting them to vengeance; on noticing that Ulysses has left the shore, she becomes furious; she makes the shadows give way to the day that would shine on her island; she turns it into an awful desert, and flies away in a chariot drawn by dragons.

In this miserable situation, the nymphs and the populace implore the gods to rescue them; Amor [Love] yields to them; he appears with Venus; he transforms the desert into delightful surroundings, and the show is ended by a ballet which underscores the common happiness.

The generally accepted claim of Gluck scholarship that the text's author Coltellini only "condensed" or "adapted" Capeci's libretto set by Scarlatti[19] cannot be established with a comparison of the two librettos. If Coltellini even had access to the older libretto, it served him mainly as the initial inspiration for compsing a fundamentally different text.

With his pre-Metastasian text overrun with details, Scarlatti's librettist places the emphasis on romantic relations between the various characters; Telemaco loves Erifile; the female slave loves the nymph Calypso. She is also loved by Calypso's brother Sikoreo, while Calypso herself has succumbed to Telemaco, who reminded her of her earlier love Ulysses. Hence she rebuffs the romantic advances of the Prince of Corinth, Adrastos, although his deceased father had intended him to be her husband. After various complications that create dramatic tension, they form the proper couples. Erifile reveals herself to be the daughter of King Idomeneo and joyfully follows the

---

[19] Cf. for example Alfred Wotquenne, *Catalogue thématique des oeuvres de Chr. W. Gluck* (Leipzig: Breitkopf & Härtel, 1904; reprint, Hildesheim: Olms, 1967), 206; Hans Joachim Moser, *Christoph Willibald Gluck* (Stuttgart: Cotta, 1940), 172; Anna Amalie Abert, *Christoph Willibald Gluck* (Munich: Bong, 1959), 151; Alfred Einstein, *Gluck: Sein Leben, sein Werke*, 2nd ed. (London: Dent, 1964), 92f., and Loewenberg, 279.

command of the gods, who had already long ago chosen her to be Telemaco's wife. Calypso obeys her father, who has risen out of the nether world, and marries Adrastos. Still a third couple, Tersite and Silvina, who brings a contrasting element of cheerfulness into the opera, comes together in the end.

Common to the librettos of Coltellini and Capeci is that the female lead character is endowed with magical powers and that one of her maidservants is later revealed to be the daughter of King Idomeneo and marries the young prince. Otherwise, however, there are considerable differences between the newer and older works: Capeci remains faithful to Fénelon, while Coltellini distances himself from many aspects of the French novel.[20] The nymph Calypso, a central figure in the earlier opera, is replaced in Coltellini's work by the sorceress Circe, and the figure of Ulysses (who is also absent from Fénelon's work) is newly introduced. The romantic relationships in the two works differ completely. In Capeci, Calypso finds herself attracted to the young Telemaco, while in Coltellini the sorceress feels passion for the older man. Finally, Gluck's librettist dispenses with every element of the story that contrasts with serious events. He strives to limit the plot to its fundamental aspects: the virtuous son's search for his father and the tragic fate of the sorceress, who is robbed of her lover. From this perspective Coltellini's attitude corresponds to the artistic principles that Gluck had realized in his *Orfeo*, even if the librettist lacked the poetic force to create a fully satisfying text.

One detail of the libretto still merits particular consideration. In the summary of the French plot given above, the intervention of Amor and Venus is portrayed, through which the author forces a happy ending to the story. In the libretto, the description of the final scene is similar, yet the reference to the love goddess Venus is absent, which indicates, along with other assertions in this article, that the reporter from the *Supplément* did not only hold fast to the printed libretto but rather also rendered the impressions he gathered at the performance. Surprisingly, however, all *Telemaco* scores end with Circe's revenge recitative (NA, 373), and Gluck scholarship has simply assumed thus far that the composer ended his opera in this manner.[21] Now, however, such a claim can hardly be maintained any longer. Even if one were to consider it possible that an eighteenth-century opera could end with a solo in the form of an accompagnato-recitative, and moreover that the hopeless devastation of an island could serve as the closing of an opera intended for a wedding celebration, the testimony of such a thorough report in the *Supplément* cannot be left out of consideration. Clearly Gluck, after composing three different works that were staged in quick succession, was so in demand that he could not find the time to compose the final ballet in *Telemaco* and instead used an older dance scene. In light of the similarities between the story endings in *Orfeo* and *Telemaco*—in both cases, the God of Love brings about a happy end, which is then celebrated with dances—the speculation that in writing his wedding opera Gluck referred to his reform opera of three years previous cannot be immediately dismissed. The fact that Angiolini directed the production of dance scenes in *Telemaco* as well as in *Orfeo* strengthens this assumption even more. When Prince Khevenhüller complains in his report of the performance of *Telemaco* that the opera is "without a new ballet," this likely means that this aristocrat, who loved visiting the theater, was irritated to find before him at such a festive occasion a dance scene with which he was already long familiar. If the final scene had been completely absent, the critic would not have complained specifically about the lack of a "new" ballet.

In the nineteenth century the common view was that Gluck's *Telemaco* was first performed in Rome in 1749-50 and subsequently in Naples as well; the performance in honor of the wedding of Joseph II, therefore, would have represented the resurrection of an older work. Thus far, no proof of any kind has been found to support the assumption that the opera existed in an earlier form, nor has anyone succeeded in uncovering the basis for this mistaken idea. On the other hand, however, it is also not entirely incomprehensible that even respected scholars would have taken this view,[22] since the work truly does contain certain stylistic characteristics that could point to its existence previous to the reform opera *Orfeo*. One would sooner expect such clear weaknesses in the libretto in an early work, for example, than in a composition by a mature artist. To a strong degree the events in *Telemaco*

---

[20] In the foreword to his libretto Coltellini writes: "Auch ich glaubte gewisser massen berechtigt zu seyn, in dieser Geschichte nach meinem Gutdünken weiter zu dichten . . ." (I, too, believed myself to have license to compose this tale further according to my own judgement . . .); cf. fig., p. 185.

[21] Cf. Moser, 175; Abert, 151-52; Einstein, 93; Rudolf Gerber, *Christoph Willibald Gluck*, 2nd ed. (Potsdam: Athenaion, 1950), 140.

[22] Cf., for example, Anton Schmid, *C. W. Ritter von Gluck* (Leipzig: Fleischer, 1854), 116, and Adolf Bernhard Marx, *Gluck un die Oper*, vol. 1 (Berlin: Janke, 1863), 188ff.

lack clarity and internal context. Not the title figure Telemaco and his beloved Asteria, but rather Ulysses and the unfortunate sorceress Circe are the actual main characters in the drama. Also the plot at the end of the first act seems to have found a satisfactory solution, to which the events of the second act are surprisingly and quite inorganically attached. In addition the composition contains pages of schematically-arranged secco-recitatives that Gluck uses along with da capo arias, as well as occasionally brilliant coloraturas that apparently represent concessions to the taste of audience and performers.

Yet it is unmistakably true that *Telemaco* cannot be counted among the early Italian compositions. Even in the libretto, though hardly satisfying overall, one notices that a student of Calzabigi was at work. In *Orfeo* the title character must twice confront the powers of darkness before attaining final victory. However, Coltellini's opera surpasses even this. Here, the sorceress Circe threatens the fate of the mortals three times, and the final, happy conclusion is brought about by Amor, just as in the example of *Orfeo*. Indications of the relation to Gluck's later grand operas reveal themselves to an even greater extent from a musical perspective. Even a piece endowed with such brilliant passages as Circe's da capo aria "In mezzo a un mar crudele" (NA, 58ff.) exudes demonic energy and wild passion. Although rare in Gluck's work, the coloraturas complete the picture of scintillating evil in a most effective manner, as is the case for the Queen of the Night's arias in Mozart. Telemaco's arias are expressive and filled with dramatic power, and the second, "Se per entro alla nera foresta" (NA, 136ff.), with its sinister combination of muted strings, oboes, and horns, is a model of impressive orchestration.

Hector Berlioz, who knew the score of *Telemaco* extremely well and admired it greatly, describes Ulysses' aria "Ah, non chiamarmi ingrato" (NA, 114ff.) with typically Romantic exuberance as "un des plus delicieux Andante qu'on ait jamais écrit," and continues:

> All that is the most irresistible in tenderness, the simplest and the most touching in grace seems to have been exhausted by the composer in order to embellish the singing of Ulysses: and surely if the King of Ithaca, in resisting the love of Circe, withstands the test of conjugal fidelity, if he responds with a refusal to the brilliant proposals of the enchantress, one must admit that his accents possess a certain sweetness and rather strongly resemble those of love, which he is happy for his own sake that his chaste spouse has no opportunity to hear. The manner in which the word "ma" is thrown out indicates all that it costs him to
>
> > Lieta veder ti bramo
> > Del mio rigor mi pento
> > Ah! vorrei dir ch'io t'amo
> > Ma . . . non lo posso dir.
> >
> > [See you happy, I yearn for you
> > My severe rigor I do rue
> > Oh! I'd like to say that I love you
> > But . . . I cannot say it.]
>
> The second part of the aria especially seems to me to sublimate Ulysses for remaining faithful. It expresses a regret so passionate, so profound . . . oh! it is admirable. I am not rich, but I would gladly give two hundred francs to hear the quivering voice of Rubini[23] singing me this very aria.[24]

Already in the previous year, in an article dedicated to Gluck, Berlioz had called attention to Asteria's monologue "Ah l'ho presente" (NA, 99ff.), the scene in which she declares her love for Telemaco:

> With what rapture did I ever sit while discovering this marvelous elegy, where the melody competes with the chords and with the orchestral textures for painting the most overpowering sadness that could break the heart of a young and beautiful woman, that of seeing her love disdained by the man whose

---

[23] Giovanni Battista Rubini (1795 or 1796-1854), known as "the king of tenors" and "Europe's nightingale," made strong use of tremolo in his singing. Cf. Hans Kühner, *MGG*, 11 (1963), cols. 1041-42.

[24] *Gazette musicale de Paris* (1835), 13.

life she had saved! ...—I have never found, even in the immense body of work that Gluck wrote since, anything simpler or more nobly beautiful than these accents of a resigned victim, whose complaint breathes out without bitterness towards a past full of poignant memories. The singing and the harmony are wed so admirably that one cannot tell if the effort results more from the one or more from the other. The instrumentation ... it is nothing; solely the stringed instruments are used. But how each part is drawn! Under the verse: "quando appannatti, e tardi pria giro gli occhi intorno" ["when clouded, and late I first turn my eyes about"], the violins unfold a long period, which the violas come to join shortly thereafter; the three parts mingle, cross, climb, and descend gently; the blood begins to circulate; life spreads more and more closely: "Pria giro gli occhi intorno"; and the singing rises little by little, comes, via a crescendo, to make an explosion on the words: "E poi gli appersi al giorno; and then they open to the light of day." A slight tone of reproach makes itself heard in the phrase: "E mi trafisse il cor" ["And my heart gave a stab"]. After a silence, Asteria rejoins on a higher tone: "O giorno!" ["Oh sweet glances!"] Third silence ... and the voice dragging itself laboriously up to its keenest note, with the words "O rimembranza!" ["Oh remembrance!"] falls back suddenly, like the choked sigh of a heart that is breaking, while murmuring: "O amor!" ["Oh love!"] and ... nothing more ... not a note of ritornello ... the orchestra stays mute ... what could he add in effect that would not have been at least useless? ... Oh well! one day in Italy I had this heart-rending piece listened to by a musician with a greatly distinguished talent; he found it insignificant, and proved its nothingness by a barrage of peremptory arguments. As of that moment onward I felt that I hated him with all of my strength; I do not believe I will ever be able to forgive him.[25]

Of even greater importance than that expressive power of individual pieces is the lively and supple arrangement of the work's music in general. Again and again secco-recitatives, *accompagnati*, and aria-like structures merge freely into one another, while occasional ensemble and choral numbers add to the solidity of the formal context. This principle of active condensation of solo and choral numbers into larger architectonic structures is used consistently by Gluck in his reform operas. Yet *Telemaco* also offers fascinating examples of this. Already at the beginning of the first act, a rondo-like scene (NA, 21ff.) is presented in which a frequently-recurring, mixed chorus alternates with a vocal trio and brief instrumental dances. The finale of the same act forms a counterpart to this scene (NA, 151ff.): after a slow introduction, a joyful chorus begins, whose music is taken up again by the chorus at the end after the introduction of various contrasting elements. In Circe's great incantation scene in the second act (NA, 207ff.) various forms of solo vocal music alternate with one another, while the dramatic power and monumental configuration of the scene are intensified further through the double insertion of choral episodes.

Gluck's *Telemaco* is unambiguously a work in which the new spirit of opera finds expression.[26] If through the incorporation of certain conventional features the score takes on a hybridized or ambiguous form, this is likely caused above all by the unsatisfactory libretto that Coltellini delivered to the composer. And since Gluck was overwhelmed with work on the three wedding pieces,[27] he clearly found no opportunity to make his wishes heard with regard to the textual form. Moreover, at this stage of his creative development the composer had outgrown such traditional compositions written for particular occasions. He took them on at that point only in exceptional cases, and his personal involvement in the process did not always come into play.

We do not know how Joseph II reacted to *Telemaco*. The public in any case had a negative attitude towards the work. The weaknesses of the libretto were obvious, and the conflicting tone of the music could fully satisfy neither listeners bound to tradition nor those with a more progressive attitude. Thus the work's stage run ended after only two performances.

Despite this, the components of the opera have continued to prove their vitality. Gluck often referred to material from his own earlier works, even in compositions from the time of his artistic mastery. However, he hardly quoted another opera to the same extent in his later production. Three arias in *Telemaco* fall back upon Gluck's Italian operas of the 1740s and 1750s.[28] On the other hand, however, material from more than dozen numbers in *Telemaco*

---

[25] *Gazette musicale de Paris* (1834), 174.

[26] In his letter to Prince Kaunitz, Calzabigi places the opera *Telemaco* in line with *Orfeo*, *Ifigenia* (by Coltellini-Traetta), and *Alceste*.

[27] Cf. Baselt, foreword.

[28] Ulysses' aria "Freme gonfio" is indebted to *Ippolito* (1745), Circe's aria "Se a estinguer non bastate" to *Antigono* (1756). Circe's aria "Se per entro alla nera foresta" is constructed on one of the composer's favorite ideas, which he already employed in *Sofonisba* (1744), *Le nozze*

recur in later operas.[29] Aside from the occasional cycle *Le feste d'Apollo*, several of Gluck's masterpieces are particularly indebted to the Viennese wedding opera. *Paride ed Elena*, *Cythére assiégée* (second version), *Alceste*, and *Iphigénie en Tauride* contain passages whose origins are traceable to this work. *Iphigénie en Aulide* is indebted to it for the fundamentals of its overture and the following scene with Agamemnon ("Diane impitoyable"); most of all, however, multiple references to the Viennese wedding opera can be found in *Armide*. The overtures of these two works correspond in their fundamental elements; in addition, the introduction to the scene between Armide and Hidraot in the second act and the subsequent duet, as well as the great dialogue between hate and the chorus in the third act contain allusions to *Telemaco*.

Such transplantation of musical ideas presumes that the situation with regard to content in both cases is fundamentally the same. This is most evident in *Armide*, the material of which is organically related to that of *Telemaco* since in both operas a sorceress, after a long struggle, must allow her beloved, the hero, to leave her. However, intimate relations can also be found elsewhere. If, for example, material from Telemaco's solo scene "Ah, che di voi m'addita" (NA, 131ff.) reappears at the beginning of the Aulian *Iphigénie*, in both cases it is a question of a mortal's lament for the cruelty of the gods. Telemaco is in despair at his inability to find his father; Agamemnon defends himself against Diana's demand that he sacrifice his daughter. If Circe's aria "Notte fedel custode" (NA, 230ff.) resonates with the solo of Pallas in *Paride ed Elena*,[30] the music in each work expresses the indignation of a goddess offended by a human. Circe's incantation scene that precedes the aria "Del orrido soggiorno" (NA, 213ff.) becomes Jupiter's incantation scene in *Le feste d'Apollo* (*Atto di Bauci e Filemone*). In the place of furies and larvae, now a thunderstorm is conjured. The singing of Asteria, "Perdo, oh Dio, l'amato bene" (NA, 336), is transformed in *Cythére assiégée* into an aria by Carite.[31] Here, as there, a maiden laments her terrible fate. Telemaco's aria "Non dirmi ch'io viva" (NA, 89ff.) provided the inspiration for a song by Orestes in *Iphigénie en Tauride*.[32] In both operas the individual finds himself in a fateful conflict with higher powers.

In the various cases in which elements of *Telemaco* influence other compositions, the relation between original and later versions is certainly not always the same. At times the relation is loose; it is closer to the continuation of an idea than the recycling of a piece. This is the case for the chorus "Ahi che fia lo sventurato" (NA, 48ff.), which influenced the chorus "O Dieux qu'allons nous devenir" in *Alceste* (act 1, scene 1). Even when Gluck allows one of his favorite ideas, the aria "Se per entro alla nera foresta" (NA, 136ff.), to resonate in *Armide*,[33] he approaches the older versions freely. Finally, Telemaco's aria mentioned above has an effect similar to that of the germ motive of Orestes' aria in the Taurean *Iphigénie*.[34]

In stark contrast to this are instances in which Gluck takes passages out of the *Telemaco* score and incorporates them into a new composition with relatively insignificant changes (transpositions, abridgements, etc.). This form of self-borrowing, primarily attributable to a lack of time, is used in particular in *Le feste d'Apollo* (1769), the last Italian occasional composition by the master, a work that is constructed in large part of older scores by Gluck.

Between these two extremes are the creative revisions that Gluck undertakes at times on passages from *Telemaco*. In these particularly significant examples of Gluck using his own material, the work in question is neither a more or less mechanical copy nor a radical reorganization. *Armide*, for example, employs as a prelude a much altered and intensified version of the overture to *Telemaco*. The Italian opera begins with an introductory Moderato, followed by an Allegro as its main part. The French work takes over this structure, but expands the contrasting sorrowful idea of the introduction (NA, meas. 12-15) from four to seven measures and inserts several important

---

d'Ercole e d'Ebe (1747), and *La clemenza di Tito* (1751). Cf. Wotquenne, 206; Klaus Hortschansky, "Parodie und Entlehnung im Schaffen Christoph Willibald Glucks" (Ph.D. diss., Universität Kiel, 1965), appendix, table 37.

[29] Cf. Wotquenne, 209-10, 213, 215-16; Schmid, 119f.; Marx, 1:193ff.; Moser, 173; Hortschansky, ibid.

[30] "Va coll'amato nel seno," act 5, scene 3. *Sämtliche Werke*, sec. 1, vol. 4, 262ff.

[31] "Le barbare me declare," act 1.

[32] "Dieux qui me poursuivez," act 2, no. 12.

[33] Duet "Esprits de haine et de rage," act 2, scene 2.

[34] Cf. also the remarks to this by Berlioz in *Gazette musicale* (1835), 12.

passages in the Allegro.[35] In particular, however, the sorrowful idea of the slow introduction returns at the end of the later work, in which Gluck both aims at a rounding-off suggestive of the form of French overtures and provides a reference to the ending of the drama, which will be tragic for the demonic seductress.

Particularly impressive is the process of refinement that led to the forming of the introduction in the overture to the Aulian *Iphigénie*. We already encounter the noble basic idea in Telemaco's arioso "Ah, qui di voi m'addita" (NA, 131ff.), and yet the power of his expression is palpably weakened through the threefold literal return of the sorrowful two-measure closing phrase. *Iphigénie* begins in much the same way, although the voice leading is brought out more clearly through the effective use of octave displacement. Instead of three repetitions of the closing phrase, here there are only two. On the other hand the entire eight-measure passage is lowered in pitch by a fourth and rendered once more in a slightly expanded form. The new version is nearly twice as long as the original; however, the considerable deepening of dramatic effect achieved through this cannot be expressed in mathematical terms.

Finally, it is notable that several particularly valuable pieces in *Telemaco* were not used in later Gluck scores. To this group belong, for example, the numbers already pointed out by Berlioz: the subtle solo by Ulysses, in which he indicates that only his sense of duty hinders him from reciprocating the passion of his seductress, and the moving scene with Asteria, which demonstrates how the young girl loses her heart to the handsome youth Telemaco after he saves her life. The fact that the composer did not transplant such passages into other scores illuminates Gluck's entire attitude toward the problem of reusing his own musical ideas. Self-quotations are not only a means for the composer to conserve time and energy; in addition to that, they give him the opportunity to refine his ideas and to bestow upon them their final imprint. The strangely ambivalent opera *Telemaco* provides the best examples of Gluck's attitude. Here are not only the valuable raw materials for later forms, but also completed jewels of the highest worth.

---

[35] The first fourteen measures are very similar in the two versions, followed by a measure in *Telemaco* that is expanded to six measures in *Armide*. The next twenty-two measures are almost identical in the two scores. Five measures follow in *Telemaco*, extended to ten in *Armide*. Ten measures follow, that again agree in both works, then four more measures in *Telemaco* that correspond to twelve measures in *Armide*. The remaining sixteen measures of the Allegro are identical in both works.

Fig. 16.2. *Telemaco*, act 1, scene 1 (Oracolo, meas. 205ff.) from the autograph fragment (cf. NA, 47)

Courtesy of Vienna, Österreichische Nationalbibliothek, Cod. 18464

Fig. 16.3. *Telemaco*, act 1, scene 1 (Oracolo, meas. 205ff.) from the score (cf. NA, 47)

Courtesy of Paris, Bibliothèque Nationale, VM 4/51

Emanuel Bach and the Music of the Viennese Classical Triad

Unpublished typescript. The version of the article published in the *Österreichische Musikzeitschrift* 6 (1988): 300-06 under the title "Carl Philipp Emanuel Bach und die Meister der Wiener Klassischen Schule" was earlier. Its reworking into a revised English translation was interrupted by the author's death in January 1989. The essay permits Geiringer to bring into play under a single roof two of his primary research areas—Haydn and the Bach family.

> The Österreichische Musikzeitschrift *also had timed the publication of an article I had written about the influence of C. P. E. Bach on the music of Haydn, Mozart, and Beethoven to coincide with my stay in Vienna* [1988].— This I Remember, *180.*

To Eugene Helm, leader of C. P. E. Bach research,
whose 60th birthday occurs in the same year 1988
as the bicentenary of the composer's death.

Carl Philipp Emanuel Bach belonged to the most successful and most influential composers of his generation. Well over five hundred of his compositions were printed in his lifetime[1]—no mean achievement in a period in which hand-written copies of music were generally used. His circle of acquaintances and close friends included some of the greatest talents and best minds of his time. Among them were musicians like the brothers Benda, Graun, Quantz, Marpurg, Agricola, Kirnberger, Mattheson, Telemann, and Reichardt; poets like Claudius, Gerstenberg, Gleim, Ramler, Voss, Hölty, Lessing, and Klopstock.[2] Bach enjoyed visiting the home of the mathematician J. G. Büsch in Hamburg and kept amiable business relations with the publishers Winter in Berlin, Breitkopf & Härtel in Leipzig, and Artaria in Vienna.

Bach's fame had spread even beyond the confines of Germany. When the famous English music historian Charles Burney visited the continent, one of his main objectives was to call on the eminent composer in Hamburg. The details of this memorable meeting, which took place in 1772, have been carefully described by Burney himself. After having heard Emanuel play, the author came to the following conclusion:

> His performance . . . convinced me . . . that he is not only one of the greatest composers that ever existed, for keyed instruments, but the best player, in point of *expression* . . . he possesses every style; though he chiefly confines himself to the expressive. He is learned, I think, even beyond his father, whenever he pleases, and is far before him in variety of modulation; his fugues are always upon new and curious subjects, and created with great art as well as genius. . . . Emanuel Bach . . . seems to have outstript his age.[3]

---

[1] Alfred Wotquenne, *Thematisches Verzeichnis der Werke von Carl Philipp Emanuel Bach (1714-1788)* (Leipzig: Breitkopf & Härtel, 1905) and *The New Grove Dictionary of Music and Musicians* (1980), s.v. "Bach, §III (9), Carl Philipp Emanuel," by Eugene Helm.

[2] Hans-Günter Ottenberg, *Carl Philipp Emanuel Bach* (Leipzig: Reclam, 1982), 88-99 and 189-213.

[3] *The Present State of Music in Germany, the Netherlands, and United Provinces*, 2nd ed., 2 vols. (London: Becket, Robson, and Robinson, 1775; reprint, New York: Broude, 1969), 2:271, 273.

Even a Frenchman who was no musician, the famous encyclopedist Denis Diderot, wrote to Bach expressing his admiration of the composer's work and asked him for some of his yet unpublished clavier music he wanted to give to his daughter, an accomplished player of keyboard instruments.[4]

Of particular interest is the impact of Bach's work on the masters of the Viennese Classical School of music, none of whom the composer had ever met in person. Even contemporary reports mention the impact of Emanuel's creations on the mind of Joseph Haydn. In particular, two men who had an opportunity to interview the composer towards the end of his life to gain biographical information provide interesting statements. Thus, the composer and painter Albert Dies who held thirty conversations with Haydn tells us:

> Haydn ventured to walk into a bookstore and ask for a good textbook of theory. The bookseller named the writings of Carl Philipp Emanuel Bach as the newest and best. Haydn wanted to look and see for himself. He began to read, understood, found what he was seeking, paid for the book, and took it away thoroughly pleased.
> That Haydn thought to make Bach's principles his own, that he studied them untiringly, can already be noted in his youthful works of the period. . . . In his opinion Bach's writings form the best, most basic textbook ever published.[5]

George August Griesinger, the diplomat and friend of Haydn, supplements this statement by reporting the enormous impression which the acquaintance with Emanuel's early sonatas made on young Haydn and quotes the composer as having said:

> I did not come away from my clavier till I had played through them, and whoever knows me thoroughly must discover that I owe a great deal to Emanuel Bach, that I understood him and have studied him diligently.[6]

Similarly, the music historian Friedrich Rochlitz reports on the basis of information he had received from Haydn's friend Abbé Stadler that Haydn had said:

> Innumerable times I played them [Emanuel's sonatas] for my own delight when I felt depressed and discouraged by worries and I always left the instrument gay and in high spirits.[7]

It is obvious that Haydn's great admiration for the work of Emanuel Bach is also reflected in his own compositions. This was already recognized in the lifetime of the two artists and led to the publication of a rather scurrilous statement. The *European Magazine* of London brought in its issue of October 1784 a friendly article about Haydn which contained the following strange assertion:

> Amongst the number of professors who wrote against our rising author was Philip-Emanuel Bach of Hamburgh (formerly of Berlin); and the only notice Haydn took of their scurrility and abuse was to publish lessons written in imitation of the several stiles of his enemies, in which their peculiarities were so closely copied, and their extraneous passages (particularly those of Bach of Hamburgh) so inimitably burlesqued, that they all felt the poignancy of his musical wit, confessed its truth, and were silent.
> This anecdote will account for a number of strange passages that are here and there dispersed throughout several of the sonatas that have been reprinted in England from the German copies. . . . The stile of Bach is closely copied, without the passages being stolen, in which his capricious manner,

---

[4] J. G. Prod'homme, "Diderot et la musique," *Zeitschrift der Internationalen Musikgesellschaft* 15 (1913-14): 156ff. and 177ff.

[5] Albert Christoph Dies, *Biographische Nachrichten von Joseph Haydn* (Vienna: Camesinaische Buchhandlung, 1810); English translation in Vernon Gotwals, *Joseph Haydn, Eighteenth-Century Gentleman and Genius* (Madison: University of Wisconsin Press, 1963), 95.

[6] Georg August Griesinger, *Biographische Notizen über Joseph Haydn* (Leipzig: Breitkopf und Härtel, 1810); English translation in Gotwals, 12.

[7] *Für Freunde der Tonkunst*, vol. 4 (Leipzig: Cnobloch, 1832), 274.

odd breaks, whimsical modulations, and very often childish manner, mixed with an affectation of profound science, are finely hit off and burlesqued.[8]

In 1785 this bizarre article was published in a German translation in *Cramers Magazin der Musik*, where Bach must have seen it, because he had in the Hamburg *Unpartheiische Korrespondent* of September 1785 the following open letter printed:

> My way of thought and my occupations have never allowed me to write against anyone: the more I was astonished about a passage in a recent article in *The European Magazine* in England, where I am accused in a mendacious crude and shameful way of having written against the good Herr Haydn. According to my news from Vienna and even from members of the Esterházi [*sic*] Kapelle who came to me, I must believe that this worthy man, whose works continue to give me much pleasure, is surely as much my friend as I his. According to my principles, every master has his true and certain value. Praise and criticism cannot change any of that. Only the work itself praises and criticizes the master, and therefore I leave to everyone his own value.
>
> C. P. E. Bach, Hamburg, 14 September 1785[9]

A direct influence of the rather personal style of Emanuel's music on the compositions of Haydn has been acknowledged by twentieth-century research. However, the opinions vary widely concerning the exact nature and the extent of this influence. Several authors, among them Schmid, Abert, Finscher, and the present writer,[10] assume that the young composer followed in numerous instances the model of the North German master. Others, like Landon, Graue and Wackernagel,[11] consider the direct influence of Emanuel as less significant and designate other models of Haydn's art. The following simple and convincing solution of the problems is offered by Tovey:

> What, then, is Haydn's real debt to C. P. E. Bach? It is a pity that the word "rhetoric" has been degraded to a term of abuse, for it means in art the perfection of which is as noble as the noblest cause in which it can be used. Rhetoric is what Haydn learnt from C. P. E. Bach: a singularly beautiful but pure rhetoric, tender, romantic, anything but severe, yet never inflated. This great and comprehensive gift is independent of all reform or progress. The example of Bach's chaotically wild rondos and fantaisias may have been necessary in order to stimulate Haydn's far more realistic sense of adventure. But of art forms, the only thing that Haydn adopted from C. P. E. Bach was this device of *Veränderte Reprise*. Its original motive arose from the fact that in any movement, sections marked to be repeated were in fact often varied by the performer on repetition, the repeats being, indeed, supposed to be prescribed for that purpose. . . .
>
> Now, how does Haydn treat Bach's reprise-device? Besides restricting its use to lyric slow movements, he shows none of the patience which enabled C. P. E. Bach to write an ornamental repeat of both parts. In the final recapitulatory stage of his movement the ornaments will combine both versions of the exposition or will otherwise throw appropriate light on it. The reprise-movements in Haydn's quartets are the slow movements of op. 9, no. 2; op. 9, no. 4; op. 20, no. 6; and op. 33, no. 3: with which the history of this art-form closes, to be reopened only once, many years later, in the most original and exquisite masterpiece of orchestration Haydn achieved, the slow movement of the ninth *London Symphony*, in B-flat [no. 102].[12]

---

[8] Reproduced in H. C. Robbins Landon, *Haydn: Chronicle and Works*, vol. 2, *Haydn at Esterháza 1766-1790* (Bloomington: Indiana University Press, 1978), 496f.

[9] Translated in ibid., 498.

[10] Ernst Fritz Schmid, "Joseph Haydn und Carl Philipp Emanuel Bach," *Zeitschrift für Musikwissenschaft* 14, no. 6 (March 1932): 299-312; Hermann Abert, "Joseph Haydns Klaviersonaten," ibid., 3, nos. 9-10 (June-July 1921): 535-52, and "Joseph Haydns Klavierwerke," ibid., 2, no. 10 (July 1920): 553-73; Ludwig Finscher, *Studien zur Geschichte des Streichquartetts*, vol. 1, *Die Entstehung des klassischen Streichquartetts* (Kassel: Bärenreiter, 1974); Karl Geiringer, in collaboration with Irene Geiringer, *Haydn: A Creative Life in Music*, 3rd ed. (Berkeley: University of California Press, 1982).

[11] Landon; Jerald C. Graue, "Haydn and the London Pianoforte School," *Haydn Studies: Proceedings of the International Haydn Conference, Washington, D.C., 1975*, ed. Jens Peter Larsen, Howard Serwer, and James Webster (New York: Norton, 1981), 422-31; Bettina Wackernagel, *Joseph Haydns frühe Klaviersonaten: Ihre Beziehungen zur Klaviermusik um die Mitte des 18. Jahrhunderts* (Tutzing: Schneider, 1975).

[12] Donald Francis Tovey, "Haydn," in *Cobbett's Cyclopedia Survey of Chamber Music*, 2 vols. (London: Oxford University Press, 1929), 2:528.

A. Peter Brown[13] supplements this somewhat restrictive observation by emphasizing that the detailed description of "Improvisation" and "Free Fantasia" in the last chapter of Bach's *Versuch über die wahre Art das Clavier zu spielen*[14] likewise influenced Haydn. It contributed to the conception of Haydn's "Capriccios" and "Fantasias" for clavier (Hob. XVII:1 and 4), string quartet (Hob. III:32/2 and 80/2), and orchestra (Hob. I:86/2).[15] The main instances of a possible direct influence were thus pinpointed.

Like Haydn, Mozart was an admirer of Emanuel's art, although his esteem was not nearly as great. Wolfgang's father Leopold, who had obviously studied Emanuel's *Versuch* when working on his own treatise for the violin, introduced the child to the art of the North German composer at a very early age. On Wolfgang's sixth name-day (31 October 1762) Leopold surprised his son with a booklet with compositions suitable for a child, among them two minuets and one march by Emanuel. Nissen, possibly on the basis of information he had received from Mozart's sister, writes that Emanuel, Hasse, Handel, and Eberlin were Wolfgang's models, which he constantly studied.[16] At the age of eleven, Wolfgang transcribed a programmatic clavier composition by Philipp Emanuel called "La Boehmer" (Wq. 117/26 [H. 81]), into the finale of a clavier concerto (K. 40). Moreover, the admiration which Mozart manifested in his early clavier compositions for the work of J. G. Eckard again leads to Emanuel, as this composer had trained himself principally by studying Emanuel's works.

As a mature artist, Mozart had new and even stronger reasons to familiarize himself with Emanuel's works. On 10 April 1782 the composer wrote to his father:

> I go every Sunday at twelve o'clock to Baron van Swieten, where nothing is played but Handel and Bach. I am collecting at the moment the fugues of Bach—not only of Sebastian, but also of Emanuel and Friedemann.

And a letter to the father, dated 24 December 1783, contains the following request:

> If you could have Emanuel Bach fugues (there are six of them, I think) copied and sent to me some time, you would be doing me a great kindness.[17]

Mozart's rondos for clavier, and in particular his phantasies, appear to have been somewhat influenced by Philipp Emanuel. With their broken chords, the predilection for harsh and daring chromatic progressions, arpeggios, and rich modulations, cadenzas in a free and improvisatory style, inserted holds and arioso-like episodes, the four clavier phantasies written between 1782 and 1785 seem to carry ideas and experiments of the North German master[18] (exx. 17.1 and 17.2). Similarly, the fragmentary piano and violin sonatas in A major and C major (K. 402 and 403), with their archaic character, are inspired by Emanuel's idiom. Hermann Abert points out that the thematic unification combined with a rather unconventional treatment of the thematic material in the final movement of the string quartet in B♭ major (K. 589) is due to Mozart's infatuation with the art of the Hamburg composer.[19] Likewise, in the finale of the String Quintet in D major (K. 593) we find a wonderful fusion of the spirit of Emanuel with Mozart's own creative power.

It is not surprising that Mozart also performed works of the composer whose creations made so strong an impression on him. In 1787 he conducted Emanuel's *Die Israeliten in der Wüste* [H.775]; and in 1788 Ramler's *Auferstehung und Himmelfahrt Jesu*, having first added an oboe and a flute part to a tenor aria in the latter oratorio. Mozart was certainly very receptive to ideas conveyed to him from the works of his peers, but the active interest he took in Emanuel's music was of unusual strength.

---

[13] *Joseph Haydn's Keyboard Music: Sources and Style* (Bloomington: Indiana University Press, 1986), 221ff.

[14] Vol. 1 (Berlin: Henning, 1753), vol. 2 (Berlin: Winter, 1762). English translation by William J. Mitchell (New York: Norton, 1949).

[15] Brown's assertion that the "Chaos" in Haydn's oratorio *The Creation* belongs in the same category is less convincing.

[16] Théodore de Wyzewa and Georges de Saint-Foix, *W.-A. Mozart: Sa vie musicale et son oeuvre, de l'enfance a la pleine maturité: Essai de biographie critique, suivi d'un nouveau catalogue chronologique de l'oeuvre complète du maitre*, vol. 1 (Paris: Desclée de Brouwer, 1936), 170.

[17] Emily Anderson, ed., *The Letters of Mozart & His Family*, 3 vols. (London: Macmillan, 1938), 3:1191 and 1291.

[18] Bernard Paumgartner, *Mozart* (Zurich: Atlas Verlag, 1940), 382.

[19] Hermann Abert, *W. A. Mozart*, rev. ed., vol. 2 (Leipzig: Breitkopf & Härtel, 1924), 717.

Example 17.1. C. P. E. Bach, Fantasia in F major, Wq. 59/5 [H. 279], meas. 27-29.

Example 17.2. Mozart, Phantasie in C major, K. 394, meas. 43-45.

An interesting little episode might also be mentioned, reported by Johann Friedrich Rochlitz:

> When Mozart, a few years before his death, stayed in Leipzig, he had, shortly before, also visited Hamburg where he had an opportunity repeatedly to hear Bach—who was already quite elderly—improvise on his Silbermann instrument. At a musical soirée in the house of [the Thomas Cantor J. F.] Doles Mozart was asked what he thought about Bach's playing—the topic of the conversation was only his playing. Mozart answered in his Viennese direct and unsophisticated manner: "He is the father, we are the boys. Whoever among us knows the proper things has learned them from him and who does not admit that, is a . . ." [Mozart's expression is unreproduceable]. "With the means he used"—Mozart continued—"we could no longer manage today; but his use of them is incomparable."[20]

This anecdote is quite characteristic, despite the fact that nothing is known about a visit which Mozart supposedly paid to Hamburg.

---

[20] Rochlitz, 308.

Beethoven was the third of the great Austrian composers who started his acquaintance with the work of Emanuel at an early age. His teacher Christian Gottlob Neefe had trained himself by studying Emanuel's *Versuch*, and Carl Czerny, who later became Beethoven's pupil, reports that the master demanded of the fledgling pianist and composer to bring a copy of the *Versuch* to his first lesson.[21] It is known, moreover, that Beethoven used the work later also in the instruction of Archduke Rudolph.[22]

In a letter to Breitkopf & Härtel in Leipzig, dated 26 July 1809, Beethoven wrote:

> I have only a few samples of Emanuel Bach's compositions for the clavier; and yet, some of them should be in the possession of every true artist, not only for the sake of real enjoyment, but also for the purpose of study.[23]

Later he wrote again:

> I should like to have all the works of C. P. E. Bach, all of which, of course, have been published by you.

And, as the publisher still did not react, the composer wrote on 28 January 1812:

> I fancy you could make me a present of C. P. E. Bach's works, for surely they are rotting with you.[24]

These letters prove both Beethoven's limited knowledge of the work of Emanuel and his eagerness to broaden his acquaintance with this music.

It might be more than a coincidence that Emanuel's clavier Concerto in D minor (Wq. 23 [H. 427]) contains a middle movement in which a delicate keyboard solo effectively contrasts with a forceful, threatening orchestra episode, an idea which is similarly used in the slow movement of Beethoven's Fourth Piano Concerto in G major[25] (ex. 17.3). Even closer seems the relationship between Beethoven's piano sonata in F minor, op. 2, no. 1, and Emanuel's clavier sonata in the same key (Wq. 57/6 [H. 173]). Passionate expression, rhythmic energy, and formal condensation characterize both works.[26] When Beethoven wrote his song "Bitten," op. 48, no. 1, on a text by Gellert, he undoubtedly knew Emanuel's setting of the same poem. There is a striking similarity between certain passages in the two songs[27] (exx. 17.4a-b).

There are other, less obvious resemblances between the works of the two composers. They include the presentation of a melody in the major mode followed by its repetition in minor, an effect which Beethoven and after him Schubert liked to use; the characteristic employment of diminished-seventh chords to produce rhetorical results; the usage of unexpected rests, of chromatic progressions and enharmonic changes; the very effective means of varying a theme through harmonic changes at its repetition in the same composition. All this points to a similarity of artistic aims, but it seems hardly justified to assume that a large scale direct influence prevailed. Beethoven stated himself that he did not know Emanuel's works too well. If he really needed models for the stylistic features he liked to use, he found them in the works of Haydn and Mozart, which he knew better and to which he was closer in every respect.[28]

After Beethoven's death the growing admiration for Johann Sebastian's monumental output hampered the full understanding of Emanuel's work. The prevailing opinion was clearly expressed in an article by Robert Schumann:

---

[21] Alexander Wheelock Thayer, *Ludwig van Beethoven*, rev. ed., ed. Elliot Forbes (Princeton: Princeton University Press, 1967), 228.

[22] Ibid., 467.

[23] Emily Anderson, ed., *The Letters of Beethoven* (London: Macmillan, 1961), 235.

[24] Ibid., 298, 355.

[25] Arnold Schering's preface to his edition of Emanuel's concerto in *Denkmäler deutscher Tonkunst*, vol. 29/30 (Leipzig: Breitkopf & Härtel, 1904-08). A quite different attempt to explain this unusual movement was made by Owen Jander, "Beethoven's 'Orpheus in Hades': The Andante con moto of the Fourth Piano Concerto," *19th Century Music* 8 (1985): 195-212.

[26] Reinhard Oppel, "Über Beziehungen Beethovens zu Mozart und zu Ph. E. Bach," *Zeitschrift für Musikwissenschaft* 5 (1922/23): 30ff.

[27] Ottenberg, 137.

[28] Heinrich Jalowetz, "Beethovens Jugenwerke in ihren melodischen Beziehungen zu Mozart, Haydn, und Phil. E. Bach," in *Sammelbände der Internationalen Musikgesellschaft* 12 (1910/11): 417ff.

> The son Emanuel inherited a beautiful talent. He polished and refined, equipped the predominant harmonies and figurations with singable melodies, but he reached his father by no means as a creative musician.[29]

Schumann obviously realized the significance of Emanuel's work, but he could not help comparing it in a disparaging manner with that of his father.

As a true Romantic artist who lacks understanding of earlier manifestations of passionate expressiveness, the poet-composer E. T. A. Hoffmann wrote:

> I realized only at a later date how ridiculous and silly these concerts were. Usually my teacher played concertos for two claviers by . . . Emanuel Bach.

Example 17.3. C. P. E. Bach, Cembalo Concerto in D minor, Wq. 23 [H. 427], movement 2, meas. 21-27.

---

[29] Robert Schumann, *Gesammelte Schriften über Musik und Musiker*, 5th ed., ed. Martin Kreisig (Leipzig: Breitkopf und Härtel, 1914), 1.

Example 17.4a. C. F. Gellert, "Bitten," C. P. E. Bach, Wq. 194/9 [H. 686/9], meas. 17-22.

Example 17.4b. C. F. Gellert, "Bitten," Beethoven, op. 48/1, meas. 26-32.

At other times he wrote:

> When such a long piece at last was finished, everybody yelled loudly and called out "Bravo, bravo, what a lovely concert. How well, how perfectly executed." Full of veneration they uttered the name of Emanuel Bach. However, the father had hammered and roared so much, I was under the impression this was hardly music which I consider to consist of heart moving melodies. It seemed to me this was only a joke, and the listeners also considered it as a joke.[30]

This phase of comparative uneasiness did not last very long. Johannes Brahms, who was an enthusiastic admirer of the work of J. S. Bach, assembled a library of works by Emanuel of a size hardly equaled by any other composer. It included a large collection of original editions and early handwritten copies, mostly sonatas and related works for clavier alone; in addition, clavier trios, clavier concertos, sacred songs, and two large scale sacred cantatas: altogether well over a hundred items.[31] Brahms was not satisfied with having a substantial number of Bach's works in his library. In 1862 he edited three of Emanuel's *Concerti per il cembalo*, Wq. 43, nos. 1, 4, and 5 [H. 471, 474-75], and in 1864 two of his *Sonatas a cembalo obligato e violin*, Wq. 76 and 78 [H. 512, 514].[32] Finally, in 1868 C. H. Bitter's pioneering two-volume work *Carl Philipp Emanuel und Wilhelm Friedemann Bach und deren Brüder* was issued. It provided a solid basis for further research on the life and work of the North German composer. The Carl Philipp Emanuel Bach research, which was to culminate in the twentieth century, had auspiciously started.

---

[30] E. T. A. Hoffmann, *Musikalische Novellen und Aufsätze*, 2 vols., ed. Edgar Istel (Regensburg: Bosse, 1919), 1:131f.

[31] Kurt Hofmann, *Die Bibliothek von Johannes Brahms: Bücher- u. Musikalienverz.* (Hamburg: Wagner, 1974), 146.

[32] Margit L. McCorkle, *Johannes Brahms, Thematisch-bibliographisches Werkverzeichnis* (Munich: Henle, 1984), 749.

Stephen and Nancy Storace in Vienna

With Irene Geiringer as co-author. Taken from *Essays on the Music of J. S. Bach and Other Divers Subjects: A Tribute to Gerhard Herz*, ed. Robert Lamar Weaver (Louisville, Ky.: University of Louisville, [1981]), 235-44, with permission. By having the stage shared by a woman musician, the Geiringers anticipate the powerful rise of feminist subject matter and methodology in American musical scholarship over the ensuing 1980s and 1990s. The piece continues to serve as a reference for the early biography of the Storaces, although not without occasionally being misinterpreted—see Jane Girdham, *English Opera in Late Eighteenth-Century London: Stephen Storace at Drury Lane* (Oxford: Clarendon Press, 1997), 13f., n. 50.

Among the friends and pupils of Mozart in Vienna, Nancy Storace and her brother Stephen are of particular interest. Nancy was the first Susanna in *Figaro*. Stephen was probably a pupil of Mozart and certainly influenced by him in his own compositions. The information available about the pair is partly sketchy and partly one-sided. An attempt was therefore made here to collect the available data and to draw a fuller picture of Stephen's and Nancy's activities in the Austrian capital, in particular of their relationship to Mozart.

Stephen, born 1762 in London, was the son of an Italian double bass player and an English mother. He was a child prodigy who, at the age of ten, could perform the most difficult violin music. When he was twelve he was sent for professional training to Naples. Later he joined his three-years-younger sister, Anna Selina, called Nancy, likewise endowed with great talent, who had gone with their mother to Venice to study singing with Sacchini. Before long Nancy won great success in Italian operatic theater. As a result the eighteen-year-old was called to Vienna to serve as "prima buffa" in an Italian troupe of singers engaged for the Viennese court theater. Such was the

This article is based primarily on the following sources: "Übersicht der Geschichte der kaiserlich königlichen Hoftheater in Wien, bis zum Jahre 1818," in *Allgemeine musikalische Zeitung* (Leipzig) 24 (1822), cols. 281-87; Hans Boas, "Lorenzo da Ponte als Wiener Theaterdichter," *Sammelbände der internationalen Musikgesellschaft* 15 (1913): 325-38; James D. Brown and Stephen S. Stratton, "Anna Selina Storace" and "Stephen Storace," in *British Musical Biography* (Birmingham: Stratton, 1897), 397-98; Giuseppe Brunati, *Gli sposi malcontenti: Opera comica* (Vienna, 1787), Vienna, Österreichische Nationalbibliothek; ibid., with German translation (Dresden, 1797), Library of Congress, Washington, D.C.; Lorenzo da Ponte, *Memorie*, 3 vols. (New York: Lorenzo & Carlo da Ponte, 1823-27); Otto Erich Deutsch, *Mozart: Die Dokumente seines Lebens* (Kassel: Bärenreiter, 1961); Alfred Einstein, "Shakespeare and Da Ponte," *Monthly Musical Record* 66 (March-April 1936): 56-57; Roger Fiske, preface to Stephen Storace, *No Song, No Supper*, Musica Britannica, 16 (London: Stainer and Bell, 1959); Fiske, "The Operas of Stephen Storace," *Proceedings of the Royal Musical Association* 86 (1959-60): 29-44; Fiske, "Storace, Stephen," *MGG*, 12 (1965), cols. 1411-13; Richard Graves, "The Comic Operas of Stephen Storace," *Musical Times* 95 (1954): 530-32; Otto Jahn, *W. A. Mozart*, 4 vols. (Leipzig: Breitkopf und Härtel, 1856-59); Michael Kelly, *Reminiscences*, 2 vols. (London: H. Colburn, 1826); Judith Ann Anderson, "The Viennese Operas of Stephen Storace" (Ph.D. diss., Catholic University of America, 1972); Alfred Loewenberg, *Annals of Opera, 1597-1940*, 2nd ed., 2 vols. (Geneva: Societas Bibliographica, 1955); Carl Ferdinand Pohl, *Joseph Haydn*, 2 vols. (Leipzpig: Breitkopf & Härtel, 1875-82); Leopold von Sonnleithner, "Materialien zur Geschichte der Oper und des Ballets in Wien," Ms., Gesellschaft der Musikfreunde, Vienna; Stephen Storace, *Gli sposi malcontenti*, Ms. score of the first Viennese performance, Vienna, Österreichische Nationalbibliothek, Ms. copies, Dresden, Sächsische Landesbibliothek, and Washington, D.C., Library of Congress; Martha Kingdon Ward, "Nancy Storace," *Musical Times* 90 (November 1949): 385-88; Alexander Weinmann, "Eine Aria von Bach," *Österreichische Musikzeitschrift* 21 (1966): 53-61; Karl Graf von Zinzendorf, "Tagebuch," Ms., Haus-, Hof-, und Staatsarchiv, Vienna.

Fig. 18.1. Anna Selina Storace, by Pietro Bettelini
Reprinted by permission of the Pictorial Collection of the Austrian National Library, Vienna

artistic standing of young Nancy that, as the Vienna court theater accounts reveal, she was granted an unusually high salary of 3247 florins a year.

On 3 April 1783 the Italian troupe started performing, and one success after another was won by Nancy who, according to Da Ponte's report, was quite idolized by the Viennese. Typical is the verdict of Count Zinzendorf, an indefatigable visitor of the theater. In his diary he described the impression Nancy made upon him: ". . . a pretty figure, sensuous, lovely bosom, beautiful eyes, a white neck, fresh mouth, immaculate skin, the naïveté and temperament of a child, sings like an angel."[1] The Hungarian poet Franz Kazinczy, who attended opera performances in Vienna, expressed a similar verdict in a more concise manner: "Storace, the beautiful songstress, bewitches eye, ear and soul."[2] Even years after Nancy's appearance in Vienna the prestigious *Allgemeine musikalische Zeitung* wrote enthusiastically about her achievements: "She united in her person, like none other alive, and only a few singers of the past, all the gifts of nature, education, and technique which one may desire for performance in Italian comic opera."[3]

---

[1] ". . . jolie figure, voluptueux, belle gorge, beaux yeux, cou blanc, bouche fraîche, belle peau, la naïveté et la petulancé de l'enfance, chante comme un ange."

[2] "Storazzi, a szép énekesné, szememet, fülemet, lelkemet, elbájolta."

[3] ". . . indem sie, wie damals keine in der Welt, und wie nur wenige jemals, alle Gaben der Natur, der Bildung und der Geschicklichkeit, die man sich nur für die itälianisch-komische Oper wünschen mag, in sich vereinigte."

However, after the brilliant success of her first months in Vienna, Nancy went through a period of bad luck and unhappiness in the years 1784 and 1785. An Irish violinist by the name of Dr. John Abraham Fisher had come to Vienna on a concert tour. He fell in love with Nancy, and through persistent pleading induced her to marry him, though he was twice her age. On 28 March 1784 their two names appeared on the program of an academy of the Vienna Tonkünstlersocietät: Nancy as a soloist in Haydn's oratorio *Il ritorno di Tobia* [Hob. XXI:1] conducted by the composer; Dr. Fisher as the performer of his own violin concerto in the intermission between the oratorio's two sections. Harmony was, however, conspicuously absent from their domestic life. Quarrels abounded, and as the tenor Kelly, who often appeared on stage with Nancy, reports in his *Reminiscences*, Fisher "had a very striking way of enforcing his opinion, of which a friend of hers [Nancy's] informed the emperor, who intimated to him, that it would be fit for him to try a change of air, and so the Doctor was banished from Vienna."[4] Nancy and Fisher were never united again, and she kept her marriage to the violinist a secret.

The disturbing events in her married life could but have an impact on Nancy's artistic work. This manifested itself in a manner quite detrimental to her brother, too. Stephen had joined his sister and mother in Vienna. The emperor, evidently at Nancy's suggestion, commissioned the young composer to write an opera for the court theater, a marvelous opportunity for a youth of twenty-three, still quite unknown in Vienna. Stephen set to work and offered a comic opera entitled *Gli sposi malcontenti*. The premiere was scheduled for 1 June 1785, as a visit by his Royal Highness the Duke of York, son ot King George III of England, was expected, and it was considered a nice compliment for the august guest to offer a work by an English composer. The highest dignitaries, including the emperor, had come to the theater to hear Storace's opera. Nancy was entrusted with the main part. However, halfway through the first act her voice failed and through the whole performance she was unable to produce a single sound. Michael Kelly, who sang the main male part, reports in his *Reminiscences*: "I never shall forget her despair and disappointment, but she was not then prepared for the extent of her misfortune, for she did not recover her voice sufficiently to appear on the stage for five months."[5]

The work that occasioned Nancy's breakdown uses a conventional, though skillfully devised, libretto. It deals with two couples who alternately quarrel and fall in love. In addition there is a comic old man, always grumbling, a rejected philanderer bent on intrigues, and a saucy chambermaid. Nancy took the part of young Eginia, who is dissatisfied with her husband and, when first appearing, complains with tears that she lost her freedom and is tied to a man she does not love. These words, perfectly fitting her own situation, seem to have so upset the singer as to produce a nervous crisis.

Despite the disastrous event at the premiere, *Gli sposi malcontenti* found its way to various operatic theaters. Prague, Leipzig, and Dresden performed the work in Italian. In a German translation it was presented at Hanover, Berlin, and Breslau, while Paris offered it in a French version. This success was mainly due to Storace's melodious and cleverly orchestrated score.

Mozart, who naturally followed every phase of Vienna's operatic life, must have felt great sympathy with Nancy's misfortune as he was strongly impressed by her talent. Her fine voice and her spirited acting were in his mind while he planned a new opera. In sketches he drafted in 1784 for an Italian comic opera *Lo sposo deluso*, Nancy's name, as "S^{ra} Fisher," appears as he meant her to interpret the main part. When she recovered from her breakdown and could sing again, Mozart, in conjunction with Salieri and a third composer by the name of Cornetti, wrote a cantata on words by Da Ponte in celebration of this happy event. Unfortunately the composition has not survived.

Nancy and Stephen played a certain part in Mozart's social life also. Kelly mentions in his *Reminiscences* a chamber music party which took place in 1786 at the Storaces. Haydn played the first violin, Dittersdorf the second, Mozart the viola, and Vanhal the cello. Paisiello and the poet Battista Casti were in the audience. Kelly could not refrain from remarking that the performers played "tolerably, but not particularly well."[6] Perhaps another member of the English group attended the performance, too: young Thomas Atwood, who studied counterpoint with Mozart and who was to develop into a composer highly respected in England for his operatic and sacred music.

---

[4] Kelly, 232.

[5] Ibid., 234.

[6] Ibid., 240f.

To write an opera for the Italian troupe was at that time Mozart's main aim. The libretto of *Lo sposo deluso* proved after all not too suitable, and it seemed doubtful whether the emperor would commission him to set it to music, a commission that under prevailing conditions was indispensable. So Mozart was assiduously on the look-out for another text. A fortunate turn of events brought him into contact with the man destined to deliver the ideal libretto to him. Lorenzo da Ponte, since 1781 engaged as poet to the imperial theater, had at first supplied librettos to the powerful court composer Antonio Salieri. When one of these works did not achieve the hoped-for success, Salieri turned to another poet, Casti. To be thus put aside made Da Ponte worry about the safety of his own position, and he approached Mozart. The sequence of events is well-known. Mozart suggested that Da Ponte adapt for him the comedy *Le Mariage de Figaro* by Beaumarchais which, since its Paris premiere in 1784, was creating a sensation everywhere because of its political candor. Da Ponte went to work, Mozart composed one scene after another, and within six weeks the opera was finished. Now the emperor's approval had to be secured, not an easy matter, as Joseph II had forbidden performance of Beaumarchais's comedy. Da Ponte, however, explained to the monarch that he had mitigated the political satire in many ways, and when several numbers of Mozart's opera were played to the emperor he gave in. Thus *Le nozze di Figaro* had its world premiere on 1 May 1786 at the Vienna Burgtheater. While at work on *Figaro*, Mozart was keenly aware of the singers to perform his opera. In order to provide an effective role for Kelly, he devised the part of old Basilio for the young tenor. More important still, he wrote the part of Susanna for Nancy Storace. It was not only ideally suited for her voice: Susanna's whole character reflects the personality of the brilliant young songstress. High-spirited, energetic, and utterly charming, Susanna seems in a way like a portrait of Nancy as she is described in contemporary reports. It was justly remarked that we owe to her some of the most exquisite sections in the opera.

The year 1786 afforded also to Nancy's brother opportunities to win laurels at the Vienna Burgtheater. According to Da Ponte's memoirs, Stephen turned to the poet as soon as work on *Figaro* was finished and asked him to write a new opera libretto for him. The emperor was willing to commission it, and Stephen suggested a work by Shakespeare for adaptation. *The Comedy of Errors* was chosen and skillfully transformed into an operatic libretto entitled *Gli equivoci*.[7] Shakespeare's five acts were condensed into two, which simplified the action and made it more exciting. Storace's familiarity with German music and, most of all, his study of Mozart's works certainly had an impact on this opera. *Gli equivoci* is not a pure comedy any more: there are also entirely serious, as well as partly serious and partly comic characters in it. The very overture seems to be influenced by Gluck's *Iphigénie en Tauride* as well as by Mozart's *Figaro*. Like Gluck's festive opera, performed 1781 in Vienna, *Gli equivoci* begins with a prelude portraying a storm at sea and preparing the first scene. At the beginning of the recapitulation the curtain rises and one observes lightning, thunder, and hail produced by the customary stage machinery. Moreover, the overture, like that to *Figaro*, employs no less than five subjects, which are not developed but later recur in slightly modified form. Apart from this piece, *Gli equivoci* has, again like *Figaro*, only one purely instrumental number, which has also a programmatic character. Either opera has four *accompagnato* recitatives. Moreover, in Storace's work the musical forms are structured more freely than in the typical Italian *opera buffa*. Minor keys, expressive chromatic progressions, bold modulation, the occasional use of uncommon instruments such as "tamburino" and "piffero" (small pipe) increase the dramatic impact of the composition. Ensembles from duets to sextets fill more than half the score. In the finale of the first act Storace divides his nine characters into groups according to their personality, as Mozart had done in the finale to the second act of *Figaro*. In addition, there are also melodic affinities to Mozart's idiom which, though to a lesser degree, may already be observed in Storace's first Vienna opera. As an example, a few measures will be quoted from the aria in *Gli sposi malcontenti*, which brought forth Nancy's breakdown (ex. 18.1). Imbued with deep feeling and tender warmth is also the beginning of the following aria from *Gli equivoci* [see fig. 18.2]. In the first opera we find moreover a tenor aria (ex. 18.2) which seems to conjure up Bartolo's aria "La vendetta" in the first act of *Figaro*. The Vienna score contains also two arias which Süssmayr had contributed for later Viennese performances. These pieces seem to fit well into Storace's score, which is not surprising as both these young composers were under Mozart's influence. As a matter of fact, Süssmayr's marchlike aria "A un onesto mercadante" (ex. 18.3) appears to be influenced by the aria in which Figaro makes fun of Cherubino. Though there is no proof that Storace stood to Mozart in the close relationship of pupil to teacher, as Süssmayr did, there are plenty of instances pointing to Stephen's artistic indebtedness to the Viennese master.

---

[7] Da Ponte employed a French translation by the title of *Les Méprises*, as he was not conversant with the English language.

Gli equivoci had its world premiere on 27 December 1786 and was repeated twice in that year and three times in 1787. Zinzendorf tersely remarked in his diary: "The music is nice, but the topic offers continuous confusion.[8] This criticism is not unjustified; however, the culprit in this case is neither Storace nor Da Ponte but Shakespeare, who introduces in his comedy two sets of twins with a resulting unending sequence of mistaken identities. In 1788 the opera was presented in a German version at Pressburg (Bratislava). Possibly at that occasion the material of the first performance was used, as the score in the Vienna National-Bibliothek contains in the music numbers, under the original Italian text, a German translation inserted by another hand. In 1793 *Gli equivoci* was performed in Leipzig and Prague (here under the title *Gli quattro gemelli*), and in 1797 Dresden offered the opera in a somewhat altered version.

Example 18.1. Stephen Storace, *Gli sposi malcontenti*, act 1, "Ah, che invan io piango," Eginia.

Example 18.2. Stephen Storace, *Gli sposi malcontenti*, "Ad un uom versato," Valente.

Example 18.3. Franz Xaver Süssmayr, insertion aria, "A un onesto mercadante."

---

[8] "Il y a de jolie musique, mais le sujet est une confusion continuelle."

Fig. 18.2. Stephen Storace, *Gli equivoci*, act 1, scene 2, no. 3
(Egeone, opening through meas. 13),
"Il ciel che tutto vede," from the Ms. score

Washington, Library of Congress

Fig. 18.2.—*Continued*

On the day before the Viennese premiere of *Gli equivoci*, Mozart noted in his thematic catalog that he had composed a scena and rondo entitled "Ch'io mi scordi di te?" for soprano, piano obbligato, and orchestra "for Mademoiselle Storace and me." On the autograph (which was lost during the last war) he notated "Composto per la Signora Storace dal suo servo e amico W. A. Mozart 26 di December 1786." Aware that the Italian troupe would have to leave Vienna before long, as their contract had expired, Mozart decided to shape for Nancy an aria from the Viennese version of *Idomeneo*, precede it by a new recitative, and replace the solo violin of the original by a piano obbligato which carries on an expressive dialogue with the soprano. Various scholars have interpreted the piano part as a secret declaration of love for the charming Nancy. For the time being we have to consider this as a poetic myth, as letters which Mozart is alleged to have written to Nancy have so far not come to light. It is certain that Mozart wanted to erect in this work (K. 505) a monument to his artistic collaboration with his Susanna, for the introductory recitative (the "scena," as the composer calls it) contains clear reminiscences of the parts of Cherubino and Susanna in *Figaro*. Moreover, Mozart must have liked appearing in a concert with the idolized star, and he wrote for himself a solo part which afforded him a good opportunity for displaying his unique pianistic mastery. There seem reasons enough for the composition of the piece. About the rest, the nature of Mozart's feelings for his Susanna, we know nothing. It seems that the work was performed by the two soloists in Nancy's farewell recital on 23 February 1787. On that evening the singer presented also a new aria titled "Schwer drückt es meine Seele dich Donaustadt zu lassen" (It weighs heavily on my soul to leave thee, city on the Danube). The work is not by Christian Bach, as the *Wiener Zeitung* noted, nor by Anfossi as C. F. Pohl assumes, but, as Graf Zinzendorf immediately recognized and noted in his diary, based on an aria in Stephen's *Gli equivoci*.

Mozart's English friends urged him to try his luck in England. Such a plan greatly appealed to him. However, it had to be shelved for the time being, as ailing Leopold Mozart was opposed to it and unable to take care of Wolfgang's children during their parents' absence. Yet plans were made for the future, and Mozart parted on the best terms from his English friends. It was quite a sizable group which left the Austrian capital on its way to London. There were the two Storaces, their mother, the ladies' favorite lap-dog, an English nobleman who was in love with Nancy, and finally Attwood and Kelly. They all made a stop in Salzburg and received a friendly welcome from

Wolfgang's father. Leopold in a letter to his daughter reported the visit: "I galloped round the town with them on Tuesday from ten to two in order to show them a few sights. We lunched at two o'clock. In the evening she sang three arias and they left for Munich at midnight! They had two carriages, each with four post-horses. A servant rode in advance as courier to arrange for the changing of eight horses. Goodness, what luggage they had! This journey must have cost them a fortune."[9]

Mozart's acquaintance with the two Storaces had certain consequences for each of the three people concerned. Mozart's plan to travel to England became known to the emperor, who decided to keep the composer in Vienna by appointing him (at long last!) *Kammermusicus* at a salary of 800 florins. It was anything but a glamorous opening, but still better than nothing.

Stephen kept the memory of his stay in the Austrian capital alive even after his return to England. He edited an extensive *Collection of Original Harpsichord Music*, which contained works of various Viennese composers. Mozart occupied a prominent place in this edition—he was represented with three piano trios in Storace's arrangement and the hitherto unprinted Rondo in F, K. 494. As a composer, too, Stephen at first tried to follow his great model. However, a new Italian opera, *La cameriera astuta*, which he wrote for the London King's Theatre, had but little success. The *Public Advertiser* criticized it for "having insufficient melodious soft Italian music" and "too much of the German style of Gluck . . . loaded with harsh terrifying music of trumpeting and drumming."[10] Likewise, Kelly's valiant efforts to have *Gli equivoci* performed in London proved unavailing. Thus, the composer decided to write stage works with English text and spoken dialogue. These compositions, which incorporate numbers from Stephen's earlier operas and in their musical idiom still follow to some extent the Viennese tradition, were at last received with enthusiastic acclaim. However, the composer was not fated to enjoy his success for a long time. He died in 1796, at the height of his creative powers, not quite thirty-four years old.

Nancy likewise was intent upon making the London public aware of Mozart's greatness. On 9 May 1789 she sang at the King's Theatre a piece from *Figaro* inserted into an opera by Gazzaniga. (It was probably the first time a number from a Mozart opera was heard in London.) On 28 February 1790 she performed in a pasticcio one aria each from *Figaro* and *Don Giovanni*. We do not know how the audience reacted to these works. By and large Nancy seemed unable to kindle enthusiasm for her interpretation of Italian opera. Apparently her style was too much influenced by Mozart and thus deviated from traditional Italian virtuosity. She therefore turned to the English stage and was highly successful at the Drury Lane Theatre and later at Covent Garden, usually appearing as a comedienne and winning the hearts of the audience with her charm and temperament. Not infrequently she could be seen as a witty and resourceful chambermaid, the role assigned to her in *Figaro*. After the death of her brother, Nancy visited the Continent again, this time concentrating on Germany and Italy. Vienna had lost its attraction for her, as neither Mozart nor her brother was there any longer. The singer retired from the stage in 1808 and spent her last years in Dulwich. She died in 1817, surviving by more than two decades the two men who had played such an important part in her life.

---

[9] ". . . den Dienstag bin von 10 uhr morgens bis 2 uhr mit ihnen in der Statt herum galloppiert um ein und anders ihnen zu zeigen. um 2 uhr speisten wir erst zu Mittag. Abends sang sie 3 Arien, und *um 12 uhr in der Nacht* sind sie nach München abgereiset. sie hatten 2 Wägen, ieden mit 2 Postpferd, ein Bedienter ritte voraus um die 8 Pferd als Currier zu bestellen. welch ein Gepäck!—diese Reise mag Geld kosten!" Translation from Emily Anderson, *The Letters of Mozart and His Family*, 2nd ed. (London: Macmillan, 1966), letter no. 545 from Leopold to his daughter, Salzburg, 1 March 1787, pp. 905f.

[10] Fiske, preface to *No Song, No Supper*, xviii; the same quotation in his *English Theatre Music in the Eighteenth Century* (London: Oxford University Press, 1973), 498f., is assigned to *The Spectator*, no. 6, in place of the *Public Advertiser*.

Part 4

On Haydn Scholars and Scholarship

Robert Sondheimer

Review of *Haydn: A Historical and Psychological Study Based on His Quartets* (London: Bernoulli, [1951]). Reprinted from *Notes* 9 (1952): 604-05, by permission of the Music Library Association. From his first review for *Notes* published in December 1946 until his last in 1989, Geiringer evaluated 129 books and scores for the journal, a figure believed to be a record—see "Notes for Notes," *Notes* 45 (1989): 733. Much of that effort was devoted to items related to Haydn and then, with the appearance of the first volumes of the new collected edition, to the activities of the newly established Haydn Institute in Cologne (see the annotation to essay 22, below).

Sondheimer (1881-1956) was an ardent advocate of the "Vorklassik." This volume constituted his principal study relating to Haydn, and its publication sparked a vigorous exchange between Geiringer's former pupil Robbins Landon and the author in the pages of the *Music Review* published around the same time as Geiringer's piece.

Robert Sondheimer has devoted a life of intensive study to that remarkable transitional phase which connects the Baroque and Classic periods. He has written on the works of preclassic composers, and his private publishing firm, the Edition Bernoulli, has printed a sizable number of symphonic works from the middle of the eighteenth century in his revisions. This new book, which he has published at the age of seventy, is a direct outgrowth of this activity. Although it bears the name of Haydn on its title page, it deals not so much with Haydn as with men like Beck, Boccherini, Sammartini, Stamitz, and Wagenseil. The unaffected admiration Dr. Sondheimer feels for the achievements of these preclassic artists leads him to show Haydn as a rather ambitious but not too gifted pupil, who zealously imitated works written by composers of the *style galant* and *Empfindsamkeit* but seldom succeeded in equaling his great masters. There can be no doubt that Sondheimer has made some interesting contributions to our knowledge about the origin of Joseph Haydn's string quartet style, but too large a part of his book is devoted to an exaggerated glorification of preclassic art with subtle hints that the author himself was the Columbus of this vast continent with its unlimited possibilities. Unfortunately Dr. Sondheimer overlooks the fact that among his fellow explorers were men like Riemann, Sandberger, Adler, Fischer, Torrefranca, Falck, Schünemann, and Kretzschmar, whose discoveries are apt to dwarf his own contributions. The Haydn expert will appreciate Sondheimer's intimate knowledge of the material he discusses; the average music lover, however, will find it difficult to bear with the book's involved diction, which seems to result from an all too literal translation of the German original.

While the author is inclined to find fault with the statements of quite a few of his fellow research students (including Marion Scott and Alfred Einstein), he is not quite infallible himself. On page 31, for instance, we find the assertion that Haydn wrote his *Seven Last Words* [Hob. XX/2] at the age of fifty; actually they were composed in 1785, when the composer was fifty-three. More surprising still is Dr. Sondheimer's remark on the same page that *The Seasons* [Hob. XXI:3] was Haydn's last sacred work. It seems hardly proper to describe as a sacred work a composition in which hunting and drinking play an important part; moreover, in 1802, one year after completing *The Seasons*, Haydn wrote the *Harmoniemesse* [Hob. XXII:14], a composition undoubtedly designated for the church.

Donald Francis Tovey

Review of *Pianoforte Trio in F-sharp Minor* [Hob. XV:26] (London: Oxford University Press, 1951). Reprinted from *Notes* 9 (1952): 644, by permission of the Music Library Association. Oxford published this edition more than a decade after the death of the brilliant English composer-pianist-scholar (1875-1940). With the financial collapse of the Haydn Society and the abandonment of its collected edition in this year, such individual efforts were the only way Haydn's unpublished music could reach the public. Geiringer closes his review with a personal comment that anticipates the wave of the early music movement that was to gain so much momentum in future decades. As fate would have it, he was to evaluate another edition of the same work almost four decades later in his last review for *Notes* (see essay 22, pp. 221-30). By that time the number of authentic keyboard trios attributed to Haydn could be increased to thirty-eight.

Haydn's thirty-one piano trios mostly belong to the category of the sonata for the clavier with the accompaniment of a violin and a violoncello *ad libitum*, so popular in the second half of the eighteenth century. Such music was primarily intended for the weak square piano of the time, and the stringed instruments had the task of emphasizing the main melodic lines. This form of composition lost its meaning with the arrival of the large and powerful piano of the Romantic period. Now there did not seem to be any point in having the violin double the right hand in unison and the cello the left hand of the piano part, and, even though most of Haydn's trios are mature works of great artistic value, they became completely obsolete. To save this exquisite music from oblivion, one would have to perform it on the tiny sweet claviers of the eighteenth century, or else to adapt it to modern instruments. Sir Donald Tovey made such an arrangement with great skill and fine tact. His basic aim was to avoid at all costs the monotonous unisons between the clavier and the stringed instruments which are a feature of Haydn's originals. This he achieved by omitting from the piano part the melodic line entrusted to the strings by inserting rests, changing unisons into octaves, etc. There can be no doubt that the resulting arrangement is more transparent and offers greater scope to modern performers than the version of the eighteenth century; and, since the *Trio in F-sharp minor* (Breitkopf & Härtel, no. 2) contains in the middle movement an Adagio which Haydn took over from his Symphony no. 102, Tovey's adaptation has many points in its favor. This writer must confess, however, that he would prefer to hear the work performed on a pre-romantic piano, so that the balance of parts, as conceived by the composer, would be restored.

Anthony van Hoboken

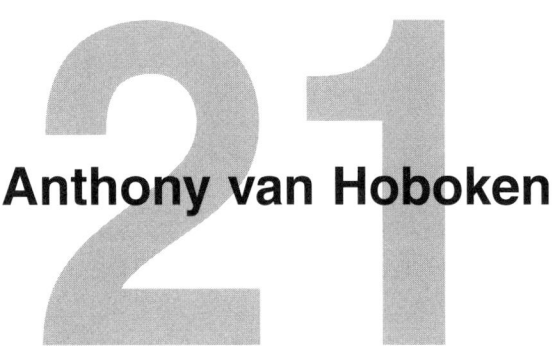

Reviews of *Joseph Haydn: Thematisch-bibliographisches Werkverzeichnis*, vols. 1-2 (Mainz: Schott's Söhne, 1957-71). Reprinted from *Notes* 14 (1957): 565-66, and *Journal of the American Musicological Society* 25 (1972): 471-73, by permission. Having vowed already in 1932 "to deprive the thematic index . . . of [its] utopian character" (essay 2, p. 17), indeed he went ahead and compiled and published in microfilm form his own thematic catalog of the folksongs in 1953, it was fitting that Geiringer review the two massive tomes edited by Hoboken, rightly referring to them as "milestones." The two reviews published fifteen years apart chronicle the long journey of Hoboken's tireless work. Now (2001), of course, with the Mozart Köchel catalog being prepared in a 7th edition, Hoboken's singular edition cries out for updating.

This is undoubtedly one of the most significant musicological publications we have witnessed in recent years. Dr. van Hoboken's book presents the results of painstaking and arduous work carried out over more than a quarter of a century. The gigantic Haydn catalog in three or possibly four sections, the first of which is now published, could only have been compiled by a distinguished scholar who gave unstintingly of his talent and his time without any thought of financial rewards.

Attempts to create thematic lists of Haydn's works go back to the eighteenth century. The composer himself, as early as 1765, set out on such a task and eventually entrusted his faithful *famulus*, Johann Elssler, Jr., with the compilation of an extensive catalog which was concluded in 1805. Unfortunately the Haydn-Elssler *Verzeichnis*, though highly important, is neither complete nor fully reliable. In the second half of the nineteenth century Carl Ferdinand Pohl began to collect on a large scale material pertaining to the life and works of Haydn. On many thousand slips of paper he noted in a tiny script every fact he had found, but the research was undertaken on so vast a scale that the scholar was not able to conclude even his biography, while only a very small part of the thematic catalog was published as an appendix to his book. Another important step was taken in our century in connection with the launching of the Haydn Collected Edition (to which so short a life span was allowed!), and scholarly thematic lists were compiled for the symphonies (Mandyczewski), piano sonatas (Päsler), and songs (Friedländer). There followed a significant contribution made by the eminent Danish scholar Jens Peter Larsen in his *Die Haydn-Überlieferung* and its companion volume *Drei Haydn Kataloge in Faksimile*. The Haydn material thus available has been brought together with infinite thoroughness by Dr. van Hoboken, whose mere achievement of working through the maze of Pohl's annotations must be regarded by anyone familiar with the material as a feat deserving fullest admiration. Moreover, an imposing amount of new data was added by Dr. van Hoboken, who had studied with never-failing perserverance the Haydn material in practically all the significant Western libraries.

This book is not arranged chronologically like Köchel's Mozart catalog, since a large part of Haydn's works cannot be ascribed with accuracy even to a certain year. The author groups the compositions according to forms and performing media: symphonies, overtures, divertimentos for four or more voices, string quartets, three-part divertimentos, string trios, duos for different instruments, concertos, marches, dances, works for different instruments with baryton, baryton trios, baryton duos, baryton concertos, divertimentos for clavier in combination with several instruments, clavier trios, clavier duos, clavier sonatas, smaller pieces for clavier two-hands, works for clavier four-hands, clavier concertos, pieces for musical clocks, *The Seven Last Words* (instrumental versions). Within each group Dr. van Hoboken uses the numbers of the collected edition or, in the absence of a twentieth-century list, the numbers of the Haydn-Elssler *Verzeichnis* of 1805. Works not figuring in either of these lists are given additional numbers and marked with an asterisk. In the case of the symphonies, for instance, the 104 works of Mandyczewski's list are followed by 105*, the *Symphonie concertante* of 1792; 106*, a lost early symphony; 107*, an early work usually considered as a partita. The authentic works are followed within each group by a list of the spurious compositions, which are designated by a letter indicating the tonality and an arabic number. Thus, in the case of the string quartets the compiler enumerates no less than 66 additional works, while the series of added symphonies goes up to 148.

For each composition the catalog supplies as far as possible the following information: the name or nickname, the date of composition, the instruments used, the incipits of each movement (including trios of minuets), documentary evidence regarding the composition, a very thorough description of the autograph whenever it has survived, a list of early manuscript copies, a list of prints (including arrangements) issued in Haydn's lifetime. There follows a section, labeled rather modestly as *Anmerkungen*, which supplies a wealth of biographical information derived from contemporary literature, Haydn's own letters, etc. In conclusion the author selects out of the various works on Haydn's music a few references to the composition in question, occasionally quoting a passage literally. Even this short survey should give an idea of the tremendous scope of the new Haydn catalog.

It is easily understandable that Dr. van Hoboken did not attempt to provide in every case a definite solution for the ticklish question of authenticity, and he emphasizes in his preface that this was not his goal. The Overture to *King Lear* (Ia:9) and the six *Feldparthien* (II:41*-46*, two of which were edited by the undersigned) are, for instance, listed as genuine although their authenticity is not generally recognized. On the other hand, the string quartet in E major (III:E2) which E. F. Schmid edited in 1936 is listed as spurious, the situation being somewhat obscured by the omission of the customary mention of the early source. Further research will have to set in at this point, and it might in some details change the picture. Yet for all further studies the new Haydn catalog provides a tool of inestimable value. Its publication may be considered a milestone in our progress towards the evaluation of a great composer undeservedly neglected in our time.

*   *   *   *

Plodding and struggling to present the catalog of a composer's works is a very peculiar kind of activity for which only a small number of scholars appear well suited. Collecting an almost endless number of data and facts about hundreds of compositions would seem to tax the patience of a saint. A new work of this kind has now been completed, and as far as dimensions go, it surpasses all its predecessors. Anthony van Hoboken's *Haydn Verzeichnis*, the second volume of which deals with the vocal compositions, has recently been published and is certainly a work of quite unusual proportions. With its 1,500 large-size pages, it is almost twice as big as Schmieder's *Bach-Werke-Verzeichnis* or Kinsky-Halm's *Das Werk Beethovens*, and this in spite of the fact that the musical incipits are presented in a single line only, while they are offered in two lines in the two earlier catalogs. Not even the enlarged latest edition of the Köchel-Mozart listing approaches the size of the *Haydn Verzeichnis*.

The student's first reaction to these facts must be amazement and admiration for the gigantic achievement. Dr. van Hoboken carried out his task single-handedly, and he was approaching his eighty-fifth birthday when the second volume of the *Haydn Verzeichnis* was finally printed.

The first volume of the Hoboken catalog, listing Haydn's instrumental compositions, was published as early as 1957. At that time the author visualized a continuation of his work in three additional volumes. The second was to contain Haydn's original vocal compositions, the third his arrangements of Scottish and Welsh folksongs as well as various lists (opus numbers used in early editions, contemporary publishers, etc.). A fourth and final volume was to present a systematic survey of the motivic material appearing in Haydn's compositions.

These plans had to be radically changed, which was no doubt one of the reasons for the long delay in the publication's progress. Haydn's folksong arrangements are presented together with the original vocal compositions in volume 2. A supplementary volume with various lists and indexes is in preparation, while the idea of a motivic survey seems to have been abandoned. Thus, for all practical purposes, work on the bulk of the Haydn catalog is now finished.

The question is bound to arise as to why the *Verzeichnis* had to assume such a huge size. The answer lies largely in the nature of the material, partly in the approach chosen by the author. To present the works in chronological order, as was done in the case of Mozart or Schubert, seemed hardly possible, as we are still unable to provide the date of origin for a large number of Haydn's compositions. Thus, as in Schmieder's *Bach-Werke-Verzeichnis*, a systematic arrangement of the works, according to categories, had to be chosen. The resulting twenty-three groups of instrumental compositions and eighteen groups of vocal works in the Hoboken catalog are bound to spread the material out somewhat, particularly since each section is preceded by a substantial stylistic and historical introduction which in one case (folksong arrangements) even grows into a well-documented monograph of close to a dozen pages.

Within several groups of vocal compositions the works are arranged in three subsections. The first contains compositions considered to be authentic. These are usually presented in the order and numbering which the collected edition or another reliable modern edition assigns to them. The second subgroup embraces works which are generally regarded as genuine, although their authenticity cannot be fully proved. Hoboken indicates them by the addition of an asterisk after the number. The third subgroup lists works assumed not to be authentic. These are arranged in the order of their keys and are designated by the key letter followed by an arabic numeral (C 1, C 2, C 3 . . . D 1, D 2, D 3, etc.). Moreover, smaller print distinguishes this third subsection from the preceding ones. Hoboken's system appears quite practical for the time being, but it might prove less satisfactory in the long run. Our ideas regarding the authenticity of Haydn's works are still subject to revision. Quite a few works which the volume of instrumental compositions considered as authentic in 1957 are no longer attributed to Haydn, while works with the derogatory letter-prefix in volume 1 of Hoboken's catalog have been admitted to the collected edition (cf. the clavier sonatas and clavier trios). Similar doubts might be raised concerning the full validity of the three categories in the case of Haydn's smaller church compositions. In spite of the highly valuable contribution by Irmgard Becker-Glauch—"Neue Forschungen zu Haydns Kirchenmusik," *Haydn-Studien* 2 (1970): 167-241—new insight into this complex field of research may well be gained in the future.

It is also regrettable that in the case of the "authentic" Masses, Hoboken deviates from the numbering system of the collected edition. After the first Mass he inserts the incipits of two Masses, now probably lost, which the collected edition had relegated to the end of their list. Apart from this change, his arrangement is the same. As a result, his no. 4 is no. 2 in the collected edition, his nos. 5 and 6 are nos. 3 and 4, and so forth to nos. 13 and 14, alias 11 and 12. In all likelihood the author was motivated by considerations of chronology. It might be argued, however, that it would have been safer to preserve the earlier, generally adopted numbering system, even though it may not reflect a strict chronological order—this all the more as details of chronology are apt to be controversial.

For each work, Hoboken supplies in the usual manner the date of composition (as far as it can be ascertained), a listing of the voices and instruments used, and the incipits of each movement or piece. Then follows a paragraph with the rather unfamiliar heading *Nachweise*. The author enumerates here the major documentation available for each composition: entries in Haydn's *Entwurf-Katalog* and the Haydn-Elssler list of 1805; references in the catalogs of the great collector of manuscripts Aloys Fuchs; and data from Fétis's *Biographie universelle*, Gerber's *Lexikon der Tonkünstler*, early Breitkopf lists, and the like. Anything helpful in establishing the position of the individual work within the composer's overall output is here assembled.

If an autograph is known, Hoboken describes it with a thoroughness quite unusual in thematic catalogs. Analytical comments of nearly half a page are the rule, but even discussions of one and one-half or two pages may be found in the section devoted to Haydn's operas. The *Photogramm Archiv*, a comprehensive collection of photographs of eighteenth- and nineteenth-century original manuscripts, which Hoboken himself had presented in 1925 to the music division of the Österreichische Nationalbibliothek, proved here of particular help to the scholar. As an example of the important dividends resulting from the author's painstaking thoroughness, the autograph fragment of the Biblioteca Centrală de Stat in Bucharest might be mentioned. According to an unconfirmed rumor, the beginning of the original manuscript of Haydn's *Great Organ Mass* [Hob. XXII:4] was preserved in Romania's capital. Hoboken managed to obtain detailed information about the mysterious fragment and discovered that it belonged to a different work, the *Mass of St. Cecilia* [Hob. XXII:5]. This composition had been assigned by Pohl to the year 1781, by Larsen to the period between 1769 and 1773. The newly found manuscript, however, bears the date 1766 in Haydn's hand. Moreover, in the composer's own catalogs the work had been listed as *Missa Cellensis* (*Mariazeller Messe* [Hob. XXII:8]). This had always been considered a *lapsus pennae* committed by the composer himself, as the well-known *Missa Cellensis* was a different composition, written in 1782. The Bucharest fragment, however, has the autograph heading *Missa Cellensis*, thus proving that the entries in Haydn's catalogs are correct. Apparently the composer had twice written Masses for the famous Austrian pilgrims' church.

The list of early copies (*Abschriften*) which Dr. van Hoboken provides for each composition is again unusually extensive. This seems justified, since in the eighteenth century a large percentage of all Haydn's music was handwritten, while much of the printed music was completely unreliable. Thus the author lists—as he states in the preface to volume 1—"the largest possible number of manuscripts whether representing genuine or doubtful, printed or non-printed compositions" (p. xv). He offers a wealth of information which is obviously unequal in value.

A similar situation prevails regarding the listing of printed editions (*Ausgaben*) in the Hoboken catalog. The scholar owns probably the finest collection of eighteenth- and nineteenth-century musical prints in private possession. As a matter of fact, the *Haydn Verzeichnis* grew out of its author's wish to create a scientific tool for the cataloging of the most problematic part of his vast holdings. Thus Hoboken lists with meticulous care the enormous number of prints from Haydn's lifetime as well as the most important modern editions. Since more than 125 contemporary firms published works by the famous Haydn, partly in their original versions and partly in various arrangements, this section of the catalog alone would fill a substantial volume.

Hoboken's comments on individual compositions (*Anmerkungen*) are also quite lavish. His statements dealing with the history of the work in question, its autograph and significant printed editions, are generously supported by excerpts from letters and other documents. A similar policy prevails in the bibliographical sections (*Literatur*). The author offers not only accurate references to a host of books and articles, but also many literal quotations and even quite extensive abstracts from some important studies. At times he also quotes contradictory observations by different authors or a questionable statement, always with the purpose of providing the reader with the broadest possible basis for reaching his own conclusions.

Proofreading for volume 2 was thoroughly done, and tiny errors like "Arie no. 16" instead of "Duett no. 16" (p. 411) and "1876" instead of "1786" (p. 422) are rare. On the other hand, a certain difficulty arises out of the author's necessarily wide use of abbreviations. In the various sections of his work he employs more than 500 different abbreviations (to my surprise I found among them no less than eleven referring to my own publications: *Geir*[1], *Geir*[2], *Geir*[3], etc.); but the key to these abbreviations is dispersed over six different lists such as "Catalogues and Libraries," "Books and Periodicals," or "General Abbreviations." It is almost unavoidable that the reader is forced to hunt through two, three, or even more of these indexes before he discovers the meaning of the particular abbreviation he is looking for, and the same process will have to be repeated by him again and again. I am therefore pleading for a single, comprehensive list of all the abbreviations to be incorporated into the planned supplement to the catalog.

Obviously, such details have no bearing on the intricate value of the whole work. With the publication of volume 2 of the Hoboken *Verzeichnis*, Haydn research has taken a decisive step forward.

Joseph Haydn Institute, Cologne

Between 1958 and 1988 Geiringer served unofficially as regular reviewer for *Notes* of the volumes of Haydn's works being produced by the Haydn Institute in Cologne. In all he reviewed fifty-eight volumes. The six reviews below have been selected because, taken together, they tell the story of the Institute over those three decades. The last three reviews, while completing the story, also contain evaluations of all of the thirty-eight piano trios. Together they form a miniature monograph on this little-known chamber repertory.

Barytontrios, Nr. 49-72, *Barytontrios, Nr. 73-96*, ed. Hubert Unverricht; *Messen, Nr. 5-8*, ed. H. C. Robbins Landon in conjunction with Karl Heinz Füssl & Christa Landon; *Lo speziale: dramma giocoso*, ed. Helmut Wirth; *Mehrstimmige Gesänge,* ed. Paul Mies; *Kanons*, ed. Otto Erich Deutsch, *Joseph Haydn Werke* XIV:3-4; XXIII:2; XXV:3; XXX; XXXI [Hob. XI:49-96; XXII:5-8; XXVIII:3; XXVc:1-9, XXVb:1-4; XXVIIa:1-10, XXVIIb:1-46]. Munich-Duisburg: Henle, 1958-59. Reprinted from *Notes* 17 (1959): 127-29, by permission of the Music Library Association.

Habent sua fata libelli. And not only is the fate of books strange, but the same may often be said about music. As a case in point, we can offer the various attempts to provide a collected edition of the works of Joseph Haydn. After the composer's death, almost a century passed before the first important enterprise got under way, and even then the Haydn *Gesamtausgabe*, published by Breitkopf & Härtel in Leipzig, made slow progress and came to a complete halt in the thirties before a dozen volumes had been issued. A second attempt was begun in 1950 by a group of music-lovers in Boston. The Haydn enthusiast H. C. Robbins Landon acted as the spark plug in this venture, with the Danish scholar Jens Peter Larsen assuming the scientific responsibility for the work. Financial difficulties, however, plagued the American Haydn Society, and its edition had to be discontinued after the publication of only four volumes. A third attempt is now being made and present indications point to its achieving full success. A Haydn Institute has been set up in Cologne with financial assistance coming from the German government, the city of Cologne, and some private sponsors. Dr. Friedrich Blume, the energetic editor of the monumental encyclopedia *Die Musik in Geschichte und Gegenwart*, is at the helm of the project and has secured the cooperation of the G. Henle Verlag of Munich (well known particularly for its edition of the Kinsky-Halm Beethoven catalog). The scientific direction is again in the competent hands of Larsen. Photographic reproductions of all the available sources are being assembled at Cologne, where all the preliminaries are worked out with meticulous care.

The six volumes issued so far represent different aspects of Haydn's creative activities. Paul Mies, the highly respected expert on the German Lied, opened the series with an edition of Haydn's delightful songs for three and four voices with clavier—some of the finest specimens of vocal chamber music the eighteenth century produced. Since the autographs of all thirteen works in the volume have been preserved in the library of the Paris Conservatory and editions of them were published in 1803 during Haydn's own lifetime, the editor did not have to face the thorny problem of inadequate sources so often encountered in Haydn research.

While these gems of vocal music are comparatively well known, the Haydn student will discover new aspects of the composer in Otto Erich Deutsch's edition of the fifty-six canons. As long ago as 1932 Deutsch pointed out that more than half the canons had been first published, out of prudery, with rather inferior texts provided by an employee of Breitkopf & Härtel. The editor has now restored the pithy texts set by Haydn, greatly adding to the attraction of these entertaining little pieces. It is to be hoped that they will achieve wide circulation in this form, especially since their performance will be facilitated by the presentation of the canons in full score without any attempt to resort to the customary (and rather annoying) condensation.

H. C. Robbins Landon prepared a volume containing the first four Masses for the Haydn Society of Boston and is continuing that series now with a volume containing Mass nos. 5 to 8. In doing so, a re-evaluation of the traditional attitude toward the publication of Classical music had to be made. Autographs are available for all four works, but they employ a sort of musical shorthand which leaves out important details of phrasing, application of text to music, and so on. It was necessary to use handwritten contemporary parts to fill the gap, and material found in the collection over which Haydn himself had presided furnished particularly important evidence. The significance for Haydn research of the Esterházy Archives formerly in Eisenstadt has only recently become fully apparent, but these Archives have now been used extensively for the present revision. (The basic importance of the Eisenstadt collection for another phase of Haydn research was emphasized by this writer in an article in the October 1959 issue of *Musical Quarterly*.)

We are grateful to Messrs. Blume and Larsen for offering us two volumes of baryton trios, those mysterious compositions to which Haydn owed a grade of prestige at the Esterházy court quite out of proportion to the artistic value of the little pieces. Prince Nicholas "the Magnificent" was a passionate amateur player of the strange cello-like instrument with its added set of sympathetic strings underneath the fingerboard, and Haydn had to produce well over a hundred works to satisfy his patron's insatiable appetite for new compositions. Hubert Unverricht, a member of the Institute's staff, served as editor of the volumes. It may be interesting to know that one of his main sources was furnished by the fine parts written by Haydn's copyist Radnitzky and preserved today at the Library of Congress in Washington. Prince Nicholas must have been a very skillful performer, if we may judge from the rather difficult baryton parts Haydn supplied for him. Figures written underneath certain notes indicate a pizzicato of the sympathetic metal strings. These strings must be plucked by the thumb of the left hand while the remaining fingers play the melody on gut strings suspended over the fingerboard. Thus all five fingers were in action, and the left hand could give no firm support to the neck—a state of affairs that would surely fill a modern cellist with dismay.

A sixth volume presents one of Haydn's works for the stage, *Lo speziale*, the *dramma giocoso* of 1768. The edition was prepared by Helmut Wirth, to whom we owe an extensive study of Haydn's operas. *Lo speziale* is perhaps the best-known of Haydn's numerous dramatic works, since it was adapted by Robert Hirschfeld in 1885 and performed in this new version at the Vienna Opera by such eminent conductors as Mahler and Weingartner. Hirschfeld's arrangement contracts the original three acts into a single act, omitting certain numbers and adding one from Haydn's opera *Orlando Paladino* [Hob. XXVIII:11]. Some sort of adaptation is required because the music to the opera is incomplete—both the beginning of the first act and large sections of the third are missing. Haydn himself may have mutilated his score and extracted certain numbers for concert performances. Thus if present-day musicians wish to make use of the highly attractive torso left to us, a version practical for performance must be devised. It may well be doubted, however, that the adaptation provided by Robert Hirschfeld should be considered as definitive.

In appearance the new collected edition is wholly satisfactory. Each volume begins with an informative preface, while the editor's detailed report on his revision is presented in a separate brochure. Unfortunately, only two of these booklets have appeared so far. If the very laudable enterprise of this new Haydn edition leaves us with a wish, it would be that shorter intervals separate the appearance of a volume from the matching report of its editor. And needless to say, should the slow trickle of new publications turn into a more substantial flow, they would be welcomed even more enthusiastically.

Barytontrios, Nr. 25-48, ed. Hubert Unverricht; *Lieder*, ed. Paul Mies; *Volksliederbearbeitungen, Nr. 1-100*; *Schottische Lieder*, ed. Karl Geiringer. *Joseph Haydn Werke* XIV:2; XXIX:1; XXXII:1 [Hob. XI:25-48; XXVIa:1-48; XXXIa:1-100; XXXIc:17]. Munich-Duisburg: Henle, 1960-61. Reprinted from *Notes* 20 (1963): 303-05, by permission of the Music Library Association.

Music friends may have followed with concern the crisis of the Joseph Haydn Institute in Cologne. Jens Peter Larsen, the eminent Haydn scholar, resigned from the editorial leadership he had given to the publication since its inception, and there seemed to be a clear danger that the new collected Haydn edition might share the fate of its two predecessors, forced, after the appearance of a few volumes, to stop their activities. Fortunately the staff of the Haydn Institute under the direction of Georg Feder rose to the occasion; these young scholars not only carried on the publication, but even accelerated, as far as this was possible, its hitherto most deliberate pace. A considerable number of volumes for which all the necessary source material has been secured is now in preparation, and everything seems to portend full success for the Institute's important task.

The editors had been wise in starting, among the earliest issues, with a systematic publication of Haydn's trios for baryton, viola, and cello. The baryton is truly a Haydn instrument. No other great composer wrote music for it, and it was therefore most fitting to present in a scholarly revision these attractive small chamber music works, many of which have never been printed before. Hubert Unverricht, formerly a staff member of the Haydn Institute and now on the faculty of the University of Mainz, has continued his presentation of these works, editing a third volume of trios, containing nos. 25-48 dating from the years 1766 and 1767. It is interesting to observe that ideas known to us from the piano sonatas often appear in a somewhat changed form in these trios, a proof that Haydn enjoyed treating the same musical subjects in different ways. Also remarkable is the Andante of Trio no. 29, employing the subject of the first aria in Haydn's comic opera *La canterina* [Hob. XXVIII:2] as the theme for five variations. This peculiar use of a vocal melody in a work of chamber music occurs here thirty years before the "Emperor" variations and more than half a century before Schubert's "Death and the Maiden" quartet and "Trout" quintet.

Scholars have for a long time been aware of the fact that the Haydn edition started in 1908 under the direction of Eusebius Mandyczewski does not satisfy the requirements of mid-century musicology. The source material was not fully known to the first editors, and their methods of text revision were at times not very rigorous. It has been found necessary to re-edit the collected works of Bach, Handel, and Mozart; and a similar course seemed imperative in the case of Haydn. Paul Mies, the distinguished Cologne scholar, who previously revised the four-part songs for the Haydn Institute, now presents Haydn's solo songs, thus replacing the volume edited by Max Friedländer in 1932. Mies divides his material into three groups. He starts with the twenty-four German songs of 1781 and 1784, which mostly dispense with a separate line for the vocal part, since it is included in the right-hand part of the keyboard instrument. The following twelve canzonettas of 1794 and 1795, on the other hand, are set to English texts; and Haydn prescribes a specific line for the vocalist's part. The revision of these thirty-six songs, which were well known in the composer's lifetime and were published in authorized editions, offered no excessive difficulties. A different situation arose, however, with regard to a number of widely dispersed individual songs presented by Mies in a third group. Here one notices the most significant deviations from Friedländer's edition. Three songs ("Liebes Mädchen, hör mir zu," "An die Freundschaft," "Die Teilung der Erde") [Hob. XXVIa:D1, D4, C1], considered by the previous editor as authentic, are now recognized as works by another composer or as arrangements not authorized by Haydn. Certain reservations are also expressed regarding the attractive farewell song Haydn is alleged to have written for Marianne von Genzinger before his departure to England. On the other hand a German first version of the English canzonetta "Content" and several song-fragments are included in the new volume.

An indirect contribution to song literature was made by Haydn in his arrangements of Scottish, Welsh, and Irish folk songs which he produced from 1791 to the last years of his life. The publishers merely supplied the vocal melody (as a rule without text) and the composer had to add the accompaniment for piano, with violin and cello parts *ad libitum*. Though Haydn may possibly have received some assistance from his pupils, he doubtless contributed decisively to the 450 arrangements that survived under his name. In this way he played a significant part in the revival of the British folk song, working in the same direction as Pleyel, Beethoven, Weber, and the poets Robert Burns, Allan Ramsay, and Sir Walter Scott.

The author of this review, who published in 1949 (*Musical Quarterly* 35) an extensive study on Haydn and the folk song of the British Isles, was invited to edit the critical edition of these songs for the Cologne Institute. The volume now presented comprises the 100 songs published in 1792 by William Napier of London. The collected edition in its musical text follows exactly the original edition, which presents each song in three lines. At the top is the violin part, in the middle is the vocal part (evidently also meant for the clavierist), and at the bottom is the figured bass. The editor had to face a rather peculiar problem, for Napier's edition was the only source available to him. There is no manuscript nor other contemporary print in existence. And, since proofreading was, as we know, rather haphazardly done in the eighteenth century, the editor had to cope repeatedly with the problem of whether to consider a bold progression as intentional or as a printer's error. Even where a mistake had been unmasked it was not always easy to reconstruct the composer's intentions. Moreover, the Scottish texts were printed quite inconsistently in Napier's edition and Dr. Paul G. Buchloh, who took care of the literary revision, was likewise faced with difficult problems. In the old edition, the first stanza of each song was printed with the music and then again on a separate page, together with the rest of the text, a practice that invariably resulted in some differences between the two versions. Moreover it seemed almost to be a rule that the same word occurred throughout the volume in various spellings. Thus the single source, which might have simplified the task for the editors, in reality posed some knotty editorial problems.

Konzerte für Klavier (Cembalo) und Orchester, ed. Horst Walter and Bettina Wackernagel; *Stücke für das Laufwerk (Flötenuhrstücke)*, ed. Sonja Gerlach and George R. Hill; *Konzerte für ein Blasinstrument und Orchester*, ed. Makoto Ohmiya and Sonja Gerlach; *Acide; und Fragmente*, ed. Karl Geiringer and Günter Thomas. *Joseph Haydn Werke* XV:2; XXI; III:3; XXV:1 [Hob. XVIII:3-4, 11*; XIX:9-18, 27-32; VIId:3*, VIIe:1*; XXVIII:1]. Munich: Henle, 1983-85. Reprinted from *Notes* 42 (1986): 847-49, by permission of the Music Library Association.

The *Joseph Haydn Werke*'s newly adopted policy of printing the critical remarks as an appendix to each volume is maintained in these recent publications. Users of the scores will certainly welcome this, as the data on which the editorial decisions are based are now readily available in concise form. The separate brochures which contained this information for earlier volumes were all too often lost. Moreover, the editors were tempted to procrastinate and present the critical remarks at a later date than the score itself. As a matter of fact, for no less than ten volumes, some of which were published in the early sixties, the important little booklet is still not available.

Students of eighteenth-century keyboard music often have difficulty determining for which particular instrument a specific composition was intended. Haydn himself added to the confusion; for example, in his draft catalog he designates the C-major concerto (Hob. XVIII:1) as a concerto "per il clavicembalo," while the work's autograph calls it "Concerto per l'organo." Georg Feder, editor-in-chief of the Haydn *Werke*, attempted to clarify the situation by stating that the normal range of the organ keyboard in Haydn's time was c to c'''. Keyboard parts keeping to this range were apparently intended for the organ, while those exceeding that ambitus were meant for harpsichord. Volume XV/2 of the new edition presents the only three concertos which—according to Feder's distinction—are intended for the harpsichord. Strangely enough, the best known of these, the Concerto in D major (Hob. XVIII:11*), is not listed in Haydn's own catalog of his work, nor has the autograph of the composition been preserved. However, the fact that it was first printed in 1784 by Haydn's Viennese publisher Artaria and copied by Radnitzky, who frequently worked for Haydn, provides sufficient proof of its authenticity.

The appendix to this volume of the new edition presents various cadenzas to individual concerto movements. Although these cadenzas are certainly not by Haydn himself, they give a good idea of how eighteenth-century artists performed this kind of music. The appendix also contains the oboe and horn parts which were added to Haydn's original string orchestra in certain early editions. The fact that different publishers provided different wind instrument parts indicates that the composer was not consulted when these arrangements were made. Finally, the appendix includes a further Concerto in G major (Hob. XVIII:9*). It is musically rather uninteresting, and no proof of its authenticity exists; there is no apparent reason why the work was included in the volume at all.

In 1926 Alfred Schnerich surprised the musical world by revealing that Haydn had written a number of compositions for musical clocks equipped with miniature mechanical flute organs. Five years later, Ernst Fritz Schmid edited these pieces in an arrangement for keyboard. The original version of the thirty-two compositions appears now in this scholarly publication. The authenticity of seventeen of these pieces can be proved by Haydn's autograph or a manuscript in the hand of his favorite copyist, Johann Elssler; the traditional attribution to Haydn of the remaining fifteen cannot be verified. From the outset, the editors have distinguished between these two groups. In each case, the source material presented includes the content of surviving manuscripts as well as transcriptions of the compositions based on the sounds produced by the three musical clocks still in existence. This method shows that the same ornaments are by no means uniform as played on different instruments. The editors also realized that, in certain cases, the levers operating the tiny pipes no longer function well; some pipes do not sound properly, while others hold the tones too long. Therefore impressions were taken from some of the original cylinders in the clocks, enabling the editors to investigate the exact positions of the pins and clamps operating the flute pipes, and thereby to assess the intended sounds. The compositions assembled in this volume may not have great musical significance, but the new publication has a special value: it provides a substantial number of eighteenth-century ornaments in a completely reliable form. The editors deserve special gratitude for their painstaking detective work.

For a long time, Haydn was thought to have written ten concertos for wind instruments and orchestra, but this formidable number has shrunk considerably, since four of the compositions have been proved to be spurious works, while four others, although well documented, seem to be irretrievably lost. Only two authentic works are known still to exist; both are preserved in Haydn's autographs belonging to the Gesellschaft der Musikfreunde in Vienna. The two works are quite different in character. One, dated 1762, uses as a solo instrument the *corno di caccia*, predecessor of the modern horn. Haydn explores the full range of the instrument, from the lowest pedal notes to the dizzy highest register. The performer for whom this work was written must have commanded outstanding technical skill, which allowed him to play this fast-moving composition on an eighteenth-century horn long before valves were invented or hand stopping was generally practiced.

Quite different in character is the *Concerto per il clarino* of 1796, the last and most significant concerto Haydn wrote. The clarino for which the work was intended was a curious invention, made toward the end of the eighteenth century. The Viennese court trumpeter Anton Weidinger, frustrated by the technical limitations of his instrument, tried to equip it with the keys that had proved so successful on woodwind instruments. In the long run, however, the new invention had no success. The keyed trumpet had to pay for its technical nimbleness—which allowed the player to perform chromatic progressions even in the lower register—with the loss of the characteristic brilliant, ringing tone quality traditionally associated with the trumpet. Weidinger's experiment was soon forgotten; since its rediscovery in our time, Haydn's lovely concerto has been played on a small valve trumpet.

The editors' task here was comparatively simple, as only one authentic source was available for each of the two works. Besides a scrupulously accurate reproduction of the autograph texts, the editors provide interesting speculations about the nature of the lost concertos, demonstrating the unlikelihood of Haydn's authorship.

The beginnings of Haydn's work for the stage have long been shrouded in darkness. The music to two early German Singspiels written for Vienna is irretrievably lost. Fragments of Italian language works written at the outset of the composer's employment at the court of Prince Esterházy survive; these remarkable torsos have now been published in the collected edition. Best preserved is *Acide*, first performed in 1762 at the festivities celebrating the wedding of Prince Esterházy's son Anton, from which a libretto, the overture, and several vocal numbers remain, including two setttings of the final vocal number. (For a later performance of the opera, the aria of the goddess Thetis, who assures a happy ending, had to be eliminated when no good contralto singer was available. Haydn wrote a completely new piece for bass voice on the text of the original aria and called the *deus ex machina* Nettuno instead of Thetis.)

Even more fragmented than *Acide* is the music to *La Marchesa Nespola* [Hob. XXX:1]. No libretto is extant, and the seven arias and one *accompagnato* recitative preserved in Haydn's own manuscript are partly incomplete. Particularly sad is the fate of a third Haydn stage work known only from the surviving aria for "Dorinda" and the following "Recitativo di Podagroso" [Hob. XXIVb:1]. The original manuscript belonged to the Viennese publisher Artaria, who presented it to his friend Aloys Fuchs. This well-known collector of autographs apparently did not think very highly of the fragment, for he dismembered it, presenting individual pages to different people. (At present the four remaining sheets are dispersed among four libraries in different countries.) Even the surviving parts have been so unfeelingly trimmed that individual measures are missing from the middle of the work. Apparently the collectors of these irreplaceable manuscripts were more interested in squeezing specimens of Haydn's handwriting into suitable frames than in preserving his music.

Examining these recent publications of the Joseph Haydn Institute, we can not help but realize the debt of gratitude we owe to the scholars who shed light into one of musicology's dark corners. Our knowledge of the singularly rich creative output of one of the Classical era's leading composers is primarily due to Georg Feder, the director of the Haydn Institute, as well as to the untiring Haydn enthusiast H. C. Robbins Landon. After the cavalier treatment accorded to Haydn's works during the latter part of the nineteenth century, their long overdue return to the focus of musical attention must certainly be most welcome.

Sinfonien um 1775-76, ed. Wolfgang Stockmeier in conjunction with Sonja Gerlach; *Klaviersonaten*, ed. Georg Feder; *Klaviertrios*, ed. Wolfgang Stockmeier; *Concerti mit Orgelleiern*, ed. Makoto Ohmiya; *Klaviertrios*, ed. Wolfgang Stockmeier; *La vera costanza*, ed. Horst Walter; *Klaviertrios*, ed. Irmgard Becker-Glauch. *Joseph Haydn Werke* I:1; XVIII:1-2; XVII:1/1; VI; XVII:2/2; XXV:8; XVII:3/3 [Hob. I:61, 66-69; XVI:1-10, 12-14, 16, 18-32, 35-39, 44-47; G1, XVII:D1; F1, XIV:5; IX:26; XV:1-2, 34-38*, 40-41*; CI, f1, XIV:1; VIIh:1*-5*; XV:5-17; XXVIII:8; XV:18-32]. Munich-Duisburg: Henle, 1970-86. Reprinted from *Notes* 28 (1972): 765-68; 34 (1977): 192-94; and 44 (1988): 812-13, by permission of the Music Library Association. The final volume of piano trios was the last item of *Joseph Haydn Werke* reviewed by Geiringer for *Notes*.

The new volumes in the Haydn Collected Edition testify again to the high scholarly standards adopted by the staff of the Joseph Haydn Institute in Cologne. Every slightest bit of evidence is checked and double-checked before it is incorporated into the printed edition, the result being utmost reliability of the finished product. The newest addition to the corpus of orchestral works is a handsome volume with five symphonies composed around 1775-76. It is edited by Wolfgang Stockmeier and Sonja Gerlach, the latter having previously published in *Haydn-Studien* an article on the chronological order of Haydn's symphonies written during the problematical period between 1774 and 1782. While previous symphony volumes were largely based on Haydn's autographs, the editors were forced here to rely mostly on secondary source material, the original manuscripts of four symphonies in this selection having been lost. There is no great masterwork in the new volume, such as we find among the symphonies written between 1768 and 1772 or the Paris symphonies of the 1780s. These are, however, attractive and well-built compositions showing the influence which Haydn's growing interest in dramatic composition exercised on his symphonic output. The enlargement of the orchestra required for opera performances is reflected in the scores (two bassoons instead of one, flute in addition to oboes). Moreover the finale of no. 67 consists of a fast section, a slow one, and a reprise-like second fast section, thus appearing like an Italian opera sinfonia of the kind Haydn himself used in his overture to *Armida* [Hob. XXVIII:12]; no. 68 has also been preserved in an abbreviated version without a minuet, as well as with shortened slow movement and finale, a form in which it might well have been employed as a prelude to an opera. Interesting coloristic effects are to be observed in these symphonies. At the end of the Adagio in no. 67, *"col legno dell' arco"* is prescribed for all the strings, creating a particularly unusual effect in the violins which are to play simultaneously *"con sordini."* The trio of the minuet in the same symphony is scored exclusively for muted violins. Moreover, Haydn prescribes scordatura for a solo violin II. It has to tune its lowest string one whole tone down, to *f*, to produce a kind of drone accompaniment to the dance tune in F major, intoned by the first violins.

Dr. Georg Feder, director of the Haydn Institute, presents the first two volumes of the composer's piano sonatas, the third and last having been offered by him as early as 1966. The whole set of fifty-four sonatas, five separate movements, and the incipits of seven—presumably lost—sonatas, is now available. Compositions entitled "Partita" or "Divertimento" are, following the traditional approach, included among the sonatas. No basic distinction is made between works designated *"per il cembalo"* and later ones assigned to *"clavicembalo ò forte piano."*

Dr. Feder's publication was preceded in this century by two other important collected editions: Karl Päsler's publication of 1918 in the old Breitkopf & Härtel *Gesamtausgabe*, and Christa Landon's *Wiener Urtextausgabe* of 1964 and 1966. They both tried to establish a chronological order of all the sonatas, but arrived at somewhat different results. Dr. Feder feels that it is virtually impossible to establish a completely satisfactory chronology of all the works, and he groups them instead in blocks of two, three, six, seven, and nine sonatas, assigned to a specific period. Volume 1 starts with nine extensive, and technically quite demanding *Frühe Sonaten,* written before 1765. They include two works, both in E♭ major, found by Dr. Feder in the Moravian Benedictine Monastery of Rajhrad (Reigern). The second group of works in the new edition consists of nine *Kleine frühe Sonaten*: simpler, shorter, and easier works intended for educational purposes, and likewise composed before 1765. A comparison of Feder's first eighteen sonatas with the early works in the two previous editions shows marked deviations. Päsler's nos. 15 and 17 are missing now, the former being an arrangement not made by Haydn, the latter a sonata of the composer's contemporary, Johann Gottfried Schwanenberger. Päsler's no. 11, which was also accepted by the *Wiener Urtextausgabe* is taken apart by Feder. He assigns the first movement to another sonata, while salvaging the second and third in the Appendix. On the other hand he includes, though with a certain reluctance, Päsler's no. 16, which Christa Landon felt unable to admit to her edition.

The third group of works in the Haydn Institute edition comprises seven sonatas composed between 1765 and 1772. It begins with a work in E minor, representing a better and more reliable version of Päsler's no. 47. Strangely enough, the magnificent Sonata in C minor [Hob. XVI:20], which according to the date on the autograph was written in 1771, is not to be found among the works Dr. Feder assembles in this group. It appears only as the last composition of volume 2. Haydn had the work printed in 1780 by Artaria in Vienna in a set of six sonatas which, with this single exception, are all undated. To Dr. Feder it seemed "advisable not to sacrifice Haydn's own method of grouping his sonatas to a basically hypothetical chronological order." An almost Spartan stoicism is here displayed, as the editor willfully ignores one of the very rare autograph dates available for one of the sonatas.

The Appendix to volume 1 presents not only the two movements from Sonata 11, but also an Allegro molto in D, an Aria in F, and a Minuetto in F#, two of which had hitherto not been printed. From Haydn's own Draft Catalog are listed the incipits of the works no longer known to exist; they were probably also composed before 1772. Thus this initial volume offers a definite picture of the present state of research in the controversial field of Haydn's early keyboard music. It is hard to imagine that future investigations could materially alter it.

Throughout the second volume of the Haydn Institute edition we find ourselves on solid ground. It contains first the six sonatas, dedicated to Prince Nicolaus Esterházy, published in February 1774 in Vienna, then the six sonatas which according to Haydn's entry in his Draft Catalog belong to the year 1776, but may well have been written earlier. They were not printed, but distributed from Vienna in handwritten copies. The aforementioned third set of six sonatas in this volume was dedicated to the sisters Katharina and Marianna Auenbrugger, two highly talented musicians who were the daughters of the famous physician Dr. Leopold Auenbrugger. Highly interesting is the Italian *Avertimento* which Haydn had printed in this edition: "Among these six sonatas there are two pieces which begin with a few identical measures, *viz*. the Allegro scherzando of no. 2 and the Allegro con brio of no. 5. The author wishes to state that he has done this on purpose, in order to demonstrate the difference in the development of the same idea." Actually the first sixteen measures of these two movements show a marked resemblance which gradually disappears as the movements progress. Haydn clearly expresses here the idea, which was to become of such great significance for him, and later for Beethoven, that the invention of a theme might be of lesser significance than its eventual elaboration.

Dr. Wolfgang Stockmeier deals with the difficult problem of separating the authentic early clavier trios of Haydn from the arrangements for cembalo, violin, and violoncello made by various other, more-or-less skilled, musicians. The result is presented in a volume containing eleven trios and one quintet (actually a trio with added horns), all written in the 'fifties and 'sixties. Even performers who think they are well acquainted with this part of the composer's chamber music will be surprised by the new publication. Only one of these twelve compositions (Hob. XV:2 in F major) is, for instance, to be found in the old three-volume set published by Peters Edition. Likewise the traditional conception that in Haydn's trios the violin is doubling the clavier, or merely providing a filling part, is not fully supported by the new volume. The trios, which the editor attempted to present in an approximately chronological order, show an increasing interplay between violin and cembalo. Frequently solos are also entrusted to the string instrument while the clavier accompanies, with chords indicated by a figured bass. Early realizations of this continuo are entered with smaller-sized notes into Dr. Stockmeier's edition. If no such filling parts were available, the editor indicates rests in the staff for the keyboard player's right hand. This is a somewhat misleading procedure, as the figures under the bass notes clearly indicate that a bass accompaniment alone was not sufficient, and Haydn desired filling middle parts to be added. The trios display, as a rule, the character of the partita or divertimento. They consist mostly of two fast movements with a minuet in the middle, the trio of the minuet being the only movement which deviates from the uniformly preserved tonic key. Haydn occasionally likes to experiment with this basic form. In no. 1 (Hob. XV:36*) a "Polones" (*sic*) in the relative minor key takes the place of the minuet. No. 7 (Hob. XV:41*) even proceeds to the four-movement structure, otherwise unusual among the composer's trios. Between minuet and finale, an Adagio in the subdominant is here included. These trios display a certain enterprise in the choice of keys. Compositions in E♭ major, F minor, A major, and E major appear in the early set. In no. 4 (Hob. XV:38*), Haydn also makes an attempt to increase the cohesion of the composition by using related material in the main subjects of the first and last movements.

Thanks to its thorough spadework, this volume provides a solid basis for the publication of the better-known trios from the 'eighties and 'nineties, for which more reliable source material is available.

* * * *

After two false starts made earlier in this century the collected edition of Joseph Haydn's works is progressing steadily. To the end of 1976 the Cologne Institute, whose goal it is to present all the works of the Viennese composer in critically revised editions, has issued exactly fifty volumes. Thus the largest and most embarrassing gap in our knowledge of Classical music is being gradually closed. Georg Feder, the Institute's farsighted director, does not recruit his collaborators from European scholars only, for several American as well as Japanese musicologists are among his helpers. In 1971 Makoto Ohmiya, of Kamakura, Japan, contributed nine Haydn Notturnos with two "lire organizzate"—cf. *Notes* 32 (1975-76): 623-25—and, more recently, five concertos for the same instruments accompanied by horns and strings.

These thirteen compositions had originally been commissioned by King Ferdinand of Naples, whose main passions in life were to hunt and to play the curious "lira organizzata." Not only Haydn, but also Franz X. Sterkel, Ignaz Pleyel, and Adalbert Gyrowetz received commissions for works of this kind. Ferdinand's "lira organizzata" represented a very rare form of a widely diffused instrument which in earlier times was mainly used by shepherds and beggars. This "lira," as the Italians called it, was a stringed instrument in which a wooden wheel rubbing the strings from underneath replaced the traditional bow. In the eighteenth century it was usually equipped with two melody strings, tuned in unison, and up to four bourdons. The melody strings were shortened by means of keys operated by the player's left hand, while his right hand turned a crank connected to the wooden wheel. In the "lira organizzata" one or two sets of organ pipes were added. The keys of the instrument were also used to admit air to the individual pipes, while the bellows were mostly operated through a special pedal. The player had several registers available since he could either employ the pipes and the strings separately or else combine them. The bourdons too could be eliminated at will. Haydn's parts offer no indications for such register changes. Yet, with their little rests, staccato marks, and dynamic alterations achieved through skillful handling of the wheel, they pose quite formidable technical problems to the performer. Thus the rather pompous designation of these chamber music compositions as "concertos" does not seem entirely out of place.

Unfortunately, the autographs of these concertos have disappeared. Haydn may have delivered them in 1786 or 1787 to the king, who could well have discarded them after use. Fortunately, the composer retained manuscripts of the works produced by an Esterházy copyist and carefully corrected by the composer himself; in one place he even inserted three pages in his own hand. This authentic copy furnished the most important source for the editor's work.

Haydn himself does not seem to have included the concertos in his own performances. He did, however, use material from these works for other compositions. The Andante and finale from Concerto no. 5 were employed in Symphony no. 89, and the Romance from Concerto no. 3 was later transformed into the Allegretto of the "Military" Symphony (no. 100), which is among Haydn's most popular compositions. None of the five concertos was published in the composer's lifetime. The first printing of one of these works took place in 1932 when this reviewer edited the Concerto with the Romance.

Wolfgang Stockmeier, who previously edited the early clavier trios, followed up this publication with trios from Haydn's middle period. The first volume contained works from the sixties and possibly even the late fifties of the eighteenth century. In the following fifteen-odd years Haydn did not write any trios, but between 1784 and 1790 a new group of more than a dozen works was created which Stockmeier has assembled in the present volume. Stylistically, the later pieces differ considerably from the earlier works. Figured basses have disappeared from the keyboard parts, the individual compositions are on the average longer, and the melodic lines more flexible, since the old-fashioned harpsichord is being replaced by the modern pianoforte; keyboard music accompanied by more or less optional stringed instruments begins to change into chamber music in which the strings compete with the keyboard. These are no longer compositions written for Prince Esterházy's musicians, but works intended for general distribution. Seven were to be printed by the important publishing house of Artaria in Vienna and three each by two London publishers, Forster and Bland. Into a special category belong two additional trios (Hob. XV:3 and 4) which Haydn sent to Forster for publication, attesting with his own signature that they were his compositions. Accordingly, the works were also printed under Haydn's name. Many years later the composer was shown, however, the first of these trios, and he declared that it was really a work by his brother Michael. On the other hand, Haydn's pupil Ignaz Pleyel had the two trios published as works of his own. For good measure, this set contained also a third "Pleyel-Trio" (Hob. XV:5) which was undoubtedly a work of Joseph Haydn. Altogether, questions of authorship were not taken too seriously in the eighteenth century.

Stockmeier's edition of the fifteen trios contained in the new volume is based on the few Haydn autographs that have survived, on the authentic copies sent to Forster for his publications, and, most of all, on the original prints. The editor did not attempt to offer a definite solution of the Joseph-Michael-Ignaz puzzle and reproduced the two controversial trios in an appendix, indicating with a question mark the likelihood of Pleyel's authorship.

While the concertos and trios did not offer too many editorial problems, the work on the opera *La vera costanza* proved to be more complicated. The editor of this volume, Horst Walter, is on the staff of the Haydn Institute itself; undoubtedly he received the active support of his colleagues in this rather tricky work. To begin with, Walter attacked a tale started by Haydn's early biographer A. C. Dies which was later enlarged by C. F. Pohl and repeated by various authors. According to this story the composer was commissioned by the emperor in 1776 to write *La vera costanza* for Vienna. Intrigues of his competitors made the performance impossible; the composer withdrew his work and had it performed in Esterháza during the spring of 1779. Walter shows, however, that every evidence points against Haydn's ever having received such a commission. He explains convincingly that *La vera costanza* was always meant for Esterháza and was not written before 1778. The Vienna performance which never materialized could only have been planned for a date after the Esterháza premiere of 1779.

A second problem resulted from the fact that the most authentic manuscript score of the opera, preserved today in Paris, is not entirely in Haydn's own hand and bears the date of 1785. The editor copes with this difficulty by explaining that the score and parts used at the premiere were probably destroyed in the great fire which ravaged the castle of Esterháza in November 1779. For a repeat performance of the opera which took place in the restored castle during the year 1785 Haydn had to reconstruct the lost score. Thus, numbers which in the meantime had been printed or preserved in manuscript could be written into the new score by copyists. The rest had to be reconstructed, with the help of the old printed libretto, by Haydn himself. How much he still remembered of the old composition, and how much he newly created in 1785, can no longer be determined.

Subsequently, Haydn's opera won great success. It was performed in various cities, and a substantial number of handwritten scores was produced. One of them, preserved today in Brussels, is particularly important as it was carefully revised and corrected by Haydn himself. It may well indicate the composer's ultimate intentions and was therefore used, together with the Paris manuscript, as a main source for the new edition.

Walter's work is not only distinguished by the aim of reproducing every measure in accordance with the definite wishes of the composer. It offers also no fewer than twelve pages of Haydn's sketches for various parts of his score. Even for his *secco* recitatives the composer made numerous sketches, always omitting the barlines which in such cases apparently seemed to him of lesser importance. This also explains a peculiarity which is apt to puzzle students of Haydn's opera scores: occasionally the composer, who is usually so neat, erroneously inserts one quarter note too many in a measure from a recitative.

In conclusion, it might again be stated that every volume published under the imprimatur of the Haydn Institute furnishes a highly reliable musical text. In later years new material might, of course, still come to light, but we need not expect that it will substantially change the features of the Haydn-mosaic which is now being assembled with such care.

*   *   *   *

This third volume of keyboard trios by Joseph Haydn concludes the publication of the composer's thirty-eight works of this genre in the Collected Edition. The volume was edited with meticulous attention to detail by Irmgard Becker-Glauch of the Haydn Institute in Cologne. It contains fourteen trios and a single violin sonata, all written between 1794 and 1796, during Haydn's second trip to England or shortly thereafter. The first editions of most of these works were consequently published in England. The trios were usually issued in sets of three, each group bearing a special dedication to a lady; possibly Haydn felt that this kind of chamber music was of greater interest to women than to men. The first two groups were inscribed to princesses in the House of Esterházy, where Haydn had served for three decades as Kapellmeister. The third group was dedicated to Haydn's English friend

Rebecca Schroeter, and the fourth to the pianist Therese Jansen-Bartolozzi. Only one trio, no. 30, bears no inscription, but no. 31 makes up for it by having two dedications: first to a Viennese pianist and later, following a command of Prince Esterházy, to the wife of a French general.

These are the most mature and also probably the best known of Haydn's piano trios. The G-major Trio, no. 25, with the "Rondo, in the Gypsies' style," even enjoys a certain popularity among amateur musicians. Haydn's own interest in these works is indicated by the fact that he considered the Adagio from no. 26 as worthy of appearing also as a movement in his London Symphony (no. 102). He prudently transposed the piece, however, from its original F♯ major to the simpler key of F major.

A composition which had been considered lost has been retrieved by Becker-Glauch; it is the so-called "Jacob's Dream," in allusion to the heavenly ladder that appeared to the patriarch. According to an anecdote reported by Haydn's early biographer Dies, the composer wrote this piece to make fun of an amateur violinist who liked to play in the highest register without commanding the necessary technical skill. Earlier researchers were unable to find this work among Haydn's compositions. The eagle eyes of this editor discovered, however, that in the autograph of the Trio no. 31 (kept on loan in the British Library), the second movement bears the very faint, almost illegible heading "Jacob's Dream." As a matter of fact, the violin part in this movement ascends to $a^{\flat\prime\prime\prime}$, a high note usually avoided by the composer. The editor also addresses a hitherto unsolved problem of Haydn research: whether or not Haydn wrote a work for violin and piano. She considers the cello part in the "Trio" no. 32, known in two slightly different versions, to be spurious. The work is therefore classified in the present edition as a violin sonata, which would make it Haydn's only composition of this kind known to us.

It is to be hoped that this handsome, well documented publication will help stimulate interest in this worthwhile, unjustly neglected genre of Haydn's compositions.

Hungarian Academy of Science

Reviews of *Haydn Compositions in the Music Collections of the National Széchényi Library, Budapest*, ed. Jenö Vécsey, rev. Dénes Bartha, trans. Sándor Országh; *Symphonie, fis-moll* [Hob. I:45]; *Haydn emlekere*, ed. Bence Szabolcsi and Dénes Bartha; *Bericht über die internationale Konferenz zum Andenken Joseph Haydns*, ed. Bence Szabolcsi and Dénes Bartha; *Haydn als Opernkapellmeister*, 2 vols., by Dénes Bartha and László Somfai, *Notes* 18 (1961): 230-32, and 19 (1961): 67-69. Reprinted by permission of the Music Library Association.

Budapest, the capital of Hungary, is gradually assuming its rightful place in Haydn research. The city which boasts ownership of the world's most important collection of works by Franz Joseph Haydn here initiates an exploration of its treasures in a series of highly significant studies. Since the end of the first world war it has housed the archives of Prince Esterházy, whose ancestors Haydn worked for during the better part of his life. Precious material was accumulated in this long period, and the Esterházys also acquired important portions of Haydn's estate after the composer's death. When the Communist government took over the large princely possessions, most of the Haydniana were transferred to the National Library in Budapest. In 1959, on the occasion of the 150th anniversary of Haydn's death, the opening of the collection in its new quarters was celebrated by an international Haydn Congress which also marked the beginning of large-scale scholarly publications.

A handsome catalog informs us about the vast extent of Haydn's compositions in the National Library. Edited by Jenö Vécsey, the distinguished head of the music division, it was printed in Budapest, first in German and then in English translation. The catalog lists autographs (among them no less than twenty symphonies, eight works for the stage, twenty operatic arias, five Masses and oratorios, etc.), contemporary manuscript copies, and printed documents. The book is generously illustrated. Not only are many autographs reproduced, but such interesting items as pages from the manuscript copy of Haydn's "Theory of Counterpoint" based on the work by Johann Joseph Fux also are shown. Quite remarkable is an excerpt from van Swieten's libretto to *The Creation* [Hob. XXI:2] containing explicit and rather clever instructions for the musical interpretation of the text which Haydn for the most part faithfully carried out.

As an example of the library's valuable holdings, a facsimile edition of Haydn's "Farewell Symphony" (no. 45 in F♯ minor) has been issued. The technique of reproduction is of the highest caliber; clarity is achieved in every detail and even subsequent inscriptions with blue pencil are realistically represented. The observer naturally looks eagerly at the poignant last movement in which the individual members of the orchestra gradually depart. The autograph strikingly conveys this bold device whose programmatic meaning we can merely conjecture. The concluding Adagio has at first all the twelve staves in the score filled. After a few pages the three bottom lines are left free. Then Haydn gradually reduces the score in the successive pages until on the very last one only four measures appear in the two violins, the empty staves giving the impression of desolate loneliness. In the first movement (meas. 150-51) there appears above the staff of the first violin the strange remark from Haydn's hand "Sapienti pauca" (an expression subsequently also used in his London diary). One finds it difficult to account for the insertion of this Latin inscription signifying "to the wise little is sufficient." The editor of the facsimile edition,

László Somfai, did not mention this point in his scholarly introduction. He has, however, according to a personal letter to me, worked out a theory which has much in its favor. A thorough scrutiny of the passage reveals that in these two measures Haydn uses instead of F𝄪 (moving towards G♯ in meas. 152) its enharmonic equivalent, G. The composer apparently implied with his words that the wise violinist would, despite the simplified notation, play the note G a little sharper so as to give it the quality necessary for a leading note.

Impressive in another way is the collection of various studies on Haydn assembled in the *Zene tudományi Tanulmányok*, vol. 8, edited by the two leaders of Hungarian musicology, Bence Szabolcsi and Dénes Bartha. On more than 700 pages illustrated by countless music quotations, facsimilia, etc., seventeen articles are offered, the Hungarian text being in each case followed by a digest in German. Particularly interesting is the presentation of the "Acta musicalia" from the Esterházy files (in the original language and in Hungarian translation) documenting Haydn's activities at the princely court and his relationship to its members. Arisztid Valkó started the publication of this source material in 1957 and has now submitted its second and final installment. Professor Bartha investigates Haydn's *Seven Last Words*, throwing new light on the composer's procedure in adapting the oratorio [Hob. XX/2] from the original instrumental work. Strips of paper pasted into the score while Haydn was at work were recently removed with utmost care, revealing a divergent earlier version underneath the definitive one. Both facsimilia and transcriptions of the respective pages are provided, allowing us interesting glimpses into the composer's workshop. László Somfai offers a penetrating study on the source material available for Haydn's string quartets, in the course of which he sums up the reasons for doubting the authenticity of the quartets op. 3. There are certainly some puzzling problems connected with this work, but Dr. Somfai's suggestion that these fine quartets (which are listed in the famous Haydn catalog of 1805) should be considered as products of talented pupils rather than of the composer himself will not easily find general acceptance. In a second study Somfai deals with the numerous arias Haydn wrote for insertion into operatic works by other composers. The article refers to a large-scale investigation of Haydn's activity as opera director, which is in preparation. One looks forward to this work which promises to offer another instance of the fruitful research now undertaken in Hungary.

*   *   *   *

In 1949 the monumental Haydn collections of Prince Esterházy were incorporated into the Budapest National Széchényi Library and thus made accessible to international research. To exhibit these treasures, and to commemorate at the same time the 150th anniversary of Haydn's death, the Hungarian Academy of Science held a Haydn Congress at Budapest in September 1959. Scholars from both East and West attended and about two dozen papers were read; these are now assembled in a handsome volume edited by the two Hungarian musicologists mainly responsible for the planning of the meeting. The majority of these papers are in German, alternating with a few in English, French, Russian, or Hungarian.

Several scholars dealt with specific sections of Haydn's output or with individual works. Thus, Karl Gustav Fellerer (Cologne) discussed Haydn's Masses, explaining the rules and regulations of the Catholic Church so far as they governed eighteenth-century sacred music and had their impact on Haydn's work. Heinrich Besseler (Leipzig) pointed out the strong influence exercised by the *Contratanz* on Classical finales. The late Ernst Fritz Schmid (Augsburg) presented an aria from Haydn's oratorio *Il ritorno di Tobia* [Hob. XXI:1], both in its original version and in a highly ornamented form preserved in the composer's hand, thus providing insight into his familiarity with the Italian embellishment technique of his time. Paul Mies (Cologne) reported on Haydn's vocal canons which reveal the composer's aim at bringing every detail of the text into full relief, while showing less concern for the intricacies of contrapuntal writing. The undersigned reported on Haydn's smaller works of sacred music preserved in the Austrian castle of Eisenstadt which has still remained Prince Esterházy's property.

Various papers dealt with Haydn's influence in different fields. His music's impact on the Czech composer Leopold Kozeluh was pointed out by Milan Postolka (Prague). Haydn's relationship to France was discussed by François Lesure (Paris), that to Russia by Tamara Livanova (Moscow) and Yuly Kremlev (Leningrad), and that to Romania by Zeno Vancea (Bucharest). The young American musicologist H. C. Robbins Landon presented a very interesting survey of Haydn sources in Czechoslovakia which had never before been systematically explored. The results of his pioneering work are sure to be beneficial to the Haydn Collected Edition.

The hosts themselves were represented by particularly noteworthy contributions. Bence Szabolcsi (Budapest) analyzed Haydn's relation to Hungarian music, explaining that for the composer—and his contemporaries—Hungarian, Slavic, Gypsy, Romanian, and Turkish music formed a single entity which supplied an unending source of stimulation. Antal Molnar (Budapest) gave a sensitive comparison of Haydn's and Mozart's artistic personalities. Possibly the most interesting report was supplied by Dénes Bartha on Haydn's activity as an opera conductor. The rich new material assembled by him and his pupil László Somfai, of which only a brief survey could be offered at the meeting, has meanwhile been presented in the second book cited above.

Up until 1959 very little had been known about Haydn's work as an opera director, since it had been difficult to get access to Prince Esterházy's collections and, moreover, the interest in his work as a composer had overshadowed that in him as interpreter. Now that the 120 scores with 90 sets of parts forming the Esterházy archives of Italian operas have been incorporated into the National Library, Bartha and Somfai have made a most careful investigation of them and reported their findings in the present book. In the years 1776-90, opera production played a very important role at the Esterházy court. The repertory was variegated, and novelties appeared six to eight times per season. Only operas in Italian were performed—Cimarosa, Anfossi, and Paisiello being most frequently heard—and the German Singspiel was excluded. It is noteworthy that no work by Mozart was heard. A production of *Figaro* was planned in 1790, but the prince's death intervened. *Don Giovanni* may have been excluded because Righini's opera on a similar plot was performed in 1781.

The demands made on Haydn as an opera director were staggering. Once a work was chosen, he had to adapt it to the specific requirements of the Esterházy theater. As a rule clarinets, trumpets, and timpani were not available, and he had to arrange the scores accordingly. On the other hand, he enriched the orchestration at times by giving the second violin and viola more important parts and adding oboes and horns where the original used strings only. In Esterháza no chorus was available; if choral numbers could not be entrusted to a group of soloists, they had to be omitted. Apart from making cuts necessitated by the limitations of his ensemble, Haydn did not hesitate to shorten—sometimes considerably—most of the operas he performed. He had no compunction even about changing the form of a number he felt to be overlong. Similar motives may have been responsible for the alterations of tempo he carried out. He liked to accelerate slow numbers, changing for instance *Larghetto* to *Andante con moto*, or even *Andante maestoso* to *Allegro vivace*. Particularly illuminating are his adaptations of the roles entrusted to the mezzo-soprano Luigia Polzelli. We know that Haydn was deeply in love with her and induced the prince to renew her contract although she was a mediocre singer. The current Italian operas offered but few arias for mezzo-soprano, and so Haydn transposed certain pieces for her and simplified others. He also composed specifically for her nearly a dozen new arias to be inserted into the operas in which she appeared in roles of minor importance.

The book provides a great deal of such interesting information, together with copious illustrations, many facsimiles and watermarks, a chronicle of opera premieres under Haydn's direction (supplementing and correcting statements of Pohl's Haydn biography), a detailed catalog of the material preserved, data on Haydn's opera ensemble, a list of the "insertion arias" contributed by Haydn to the operas of other composers, and—in the latest fashion—a recording of two newly found pieces ("Scena di Pedrillo" from *La circe* [Hob. XXIVb:1] of 1789, and cavatina "Quando la rosa" [Hob XXIVb:3] from *La Metilda ritrovata* of 1779), one of them also presented in full score.

This is indeed a highly significant study, throwing light on an important aspect of Haydn's activities and drawing attention to a number of attractive Haydn compositions which are still insufficiently known.

H. C. Robbins Landon

Reviews of *Haydn: Chronicle and Works*, 5 vols. (Bloomington: Indiana University Press, 1976-80). Reprinted from *Notes* 34 (1977): 56-58; 35 (1978): 296-98; and 38 (1981): 60-61, by permission of the Music Library Association.

> *Perhaps my most brilliant student was H. C. Robbins Landon, who came to me because he was very interested in Haydn and had read my Haydn book published in 1932. Landon worked with me on Haydn's symphonies, which resulted many years later in his monumental monograph on this topic.... Paraphrasing a widely known saying by the wealthy banker, Mendelssohn, "I am nothing but the son of my father [the famous philosopher Moses Mendelssohn] and the father of my son [Felix Mendelssohn-Bartholdy]," I said, "I am nothing but the pupil of my teacher* [the great Curt Sachs] *and the teacher of my pupil* [Robbins Landon]."—This I Remember, *99-100.*

In 1867 the study *Haydn in London* by the organist and music critic Carl Ferdinand Pohl was published. The work found a very friendly reception, and its author was invited to write a full-size life of Haydn. Rather reluctantly Pohl accepted, and in 1875, after very extensive preparatory research, the first volume of his Haydn biography appeared in print.

A century has passed since, and a new Haydn biography, conceived on the largest possible scale, is making its appearance. Once more the initial study is devoted to the composer's stay in England. The author of this highly ambitious work is a native of New England who has taken up residence in Europe. In retrospect it appears as if all his previous publications were intended as a kind of preparation for this supreme effort. The collected Haydn symphonies, the composer's Masses, eight of his operas, numerous piano trios, string quartets, concertos, divertimentos, arias, etc. were edited by Landon in a form which was both scholarly and serviceable for practical purposes. Accordingly, a host of performances and new recordings originated from these publications. Landon's editions were underpinned by a substantial number of musicological studies. Foremost among them the monograph on Haydn's symphonies ought to be mentioned, a gigantic work of some 900 pages, the outsize volume measuring more than three inches from cover to cover. *The Collected Correspondence and London Notebooks* (Fair Lawn, N.J., 1959) of Haydn in an excellent English translation by Landon provided the basis for a subsequent publication of the original sources. There are, moreover, a lavishly illustrated work on Beethoven, Landon's *Essays on the Viennese Classical Style* (New York, 1970), and the *Haydn Yearbook*, whose main editor Landon has been since its inception in 1962.

This new Haydn biography is projected to appear in five volumes: 1) *Haydn: The Early Years* (1732-65), 2) *Haydn at Esterháza* (1766-90), 3) *Haydn in England* (1791-95), 4) *Haydn: The Years of "The Creation"* (1796-1800), 5) *Haydn: The Late Years* (1801-09).

It might seem strange that Landon began the publication of his work with its third volume. However, very practical considerations were responsible for this decision. Without actually stating it, the author subdivided his gigantic topic into two main sections: the formative years (to 1790) and the years of consummate mastery (after 1791). During the second of these periods Haydn wrote the symphonies, oratorios, Masses, and other works that are best known today. In addition, abundant documentary evidence is available for these years that span a brilliant period of English cultural life. It thus seemed justified to start the monumental publication with its second half, opened up by a volume on Haydn in England. The production of the following two volumes is also well advanced, and their publication may be expected in not too distant a future. The situation is different in the case of the first two volumes, which deal with Haydn's formative years. Here the documentary material is not yet completely available, and further research, particularly in the Esterházy archives, seems necessary. Moreover, various problems of authenticity and chronology of known compositions must still be solved before definite results can be offered in a biographical study. It would therefore hardly seem realistic to count on an early completion of this gigantic project.

Landon's *Haydn in England*—like the rest of his work—is in two parts: Chronicle and Works. In the Chronicle the author offers primarily documents, such as letters and extracts from diaries, newspaper announcements, and reviews of concerts, as well as excerpts from various books and pamphlets. Remarks and conclusions drawn by the author himself are comparatively rare. Landon is basically concerned with facts, and he leaves no stone unturned to discover every bit of evidence. Limitations of space do not seem to exist for the author and his publishers. Not only are announcements and reviews of the Salomon Concerts, presided over by Haydn, reproduced, but also those of the competing Professional Concerts. To an article by Dr. Burney attacking a conservative critic of Haydn's music well over four pages are devoted. There is also a rather lengthy discourse in which Landon—quoting seven different sources—proves that the Viennese waltzed as early as 1792, to Haydn's *Deutsche Tänze* [Hob. IX:12]. It seems doubtful whether this contention required such weighty evidence. According to Mosco Carner—"Walzer," *MGG*, 14 (1968), col. 225—it is a "generally accepted fact" that waltzes appeared between 1770 and 1780. Even more to the point is the statement in Hugo Riemann's *Musiklexikon—Sachteil* (1967), p. 1061—that the waltz originated from the *Deutscher Tanz* in Austria and Bavaria during the last quarter of the eighteenth century.

Landon is a superb translator. He knows how to reproduce not only the content but also the flavor of eighteenth- and early nineteenth-century documents. Throughout the work he quotes sections from the first German biographies of Haydn by Griesinger and Dies in his own English version. Similarly, numerous letters by Haydn and entries into his diaries are presented in Landon's translation. In the case of quotations from Griesinger and Dies the author refers to the page numbers in modern reprints of the original German texts. When quoting Haydn's own letters and diaries, however, Landon does not refer to the original German, Italian, or French wording, but to his own earlier publication in English. This is in spite of the fact that the sources themselves are accessible in a modern edition prepared, on the basis of Landon's collection, by Dénes Bartha (Kassel, 1965). The preface to Landon's book refers to this original-language edition, but it is not entered into the list of biographical sources and is hardly referred to in the volume itself.

Landon's work, with its accumulation of documentary evidence, is intended primarily for the scholar. However, the amateur will likewise find in it much of interest. There is, for instance, such a delectable morsel as the exchange of invectives between Haydn's librettist, Badini, and a titled lady, published in the London *Oracle*. Another documentation is rather touching. The author informs us that after the death of Mozart a Graduale by the Salzburg composer was performed in the Eisenstadt Pfarrkirche and the musicians wrote into the manuscript parts brief prayers for the soul of the defunct. Landon adds: "They knew what a loss the world had suffered for they had been trained by one of Mozart's greatest admirers." As a postscript we might state: Who, but Landon, would have thought of examining the parts of a Mozart Graduale in the Eisenstadt church? Into the same category belongs Landon's finding an announcement in the London *Morning Herald* of 16 March 1799 that Haydn had written a new violin concerto for his friend Barthelemon. Nothing further is known about this concerto, but it seems amazing that Landon examined English newspapers published four years after the composer had left the English capital.

Almost half the book is devoted to an analysis of Haydn's works produced between 1791 and 1795. Landon deals with each composition separately. He provides all the catalog information concerning the various sources of individual compositions (much of it in conformity with Hoboken's catalogs), ventures into the thorny field of chronology, deals with textual problems and their consequences for the interpretation of the compositions, and interprets, with the help of well over 200 music examples, peculiarities of formal construction, the application of harmonic and contrapuntal devices, as well as special coloristic and orchestral effects. Most of all, Landon explains the position of individual works or groups of works within Haydn's oeuvre and, beyond that, in the history of music. Altogether, the author's broad musical knowledge, his enthusiastic approach to the art of Haydn, and his special gift for vivid and penetrating expression combine to provide a highly significant account of the composer's work. Students of Haydn's compositions will again and again consult these chapters in Landon's book and will be helped by the competently assembled index.

Inevitably there are also some small details which the author might want to change in a later edition. The contention that Haydn used for his opera *L'anima del filosofo* [Hob. XXVIII:13] the overture to *Windsor Castle* can no longer be upheld (cf. Hob. I, p. 279, and II, p. 435, as well as *Haydn Werke* XXV/13, p. viii). The well-known story which Landon repeats about Haydn's having published trios by Pleyel under his own name might have read somewhat differently if the author had also reported the little-known end of this episode: in 1799 Pleyel took his revenge on his former teacher by having his publishing house print a trio of Haydn as a composition of his own (cf. *Haydn Werke* XVII/2, Kritischer Bericht, p. 13). It might also be mentioned that the "Preussische Staatsbibliothek," Berlin, to which Landon refers several times, no longer exists. It was divided into "Deutsche Staatsbibliothek" in East Berlin, and "Staatsbibliothek, Preussischer Kulturbesitz" in West Berlin.

Such small matters have no bearing on the overall importance of Landon's book. No doubt the author has made a contribution of unusual merit. All criteria seem to indicate that with *Haydn in England* the publication of the definitive Haydn biography has started.

*   *   *   *

In 1976 the third volume of Robbins Landon's Haydn biography appeared in print. It was entitled *Haydn in England* and covered the highly important years 1791 to 1795—cf. *Notes* 34 (1977/78): 56-58. The fourth and fifth volumes of the biography have followed in quick succession. They deal with the end of Haydn's career, the last years of his life which he spent primarily in Vienna. Thus the short period—hardly more than a dozen years—in which Haydn's most famous works originated is now completely treated in Landon's biography. Two additional volumes (*Haydn: The Early Years* and *Haydn at Eszterháza*), describing the formative years in the composer's artistic development, are to follow.

The organization of volume 4, dealing with the years of *The Creation* [Hob. XXI:2], closely resembles that of the preceding volume; about half the space is devoted to the chronicle, the remainder to an analysis of the works. In contrast to the earlier tome, however, with its clear separation of the biographical and musical sections, the new volume deals with both the life story and the respective compositions of each year. This method is better suited to provide an idea of the stupendous productivity of the old composer. In 1796, for instance, the man of sixty-four completed the choral version of *The Seven Last Words* [Hob. XX/2] and wrote two great Masses, a number of part songs, the trumpet concerto [Hob. VIIe:1], and various piano trios. At the same time the ideas for *The Creation* were taking shape in his mind.

Landon continues the same method at the beginning of the fifth volume, covering the last nine years of the composer's life. However, Haydn's productivity was gradually drying up. In 1803 he worked only on a single string quartet [Hob. III:83], which he was unable to complete. As Haydn did not compose any more during the last six years of his life, the analysis of the works in this volume is comparatively short. Landon profits from this fact by including a number of important catalogs, partly discovered by the scholar himself and published for the first time. We find there Elssler's catalog of Haydn's music library (including numerous items by other composers), Haydn's own catalog of his libretto collection, and finally the catalog of Haydn's artistic effects (comprising also a number of engravings and a live parrot) made after the composer's death. Haydn's first will of 1801 and his last will drawn up eight years later are reproduced in English translation. There follows an appendix on "Haydn and Posterity," and finally a huge bibliography, filling thirty-eight pages, intended not only for this volume, but also for the whole work. It lists, apart from books and studies, important handwritten library catalogs and eighteenth-century periodicals and journals, as well as critical editions of Haydn's works (among them more than ninety items edited by Landon himself!). One wonders, however, whether even this gargantuan bibliography will not need some supplementation when the two remaining volumes of Landon's work are finally released.

Volumes 4 and 5 describe in great detail the conditions under which the composer lived and worked after his return from England. Two introductory chapters dealing with Vienna's musical life, as well as with Eisenstadt and the Esterházys, lead up to the description of biographical events. As in the third volume, the author consults all available sources to document his chronicle: articles in periodicals and newspapers, letters, diaries, and memoirs. A number of recent studies published in *The Haydn Yearbook*, of which Landon again is the guiding spirit, proved to be particularly helpful. Repeatedly he quotes Radant's publication of the diaries of Joseph Carl Rosenbaum, an Esterházy employee, and the diary of Count Zinzendorf, a regular patron of Vienna's musical performances, presented by Edward Olleson. All the material that seems of some significance to the author is carefully assembled, but the reader might at times wonder whether every item reported is really essential. This applies, for instance, to the description of the amorous escapades of Prince Esterházy and other noblemen of the time (volume 4, p. 46) or to the nauseating details concerning the theft of Haydn's head from the grave several days after the burial (volume 5, p. 388).

The analysis of the works in these two volumes is even more interesting than it was in volume 3. In the earlier book the author dealt primarily with the London symphonies, works he had previously treated in his mighty tome, *The Symphonies of Joseph Haydn*. Volumes 4 and 5, on the other hand, present new material, in many cases supplied by the author for the first time. Dealing with the texts of the two great oratorios, Landon offers a fascinating juxtaposition of diametrically opposed viewpoints by two scholars (Martin Stern and Olleson) concerning the origin of the libretto to *The Creation*. In the case of *The Seasons* [Hob. XXI:3] Landon himself provides a thoughtful comparison between the poem of Thompson and the libretto by van Swieten. He also enumerates the various recommendations van Swieten made for the composition of the two oratorios, stating in each case whether Haydn accepted the advice. The surviving sketches to the two oratorios are thoroughly listed and analyzed. Thus, no less than seven substantial sketches in full score for "Chaos" in *The Creation* are reproduced, filling seventeen pages of the printed book. Throughout his analyses Landon is concerned with an enumeration of the authentic sources for the works under discussion. He deals with problems of notation, musical form, key structure, symbolism, orchestration, and contrapuntal devices; and he even pays heed to Schenker's analytical theories. Every number, including recitatives, and each movement in instrumental compositions, are thoroughly analyzed. The reader is overwhelmed by the authors wide knowledge and his unfailing memory which enable him to refer in his treatment not only to an abundance of earlier Haydn works, but also to the output of contemporary composers, foremost among them Mozart and Beethoven.

The fact that Landon was one of the editors of *The Mozart Companion* and had written *Beethoven: A Documentary Study* has enriched his Haydn work. One of the most interesting features of the fourth volume is the description of the ambiguous relationship between Haydn and Beethoven. Landon points out that Beethoven learned far more from Haydn than from Mozart in matters of orchestration, and especially that the younger composer's use of the clarinet closely follows Haydn's ideas. The author also shows that in his first years in Vienna Beethoven avoided entering into direct competition with Haydn and only gave up all restraint when Haydn stopped composing.

These volumes, with their abundance of technical information, do not provide easy reading. However, the music friend can not help delighting in felicitous remarks found all over the work. When discussing the "Dona nobis" in the *Missa in tempore belli* [Hob. XXII:9] Landon remarks that "Haydn created a new church music style as immediately influential as it was to become lastingly controversial." Of *The Creation* he writes: "This work is of the same stuff as *Die Zauberflöte* and *Fidelio*, representatives of a great humanitarian era in Central Europe, a golden age of freedom, cultivation of intellect, and true sophistication which was soon to disappear forever."

Considering the encyclopedic treatment of Haydn's music in Landon's magnum opus, it would seem impossible that he could have slighted any aspect of the composer's output. Yet, with a few deprecatory remarks he dismisses a type of composition which engaged Haydn's attention for over a decade: his arrangements of folksongs of the British Isles. It is true that not so much artistic reasons as philanthropic and, later, financial inducements prompted Haydn to produce these settings; true that he never saw the texts of these songs and that, in the words of Landon, his arrangements "fill twentieth-century folksong experts with horror"; true finally that he accepted the help of students who did some of the work which was eventually published under his name. On the other hand it can not be ignored that Haydn himself, without helper, produced more than 250 of these arrangements, a fact that is also proven by the survival of several autographs. We cannot expect the composer to embrace ideas yet unknown to his generation and should rather enjoy these settings for voice and instruments which still reflect Haydn's skill and charm. At least a brief chapter might have been assigned to these modest compositions in Landon's huge work.

Another lacuna seems puzzling: the author deals only quite briefly with the famous *Haydn-Verzeichnis*, the catalog completed in 1805 by Elssler that forms one of the cornerstones of all Haydn research. On page 294 of the fifth volume Landon remarks rather casually: "This is no place to enter into a full discussion of *HV*," and he refers the reader to Larsen's classic *Die Haydn-Überlieferung*, which deals extensively with the problem. Even if we ignore the fact that Larsen's brilliant book was written in German and has been out of print for several decades, it would seem imperative that the most comprehensive work on Haydn yet published *should* include a full discussion of so basic a research tool.

On the whole the new Haydn biography is extremely well set and carefully corrected. There are, however, some minor oversights which might be corrected in the next list of errata. For example, Landon refers consistently to Eusebius *von* Mandyczewski (volume 4, pp. 350, 392; volume 5, pp. 115, 123). The famous Schubert and Haydn scholar was certainly in heart and spirit a nobleman, but actual aristocratic rank was never conferred upon him; thus, the little word *von* ought to be removed from his name. A mixup of two musical examples occurred in volume 5, page 142. Here the music of examples 3 and 4 was erroneously swapped while the texts remained in the right place. The meaning of the paragraph is thus lost.

These minute reservations are, however, of little significance considering the great importance of Landon's achievement. After *Haydn in England* was published, the American Musicological Society conferred on it the prestigious Kinkeldey award. The same quality of excellence also distinguishes the present pair of volumes. All three were produced by a man of unusual talent and encyclopedic knowledge, a compulsive worker who has devoted his full time—without interference of teaching or administrative duties—to research. He has also shown special talent in persuading his publishers to impose no limitations of space on his books, to adorn the volumes with numerous large-scale illustrations (some of them in full color), and to tolerate countless music examples, at times covering several pages—features which Landon's colleagues cannot help observing with an admiration strongly tinged with envy. Last, but not least, one of the roots of Landon's success is his single-minded obsessive interest in the art and culture of the Classical period and specifically the music of Joseph Haydn. This writer remembers that, when in 1945 Robbins Landon became his student at Boston University, the youth of nineteen knew exactly what he wanted, and he postulated to write a term paper on Haydn's symphonies!

This leads me to a slightly embarrassing confession. When I opened volume 5 I noticed that Landon had dedicated it to me and to my wife. At first I thought that this might disqualify me as a reviewer. But since my report on volume 3 was printed quite some time ago, and even numerous remarks on the fourth volume were drafted before I saw the fifth, I changed my mind. After all, having been active in Haydn research for close to half a century, I felt in duty bound to signal the appearance of this work which should leave its mark on our discipline for years to come.

*   *   *   *

"Accomplished is the mighty work." These words from Haydn's *Creation* may have crossed the mind of music lovers when the final volume of H. C. Robbins Landon's Haydn biography came off the press. A mighty work this is indeed. Not often has a monograph of similar dimensions been devoted to a single musician.

Landon's biography consists of no less than five large-size volumes with altogether 3200 pages including around 1½ million words, 265 illustrations, and over 1200 music examples, many covering several pages.

Unusual as the work's size is also the history of its publication. In 1976 the biography's third volume *Haydn in England* was issued, introducing the composer at the ripe age of fifty-nine. There followed volumes 4 and 5, covering the last decades of Haydn's life. Thereupon Landon reversed his procedure. Volume 2, covering the twenty-four important years Haydn served at the castle of Esterháza, was released in 1978, and at the end of 1980 appeared volume 1 dealing with the composer's youth and the beginning of his career.

It was certainly worthwhile to wait several years for this first volume, which offers a substantial amount of valuable new material. Landon not only unearths much hitherto-unknown information about the surroundings in which Haydn spent his early years, he also throws new light on the most obscure period of Haydn's creative activity. The author thoroughly analyzes the works of older masters which young Haydn is sure to have heard or performed, and he explains their influence on the receptive mind of the budding composer. Much new information on Haydn's artistic relationship to men like J. G. Reutter, Jr., Wagenseil, Gassmann, Holzbauer, Hasse, Caldara, Galuppi, and others is provided, while Hugo Riemann's shaky theory of the influence the Mannheim composers exerted on Haydn is definitely refuted. Landon also attempts to revise our conception of the composer's early work. He introduces—though not without reservation—hitherto-unknown works such as a Cassatio in D major for four horns and strings [Hob. II:D22 Add.], or a keyboard trio in the same key, both found in Czech libraries, and he painstakingly examines well-known works whose authenticity has been doubted. On the basis of the Fürnberg-Morzin collection of Haydn's symphonies preserved today in the Hungarian castle of Keszthely, he establishes a tentative new order of Haydn's early symphonies which is likely to produce some raised eyebrows among experts. Using the numbers of the Hoboken catalog, Landon's arrangement is: 1, 37, 18, 19, 2, 108, 16, 17, 15, 4, 10, 32, 5, 11, 33, 27, 107, 3, 20.

As the title indicates, Landon's study is divided into two main sections: Chronicle and Works. The Chronicle describes in the most elaborate manner not only the composer's life, but also his dwelling places, the personalities with whom he came into contact, and the cultural and social atmosphere in which his life unfolded. Although Landon is an excellent stylist who expresses himself in a most felicitous manner, in the Chronicle he avoids using his own voice, as far as this is possible. He presents a great deal of well-known source material—for instance the Haydn letters he had previously offered in print in his own English translation—augmenting it with valuable new discoveries. Even peripheral material which has only an indirect bearing on the specific topic is introduced repeatedly and greatly enriches the overall picture. It may be wondered whether the author, in his enthusiasm for documenting every detail of Haydn's life, does not occasionally go a bit too far. Haydn had many good friends and was on excellent terms with his musicians. Is it really necessary, whenever he served as godfather to a newborn child or as witness at a wedding, to reproduce the whole cumbersome Latin entry from the church register? In the case of a document issued in 1762 by Prince Esterházy to reorganize his musical establishment, Landon offers at first a summary translation of its German text. Next follows a draft of the same document, both in facsimile and in printed German transcription, and finally the definite version is presented in German. Thus, with certain modifications, the same act appears four times.

The author sets himself the task of dealing with all of Haydn's compositions. He discusses the source material for individual works (often supplementing and correcting the information provided by Hoboken's Haydn catalog) and offers important stylistic analyses. Valuable essays on the last oratorios, symphonies, string quartets, piano sonatas, trios, and so forth are provided in the last three volumes. Unfortunately this method is not applied in the second volume, which deals—at least as far as the composer's productivity is concerned—with the richest harvest in the artist's life. Landon explains that he has had to adopt this attitude for reasons of space: "We have forced ourselves to treat the whole of Haydn's musical life as a *crescendo* and to expand the detail as we move forward. . . . Thus the treatment of Haydn's music in this volume is of necessity a survey rather than a detailed analysis in depth" (p. 227).

It is not quite easy for the reader to accept this train of thought while considering the generous proportions prevailing in other parts of Landon's biography. One might have preferred to see the second volume subdivided so that full justice were done to Haydn's music written in the quarter of a century between 1766 and 1790. Moreover, the scholar's claim that the detail expands as the biography moves forward does not really seem to be consistently applied. Early pieces of quite modest musical value are treated at much greater length than important compositions of the middle period. Thus, while the dramatic fragment *La Marchesa Nespola* [Hob. XXX:1] of 1762 is discussed in thirteen pages, *Il mondo della luna* (1777) [Hob. XXVIII:7] receives less than three pages of coverage, and the magnificent *Armida* (1784) [Hob. XXVIII:12] scarcely more. To the *Missa brevis "Rorate coeli"* [Hob. XXII:3], a work of doubtful authenticity, written 1748-49, volume 1 devotes six pages; to the frequently performed *Missa Sancti Joannis de Deo* [Hob. XXII:7] of about 1777, volume 2 gives a single page. We can only hope that Landon is to make up for this parsimony and present us with a monograph on Haydn's vocal compositions similar to his valuable study devoted to the symphonies.

Such peculiarities of the monumental work must not detract, however, from our admiration and appreciation of its overall significance. Praise is also due to the handsomely reproduced illustrations, the variety of which testifies once more to Landon's remarkable ability to track down unusual material. His Haydn biography has not only enriched our knowledge of the composer's life and work immensely, it also represents a major contribution to the history of eighteenth-century music and culture.

Bibliography of the Works of Karl Geiringer Relating to Haydn

Compiled by David Malvinni and Martin Silver

Articles

"Das Haydn-Bild im Wandel der Zeiten." *Die Musik* 24 (1932): 430-36.
"Haydn Sketches for 'The Creation.'" Trans. Manton Monroe Marble. *Musical Quarterly* 18 (1932): 299-308.
"Haydn und England." *Österreichische Kunst* 3 (1932): 36-37, 43-45.
"Joseph Haydn und die Oper." *Zeitschrift für Musik* 99 (1932): 291-94.
"Haydn und England." *Haydn-Festschrift*. Vienna: privately printed, 1932.
"The Cantatas and Oratorios of Haydn's Youth." Trans. H. B. Weiner. *Musical Opinion* 61 (1938): 497-98.
"Joseph Haydn." *The International Cyclopedia of Music and Musicians*, ed. Oscar Thompson, 764-69. New York: Dodd, Mead, 1939.
"Haydn as an Opera Composer." *Proceedings of the Royal Musical Association* 66 (1939-40): 23-32.
"Joseph Haydn." *Grove's Dictionary of Music and Musicians*. 4th ed., ed. Henry Cope Colles. London: Macmillan, 1940.
"The Operas of Haydn." *Musical America* 60 (1940): 5, 38.
"A Historic Musical Friendship: Haydn and Mozart in Their Personal Relations." *Etude* 59 (1941): 807-08, 856.
"Joseph Haydn's Scottish and Welsh songs." *Proceedings of the Music Teachers National Association, Pittsburgh* 41 (1947): 235-44.
"Haydn and the Folksong of the British Isles." *Musical Quarterly* 35 (1949): 179-208.
"The Small Sacred Works by Haydn in the Esterházy Archives at Eisenstadt." *Musical Quarterly* 45 (1959): 460-72.
"Haydn, Werk, und Künstler." *Neue Zeitschrift für Musik* 120 (1959): 251-54.
"Joseph Haydn." *Hugo Riemann Musik-Lexicon*. 12th ed., ed. Wilibald Gurlitt. Vol. 1, 750-54. Mainz: Schott, 1959.
"Joseph Haydn als Kirchenmusiker: Die kleineren geistlichen Werke des Meisters im Eisenstädter Schloss." *Kirchenmusikalisches Jahrbuch* 44 (1960): 54-61.
"Sidelights on Haydn's Activities in the Field of Sacred Music." In *Bericht über die Internationale Konferenz zum Andenken Joseph Haydns, 17.-22. September 1959*, ed. Bence Szabolcsi and Dénes Bartha, 49-56. Budapest: Académiai Kiadó, 1961.
"Eigenhändige Bemerkungen Haydns in seinen Musikhandschriften." In *Anthony van Hoboken: Festschrift zum 75. Geburtstag*, ed. Joseph Schmidt-Görg, 87-92. Mainz: Schott, 1962.
"Joseph Haydn, Protagonist of the Enlightenment." *Studies on Voltaire and the Eighteenth Century* (Institut et Musée Voltaire, Geneva) 25 (1963): 683-90.
"Gluck und Haydn." In *Festschrift Otto Erich Deutsch zum 80. Geburtstag*, ed. Walter Gerstenberg, Jan La Rue, and Wolfgang Rehm, 75-81. Kassel: Bärenreiter, 1963.
"Anthony van Hoboken zum 80. Geburtstag." *Neue Zürcher Zeitung* 23 (1967): 9.
"Haydns Werk im Lauf der Jahrhundert." *Neue Zürcher Zeitung* 193 (1972): 43-44.
"From Guglieimi to Haydn: The Transformation of an Opera." In *International Musicological Society: Report of the Eleventh Congress, Copenhagen, 20-25 August 1972*, ed. Henrik Glahn, Søren Sørenson, and Peter Ryom, 391-95. Copenhagen: Wilhelm Hansen, 1974.
"Joseph Haydn." *The New Encyclopaedia Britannica*. 15th ed. Vol. 8, 680-84. Chicago: Encyclopaedia Britannica, 1974.

"Haydn and His Viennese Background"; "The 'Comedia la Marchesa Nespola': Some Documentary Problems"; "Remarks on the Early Masses"; "Stylistic Change in Haydn's Oratorios: 'Il Ritorno di Tobia' and 'The Creation.'" In *Haydn Studies: Proceedings of the International Haydn Conference, Washington, D.C., 1975*, ed. Jens Peter Larsen, Howard Serwer, and James Webster, 3-13, 53-55, 204-05, 392-93. New York: Norton, 1981.

"Preface" to *Haydn Commemorative Issue of the Musical Quarterly, April 1932*, ed. Paul Henry Lang. New York: Da Capo, 1983.

"Problems of Authenticity and Chronology." In *Joseph Haydn: Bericht über den internationalen Joseph Haydn Kongress, Vienna, September 1982*, ed. Eva Badura-Skoda, 5-12. Munich: Henle, 1986.

Books

With Hedwig Kraus. *Führer durch die Josef Haydn Kollektion im Museum der Gesellschaft der Musikfreunde in Wien*. Vienna, mimeograph, 1930. 2nd ed., 1932.

_____. *Joseph Haydn: Katalog einer Zentenarausstellung*. Vienna: [n.p.], 1932.

Joseph Haydn. Die grossen Meister der Musik. Ed. Ernst Bücken. Potsdam: Athenaion, 1932.

Haydn: A Creative Life in Music. New York: Norton, 1946. 2nd ed., rev. and enlarged with Irene Geiringer. Garden City, N.Y.: Doubleday, 1963. 3rd ed. Berkeley: University of California Press, 1982.

A Thematic Catalogue of Haydn's Settings of Folksongs from the British Isles. Studies in Musicology, series A, 2. Superior, Wisc.: Research Microfilm Publishers, 1953.

With Irene Geiringer. *Joseph Haydn: Der schöpferische Werdegang eines Meisters der Klassik*. Mainz: Schott, 1959. 2nd ed., rev. and enlarged. Mainz and Munich: Wilhelm Goldmann and Schott, 1986.

Brochure Notes

Keyboard Sonatas no[s]. 1-10. Sylvia Marlowe, harpsichord. Haydn Society, Boston, HSLP 3037, 1951.

Symphony no. 61 in D major (1776). Cond. Mogens Wöldike. Chamber Orchestra of the Danish State Orchestra. Haydn Society, Boston, HSL 1047, 1952.

Symphony no. 49 in F minor: "La passione" (1768); Symphony no. 73 in D major: "La chasse" (1781). Cond. Harry Newstone. Haydn Orchestra, London. Haydn Society, Boston, HSLP 1052, 1952.

Missa Sancti Bernardi de Offida: "Heiligmesse" (1796). Cond. Mogens Wöldike. Copenhagen Boys' and Men's Choir. Danish Royal Opera Orchestra. Haydn Society, Boston, HSL 2048, 1952.

Arianna a Naxos (1789) and English Songs (1791-1796). Jeannie Tourel, mezzo-soprano, and Ralph Kirkpatrick, piano. Haydn Society, Boston, HSL 2051, 1952.

The Complete String Quartets of Joseph Haydn. Schneider Quartet. Haydn Society, Boston, HSQ-A, E-H, L-M, [1952-54].

Missa Brevis Sancti Joannis de Deo: "Kleine Orgelmesse"; Songs for Mixed Voices (1796). Cond. Mogens Wöldike. Copenhagen Boys' and Men's Choir. Chamber Orchestra of the Palace Chapel, Copenhagen, and Chamber Choir of the Danish State Radio. Haydn Society, Boston, HSL 2064, 1953.

London Symphonies. Cond. Hermann Scherchen. Vienna Symphony and Vienna State Orchestras. Westminster, 6601, [1955].

The Salomon Symphonies. Cond. Sir Thomas Beecham. Royal Philharmonic Orchestra. Capitol GCR7127-7198, [1958-60]; also issued on Angel S 36242-44, S 36254-56.

Trumpet Concerto; Divertimenti. Cond. Kurt Redel. Bernard Jeannoutot, trumpet. Pro Arte Chamber Orchestra of Munich. Angel S 36148, [1963].

Mass no. 4 in G major (Missa St. Nicolai). Cond. George Barati. Akademie-Kammerchor, Vienna, and Vienna State Opera Orchestra. Lyrichord LL 114, [1963].

Mass no. 12 in B-flat major (Harmoniemesse). Cond. George Barati. Akademie-Kammerchor, Vienna, and Vienna State Opera Orchestra. Musical Heritage Society MHS 865S-66S, [1968].

Symphony no. 93 in D; Symphony no. 96 in D ("Miracle"). Cond. Erich Leinsdorf. Boston Symphony Orchestra. RCA Victor LSC 3030, [1968].

Symphonies no[s]. 1-19, 46-59. Cond. Ernst Märzendorfer. Vienna Chamber Orchestra. Musical Heritage Society OR H 201-6, OR H 219-25, [1970-76].

Orlando Paladino. Cond. Antal Dorati. Elly Ameling, soprano, and others. Kammerorchester Lausanne. Philips 6707 029, 1977.

Editions

Notturno 5 für zwei Violinen, Flöte und Oboe, zwei Hörner, zwei Violen, Violoncello und Kontrabass. Vienna: Universal Edition, 1931.

Divertimento III in E♭ [2 oboes, 2 clarinets, 2 bassoons, 2 horns]. Vienna: Universal Edition, 1931.

Divertimento Es-dur für vier Streichinstrumente. Nagels Musik-Archiv, 84. Hannover: Nagel, 1931.

"Baryton-Trio Nr. 96 für den praktischen Gebrauch eingerichtet." *Zeitschrift für Musik* 79 (1932), Beilage 4.

With Irene Geiringer. *Amors Pfeil für Sopran und Klavier oder Orchester.* Berlin: Edition Adler, 1932.

Allegro con variazioni [from Barytontrio no. 95]. In *Haydn-Festschrift*, 44-45. Vienna: privately published, 1932.

Divertimento (Feldpartita) B dur für 8 stimmigen Bläserchor. Leipzig: Fritz Schuberth, 1932.

Divertimento in G dur (1786). Berlin: Edition Adler, 1932.

Partita in F per flauto, oboe, 2 corni, 2 violini, 2 viole, violoncello e contrabassa. Vienna: Universal Edition, 1932.

Trio für Violine, Viola, und Cello (Barytontrio Nr. 82). Das Hauskonzert, 10. Copenhagen: Wilhelm Hansen, 1933.

Adagio and Presto for Strings, Flute and Harp. London: Novello, 1940.

La canterina [piano-vocal score]. New York: Music Press, 1946.

Harmonie in der Ehe [Harmony in marriage]. Text by Johan Nikolaus Goetz, trans. Henry S. Drinker. New York: Music Press, 1946.

Song of Thanks to God. Text by J. F. Gellert, trans. Henry S. Drinker. New York: Music Press, 1946.

Eveningsong to God [Abendlied zu Gott]. Trans. Henry S. Drinker. New York: Boosey & Hawkes, 1949.

To the Women [An die Frauen]. Trans. Henry S. Drinker. New York: G. Schirmer, 1951.

Eloquence. New York: Carl Fischer, 1958.

The Old Man. New York: Carl Fischer, 1958.

We Seek Not God, Our Lord or Glory [Non nobis Domine]. Concordia Motet Series. St. Louis: Concordia, 1960.

Volksliedbearbeitungen: Nr. 1-100, Schottische Lieder. Kritischer Bericht with Paul G. Buchloh. Joseph Haydn Werke, XXXII, 1. Munich-Duisburg: Henle, 1961.

Orlando Paladino: Dramma eroicomico, Libretto von Nunziato Porta. Kritischer Bericht. Joseph Haydn Werke, XXV, 11. 3 vols. Munich-Duisburg: Henle, 1972-73.

Symphony no. 103 in E-flat Major ("Drum Roll"): Historical Background, Analysis, Views and Commentary. Norton Critical Scores. New York: Norton, 1974.

La canterina = The Songstress: Opera Buffa in Two Acts [vocal score], trans. Carl Zytowski. Bryn Mawr, Pa.: Theodore Presser, 1980.

Orlando Paladino: Dramma eroicomico, 1782 [vocal score]. German trans. with Ruth Michaelis. Kassel: Bärenreiter, 1982.

With Günter Thomas. *Acide und andere Fragmente italienischer Opern um 1761 bis 1763.* Joseph Haydn Werke, XXV, 1. Munich: Henle, 1985.

Reviews

Karl Kobald, *Joseph Haydn: Bild seines Lebens und seiner Zeit.* Vienna and Leipzig: Epstein, 1932. *Die Musik* 24 (1932): 935-36.

Leopold Nowak, *Joseph Haydn: Leben, Bedeutung und Werk.* Vienna: Amalthea, 1950. *Notes* 8 (1951): 711-12.

Robert Sondheimer, *Haydn: A Historical and Psychological Study Based on His Quartets.* London: Bernoulli, 1951. *Notes* 9 (1952): 604-05.

Pianoforte Trio in F-sharp Minor, ed. Donald Francis Tovey. London: Oxford University Press, 1951. *Notes* 9 (1952): 644.

Harpsichord Concerto in D; Trumpet Concerto in E-flat. George Eskendale, trumpet, Erna Heiller, harpsichord; Vienna State Opera Orchestra, cond. Franz Litschauer. Vanguard VRS-454. *Musical Quarterly* 41 (1955): 402-04.

Fünf Eisenstädter Trios, ed. Adolf Hoffmann. Wiesbaden: Breitkopf & Härtel, 1954. *Notes* 13 (1956): 340.

Anthony van Hoboken, *Joseph Haydn: Thematisch-bibliographisches Werkverzeichnis.* Vol. 1. Mainz: Schott, 1957. *Notes* 14 (1957): 565-66.

"Grosstat eines Gelehrten: Das Haydn—Werkverzeichnis Anthony van Hobokens." *Neue Zeitschrift für Musik* 18 (1957): 693-94.

Messe B-Dur, Schöpfungs-Messe [Faksimile]. Munich-Duisburg: Henle, 1957. *Sextet no. 14, E-flat, for Violin, Viola, Violoncello, Oboe, Horn, and Bassoon*, ed. Kurt Janetsky. London: Musica Rara, 1957. *Notes* 15 (1958): 644.

Barytontrios, Nr. 49-72; *Barytontrios, Nr. 73-96*, ed. Hubert Unverricht; *Messen, Nr. 5-8*, ed. H. C. Robbins Landon in conjunction with Karl Heinz Füssl & Christa Landon; *Lo speziale: dramma giocoso*, ed. Helmut Wirth; *Mehrstimmige Gesänge*, ed. Paul Mies; *Kanons*, ed. Otto Erich Deutsch. Joseph Haydn Werke, XIV, 3-4; XXIII, 2; XXV:3; XXX; XXXI. Munich-Duisburg: Henle, 1958-59. Notes 17 (1959): 127-29.

La canterina, ed. Dénes Bartha; *Die sieben letzten Worte unseres Erlösers am Kreuze: Orchesterfassung, 1785*, ed. Hubert Unverricht. Joseph Haydn Werke, XXV, 2; IV. Munich-Duisburg: Henle, 1959. Notes 18 (1960): 125-26.

Haydn Compositions in the Music Collections of the National Széchényi Library, Budapest, ed. Jenö Vécsey, rev. Dénes Bartha, trans. Sándor Országh. Budapest: Académiai Kiadó, 1960. *Symphonie, fis-moll*. Budapest: Académiai Kiadó, 1959. *Haydn emlekere*, ed. Bence Szabolcsi and Dénes Bartha. Budapest: Académiai Kiadó, 1960. Notes 18 (1961): 230-32.

Dénes Bartha and László Somfai, *Haydn als Opernkapellmeister*. Budapest: Académiai Kiadó, 1961. *Bericht über die internationale Konferenz zum Andenken Joseph Haydns*, ed. Bence Szabolcsi and Dénes Bartha. Budapest: Académiai Kiadó, 1961. Notes 19 (1961): 67-69.

Barytontrios, Nr. 25-48, ed. Hubert Unverricht; *Lieder*, ed. Paul Mies; *Volksliederbearbeitungen, Nr. 1-100*; *Schottische Lieder*, ed. Karl Geiringer. Joseph Haydn Werke, XIV, 2; XXIX, 1; XXXII, 1. Munich-Duisburg: Henle, 1960-61. Notes 20 (1963): 303-05.

Die sieben letzten Worte unseres Erlösers am Kreuze, ed. Hubert Unvericht; *Londoner Sinfonien, 4. Folge*, ed. Hubert Unvericht; *Streichquartette, opus 9 and opus 17*, ed. Georg Feder; *L'incontro improvviso*, ed. Helmut Wirth; *Il ritorno di Tobia*, ed. Ernst Fritz Schmid. Joseph Haydn Werke, XXVIII, 2; I, 18; XII, 2; XXV, 6. Munich-Duisburg: Henle, 1961-63. *Symphony no. 89, F major*, ed. H. C. Robbins Landon. London: Eulenburg, 1962. *Overture to the opéra comique "Die Feursbrunst."* London: Eulenburg, 1962. *Symphony no. 70, D major*, ed. Fritz Kneusslin. Basel: Kneusslin, 1962. Notes 20 (1963): 556-58.

Joseph Haydn, *Gesammelte Briefe und Aufzeichnungen: Unter Benützung der Quellensammlung von H. C. Robbins Landon*. Kassel: Bärenreiter, 1965. Journal of the American Musicological Society 19 (1966): 251-54.

L'incontro improvviso, ed. Helmut Wirth; *L'infedeltà delusa*, ed. Dénes Bartha and Jenö Vécsey; *Messen, Nr. 9-10*, ed. Günter Thomas; *Sinfonien 1764 und 1765*, ed. Horst Walter. Joseph Haydn Werke, XXV, 6; XXV, 5; XXIII, 3; I, 4. Munich-Duisburg: Henle, 1963-65. Notes 22 (1966): 1308-11.

Il ritorno di Tobia, ed. Ernst Fritz Schmid; *Armida*, ed. Wilhelm Pfannkuch; *Messe Nr. 11, "Schöpfungsmesse,"* ed. Irmgard Becker-Glauch; *Messe Nr. 12, "Harmoniemesse,"* ed. Friedrich Lippmann; *Klaviersonaten, 3*, ed. Georg Feder; *Sinfonien 1767-1772*, ed. Carl-Gabriel Stellan Mörner; *Sinfonien 1773 und 1774*, ed. Wolfgang Stockmeier; *Londoner Sinfonien, 3*, ed. Horst Walter. Joseph Haydn Werke, XXVIII, 1; XXV, 12; XXIII, 4; XXIII, 5; XVIII, 3; I, 6; I, 7. Munich-Duisburg: Henle, 1963-67. Notes 25 (1968): 319-22.

Konzerte für Violine und Orchester, ed. Heinz Lohmann und Günter Thomas; *Werke mit Baryton*, ed. Sonja Gerlach; *Barytontrios Nr. 97-126*, ed. Michael Härting and Horst Walter; *La fedeltà premiata: dramma pastorale giocoso*, ed. Günter Thomas; *Applausus*, ed. Irmgard Becker-Glauch and Heinrich Wiens. Joseph Haydn Werke, III, 1; XIII; XIV, 5; XXV, 10; XXVII, 2. Munich-Duisburg: Henle, 1968-69. Notes 28 (1971): 105-07.

Sinfonien um 1775-76: Kritischer Bericht, ed. Wolfgang Stockmaier and Sonja Gerlach; *Klaviersonaten*, ed. Georg Feder; *Klavier-Trios: Kritischer Bericht*, ed. Wolfgang Stockmaier. Joseph Haydn Werke, I, 11; XVIII, 1-2; XVII, 1. Munich-Duisburg: Henle, 1970. Notes 28 (1972): 765-68.

Anthony van Hoboken, *Joseph Haydn: Thematisch-bibliographisches Werkverzeichnis*, vol. 2 (*Vokalwerke*). Mainz: Schott, 1971. Journal of the American Musicological Society 25 (1972): 471-73.

Haydn-Studien, I-II. Munich-Duisburg: Henle, 1965-70. Notes 29 (1972): 51-52.

Pariser Sinfonien, ed. Hiroshi Nakano; *Frühe Streichquartette*, ed. Georg Feder and Gottfried Greiner; *Philemon und Baucis, oder Jupiters Reise auf die Erde*, ed. Jürgen Braun. Joseph Haydn Werke, I, 12; XII, 1; XXIV, 1. Munich-Duisburg: Henle, 1971-73. Notes 31 (1975): 845-47.

Notturni mit Orgelleiern: Kritischer Bericht, ed. Makoto Ohmiya; *Streichquartette "op. 20" und "op. 33,"* ed. Georg Feder and Sonja Gerlach; *Le pescatrici: Kritischer Bericht*, ed. Dénes Bartha, Jenö Vécsey, and Maria Eckhardt; *L'anima del filosofo, ossia Orfeo ed Eurydice: Kritischer Bericht*, ed. Helmut Wirth. Joseph Haydn Werke, VII; XII, 3; XXV, 4; XXV, 13. Munich-Duisburg: Henle, 1972-74. Notes 32 (1976): 623-25.

H. C. Robbins Landon, *Haydn in England, 1791-1795* (Haydn: Chronicle and Works, vol. 3). Bloomington: Indiana University Press, 1976. Notes 34 (1977): 56-58.

Concerti mit Orgelleiern, ed. Makoto Ohmiya; *Klaviertrios, 2*, ed. Wolfgang Stockmeier; *La vera costanza*, ed. Horst Walter. Joseph Haydn Werke, VI; XVII, 2; XXV, 8. Munich-Duisburg: Henle, 1975-76. Notes 34 (1977): 192-94.

H. C. Robbins Landon, *Haydn: The Years of The Creation, 1796-1800* (Haydn: Chronicle and Works, vol. 4); *The Late Years, 1801-1809* (Haydn: Chronicle and Works, vol. 5). Bloomington: Indiana University Press, 1977. Notes 35 (1978): 296-98.

_____, *Haydn: The Early Years, 1732-1765* (Haydn: Chronicle and Works, vol. 1); *Haydn at Eszterháza, 1766-1790* (Haydn: Chronicle and Works, vol. 2). Bloomington: Indiana University Press, 1980 and 1978. *Notes* 38 (1981): 60-61.

Michael C. Bryant and Gary W. Chapman, *A Melodic Index to Haydn's Instrumental Music*. New York: Pendragon Press, 1982. *Notes* 41 (1984): 70-71.

Applausus: Kritischer Bericht, ed. Heinrich Wiens and Irmgard Becker-Glauch; *Le pescatrici*, ed. Dénes Bartha, Jenö Vécsey and Maria Eckhardt; *Streichquartette "op. 64" und "op. 71/74,"* ed. Georg Feder and Isidor Saslav; *Barytontrios Nr. 1-24: Kritischer Bericht*, ed. Jürgen Braun and Sonja Gerlach; *Konzerte für Violoncello und Orchester*, ed. Sonja Gerlach; *Concertante*, ed. Sonja Gerlach; *Il mondo della luna*, ed. Günter Thomas. Joseph Haydn Werke, XXVII, 2; XXV, 4; XII, 5; XIV, 1; III, 2; II, XXV, 7. Munich-Duisburg: Henle, 1969-82. *Notes* 41 (1984): 151-54.

Konzerte für Klavier (Cembalo) und Orchester, ed. Horst Walter and Bettina Wackernagel; *Stücke für das Laufwerk (Flötenuhrstücke)*, ed. Sonja Gerlach and George R. Hill; *Konzerte für ein Blasinstrument und Orchester*, ed. Makoto Ohmiya and Sonja Gerlach; *Acide und andere Fragmente italienischer Opern um 1761 bis 1763*, ed. Karl Geiringer and Günter Thomas. Joseph Haydn Werke, XV, 2; XXI; III, 3; XXV, 1. Munich: Henle, 1983-85. *Notes* 42 (1986): 847-49.

Streichtrios, vol. 1, ed. Bruce Macintyre and Barry Brook. Joseph Haydn Werke, XI, 1. Munich: Henle, 1986. *Notes* 43 (1987): 923-24.

Joseph Haydn: Bericht über den internationalen Joseph Haydn Kongress, Vienna, September 1982, ed. Eva Badura-Skoda. Munich: Henle, 1986. *Notes* 44 (1988): 475-76.

Klaviertrios: Kritischer Bericht, vol. 3, ed. Irmgard Becker-Glauch. Joseph Haydn Werke, XVII, 3. Munich: Henle, 1986. *Notes* 44 (1988): 812-13.

Indexes

Names and Places

PAGE NUMBERS IN BOLDFACE REFER TO MUSIC EXAMPLES; THOSE IN ITALICS REFER TO FIGURES

Abert, Hermann, 97, 197-98
Addison, Joseph, 175
Adler, Guido, xvii-xviii, 181, 213
Agricola, Johann Friedrich, 195
Ahren-August, Therese, xxii
Albrechtsberger, Johann Georg, 74n
Algarotti, Francesco, 174, 176-78
Allan, Jean M., 104n
Altmann, Wilhelm, 148
Amalia, Archduchess, 181
American Academy of Arts and Sciences, xvii
American Musicological Society, xvii, 239
Amsterdam, 7
Anfossi, Pasquale, 77, 208, 233
Angiolini, Gasparo, 177, 183, 187
Appel, Richard, 104n
Arbesser, Ferdinand, 35
Arend, Max, 172n
Ariosto, Lodovico, 98
Arnold, Samuel, 105
Artaria, Carlo, 36
Artaria, Francesco, 36
Artaria (publisher), 10, 36, 72, 111, 145, 155, 195, 224-25, 227-28
Asplmayer, Franz, 28, 143
Attwood, Thomas, 205, 209
Auenbrugger, Katharina von, 227
Auenbrugger, Leopold von, 227
Auenbrugger, Marianna von, 227
Augsburg, 101, 232
Austria, xvii, xix, xxii, 3, 5-6, 8, 10, 19, 26, 67, 69, 70, 97, 100, 133, 146, 154, 236

Bach, Carl Philipp Emanuel, 4, 10, 28, 55, 136-37, 139-40, 143, 145, 195-98, **199**, 200-02, 223
Bach, Johann Christian, 98, 208
Bach, Johann Sebastian, xx, 135, 137, 198, 202
Bach, Wilhelm Friedemann, 198
Bach family, 195
Badini, Carlo Francesco, 98, 101, 236
Badura-Skoda, Eva, xx, 27
Badura-Skoda, Paul, xx

Bärenreiter Verlag, 97
Balet, Leo, 17
Bartha, Dénes, 41n, 77, 172, 232-33, 236
Barthélemon, François Hippolyte, 105, 236
Bartolozzi, Gaetano, 105
Bavaria, 236
Beaumarchais, Pierre-Augustin Caron de, 206
Beck, Franz Ignaz, 213
Becker-Glauch, Irmgard, 41n, 67, 103, 219, 229-30
Beethoven, Ludwig van, 3, 7-8, 11, 27, 40, 45, 68, 106, 110n, 120n, 126, 129, 131, 133, 135, 144-46, 148, 152-54, 176, 195, 200, 221, 223, 227, 235, 238
Benda brothers, 195
Benedict XIII, Pope, 162
Bent, Margaret, xx
Bergen (Rügen), 10
Berlin, xvii, 55, 101, 137, 195-96, 237
    Staatsbibliothek zu Berlin (Deutsche Staatsbibliothek; Preussische Staatsbibliothek; Staatsbibliothek, Preussischer Kulturbesitz), 42n, 45n, 89, 165n, 237
Berlioz, Hector, 181, 188, 190-91
Bertoni, Ferdinando Giuseppe, 178n
Besseler, Heinrich, 232
Bettelini, Pietro, *204*
Biba, Otto, xx, xxii
Biber, Heinrich, 19, **20**
Biggs, E. Power, 35n
Bitter, Carl Hermann, 202
Bland, John, 228
Blandford, Walter F. H., 104n
Blinoni, Nicodemo, 169
Blume, Friedrich, 221-22
Boccherini, Luigi, 145, 213
Bohemia, 4, 10, 97
Boieldieu, François-Adrien, 183
Bologna, 55, 183n
Bonaparte, Napoleon, 8-9
Bonn, 6
Boston, 9, 221
    Haydn Society, 9, 68n, 133, 174n, 215, 221-22
    Public Library, 104n
    University, xix, 104n, 239

Botstiber, Hugo, xviii, 17, 71n, 112
Brahms, Johannes, xix-xx, 3, 17, 27, 40, 138, 141-42, 173n
Bratislava. See Pressburg
Braunschweig (Brunswick), 100, 183
Breitkopf & Härtel (publisher), xviii, 68, 72, 89, 113, 149, 174n, 195, 200, 219, 221, 226
Bremen, 101
Breslau, 101, 205
Brion, Marcel, 27
Broughton, C. R., 111
Brown, A. Peter, 198
Bruckner, Anton, 3, 27, 40, 72
Brühl, Count Karl Friedrich Moritz Paul von, 171
Brünn (Brno), 101
Brussels, 229
Bucharest, 220, 232
    Biblioteca Centrală de Stat, 219
Buchloh, Paul G., 224
Budapest, 41n, 67, 101, 181, 231-33
    Hungarian Academy of Science, 232
    National Széchényi Library, 95, 231-33
    Országos Széchényi Könyvtár, 42n, 43n, 67n, 69n
Bücken, Ernst, xviii, 9
Büsch, Johann Georg, 195
Bukovina, xviii
Burgenland, 67
Burgundy, Duke of, 183
Burkart, Leonard, 104n
Burnacini, Ludovico, 27
Burney, Charles, xx, 6, 55, 171, 182, 195, 236
Burns, Robert, 106, 123, 223
Bustelli, Giuseppe, 99-100

Caccini, Francesco, 178
Cádiz, 5, 149-50
Caffé, Daniel, *13*
Caldara, Antonio, xviii, 19, **24**, 28, 138, 240
California, xx
Calzabigi, Ranieri de', 174, 177-79, 182n, 183, 188, 189n
Capeci, Carlo Sigismondo, 183, 186-87
Carner, Mosco, 236
Carter, Charles Thomas, 105
Casti, Battista, 205-06
Cavalli, Pier Francesco, 27
Cernauti, xviii-xix
Cervantes, Miguel de, 89
Český Krumlov (Krumau), 99
Cesti, Antonio, 27
Charles, King of Spain, 149
Charles VI, Emperor of Austria, 176
Charlotte, Archduchess of Austria, 181
Charlotte Sophia, Queen of England, 105n
Charlottenburg Palace (Copenhagen), 165
Chernovtsy. See Cernauti
Christian VIII, King of Denmark, 165
Cimarosa, Domenico, 233
Claudius, Mathius, 195
Clemens XI, Pope, 162n
Clementi, Muzio, 141

Clinton, N.Y., Hamilton College, xix
Cobbett, Walter Wilson, 144
Cologne, 41n, 101, 221, 223, 232
    Joseph Haydn Institute, xxii, 67, 68n, 103, 213, 221-23, 225-29
Coltellini, Marco, 182-84, 186-89
Cornetti, Paolo, 205
Coutts, Thomas, 109n, 111n
Cramer, Carl Friedrich, 142
Czechoslovakia, 232
Czernowitz. See Cernauti
Czerny, Carl, 200

Dance, George, *16*
Dancourt, Louis Hurtaut, 85
Da Ponte, Lorenzo, 204, 206-07
Darmstadt, Hessische Landesbibliothek, 70n
Dercy, Paul, 183
Desing, Abbot Anselm, 26
Deutsch, Otto Erich, 17, 36n, 221
Diderot, Denis, 174, 176, 196
Dies, Albert Christoph, 35, 196, 229, 236
Dittersdorf, Carl Ditters von, 171, 205
Doles, Johann Friedrich, 199
Dresden, 101, 205, 207
Dreyfus, Laurence, xx
Duke of York, 6, 205
Dulwich, 210
Dunfernline, Limekilns (Scotland), 106
Durazzo, Count Giacomo, 177
Dvořák, Antonin, 36

Eberlin, Johann Ernst, 198
Eckard, Johann Gottfried, 198
Edinburgh, 104n, 106, 109, 111, 120
Einstein, Alfred, xvii, 159, 213
Eisenstadt, 4, 35, 42n, 45n, 63, 67-70, 71n, 72-73, 75, 77, 222, 232, 236, 238
    Brothers of Mercy, 73
    Esterházy Archives, 72n, 73n, 222, 231-33, 236
    Haydn Museum, 69
    Pfarrkirche, 75, 236
Elisabeth, Archduchess, 181
Elizabeth Christiane, Dowager Empress, 19
Elssler, Johann Jr., 113-14, 154, 217, 224, 237, 239
Elssler catalog, 68-69
Engel, Carl, xviii
Engelke, Bernard, 103n
England, 5-7, 10, 36, 45, 55, 63, 78, 97, 105, 126, 129, 131, 146, 150, 152, 154, 176n, 196-97, 209-10, 223, 229, 235-36, 238
Erdödy, Count Joseph, 152
Esterháza, 5, 27, 35-36, 77, 95, 100, 172-74, 229, 233, 239
    Theater (Opera House), 5, 97, 233
Esterházy, 4-7, 10, 36, 42n, 63, 67, 70, 74, 77, 97, 101, 113, 171, 222, 228-29, 232-33, 238
Esterházy, Prince (d. 1989), 68n
Esterházy, Prince Nicolaus (Miklós) I the Magnificent, 5, 6, 28, 35, 73, 77, 91, 100, 125, 172, 174, 222, 225, 227, 230, 238, 240
Esterházy, Prince Nicolaus (Miklós) II, 7, 36
Esterházy, Prince Paul Anton (Pál Antal), 4, 6, 10, 225

Falck, Martin, 213
Fauxbourg, 26
Feder, Georg, 223-28
Fellerer, Karl Gustav, 232
Fénelon, François de Salignac de la Mothe, 183, 187
Feodorovna, Grand Duchess Maria, 171
Ferdinand III, Grand Duke of Tuscany, 178, 179n
Ferdinand IV, King of Naples, 5-6, 10, 228
Fétis, François-Joseph, 219
Finscher, Ludwig, 197
Firestone, Elizabeth C., 108n
Fischer, Wilhelm, xvii, 35n, 213
Fischer von Erlach, Johann Berhard, 26
Fisher, John Abraham, 205
Fitz, Oskar, 17
Flamm, Antonia, 89
Florence, 179n
Forconi, Alipio, 176
Forini, Elisabeth, 78
Forster, William, 228-29
France, 3, 5, 10, 55, 63, 162, 164-65, 168, 179, 183, 232
Frankfurt, 6, 101, 181-82
Franz Eugen, Duke of Württemberg, 141
Franz II, Emperor of Austria, 6, 133, 154
Fraser, William, 105n
Fratres Misericordiae. *See* Vienna, Brothers of Mercy
Frederick II, "The Great," King of Prussia, 55, 137, 145
Frederick William II, King of Prussia, 145-46
Freeman, Estelle Reemie, 104n
Freud, Sigmund, xix
Frieberth, Joseph, 72, 85, 150
Frieberth, Karl, 172
Friedländer, Max, 217, 223
Fries and Co. (bank), 109-11
Frisch, Walter, xx
Fuchs, Aloys, 219, 225
Fuchs, Ingrid, xx
Fürnberg, Karl Joseph von, 4, 9, 133, 240
Fux, Johann Josef, 28, 55, 138, 231

Gál, Hans, 89, 104n
Galli, Amintore, 11
Galli-Bibiena, Francesco, 27
Galliard, Johann Ernst, 183
Galuppi, Baldassare, 240
Gardiner, George, xviii-xix, xxii
Garrick, David, 182
Gassmann, Florian Leopold, 240
Gazzaniga, Giuseppe, 210
Geiringer, Bernice, xvii n, xx, xxii
Geiringer, Irene, xviii-xx, xxii, 97
Geiringer, Karl, xvii-xxii, 9, 19n, 55, 67, 77, 103, 133, 159, 171, 181, 195, 197, 203, 213, 215, 217, 221
Gellert, Christian Fürchtegott, 200, 202
Geneva, Institut et Musée Voltaire, 55
Genzinger, Marianne von, 36, 172n, 223
Genzinger, Peter von, 36
George III, King of England, 205
Gerber, Ernst Ludwig, 219
Gerber, Rudolf, 181

Gerlach, Sonja, 226
Germany, xxii, 5-7, 63, 89, 97, 150, 154, 195, 210
Gerstenberg, Heinrich Wilhelm von, 195
Gertruydenberg (treaty, 1710), 162n
Gillesberger, Hans, 36n
Gleim, Johann Ludwig, 195
Gluck, Christoph Willibald, xix-xxi, 27, 89, 91, 98, 141, 144, 165, 171-74, 177-79, 181-83, 186-91, 206, 210
Goethe, Johann Wolfgang von, 56, 125, 137
Göttweig. *See* Zwettl
Goeyens, Alphonse, 17
Goldoni, Carlo, 78, 85, 89
Gottsched, Johann Christoph, 176
Graue, Jerald C., 197
Graun brothers, 195
Graz, 101
Great Britain, xxii
Grenoble, xix
Griesinger, Georg August, 45, 63, 196, 236
Griffin, W., 98
Grundmann, Johann Basilius, 9
Guadagni, Gaetano, 182
Gülzow, A., 17
Guglielmi, Pietro Alessandro, 97-101
Gumpendorf, 7, 36
Gyrowetz, Adalbert, 228

Haas, Robert, xvii, 27
Hadden, James Cuthbert, 104
Hainburg, 3-4, 9
Halm, Hans, 218, 221
Hamburg, 55, 101, 142, 195-99
Handel, George Frideric, 7, 98, 105, 133, 176, 198, 223
Hanover, 101, 205
Hapsburg, 26, 181
Hardy, Thomas, *2*
Harich, János, 68n, 73n, 172
Hasse, Johann Adolf, 72-73, 174, 183, 198, 240
Hawlin, Elisabetha, 168n, 169
Haydn, Joseph, xvii-xviii, xx-xxii, 1, *2*, 3-11, *12-15*, 16, *16*, 18-19, 26-28, **29**, 35-37, 40-46, 49-53, 55-56, 63-64, 67-78, 85, 89, 91, 97-98, 100-01, 103-14, 118-23, 125-31, 134-55, 171-74, 195-98, 200, 213, 215, 217-33, 235-39, 240
Haydn, Maria Anna, 6
Haydn, Michael, 74, 228
Heckenauer, C., 169n
Heckmann, Harald, 172n
Heideloff, Karl Alexander von, 16
Helfert, Vladimir, 169
Helm, Eugene, 195
Helms, Marianne, 67
Henle, G. (publisher), 221
Henry IV, King of France, 163
Hertzmann, Eric, xix
Hildebrandt, Johann Lukas von, 26
Hill, Richard S., 104n
Hirschfeld, Robert, 222
Hoboken, Anthony van, xviii, 73, 103, 217-20, 236
Hölty, Ludwig Christian Heinrich, 195
Hoffmann, E. T. A., 183, 201-02

252   Names and Places

Hoffmeister, Franz Anton, 183n
Holland, 5, 10
Holzbauer, Ignaz, 240
Hopkinson, Cecil, 104
Huber, Thaddäus, 143
Hughes, John, 183
Hughes-Hughes, Augustus, 104, 112
Hugo Capet, King of France, 163
Hungary, 5, 26, 67, 126, 149, 231-32

Ignaz, Joseph Michael, 229
Ihrwach, Sebastian, *15*
Ireland, 106
Isabella of Parma, wife of Joseph II, 181
Italy, 3, 18, 28, 55, 63, 78, 161-62, 210

Jaffé, M., *14*
Jahn, Otto, 17
Jansen-Bartolozzi, Therese, 230
Japan, 228
Jaroměřice, 169
Jenkinson, Mr., 111
Jommelli, Niccolò, 89, 99, 174
Jordan, Dora, 108
Joseph-Friedrich, Prince of Sachsen-Hildburghausen, 171
Joseph II, Emperor of Austria, 26, 181, 187, 189, 206
Josepha, Archduchess of Austria, 181

Kamakura, 228
Kassel, 97
Kaunitz, Prince Wenzel Anton, 182n, 183n, 189n
Kazinczy, Franz, 204
Kelly, Michael, 205-06, 209-10
Keszthely, 240
Khevenhüller-Metsch, Prince Johann Joseph, 182, 187
Kidson, Frank, 112
King, Alec Hyatt, 104n
Kinsky, Georg, 218, 221
Kirnberger, Johann Philipp, 195
Klopstock, Friedrich Gottlieb, 195
Köchel, Ludwig von, 217
Köln. *See* Cologne
Königsberg, 101
Kozeluch, Leopold, 106, 232
Kratochwil, Antonio, 168-69
Kraus, Hedwig, xviii
Krause, Christian Gottfried, 176
Kremlev, Yuly, 232
Kretzschmar, Hermann, xvii, 213
Krottendorffer, Joseph, 74n
Kurz-Bernardon, Johann Joseph Felix von, 27, 134

Landon, Christa, 226
Landon, H. C. Robbins, xx-xxii, 9, 68n, 126, 133, 173n, 174, 197, 213, 221-22, 225, 232, 235-40
Landshoff, Ludwig, 17
Lang, Paul Henry, 67, 126
Larsen, Jens Peter, 9, 71n, 73-74, 104n, 112n, 113, 217, 219, 221-22, 239

Leipzig, xviii, 101, 113, 174n, 195, 200, 205, 207, 221, 232
Leningrad, 232
Lenzewski, Gustav, 17
Leopold, Archduke, 181
Le Sueur, Jean-François, 183
Lesure, François, 232
Lessing, Gotthold Ephraim, 195
Leszinskas, Marie, 162n
Levin, Robert, xx
Lichtenwanger, William, 104n
Limekilns. *See* Dunfermline
Livanova, Tamara, 232
Lockwood, Lewis, xx
London, xix, 6-7, 10, 27, 36, 42-43, 45, 73, 91, 98-99, 104n, 105, 125-26, 131, 173n, 174, 183, 203, 209, 223, 228, 238
    BBC, xix
    British Library (British Museum), 103-04, 108, 112-14, 122
    Covent Garden, 210
    Drury Lane Theatre, 210
    King's Theatre, 6, 78, 97-99, 210
    Queen's Theatre, 183
    Royal College of Music, xix
    Sacred Harmonic Society, 89
    Westminster Abbey, 7
Lorenzi, Giambattista, 85
Louis Charles (son of Louis XVI), 159
Louis Philippe (citizen-king), 162
Louis XIV, King of France, *160*, 183
Louis XV, King of France, *160*, 162
Louis the Great, King of France, 163, 168
Louis XVI, King of France, 159, *160*, 162, 165
Ludwig, Friedrich, xvii
Lukaveč (Bohemian castle), 4, 35
Lully, Jean-Baptiste, 17, 98, 173-74

Mahler, Gustav, 27, 40, 222
Mainz, xviii
    University, 223
Mandyczewski, Eusebius, xviii, 17, 19n, 45, 103n, 133, 159, 217-18, 223, 239
Mannheim, 97, 101, 240
Marcello, Benedetto, 175-76
Maria Amalia, Archduchess, 181
Maria Anna, Archduchess, 19
Maria Theresa, Empress of Austria, 5, 19, 28, 77, 85, 173
Marpurg, Friedrich Wilhelm, 195
Martin y Soler, Vincente, 89
Martini, Padre Giovanni Battista, 55
Mattheson, Johann, 55, 195
Mendelssohn, Abraham, 155
Mendelssohn, Fanny, 154
Mendelssohn, Felix, 125, 154-55, 235
Mendelssohn, Moses, 235
Menel, Mr. (cellist), 128
Metastasio, Pietro, 27-28, 164-65, 167-68, 176, 178-79, 181n
Mies, Paul, 223, 232
Milton, John, 7
Mitscha, Franz, 168-69
Mitscha, Johanna, 168-69
Molnár, Antal, 233

Monn, Matthias Georg, 28, **32**, 35n
Montagu, Lady Mary Wortley, 26-27
Monteverdi, Claudio, 17, 178
Moravia, 169
Morzin, Ferdinand Maximilian von, 4, 6, 9, 28, 35, 240
Moscatelli, Peter, 181
Moscheles, Ignaz, 154
Mozart, Leopold, 198, 209-10, 223, 233
Mozart, Nannerl, 198
Mozart, Wolfgang Amadeus, 3, 5, 11, 16-17, 27, 35-36, 45, 63, 78, 89, 91, 95, 97, 129, 138, 141, 144-46, 148, 172, 176-77, 188, 195, 198, **199**, 200, 203, 205-06, 209-10, 217, 219, 236, 238
Munich, 101, 210, 221

Nancy 175
Napier, William (publisher), 104-06, 111-14, 118, 122-24
Naples, 165, 169, 187, 203
Napoleon, 8-9
Naumburg, 183
Neefe, Christian Gottlob, 200
Neidl, Johann, *14*
Nettl, Paul, 19n
Neubauer, Friedrich Ludwig, *15*
Neukomm, Sigismund, 103, 112
New York Public Library, 104n
Nissen, Georg Nikolaus, 198
Norton, W. W. (publisher), xx
Noverre, Jean-Georges, 177-78
Nürnberg. *See* Nuremberg
Nuremberg, 101

Odo, Pater, 69
Österreichische Nationalbibliothek. *See* Vienna, Austrian National Library
Oettingen-Wallerstein, Prince Ernst, 141
Ohmiya, Makoto, 228
Oldman, Cecil Bernard, 104
Olleson, Donald Edward, 238
Olmütz, 169
Ordoñez, Carlo, 171
Országos Széchényi Könyvtár. *See* Budapest
Oxford University, 6

Päsler, Karl, 217, 226-27
Paisiello, Giovanni, 99, 165, 205, 233
Palatine, 162n
Pannini, Giovanni Paolo, 159, *160*, 162-63, 164n, 165
Paris, 7, 72, 99, 125, 159, 181n, 205, 226, 229, 232
    Bibliothèque Nationale, 98, 112
    Conservatoire National de Musique, 53n, 98, 112, 114, 173n, 221
    Louvre, 159, 162
    Sorbonne, 162
Parma, 169, 172
Passau, 150
Paul, Grand Duke of Russia, 141, 171
Pergolesi, Giovanni Battista, 78
Peri, Jacopo, 178
Philipp August II, King of France, 163

Piccinni, Niccolò, 99
Pisk, Paul Amadeus, 89
Pleyel, Ignaz, 6, 106, 150, 223, 228-29, 237
Pohl, Carl Ferdinand, xviii, 9, 17, 46, 67, 73, 208, 217, 219, 229, 233, 235
Poland, 162n
Polignac, Melchior de, 162, 164
Polzelli, Luigia, 6, 233
Pope, Alexander, 27
Porpora, Nicola, 4, 28, 171
Porta, Nunziato, 85, 99-101
Poštolka, Milan, 232
Praetorius, Michael, 17
Prague, 95, 100-01, 172n, 205, 207, 232
    Theater, 99
    University Library, 99
Prehauser, Gottfried, 27
Pressburg (Bratislava), 101, 207
Preussische Staatsbibliothek. *See* Berlin
Primakov, Vassily, xx
Prince of Wales, 6
Pustelli. *See* Bustelli
Puttini, Francesco, 85

Quaglio family, 183
Quantz, Johann Joachim, 55, 195
Questenberg, Johann Adam, 169
Quinault, Philippe, 173

Radant, Else, 238
Radnitzky, Johann, 113, 222, 224
Raffael, Ignaz Wenzel, 71
Rajhrad (Reigern), 226
Rameau, Jean-Philippe, 55, 89, 98
Ramler, Karl Wilhelm, 195, 198
Ramsay, Allan, 223
Regensburg Library, 173
Reichardt, Johann Friedrich, 195
Reutter, Georg von, the Elder, 28, 35, 165-66
Reutter, Johann Adam Georg von, the Younger, 240
Riemann, Hugo, 213, 236, 240
Righini, Vincenzo, 233
Rochefoucauld, Cardinal de, 159, *160*
Rochlitz, Friedrich, 196, 199
Roesler, Johann Carl, *13*
Rohrau, 3, 8
Romania, 219, 232
Rome, 28, 162, 164, 169, 183, 187
    Académie de France, 163
    Accademia degli Arcadi, 175
    French National Church of St. Louis, 163
    Teatro Argentina, 159, *160*
Rosen, Charles, xx
Rosenbaum, Joseph Carl, 238
Rott, Franz, 172n
Rousseau, Jean-Jacques, 55-56, 176-77
Rubini, Giovanni Battista, 188
Rudolph, Archduke, 200
Russia, 10, 232

Saarbrücken, Hochschule für Musik, xix
Sacchini, Antonio, 203
Sachs, Curt, xvii, 235
St. Johann (Bohemia), 10
St. Louis, King of France, 163
St. Louis, Missouri, 181
St. Petersburg, 7, 177, 183. *See* Leningrad
Salieri, Antonio, 205-06
Salomon, Johann Peter, 6, 42, 125-26, 236
Salzburg, 16, 35, 75, 97, 209
Sammartini, Giovanni Battista, 213
Sandberger, Adolf, xx, 213
Santa Barbara, xvii, xx
Saxe, Marie-Josèphe de, 159, *160*, 162n
Scarlatti, Alessandro, 183, 186
Scheffstoss, Anton, 72
Scheibe, Johann Adolph, 176
Schenker, Heinrich, 238
Schering, Arnold, xvii, 200
Schikaneder, Emanuel, 183
Schiller, Friedrich von, 169
Schmid, Ernst Fritz, 17, 36, 197, 218, 224, 232
Schmieder, Wolfgang, 218-19
Schneider, Michael, 35n
Schnerich, Alfred, 17, 104, 114, 224
Schoenberg, Arnold, 40
Schofield, Bertram, 104n
Schott's Söhne, B. (publisher), xviii
Schrade, Leo, xix
Schroeter, Rebecca, 230
Schubert, Franz, 3, 40, 125, 148, 154, 176, 200, 219, 223, 239
Schünemann, Georg, 46, 161n, 213
Schürmann, Georg Caspar, 183
Schultz, Helmut, 43n
Schumann, Robert, xx, 11, 200-01
Schuster, Bernhard, 77
Schwanenberger, Johann Gottfried, 226
Scotland, 106-07
    Board of Trustee for the Encouragement of Arts and Manufactures, 106
Scott, Marian, 133, 213, 223
Scott, Walter, 105n, 106
Sebestyen, Janós, 35n
Seckau, 73
Shakespeare, William, 206-07
Shapiro, Bernice. *See* Geiringer
Shield, William, 105
Simrock (publisher), 72
Society of Friends of Music. *See* Vienna
Somfai, László, 43, 77, 172, 232-33
Sondheimer, Robert, 213
Sor, Ferdinand, 183
Spain, 5, 10, 63, 149
Speck, George, 183
Spitta, Julius August Philipp, 17
Spivacke, Harold, 104n
Sprague Smith, Carleton, 104n
Staatsbibliothek, Preussischer Kulturbesitz. *See* Berlin
Stadler, Abbé Maximilian, 196

Stadlmayr, Johann, 28
Staempfli, Jacob, 19n
Stamitz, Johann, 213
Starzer, Joseph, 171
Stekel, Eric-Paul, xix
Stekel, Irene. *See* Geiringer
Stekel, Wilhelm, xviii-xix
Sterkel, Johann Franz Xaver, 228
Stern, Martin, 238
Stockholm, 7
Stockmeier, Wolfgang, 226-29
Storace, Nancy (Anna Selina), 203-06, 209-10
Storace, Stephen, 43, 203, 205-07, *208-09*, 209-10
Stranitzky, Josef Anton, 27
Straton, Alexander, 106
Strauss, Christoph, 28
Stuart, Charles, 106, 108-09, 111
Süssmayr, Franz Xaver, 206
Suvarov (Russian army general), 40
Swieten, Gottfried van, 7, 120, 150, 198, 231, 238
Szabolcsi, Bence, 232-33

Taplow, 105
Tartaglini-Tiboldi, Rosa, 183
Telemann, Georg Philipp, 195
Tesi-Tramontini, Vittoria, 183
Teyber, Elisabeth, 183
Thibaut, Anton Friedrich Justus, 16
Thomas, Günter, 77
Thomson, George, 104, 105n, 106-07, *107*, 108-14, 118-23
Thomson, Georgina, 109-10
Thomson, James, 7, 238
Tibaldi, Luigi, 183
Tomasini, Elisabeth, 70
Tomasini, Josepha, 70
Tomasini, Luigi, 70, 143
Torrefranca, Fausto, 213
Tovey, Sir Donald Francis, 130, 140, 155, 197, 215
Traetta, Tommaso, 174, 183n
Travaglia, Pietro, 85
Trière, Philippe, *13*
Tübingen, Universitätsbibliothek, 41n, 43n, 70n
Tureck, Rosalyn, xx

United Kingdom, 106
United States, xix, xxii, 126, 128, 149
Universal Edition (publisher), 24
University of California, Santa Barbara, xix-xx, xxii, 19
    Arts Library, xix
Unverricht, Hubert, 222-23
Utrecht (treaty, 1712), 162n

Valkó, Aristid, 232
Vancea, Zeno, 232
Vanhal, Johann Baptist, 205
Vécsey, Jenö, 231
Venice, 28, 169, 176, 203
Verdi, Giuseppe, 125

Versailles, 5
Vienna, xvii-xx, 3-4, 7-10, 19, 26-28, 35-36, 40, 55, 63, 71-72, 77, 100-01, 103, 106, 123, 133-34, 141, 145, 155, 159, 169, 171-72, 176-78, 181, 195, 197, 203-05, 208, 210, 225, 227-29, 237-38
    Austrian National Library, 27, 43n, 45n, 46, 99n, 169, 207, 219
    Brothers of Mercy (Fratres Misericordiae; Barmherzige Brüder), 72n
    Burgtheater, 40, 182, 206
    Court Opera, 91, 203-04, 222
    Gesellschaft der Musikfreunde (Society of Friends of Music), xviii, xx, 41n, 46n, 68n, 141, 165, 167, 225
    Kärntnerthortheater, 35
    Karlskirche, 28
    La Favorita, 27
    Musikverein, xviii, 15
    St. Stephen's Cathedral, 4, 9, 19, 27-28, 133
    Schönbrunn Palace, 181, 183n
    Tonkunstlersocietät, 205
    University, xix
Vinci, Leonardo, 159, 164-66, 169
Vitali, Carlotta, 104n
Voltaire, François Marie Arouet de, 55, 177
Voss, Johann Heinrich, 195

Wackernagel, Bettina, 197
Wagenseil, Georg Christoph, 28, 213, 240
Wagner, Peter, xvii
Wales, 106
Walter, Horst, 229
Washington, D.C., 19, 103
    Kennedy Center, 19
    Library of Congress, 19, 103-04, 113, 173n, 222
Watteau, Jean-Antoine, 128
Webb, Daniel, 56
Weber, Carl Maria von, 106, 223
Weckerlin, Jean-Baptiste, 112
Weidinger, Anton, 225
Weigl, Anna Maria, 72n, 171
Weigl, Joseph Franz, 72, 143
Weingartner, Paul Felix, 222
Weinzierl (castle, Austria), 133-34, 136
Weismann, Wilhelm, 17
Wellesz, Egon, xvii
Werner, Gregor Joseph, 68n
Whyte, William, 104, 109, 111-14, 118, 123
Wiener Philharmonischer Verlag, xix
Winter (publisher), 195
Winterthur, Rychenberg Foundation, 42n
Wirth, Helmut, 77, 172n, 174n, 222
Wolf, Johannes, xvii
Wolf, Sándor, 42n, 45n, 69
Wolff, Christoph, xx
Wyzewa, Théodore de, xx, 56

Yale University, xxii
Yriarte y Oropesa, Tomás de, 10, 149

Zeno, Apostolo, 27, 176
Zinzendorf, Count Friedrich von, 182, 207-08, 238
Zitterer, Johannes, *14*
Zweig, Stefan, 42n
Zwettl (abbey, Austria), 42, 68-69, 72

Compositions by Haydn

P<small>AGE NUMBERS IN BOLDFACE REFER TO MUSIC EXAMPLES; THOSE IN ITALICS REFER TO FIGURES</small>

Agite properate (Hob. XXIIIa:2), 71-72, **71**
Allmächtigen Preis dir und Ehre! See *O Jesu te invocamus*
Animae Deo gratiae. See *Agite properate*
Applausus (Hob. XXIVa:6), 41-42, 68-69, 71n
Aria (for "Dorinda") and "Recitative di Podagroso" (Hob. XXIVb:1), 225, 233
Aria de adventu. See "Mutter Gottes"
Aria de tempore. See "Dictamina mea"

Capriccio for keyboard (Hob. XVII:1), 198
Cassation in D (Hob. II:D22 Add.), 240
"Concertantes jugiter per calamitatem" (B.-Gl. B/6/c), 73, **73**
Concertos:
    clarino (trumpet) (Hob. VIIe:1), 17, 224-25, 237
    corno di caccia (Hob. VIId:3*), 43, 224-25
    hurdy-gurdy. *See* lire organizzata
    keyboard (Hob. XVIII:3-4), 224
        in C major (Hob. XVIII:1), 28-31, **29-31**, 224
        in D major (Hob. XVIII:11*), 224
        in F major (Hob. XVIII:F1), 17
    lire organizzate (Hob. VIIh:1*-5*), 5, 226, 228
        in F major (Hob. VIIh:5*), 228
        in G major (Hob. VIIh:3*), 17, 130
Contredanse (Hob. IX:29), 17

Des Staubes eitle Sorgen. See *Insanae et vanae curae*
Destatevi o miei fidi (Hob. XXIVa:2^d), 73
Deutsche Tänze (Hob. IX:12), 17, 36, **37-39**, 236
"Dica pure." *See* Doubtful and Spurious Works
"Dictamina mea" (B.-Gl. B/6/b), 69
Divertimento in F major (Hob. II:23), 43

Ens aeternum (Hob. XXIIIa:3), 72

Fantasia for keyboard (Hob. XVII:4), 198
Feldparthien. See Doubtful and Spurious Works
56 Canons (Hob. XXVIIa:1-10, XXVIIb:1-46), 221
    Die zehn Gebote (Hob. XXVIIa:1), *11*
folk song arrangements (Hob. XXXIa-b), 115-17, 218, 222, 238
    "Bannocks o' Barley Meal" (Hob. XXXIa:171), 122
    "The Birks of Invermay" (Hob. XXXIa:187), 120-21, **121**
    "The Blue Bells of Scotland" (Hob. XXXIa:176), 108, 113, 122
    "The Bonnie Wee Thing" (Hob. XXXIa:102), 120, 122, **122**
    "Cauld Kail in Aberdeen" (Hob. XXXIa:55bis), 120-21, **121**
    "Fair Helen of Kirkconnell" (Hob. XXXIa:236), 118, **118**
    "Fy Gar Rub" (Hob. XXXIa:7), 118-19, **119**
    "Kilicrankie" (Hob. XXXIa:169), 122
    "Maggie Lauder" (Hob. XXXIa:35), 122
    "Muirland Willy" (Hob. XXXIa:242), 119-20, **119-20**
    "My Love Is But a Lassie Yet" (Hob. XXXIa:194), 122
    "On Ettrick Banks" (Hob. XXXIa:151), *123*
    "Robin Adair" (Hob. XXXIa:202), 121-22, **121-22**
    "Roslin Castle" (Hob. XXXIa:191), 120-21, **121**
    "Saw Ye My Father?" (Hob. XXXIa:5), 122-23
    "Wandering Willie" (Hob. XXXIa:257bis), 112

German dances. *See Deutsche Tänze*
"Gott erhalte Franz den Kaiser" (Hob. XXVIa:43), 7, 40, 154

Im Augenblick. See *Insanae et vanae curae*
Insanae et vanae curae (B.-Gl. B/8), 69-70

Lauda Sion salvatorem. See Doubtful and Spurious Works
Litaniae de B.V.M. See Doubtful and Spurious Works

Masses:
    Cellensis (Mariazellermesse) (Hob. XXII:8), 219-20
    Cellensis (Sanctae Caeciliae) (Hob. XXII:5), 63, 219-20
    Grosse Orgelmesse (Hob. XXII:4), 74, 219
    Harmoniemesse (Hob. XXII:14), 45-46, 213
    In tempore belli (Hob. XXII:9), 238
    Missa brevis in F major (Hob. XXII:1), 35
    Sancti Johannis de Deo (Kleine Orgelmesse) (Hob. XXII:7), 17, 73-74, 240
Mehrstimmige Gesänge. See Vocal works with keyboard
Minuets (Hob. IX:11), 36. *See also* Doubtful and Spurious Works
Motetto di Sancta Thecla (Hob. XXIIIa:4*), 75-76, *75*
"Mutter Gottes, mir erlaube" (Hob. XXIIId:2), 70

"Nelson" aria (Hob. XXVIb:4), 17
Non nobis Domine (Hob. XXIIIa:1), 71
Notturnos for 2 lire organizzate (Hob. II:25*-32*), 17, 228

258   Compositions by Haydn

O Jesu te invocamus (B.-Gl. B/6/d), 68-69, **68**
"Offertorio de Sancto vel Sancta." *See* "Concertantes jugiter"
Operas:
   Acide (Hob. XXVIII:1), 77-78, 172, 225
   L'anima del filosofo (Hob. XXVIII:13), 78, 89, 91-95, **92-95**, 98, 174, 237
   Armida (Hob. XXVIII:12), 5, 42, 89-90, **90**, 173-74, 226, 240
   La canterina (Hob. XXVIII:2), 5, 78-86, **79-85**, 91, 172, 223
   La fedeltà premiata (Hob. XXVIII:10), 85
   L'incontro improvviso (Hob. XXVIII:6), 85, 88-89, 91, 172
   L'infedeltà delusa (Hob. XXVIII:5), 85-86, **86-88**
   L'isola disabitata (Hob. XXVIII:9), 5, 89, 91, 173
   Der krumme Teufel (The Limping Devil) (Hob. XXIXb:1a), 78, 134
   Lo speziale (Hob. XXVIII:3), 5, 16, 85, 89, 91, 222
   La Marchesa Nespola (Hob. XXX:1), 225, 240
   Il mondo della luna (Hob. XXVIII:7), 85, 89, 91, 240
   Orfeo ed Euridice. See L'anima del filosofo
   Orlando Paladino (Hob. XXVIII:11), xix-xx, 5, 65, 77, 85, 89, 97, 100-01, 222
   Lo pescatrici (Hob. XXVIII:4), 85
   Philemon und Baucis (Hob. XXIXa:1,1a), 173
   La vera costanza (Hob. XXVIII:8), 35, 85, 89, 226, 229
Oratorios:
   The Creation (Hob. XXI:2), 7-8, 10-11, 17, 27, 40, 44-53, **46-53**, 63-64, 105n, 120, 152, 231, 237-39
   Il ritorno di Tobia (The Return of Tobias) (Hob. XXI:1), 35, 50, 70, 205, 232
   The Seasons (Hob. XXI:3), 7, 10, 17, 27, 40, 45-46, 120, 127, 129, 145, 213, 238
   The Seven Last Words (Hob. XX/2), 5, 36, 150, 213, 232, 237

Pieces for a Musical Clock (Hob. XIX:9-18, 27-32), 17, 42, 224-25

Quae res admiranda (B.-Gl. B/6/a), 69
"Quando la rosa" (Hob. XXIVb:3), 233

Requiem. *See* Doubtful and Spurious Works
The Return of Tobias. See Oratorios

Salve Regina:
   in E major (Hob. XXIIIb:1), 35, 70
   in G minor (Hob. XXIIIb:2), 41, 70-71
"Scena di Pedrillo." *See* Aria and recitative
Scottish Songs. *See* folk song arrangements
6 Airs with Variation, 104, 113, 122-23. *See also* folk song arrangements
Sonatas for keyboard (Hob. XIV:1, 5; XVI:1-10, 12-14, 16, 18-32, 35-39, 44-47, G1; XVII:D1), 10, 226-27
Songs (Hob. XXVIa:1-48), 222-23
Stabat Mater (Hob. XXbis), 72-73
String Quartets:
   op. 1, 16, 134
   op. 2, 134-37, **134-37**
   op. 3. *See* Doubtful and Spurious Works
   op. 9, 197
   op. 17, 41, 141
   op. 20, "Sun," 41-44, 137-41, **139-40**, 145-46, 148, 153, 197-98
   op. 33, "Russian," 56, **62-63**, 141-46, **142-45**, 197
   op. 50, 135, 142, 145-49, **146-49**
   op. 51, "The Seven Last Words of the Savior on the Cross," 36, 138, 149-52, **150-52**, 217
   op. 64, 42, 136, 142
   op. 76, 7, *12*, 122n, 135, 152-55, **153-55**, 198, 223
   op. 103, 237
Stücke für das Laufwerk. See Pieces for a Musical Clock
Svanisce in un momento. See Insanae et vanae curae
Symphonies:
   no. 1, 4, 56-59, **57-58**
   no. 8, "Le Soir," 56, **60**
   no. 13, 43
   no. 42, 43-44
   no. 45, "Farewell," 11, 43, 231
   no. 49, "La Passione," 56, **58-59**, **61-62**, 173
   no. 50, 42
   no. 62, 42
   no. 70, 43
   no. 85, "La Reine," 130
   no. 86, 198
   no. 89, 228
   no. 93, 126
   no. 94, "Surprise," 6, 36, 43n, 126-27, *127*
   no. 95, 126, 128
   no. 96, "Miracle," 126, 128
   no. 97, 42, 128-29
   no. 98, 129
   no. 99, 129
   no. 100, "Military," 6, 129-30, 228
   no. 101, "Clock," 6, 43n, 130
   no. 102, 130, 197, 215, 230
   no. 103, "Drum Roll," 6, 128, 130-31, 145, 148
   no. 104, 131
   nos. 61, 68-69, 226
   nos. 82-87, "Paris," 5, 226
   nos. 93-104, "London," 125-26, 131
   nos. 105*-107*, 218

Te Deum (Hob. XXIIIc:2), 72
Trios:
   baryton, viola, and violoncello (Hob. XI:25-96), 221-23
      in A major (Hob. XI:1), 17
      in A major (Hob. XI:5), 171-72, **172**
      in A major (Hob. XI:29), 172n, 223
      in A major (Hob. XI:94), 43
      in C major (Hob. XI:101), 43
      in C major (Hob. XI:109), 43
   keyboard, violin, and violoncello (Hob. XV:1-2, 5-32, 34-38, 40-41, Cl, f1), 226
      in B♭ major (Hob. XV:38*), 227
      in E♭ major (Hob. XV:30), 230
      in E♭ major (Hob. XV:36*), 227
      in E♭ minor (Hob. XV:31), 230
      in F major (Hob. XV:2), 227
      in F♯ minor (Hob. XV:26), 215, 230
      in G major (Hob. XV:5), 229
      in G major (Hob. XV:25), 229-30
      in G major (Hob. XV:32), 230
      in G major (Hob. XV:41*), 227

two flutes and violoncello (Hob. IV:1-4*), 17
  in G major (Hob. IV:4*), 45
two violins and violoncello (Hob. V:3-4, 8, 17, 20, Es1, G2, A1), 17

vocal works with keyboard (Hob. XXVb:1-4; XXVc:1-9), 221

Zingarese (Hob. IX:28). *See* Doubtful and Spurious Works

Doubtful and Spurious Works Attributed to Haydn

PAGE NUMBERS IN ITALICS REFER TO FIGURES

"An die Freundschaft" (Hob. XXVIa:D4), 223
Ave Regina in F major (Hob. XXIIIb:6*), 74-75

Concerto for keyboard in G major (Hob. XVIII:9*), 224

"Dica pure" (Hob. XXIVb:8) (P. Anfossi), 77, 89, *91*

Feldparthien (Divertimentos) (Hob. II:41*-46*), 17, 218

Lauda Sion salvatorem (Hob. XXIIIc:6*), 70
"Liebes Mädchen, hör mir zu" (Hob. XXVIa:D1), 223
Lytaniae de B.V.M. (Hob. XXIIIc:C2), 73-74, *74*

Minuets (Hob. IX:20), 17
Missa Rorate coeli desuper (Hob. XXII:3), 35, 240

Overtures:
    King Lear (Hob. Ia:9), 218
    Windsor Castle (J. P. Salomon), lost, 237

Requiem (Hob. XXIIa:c1), 17

"St. Anthony Chorale" (Hob. II: 46/ii), 17
String Quartet in E major (Hob. III:E2), 218
String Quartets, op. 3, 232

"Die Teilung der Erde" (Hob. XXVIa:C1), 223
Trios for keyboard, violin, and violoncello (Hob. XV:3-4), 228

Zingarese (Hob. IX:28), 17